Bitter Fruits of Bondage

Carter G. Woodson Institute Series
Reginald Butler, Editor

Armstead L. Robinson

BITTER FRUITS OF BONDAGE

The Demise of Slavery and the Collapse of the Confederacy, 1861–1865

UNIVERSITY OF VIRGINIA PRESS   CHARLOTTESVILLE AND LONDON

University of Virginia Press

© 2005 by the Rector and Visitors of the University of Virginia

All rights reserved

Printed in the United States of America on acid-free paper

First published 2005

9 8 7 6 5 4 3 2 1

Library of Congress Cataloging-in-Publication Data

Robinson, Armstead L.

Bitter fruits of bondage : the demise of slavery and the collapse of the Confederacy, 1861–1865 / Armstead L. Robinson.

p. cm. — (Carter G. Woodson Institute series)

Includes bibliographical references and index.

ISBN 0-8139-2309-3 (cloth : alk. paper)

1. Slavery—Confederate States of America. 2. Confederate States of America—History. 3. Confederate States of America—Social conditions. I. Title. II. Series.

E453.R63 2005

973.7′13—dc22

2004010080

Contents

Armstead L. Robinson, Historian of the Confederate States of America

Joseph P. Reidy

Armstead Robinson's study of the Civil War reexamines why the Confederacy lost. With a geographical focus on the Mississippi River Valley, which occupied more than half the land mass of the Confederate States of America, and a chronological focus on the years 1860 through 1863, the book explores how the unforeseen circumstances of war strained the antebellum class structure of the plantation South.

Carefully reconstructing the dynamic interaction between military events and public policy, Robinson's account concludes that simmering tensions between nonslaveholders and smallholding yeoman farmers, on the one hand, and wealthy slaveholding planters, on the other, undermined Confederate solidarity on both the home front and the battlefield. Amid a mass movement of the enslaved in pursuit of freedom, Confederate leaders labored in vain to reconcile the often contradictory claims of military exigency and political ideology. Their inability to do so during the war's first two years cost them dominion over the vast territory extending from the Appalachian Mountains to the Mississippi River and denied them access to their breadbasket in the trans-Mississippi states. Though far from guaranteeing ultimate defeat, this sequence of events exposed cracks in the social foundation of every Confederate state and of the Confederacy itself.

When Robinson began the study some thirty years ago, the field of social history was in its infancy. As both participants in and interpreters of the popular movements against racial segregation and the Vietnam War, early practitioners strove to demonstrate the influence of ordinary people on the historical process. Influenced by Karl Marx and the Marxist intellectual tradition, they emphasized the process of class conflict both as a major motive force in history and as a means of examining the role of ordinary people in making history. Social science methodology and computer technology made generating composite profiles of large groups possible. Robinson perceived how social history could provide fresh insight into the traditional subjects of politics and war that had preoccupied historians from Herodotus onward. He drew additional inspiration from the civil rights movement and from a number of scholars whose work had helped energize the movement. Two men, Charles H. Wesley and W. E. B. Du Bois, are particularly noteworthy in this regard. Wesley's *The Collapse of the Confederacy* (1922) provided a framework for analyzing the military and political history of the Confederate States of America, and Du Bois's *Black Reconstruction* (1935) explored how the enslaved helped bring about the destruction of slavery. Finally, Robinson's mentors at Yale and Rochester, including C. Vann Woodward, Eugene D. Genovese, Herbert G. Gutman, and Stanley Engerman, likewise influenced his approach to the study of history.

From all these influences, Robinson developed a commitment to the historian's craft and to the painstaking identification and analysis of evidence from primary sources. While not neglecting the standard array of books, newspapers, and other printed materials, he paid special attention to the official military and political records of the United States and Confederate States governments housed at the National Archives in Washington and to the correspondence of governors and other state-level officials in the archives of the Confederate states. A protégé of Sara Dunlap Jackson, the legendary archivist of Civil War military records at the National Archives, Robinson left no military record, however seemingly obscure, unexamined. This grounding in contemporary sources makes his work as fresh today as it was in 1977 when he completed his doctoral dissertation at the University of Rochester under Genovese. More than simply modeling his work on the emerging intellectual framework of social history, Robinson helped to define it, with consequences that affected both the specific field of Civil War scholarship and the broader one of African American history. Virtually every page of this book gives evidence of his skill and passion. He set a standard that few Civil War scholars have equaled and none has surpassed.

By arguing that internal class conflict associated with slavery fatally weakened the Confederacy, Robinson's interpretation appears to run counter to influential recent works, particularly that of Gary W. Gallagher. Building upon ideas that James M. McPherson and others had begun to explore over the past two decades, Gallagher's *The Confederate War* (1997) offers a comprehensive argument that Confederate nationalism transcended class lines and that it burned hotly as long as Robert E. Lee's Army of Northern Virginia remained in the field. Not denying discontent within the Confederacy, Gallagher points out that much of it was aimed against politicians who, in the popular view, hampered the success of the armed struggle for independence even while imposing hardship on the civilian population. And despite the staggering toll in life and territory as the war continued, civilian morale remained remarkably high until Lee's surrender at Appomattox. Following Gallagher's lead, other scholars have stressed the resiliency of Confederate nationalism. In the face of increasing privation and the growing specter of defeat, Confederate civilians demonstrated strong support for the cause of independence and the government and armed forces that fought to achieve it. In the view of these scholars, suffering strengthened the resolve to resist.

Robinson's work anticipates many of the central arguments of these recent debates, but with a twist. Proud Southerner that he was, he appreciated the breadth and depth of support for the Confederate government, its armed forces, and the political ideology of independence. What most fascinated him as a student of political movements was the rapid disintegration of Confederate nationalism after Lee's surrender. In other relevant wars of national liberation, such as the Netherlands in the sixteenth and seventeenth centuries and Vietnam in the twentieth, the struggle for national independence persisted despite the superior economic and military power of the foe, battlefield defeats, and growing deprivation among the civilian population—precisely the same factors often cited to explain why the Confederate struggle ended so abruptly. Rejecting the hypothesis that long odds necessarily sapped the will to resist, Robinson looked beneath the surface experiences of war to probe the effects of military events on the society's underlying social relationships, which in the Confederate South stood on the foundation of slavery.

Leaving the Union to form an independent slaveholding republic posed more than military challenges to Confederate leaders. Ideologically, they had to reconcile the apparent contradiction that the freedom of white citizens required the bondage of black noncitizens. This dilemma was not new, and for over a century a number of the most gifted intellectuals and statesmen in the Atlantic basin had grappled with it. The proslavery ideology that emerged from this debate was a sophisticated blend of historical, sociological, biological, and theological reasoning that Confederate ideologues and policy makers relied on implicitly to justify secession. The theory also served to explain away the fear of potential class conflict within the slaveholding republic, projecting a vision of organic harmony that stood in sharp contrast to the self-destructive tendencies within societies based on personal freedom and compensated labor. Unrest on the part of the enslaved had no more place in a well-ordered slave society than did jealousy and strife between free slaveholders and free nonslaveholders. Of questionable validity in times of peace, the theory met its true test during the Civil War.

While focusing on the dynamic relationship between ideology and practice, Robinson did not attempt to prejudge the outcome. He fully acknowledged the astuteness of Confederate policy makers and recognized how the budding nation's defensive posture against the assaults of an invading foe could galvanize public resistance. At the same time, he examined the potentially conflicting demands of mobilizing for war on the one hand and protecting slave property on the other. The imposition of a draft in 1862 illustrated the difficulties Confederate leaders faced in attempting to ensure manpower for the army while ensuring the security of slave plantations and the productivity of their labor force. In short order, contemporaries came to view the draft as a measure designed to favor large slaveholders at the expense of ordinary citizens.

This appearance of favoritism held the potential to widen the cracks inherent in slave society and undermine the high level of popular morale present at the start of the war. Robinson's study charts the dynamic relationship between home front and battlefield in the states of the Mississippi Valley between 1861 and 1863, as Confederate officials grappled with these interdependent challenges. Two trends stand out: wholesale desertion of tens of thousands of slaves from their masters, and the growing sense among smallholding and nonslaveholding Confederates that they were sacrificing their lives and property more to maintain the privileges of wealthy slaveholders than to achieve independence. The major Confederate defeats in the western theater during 1863—Vicksburg and Missionary Ridge—were directly attributable to the growing disenchantment and the internal class conflict that underlay it. The loss of the west had two major consequences. First, it enabled Union military strategists to encircle the Confederate strongholds in Georgia, the Carolinas, and Virginia. Second, it produced new strains along social class lines in the states east of the Appalachians.

From the early days of his research, Robinson paid special attention to the internal political and military dynamics of wars for national liberation, a preoccupation that he shared with intellectuals of all political leanings during the Vietnam era. As he revised the completed dissertation for publication, he shifted some of the emphases of his original findings and explored new areas of interest in Civil War scholarship. Specifically, he strove to comprehend the underlying causes of the Civil War and the phenomenon of Confederate nationalism. The Neilson Lectures he delivered at Smith College, which he envisioned as introductory chapters to the book manuscript but which were incompletely developed at the time of his death—they have been condensed to form chapter 1 of the present work—demonstrated this evolving interest. More important, as he worked at revising the study he assumed growing professional responsibilities, particularly those associated with the Carter G. Woodson Center at the University of Virginia, for which he served as founding director until his death. Through the center's programs, most significantly its pre- and postdoctoral research fellowships, Robinson's influence has reached far beyond the Civil War and even the United States. Yet his most enduring legacy will likely be that of historian of the Confederate States of America.

Armstead L. Robinson, Historian and Discipline Builder

Barbara J. Fields

Bitter Fruits of Bondage, Armstead L. Robinson's massive study of the collapse of the Confederacy, began its life as a doctoral dissertation. It was born of an interest in the history of Afro-Americans that started at Yale when Armstead was an undergraduate scholar-of-the-house, working under the supervision of C. Vann Woodward. Pursuing graduate study under Eugene D. Genovese during the heyday of history at the University of Rochester, he received strong reinforcement for intellectual habits to which he was by then already inclined: analytical ambition, broad geographic coverage, exhaustive archival work, and a taste for international and intertemporal comparison. Inclination and training alike, therefore, encouraged him to measure the war experience of the Confederacy against that of slave societies in classical antiquity and that of Vietnam in his young adulthood. His zest for new methods and his ludic delight in high-tech gadgetry (cars as well as computers) also received reinforcement at Rochester—as to the computers, anyway—in the person of Stanley Engerman, and found an outlet in the mathematical models and now-dated enthusiasm for "high-speed computers" that supplement the argument of *Bitter Fruits of Bondage.* Mainly, however, the book reflects Armstead's quest, still in vigorous progress at the time of his death, to fit method with material in the study of Afro-America.

An Afro-American from Tennessee, Armstead Robinson came of age intellectually at a time when Afro-Americans from the South were at last free to be Southerners. Once Jim Crow was dead (at least as a legally sanctioned regime), it became possible to be both Afro-American and Southern without a disabling sense of irony or paradox in the combination. The scholarly accomplishments for which Armstead will be best remembered—Afro-

American studies as an academic discipline and his mammoth, ever-changing study of the Confederacy—are products of what was enabling, rather than disabling, in that ironic and paradoxical combination. His undergraduate senior thesis, which explored the experience of Afro-Tennesseans in slavery and emancipation, displayed the moral and intellectual urgency of one conscious of being their historical legatee. And having matured amid the segregationists' battle cries of "our Southern way of life" and "states' rights," words as potent in his youthful present as in the historical past with which he wrestled as a mature scholar, Armstead would eventually, in *Bitter Fruits,* attribute the failure of the Confederacy to slavery ("our Southern way of life") and states' rights.

Untangling the relationship between slavery, the Confederacy, and the Afro-American experience—an effort simultaneously of engagement and detachment—required Armstead to imagine and bring into being an academic vehicle, Afro-American studies, adequate to the task. In the first place, the task presented an intellectual challenge for which existing norms of American historical writing offered few guidelines. For the Afro-American experience, though rooted in the most ancient of social arrangements—slavery—nevertheless underpinned the most modern of social arrangements, capitalism. Understanding an experience founded on such a paradox meant coming to terms with contradiction and contrariety against a historiographical tradition long dominated by reflexive positivism and epistemological innocence. In practical terms, it also required mastering the scholarly literature on two complex subjects, capitalism and slavery, a mastery that entailed crisscrossing academic disciplines and escaping the confines of United States–centered parochialism.

Nor was the challenge purely intellectual. It also required that long-standing conventions of racecraft in the American academy be overturned, conventions that regarded Afro-Americans as a unicellular organism floating beyond the main currents of national and international affairs, an exception to history rather than a part of it. Afro-American studies as Armstead came to conceive it thus challenged both prevailing habits of thought—the common sense of the academy—and entrenched patterns of conduct: security patrols along departmental boundaries; a casual, often unconscious, racism toward faculty and students of African descent; and the automatic relegation of anything touching on Afro-Americans to an institutional back room where resources and respect were in equally short supply.

From the time, therefore, of his precocious efforts as a Yale undergraduate, which led to a conference and the landmark publication, *Black Studies in the University,* Armstead understood that the practical work of building Afro-American studies programs would need as much vision and finesse as the intellectual work of pursuing the studies themselves. So he set about perfecting the necessary practical skills. His shrewdness in managing administrators, bureaucrats, and students was almost uncanny, as was his brilliance in difficult negotiations. He was in frequent demand as a mediator on college campuses, legendary for the calm articulateness with which he could summon warring parties to agreement on his summary of disputed facts. Perhaps those talents owed something to the clerical atmosphere in which he was raised: His father, uncles, and various grand- and great-grandfathers and -uncles were Lutheran pastors, and he himself briefly attended divinity school. Whatever the source of his talent as an administrator, Armstead became an expert in the ways of university politics and university bureaucracies.

It is a commonplace of the university campus that those who are most adept at administration are the ones others most distrust in administrative positions—and for good reason. The ablest administrators tend to be valuers of process over result, influence-dealers, revelers in gossip and turmoil, seekers of power for its own sake. Armstead was never of that number. Though he mastered (none better) the arts of bureaucratic parry and thrust, he never practiced them for their own sake. It was not a fiefdom he sought to build, but a new intellectual discipline. The administrative task of building Afro-American studies was not, therefore, a sidelight or supplement to Armstead's "own" work but an integral and organic part of it, each the condition for the other.

Not that the two proceeded smoothly together, without friction or cost. *Bitter Fruits of Bondage* had to compete for Armstead's time with the open-ended task of nurturing Afro-American studies, protecting it from the cheerful incompetence of well-meaning friends as well as from the calculated hostility of well-placed enemies. Inevitably, one who combined Armstead's intellectual vision with his practical skill at university administration and politics faced limitless demands on his time. Everyone wanted to draw on his expertise, and his generosity usually outran his instinct for self-protection. A young scholar negotiating a first appointment, a friend embattled with hostile colleagues or administrators, a student or junior colleague deciding where to publish a first book could claim Armstead's attention because, for him, the collective endeavor of Afro-American studies ranked equally with his individual projects.

Nor could Armstead bring himself to take the expected and conventional next step after completing a doctoral dissertation—revising it into a book—in an expected or conventional way. There was always another archive to visit, another letter or general order rumored to exist somewhere, another computer technique or quantitative model to test, another argument to try out. For example, Armstead proved to his own satisfaction, by means of a computer model, that there was indeed a structural food shortage in the Confederacy. Possibly no one doubted it except a few literal-minded statisticians who discounted the Confederate women's bread riots or the "cornstalk furloughs" taken by Confederate deserters upon receiving news of hunger at home, but Armstead the archival historian, unfashionably devoted to empirical evidence, shared a central nervous system with Armstead the high-tech enthusiast, determined to "predict" by means of computer-generated quantitative models what documentary evidence told him was true. He also read every regimental history, every soldier's letter, every governor's papers, and every newspaper he could get hold of, as well as milking the military records in the National Archives for everything they would yield. By such steps, the book grew, and so did Armstead. The two kept outgrowing each other, so that when Armstead died prematurely in 1995, the book was still evolving. The current volume is thus, in a sense, artificial, representing as it does an evolution abruptly terminated by the author's mortality rather than by his decision.

The dissertation, meanwhile, has lived its own life, distinct from that of the book Armstead was still revising at the time of his death, and exerting an influence on historical literature greater than that of many published books. Citations in scholarly publications hint at the extent of that influence. A truer measure, however, is the way Armstead's arguments and the weight of his archival material have led other scholars to echo his questions, borrow his examples, and follow his road map to the sources. Armstead was not the first to grasp that slavery was the root cause of the Civil War or that slaves and common soldiers played a role in the undoing of the Confederacy: W. E. B. Du Bois, Charles Wesley, and Bell Irvin Wiley pioneered such arguments, although they attracted few imitators until much later. Armstead's originality lay in making the interconnections among slavery, slaves, soldiers, and the collapse of the Confederacy an explicit object of investigation and in pursuing those interconnections with extraordinary—and equal—emphasis upon analytical and empirical rigor. All who tackled such questions after him have been indebted, directly or indirectly, to his example.

Armstead's nose for a good story and eye for a telling detail, together with his vacuum-cleaner thoroughness in the archives, made his dissertation a cornucopia for others. Who else would have unearthed, from an obscure regimental history, an anecdote about Union soldiers cheering with relief as they crossed from Kentucky to Tennessee—pleased to be at last in a Confederate state where they could treat obstructionist slaveholders as the enemy.

If Armstead had lived to finish his book himself, it would have taken a form to which posthumous editing, unfortunately, cannot aspire. Inevitably, the editors have been obliged to make decisions that the author might have made differently or, more likely, would not have faced at all. For the editors have had to choose between divergent arguments, unequally developed and documented, that the author did not live to reconcile or transcend. The more recent material, delivered as the Neilson Lectures at Smith College— which appears here in condensed form as chapter 1—differs in interpretation and emphasis from the older chapters. Perhaps, had he lived, Armstead would have truncated or abandoned the original argument; or perhaps he would have reconsidered the new. It has seemed to the editors, however, that Armstead's work—despite the inevitable flaws of posthumous collaboration—ought to be made available in published form to the audience of scholars and interested general readers for which he intended it.

Publisher's Note

At the time of his premature death in 1995, Armstead Robinson was an associate professor of history at the University of Virginia and the director of the Carter G. Woodson Institute for Afro-American and African Studies, which he founded. For almost twenty years, Professor Robinson had been working on the manuscript of a book on the Civil War. In 1996 his widow, Mildred Robinson, brought her husband's 1,200-page work in progress to the University of Virginia Press.

The manuscript the Press received was made up of three parts, completed in 1982, 1984, and 1991, respectively. The historians Stanley Engerman, Eugene Genovese, Joseph Reidy, and Barbara Fields commented on various drafts; Professors Fields and Reidy also supplied introductory essays for the book. With the scholarly assessments—and virtually everything Armstead Robinson had ever written—in hand, renowned editor Jeannette Hopkins took on the task of rendering the manuscript into publishable form. She sorted through multiple, often undated drafts, deciding which were the most current and best reflected the author's intentions regarding the sequence and shape of the book. Removing repetitions while integrating the separate parts into a single coherent whole resulted in a manuscript that was over a third shorter than the original.

Inevitably, there were problems that could not be solved. While every effort was made to discern and adhere to the author's intentions, the results would have fallen short of the mark even if some of those intentions had not been at odds with others or had not changed over time. Not only was the most recently completed segment, based on the Neilson Lectures which the author delivered at Smith College in 1991, less developed than previously written portions of the work, it represented a new departure. Since it focused on Confederate nationalism, integrating this section into the book would have required recalibrating the author's evidence and arguments regarding conflicts dividing the Confederacy—a task beyond the powers and province of even the most talented scholar or editor. Accordingly, only those portions of the Neilson Lectures that cohered with the main body of the work were incorporated into it. Assisting Jeannette Hopkins, researcher John Kirn checked facts, quotations, and myriad other details. Regrettably, several maps and an appendix elaborating Robinson's computer model could not be found. Few historians can rival the thoroughness and accuracy of Robinson's archival research, but some notes were lost or incomplete, and Kirn and others were unable to track down all of the missing sources. Rather than indicate each omission, we have opted to cite the sources that Robinson did provide or that we were able to reconstruct. In these difficult circumstances, the final preparation and copyediting of the manuscript required an unusually high level of expertise. This was provided by another top-flight editor, Ruth Melville. Adding to his long list of invaluable contributions, Joseph Reidy generously reviewed and offered advice on the edited manuscript, the proofs, and the index.

Mildred Robinson's gentle but unrelenting determination was essential to bringing this book into print. Edward Ayers, a professor of history and now dean of arts and sciences at the University of Virginia, played an early and continuing role in securing the financial and institutional support critical for the project. The Press is grateful for financial support from the University of Virginia, in particular from the Office of the President, the Corcoran Department of History, and the Carter G. Woodson Institute for Afro-American and African Studies. Their efforts, and those of all the individuals named above, have made possible the posthumous publication of Armstead Robinson's life work.

Bitter Fruits of Bondage

Introduction

Recently I delivered a lecture on the rise and the demise of the Confederacy at the shrine of the "Lost Cause," the Museum of the Confederacy in Richmond, Virginia. Given the topic, my affiliation with the University of Virginia history department, and the similarity between my first name and the surname of a quite prominent clan of the First Families of Virginia, the Armisteds, this particular lecture attracted a much larger than usual gathering of Civil War buffs. The history department of Virginia Commonwealth University was host. Many of my audience, mostly academics, no doubt expected, from the announcement, an updated version of the prevailing orthodoxy about the war. But the version of "The War" I presented bore little relationship to the traditional account. My thesis was that Southern defensiveness about slavery had precipitated the war and that Confederates were defeated because, in the end, white Southerners had lacked the will to go on and that massive desertion and disaffection had robbed the Confederacy of the human resources it needed to stave off defeat. In subsequent years, I discovered to my surprise that many younger Southerners, too, experienced distress similar to that of my audience in Richmond. The student evaluation of my course warned others at the University of Virginia to "avoid this class unless you are a dyed-in-the-wool-born-Yankee."

Yet intolerance for new perspectives on the American Civil War knows no sectional boundaries. When I presented the same lecture to faculty at the Massachusetts Institute of Technology, less than a month after my appearance in Richmond, I argued as before that the outbreak of the war can be understood only as the logical outgrowth of Southern refusal to accede peacefully to the rapid ascension to national power of a Republican Party that in 1860 elected Abraham Lincoln its first president. In place of a policy allocating separate parts of the national territory for slave and free-soil settlement, the Republicans had demanded that Southerners abandon all future claims to the

American frontier. Anyone truly loyal to American values was honor-bound to put slavery "on course to Ultimate extinction." The imputation that Southerners must accept second-class citizenship because of the essential "evil" of the institution of slavery was an argument self-respecting Southern whites could not accept. They felt they had no choice but to invoke the right to "alter and abolish" a government harmful to their interests, a right inherited from the American Revolution and the Declaration of Independence, and to create a Confederate States of America to defend "life, liberty and the pursuit of happiness." Although Northern Republicans disclaimed any "intent" to disturb slavery where it was already entrenched, denying slavery the right to expand meant the institution would gradually die if its limits were confined.

It seems to me that pious evasions of the full consequences of Northern racialism undermine the force of Northerners' criticisms of white Southerners, particularly since on the eve of the Revolution chattel slavery was a legal institution in all thirteen of the original colonies. When I concluded my talk at MIT with the comment that the Northern edge in manpower and the edge in economic resources were probably not the decisive factors in Confederate defeat, a colleague rose and asked, "How can YOU, of all people, be so pro-Southern? How can YOU blame us for the war? After all, didn't the Northern victory free YOUR people?"

I had been accused in the South of being anti-Southern for the same paper that, in the North, prompted accusations of an anti-Northern bias. I realized that many Southerners maximize their claim to principled heroism by minimizing the role of slavery in their decision to secede, while many Northerners castigate the South for its proslavery stance while ignoring their own racialist power grab in driving Southerners to the wall. Memories of the Civil War are alive in the imaginative realm of each region, fed by partisans North and South. Fortunately, my father had warned me, more than once, that attracting fire from both sides of a heated conflict, while searing, is generally the surest sign that one is closing in on the truth.

Writing on the occasion of the 1961 centennial, the poet and novelist Robert Penn Warren argued persuasively in *The Legacy of the Civil War: Meditations on the Centennial* that the nation was not a nation until the Civil War:

> The Civil War is, for the American imagination, the great single event of our history. Without too much wrenching, it may, in fact, be said to *be* American history. Before the Civil War we had no history in the deepest and most inward

sense. There was, of course, the noble vision of the Founding Fathers articulated in the Declaration and the Constitution—the dream of freedom incarnated in a more perfect union. But the Revolution did not create a nation except on paper. . . . The vision had not been finally submitted to the test of history. There was little awareness of the cost of having a history. The anguished scrutiny of the meaning of the vision in experience had not become a national reality. It became a reality, and we became a nation, only with the Civil War.

The Civil War is our only "felt" history—history lived in the national imagination. This is not to say that the War is always, and by all men, felt in the same way. Quite the contrary. But this fact is an index of the very complexity, depth, and fundamental significance of the event. It is an overwhelming and vital image of human and national experience.[1]

The Public Broadcasting System's 1990 series *The Civil War* and the 1989 movie *Glory,* about the heroic sacrifice of black soldiers, reaffirm Warren's powerful insight that the Civil War is "an overwhelming and vital image of human and national experience."

The most salient explanation for the general persistence of interest in the Civil War stems from the fact that defeat of the South preserved the national unity, giving the Northern victory a divine sanction in the light of history. The majority of Americans came to see the victory of the North as morally just and inevitable. This sense of inevitability pervades Civil War studies; most Civil War buffs argue that the South lost because it never had a real chance for military victory. Did the North not have overwhelming advantages in both military manpower and industrial resources? Orthodox wisdom concludes that a combination of superior Northern resources and strategic Southern blunders virtually assured the victory of the Union side. Still, the North, too, committed grievous strategic errors, and the Southern army was one of the finest in the world of its day. A viable theory of the causes of the beginning and the ending of the American Civil War must explain the intensification of sectional conflict that, more than any other factor, produced the political crisis of the 1850s that led to four years of devastating warfare.

Recent histories of the Civil War concede the causal role of social factors in the defeat of the South but conclude that in the final analysis the outcome was determined by the "God of Battles." I believe, on the contrary, that the process of social change initiated during the birth of Confederate nationalism undermined the social and cultural foundations of the Southern way of life so thoroughly as to change the "peculiar institution" of slavery from being its cornerstone to a millstone. This theory breaks sharply with Civil War orthodoxy.

The will to sustain the fight against great odds can transform the meanings of "strength" and "weakness" so as to enable an underdog to gain both military victory and national independence. Because the antebellum way of life proved unable to adapt successfully to the rigors of war, the South had to fight its struggle for nationhood against mounting odds. I hope, in telling the story of how the War for Southern Independence affected slavery, the central institution of the Confederacy, to show how changes within that institution sparked the internal social conflicts that in the end undermined the Confederacy.

This study does not pretend to be the long-awaited history of the Confederacy. Standard topics such as the military and diplomatic history of the wartime South are mentioned here only as they touch on the emergence of Confederate defeatism. Other traditional issues—such as the debate over the character and quality of Jefferson Davis's leadership—receive somewhat more attention but are approached from the same perspective, that is, as they contribute to an understanding of the Confederate defeat. My focus on Southern defeatism reflects my judgment that the most significant fact about the Confederacy was not that it succeeded in accomplishing something but rather that its revolution was, finally, aborted.

Historical analysis involves more than recording the competing points of view among a random selection of surviving contemporary accounts. So, for example, excerpts from three war diaries all attest to the cohesive unity of the Southern population in the Tennessee River Valley region, but all three appear to invalidate the testimony of Joshua Burns Moore, of northern Alabama, that wealthy slaveholders avoided military service ostensibly to protect their human property at home (see chap. 6). Which of these seemingly conflicting views most closely approximates the truth? To help resolve the apparent contradictions among anecdotal accounts, I have constructed a mathematical model of the social structure and economy of the Confederacy from data provided by the U.S. Census for 1860.[2]

Chief among the questions clarified for me by the computer model were these: Were the racial and class groups within Southern society distributed uniformly or did they tend to cluster? If clustering occurred, what special characteristics of economic regionalism were produced and what effects did they have on the Confederate war effort? Did wartime mobilization affect various regions within the Confederacy in similar ways? Could all feed their stay-at-home populations and at the same time contribute to the support of their armies in the field? And were the effects of Confederate draft laws distributed evenly among economic regions?

Or were poorer soldiers justified in complaining, as they did, that the supposedly egalitarian struggle for Southern independence had been transformed by the slaveholders into "a rich man's war and a poor man's fight"? My claim that the Confederacy lost its popular will for independence primarily because of internal racial and class dissension is consistent with the economic and social structures illuminated by the mathematical model.

Most Americans, no doubt, imagine the prewar South as a region thickly dotted with immense plantations on which most of the black and white populations worked and lived. But, on the contrary, while slaves made up 40 percent of the total population of the South, only 25 percent of free families, most of them white, owned any slaves at all, and fully one-half of this minority held fewer than five slaves. Only an owner of twenty or more slaves, and of substantial land, could qualify as a planter, and fewer than 10 percent of slaveholding families qualified. The plantation elite of the antebellum South made up less than 3 percent of the free population in the region and less than 2 percent of the total free and slave populations combined. Only a tiny elite, in fact, controlled the plantations that dominated Southern society and economy. And because agricultural production depended, in part, on soil fertility, and because the plantations tended to be clustered along the fertile river valleys and in the "black prairies"—the regions with the richest soil—the vast number of slaves lived in isolation from the nonslaveholding majority. Indeed, one of the most obvious features of Southern uniqueness proved to be this internal regionalized geography wherein commercialized, slave-based agriculture, directed by a relatively small planter elite and its allies, dominated the "Black Belt," and a subsistence-oriented sector, populated largely by white yeoman farmers, predominated elsewhere. Even at birth, the Confederacy contained within its borders all the seeds of dangerous racial and class dissensions.

My study of the fault lines of the Confederacy concentrates especially on the Mississippi Valley, on the region drained by the Mississippi River and its tributaries, an area stretching from western Virginia to eastern Texas, with some attention to parallels elsewhere in the wartime South. I decided to concentrate on the Mississippi Valley rather than study the whole of the Confederacy, first, because it seemed clear that in the Mississippi Valley rampant defeatism imposed the greatest military havoc on the Southern cause. The collapse of the western front, for example, allowed General William Tecumseh Sherman to sweep from Chattanooga past Atlanta to Savannah in 1864 and then northward toward Virginia, a thrust that severed General Robert E. Lee's supply lines and cut off his line of retreat. When combined with General Ulysses S. Grant's victory at the Battle of Five Forks, Sherman's northward thrust compelled Lee to surrender at Appomattox. The social background of the military history of the western front is of paramount importance in the Confederate defeat. I believed that linking wartime social change to the military collapse of the Confederacy would best be accomplished by investigating an area where social conflict exerted a determining influence on the war effort. Thus I chose nine states—Alabama, Arkansas, Kentucky, Louisiana, Mississippi, Missouri, Tennessee, Texas, and West Virginia (formed during the war)—plus the territory of Oklahoma, for intensive research on the processes of wartime social change.

Charles H. Wesley's comparative mode of analysis proved invaluable in linking wartime social change to the collapse of the Southern war effort. His reference to the Dutch Revolution led me to the debates about developments within Spanish society during the Thirty Years' War. In the vast literature on the causes of the collapse of the Spanish empire, much like the historiography of the Confederacy, explanations for its demise include a virtual laundry list of "causes." Reflecting on the multiplicity of these "causes," Jaime Vicens Vives argues convincingly, "We must point out . . . that these 'causes of decadence' are too numerous for us not to suspect in them the presence of stronger reasons; that is the general economic crisis of the seventeenth century in which converged (in the case of Spain) political incompetence, incapacity of production, and social disintegration." Might not the concept of a Confederate "general crisis" provide a theoretical framework that could explain its collapse?[3]

In the case of Spain during the Thirty Years' War, a theory of "general crisis" provides a powerful explanatory model. Josef Polisensky's challenging study of that war builds on the concept of a general seventeenth-century crisis. He argues that "a crisis is the culmination of ever deepening internal conflicts within the infrastructure of a given society which leads to a sudden collapse of existing economic, social, cultural and political relationships and whose consequences will be either regression—regional or general—or on the other hand a powerful step forward in the development of that society."4 Did the Confederate States of America experience a broad enough spectrum of internal conflicts to warrant describing those conflicts in similar terms?

In the Confederacy's experience with internal conflict we find abundant evidence of massive breakdowns in the political, social, economic, and cultural arenas of Southern life. Eventually, Jefferson Davis faced a rebellious vice president, a dissident and querulous Congress, and the refusal by at least three state governors (Zebulon Vance in North Carolina, Joseph Brown in Georgia, and Pendleton Murrah in Texas) to acknowledge his presidential authority. Rampant, and often violent, antiwar and antidraft movements, coupled with an epidemic of social banditry, signaled the disintegration of social order in a number of the Confederate states. So, too, the early collapse of the Confederate economy produced a subsistence crisis; the resulting difficulty in supplying food for either the army in the field or the civilians at home is widely recognized. And most fundamentally, the erosion of popular faith in the Southern cause brought about a disaffection so widespread as to amount to a surrender of the will to national independence.

The Confederate government in Richmond never found an effective strategy to enable the Southern revolution to preserve slavery while retaining the allegiance of its white nonslaveholding yeoman majority. In late March 1865 the Richmond regime undertook the risky but desperate maneuver of recruiting slaves as soldiers, implicitly promising freedom to those who would serve. But long before the initiative might have fortified the Confederacy's depleted ranks, in quick succession Lee abandoned Richmond and then surrendered to Grant at Appomattox. The Confederacy failed because its government failed to sustain the popular support it enjoyed at its birth; this failure in turn resulted from its failure to reconcile the conflicting interests of its own competing social and economic classes. As a result, independence slipped away, and slavery came to a rancorous end. The Cause failed entirely. Out of this failure would emerge unresolved prospects, problems, tragedies, and enigmas that continue to afflict the Union and the entire modern world.

"A Nation . . . Is Not Beaten Until Its Spirit Is Broken"

Southerners began the Civil War with the martial fervor of newborn nationalism. Yet their spirit waned and their struggle failed in situations where other wars for national independence had managed to persevere. Speaking to the Confederate Congress in January 1863, Jefferson Davis said, "These Confederate States . . . have afforded another example of the impossibility of subjugating a people determined to be free; and have demonstrated that no superiority of numbers or available resources can overcome the resistance offered by such valor in combat, such constancy under suffering and such cheerful endurance of privation as have been conspicuously displayed by this people in defense of their rights and liberties." Charles Wesley's observations of more than fifty years ago retain their cogency today, parallelling closely Davis's vision of how the South might have won its independence:

> Clearly more important than numbers and resources—as weighty as they may be in the final result—are the morale of the people and their attitude toward war. . . . A nation like an individual is not beaten until its spirit is broken. . . . Truly as in other wars for independence, the government denying this right was superior in all things, but in this case the people who were seeking independence seemed powerless to use the nucleus given them for the building up of a greater resistance.[5]

What transformed the fervor of the secessionist effort and the first Confederate victory at Bull Run into the bitter defeatism and powerlessness of Appomattox? Did the series of setbacks over four years, despite significant battlefield victories, sap the popular will in the South, or did the withering of Confederate patriotism lead to the collapse of Southern armies on the field of honor?

I believe that the keys to understanding the defeat of the South lie along the racial and class fault lines of the Confederacy's social structure. Although years of struggle had taken a fearful toll, even after Appomattox the Confederacy retained substantial military potential that Davis would seek to turn toward guerrilla warfare. Lincoln encountered enormous difficulty in sustaining the war effort in the North; how would the Union side have responded if confronted by a Southern will as persistent as that which confronted the Spanish in the United Provinces from 1568 through 1648? "War weariness" alone cannot provide a convincing explanation for the South's loss of their war for national independence in a mere four years.

Students of the Confederacy have generally tended to pay scant attention to wartime social change within the Southern states after the Southern revolution emerged as a massive popular movement. The origins of Southern defeatism, I suggest, lay in the conflicting interests in wartime of social groups within the South itself. Despite the richness of historical scholarship on slavery in the antebellum South produced over the last half century, scholars have still not fully explored aspects of slavery during the war that Bell Irvin Wiley and W. E. B. Du Bois identified in the 1930s and 1940s.[6] I myself had first intended to study how the Civil War crisis brought about the end of slavery, but as my research progressed, it became increasingly clear to me that the devolution of wartime slavery retarded the South's capacity to make war, a finding that contradicted some historians' interpretation that slavery served as a principal source of Southern strength, particularly in the first two years of the war. My research suggested, to the contrary, that wartime slavery began to erode the South from within even before fighting began, and forced the Confederate government to distort its own strategic plans to meet the North's military challenge with efforts to shore up the Southern revolution. I came to believe that the wartime demise of slavery was decisive in turning the South away from victory and toward defeat. It affected the course of the war as much as the war affected slavery.

Before the onset of combat, the possibility of even a brief military struggle had alarmed the economic elite of the Confederacy—slaveholders in a society constantly sensitive to the threat of slave insurrection. John Brown's abortive raid on Harpers Ferry heightened that fear. The wartime measures the Confederacy undertook to sustain slavery and to prevent slave revolt undercut its efforts to defend the Southern heartland against Northern invaders. So, too, a growing alienation from the Confederate cause by nonslaveholders, the vast majority of the military population of the South, proved critical. Many whites who owned no slaves—the overwhelming majority in the South—discovered that they were expected to fight to save slavery and to replace with their own bodies slaveholders and overseers who avoided military service and stayed on the plantations to keep black slaves in line. And out of that alienation came a defeatism that destroyed the Confederate cause. Nonslaveholders, through desertion and draft resistance, demonstrated their unwillingness to fight to protect the interests of the slaveholding elite, and as they deserted the Confederate cause the dream of a Southern republic dissolved in a collapse of the popular will. The desertion of nonslaveholders transformed the Confederacy from a popular crusade into the Lost Cause.

My perspective on fear of slave insurrection as the progenitor of class conflict within the Confederacy breaks sharply with traditional explanations of Confederate defeat. Not only have the military side effects of slaveholders' anxiety about insurrection generally escaped the notice of historians, but the most serious students of Confederate draft resistance insist that the mass of Southerners remained loyal to the Cause until the bitter end. Albert B. Moore concludes, "The dereliction of many sets in a brighter light the heroic devotion of the masses. The unsurpassed sacrifices and heroism of the Southern armies and civilian population—the proudest and most sacred tradition of the South—stands unassailed."[7] To argue, as I do, that a class conflict based on defense of slavery eroded the Southern will to national independence is to confront directly the heritage of the Lost Cause.

If this general trend played out over the course of the war, with accelerating impact after the summer of 1864, its outline was clearly visible in the Mississippi Valley during the first two years of the war. The diary of Joshua Burns Moore, who lived in the Tennessee River Valley region of northern Alabama, provides one of the clearest descriptions of the connection between wartime social change and class conflict within the Confederacy. Moore professed shocked amazement that, even before the Yankee forces arrived, many wealthy pro-Confederates avoided the rigors of Southern military life, opting to remain close to home to protect their property interest, especially their human property. Moore asked of these well-to-do fair-weather secessionists, "Do they expect the poor people are fools, not to draw their own conclusions from their actions?" When a Union naval flotilla attacked northern Alabama in 1862, many plantation owners abandoned the area, taking their slaves and other chattel property beyond the reach of the invaders. During the two months when Union forces occupied northern Alabama, large numbers of slaves seized the opportunity for freedom; slaveholders, who thought they knew their blacks so well, were stunned. Moore, reflecting on the future of the Southern revolution, wrote:

> The object of the war, says Mr. Lincoln, is the restoration of the Union as it was. He may think so, and doubtless does. But from the very nature of the conflict, so sure as the war continues, it is the death blow to negro slavery. There are but some or a little over 300,000 men taking all the slave states that are interested in it (that is owners of slaves), now men who have no interest in it are not going to fight through a long war to save it—never. They will tire of it and quit. If the Southern states return to the Union by some kind of compromise, this may save it. If the North puts forth their whole strength, it is gone forever.[8]

Moore had grasped the central reality of the Confederate experience: as slavery went, so went the War for Southern Independence. Moore drafted his views during the spring of 1862, long before tidal waves of defeatism and desertion sapped the military strength of the Southern revolution. To the extent that slavery caused the war, the wartime erosion of slavery could not but bring the Confederate revolution down.

The peculiar configuration of Confederate mobilization, the genesis of popular discontent with the war effort, the failure of agricultural adjustment, the birth of states' rights ideology, the halting attempts by Jefferson Davis to cope with rampant internal dissension, the disintegration of Confederate society: all these emanated from the Confederacy's failure to preserve the stability of its home front. The Civil War South discovered that it could not sustain wartime slavery and simultaneously retain the allegiance of the nonslaveholding majority. The War for Southern Independence ruptured its antebellum consensus and with that rupture came its defeat.

Chapter One   A "Most Un-Civil War"

Slavery and a Separate Nation

A t 3:20 A.M. on Friday, April 12, 1861, a delegation of three men from the newly declared independent state of South Carolina rowed out into the harbor of Charleston to Fort Sumter, perched on a man-made island. They carried a written demand to the garrison commander to surrender within the hour or face massive bombardment. Ever since South Carolina's secession on December 20, 1860, Major Robert Anderson had refused to surrender the Union claim. He would not surrender now. At 4:30 A.M., cannon no. 1 of the Palmetto Guard's Cummings Point battery at Fort Johnson fired a solitary signal shot at Fort Sumter, the fiery arc rising high above the harbor. The honor of touching off the spark had been granted to a Virginia patriot, Edmund Ruffin of the Palmetto Guard, in honor of his long advocacy of the cause of Southern nationalism and independence.

Over the next day and a half, the outgunned Union defenders fought bravely. At 1:00 P.M. on Saturday, April 13, a Southern shell severed the pole that bore Fort Sumter's flag. Distressed at the sight of Old Glory fluttering to the ground, Senator Louis T. Wigfall of Texas rowed out on his own to urge surrender. Major Anderson, assessing the damage and dwindling supplies, agreed to Wigfall's plea, on the condition that his command be permitted to strike its colors in a formal hundred-gun salute to the flag. This ritual act of surrender became a deeply symbolic first shedding of blood when a cannon at the fort exploded, killing one soldier and wounding six others. The garrison buried its fallen comrade and abandoned the fort, and the Confederate flag and the Palmetto flag of South Carolina were hoisted together in place of Old Glory.[1]

Emma Holmes, the daughter of a Charleston physician, who lived within earshot of the fort, wrote in her personal account of the bombardment,

"Though every shot is distinctly heard & shakes our house, I feel calm and composed." "There are some few ladies who have been made perfectly miserable and nearly frantic by their fears of the safety of their loved ones, but the great body of citizens [seems] to be so impressed with the justice of our cause that they place entire confidence in the God of Battles. Every day brings hundreds of men from up country, & the city is besides filled with their anxious wives and sisters and mothers, who have followed them."[2]

The rapid diffusion of information about the surrender in Charleston harbor by telegraph, steam-driven printing press, and railroad stoked the fires of nationalism in both the North and the South. The day after the country's colors were struck, President Abraham Lincoln, in his dual capacities as president and commander in chief, dispatched telegrams to the governors of all thirty-three states to inform them that "the laws of the United States have been . . . and now are opposed, and the execution thereof obstructed . . . by combinations too powerful to be suppressed" by available forces. He called on the governors to send seventy-five thousand troops: "I appeal to all loyal citizens to . . . aid this effort to maintain the honor, the integrity, and the existence of our National Union, and the perpetuity of popular government; and to redress wrongs already long enough endured." "The heather is on fire," wrote an observer in Boston. "I never knew what a popular excitement can be. . . . The whole population, men, women and children, seems to be in the streets with Union favors and flags."[3]

Over the next four years, the clash between competing nationalisms was to attain a scope and intensity that made it the world's most massive military conflict from Waterloo to the outbreak of the First World War. More than three million men in a total population of thirty-three million persons, North and South, responded to calls for mobilization. More than six hundred thousand of these would die in the four years of the war, the total number of dead exceeding the combined total of all other American wars (up to the Vietnam War). The war preserved the national union but at a cost no one could have foreseen in the balmy days of April 1861 when the three officials of the new Confederacy rowed out to Fort Sumter to demand that a "hostile" power surrender that tiny spot of South Carolina's sovereign territory.

"This Mighty Question": Slavery as the Core Issue

Historians dispute whether the Civil War between the Union and the Confederacy was inevitable. And if it *was* inevitable, why didn't it begin until

1861 instead of in the 1850s, during the civil strife in "Bleeding Kansas," or during the furor over the Kansas-Nebraska Act, or after the controversial admission of California to the Union, or in the 1840s or 1830s during the Wilmot Proviso debates, or in 1833 during the Nullification Crisis, or even in 1820 when the debate over the admission of the state of Missouri was engaged? And why did the war happen at all? Was it merely a contingency stumbled into by blundering statesmen too maladroit to devise acceptable compromises? Or was the war about issues so fundamentally in conflict in American society that war alone seemed able to resolve them?

Too many contingencies existed for the single outcome of war to have been predetermined, yet eventual war was irrepressible, I believe, as long as the nation remained part slave and part free. In the single decade of the 1850s, a sequence of partisan realignments had led to the collapse of three national parties—the Whigs, the Know-Nothings, and the Democrats—and the meteoric rise of a fourth, the Republicans, formed specifically in response to the crisis of slavery. A new political coalition, put together out of the debris left over from the collapse of the Whigs and then of the Know-Nothings, failed when its Northern and Southern wings could find no common ground on the issue of slavery. Radical urban antislavery Democrats abandoned their own party after passage of the Kansas-Nebraska Act of 1854. The polyglot assemblage of party refugees formed the Republican Party, and within a few years Abraham Lincoln became its spokesman.

In the pivotal Illinois 1858 senatorial race between Republican Abraham Lincoln and Democrat Stephen A. Douglas, slavery was also the dominant issue. Lincoln's speech at Chicago in July called slavery "this mighty question upon which hang the destinies of the nation." He placed his opponent, Douglas, in "the slavery extension camp of the nation." "The Republican party is made up," he said, "of those who, as far as they can peaceably, will oppose the extension of slavery, and who will hope for its ultimate extinction." Douglas acknowledged the centrality of the sin of slavery but blamed the Republicans for it: "The slavery question has now become the leading and controlling issue; that question on which you and I *agreed*, on which the Whigs and Democrats united, has now become the leading issue between the national Democracy on the one side, and the Republican or Abolition Party on the other."[4]

Lincoln had accepted his party's 1858 nomination for election to the U.S. Senate with words that have echoed down the century and a half that followed:

I believe this government cannot endure permanently half *slave* and half *free*. I do not expect the Union to be dissolved. I do not expect the house to fall; but I do expect it will cease to be divided. It will become all one thing or all the other. Either the opponents of slavery will arrest the further spread of it, and place it where the public mind shall rest in the belief that it is in course of ultimate extinction; or its advocates will push it forward, till it shall become alike lawful in all the States, old as well as new—North as well as South.[5]

Although Lincoln lost the Illinois senatorial race by a narrow margin, his campaign performance had transformed him into a national figure and would catapult him into the presidency itself scarcely two years later. He risked his own political future on the single issue of opposition to the expansion of slavery, encouraging his party to bolster the support of disaffected Democrats who were drawn to the Republicans "for the sole object of preventing the spread, and nationalization of slavery." In Columbus, Ohio, in a midwestern lecture tour in the fall of 1859, Lincoln said that "the chief purpose of the Republican organization was the effort to prevent the institution of slavery being spread out and extended, until it is ultimately alike lawful in all the States of this Union."[6]

The forty years separating the Missouri Compromise of 1820 from the secession crisis of 1860 and 1861 had seen mass cultural transformations of abolition and antislavery in the North, and of proslavery and Southern nationalism in the South. National churches had fractured along sectional lines, and Southerners opposed to abolitionism withdrew from contact with their fellow citizens to the North. Southern legislatures had erected barriers to the importing of potentially seditious publications from the North, and the antebellum Southern gentry turned instead toward England and Europe as sources of cultural stimulation.

By 1850, in the free and the slave states, free males from the young generation had accounted for 33 percent of eligible voters; by 1860 they were 66 percent. The alienation of this fighting generation, North and South, along sectional lines is a significant, and poorly understood, cause of the Civil War. These young men found mobility increasingly problematic, especially because movement to the western frontier had become less feasible on economic grounds. Beginning in the 1840s, aridity had altered the economics of frontier farming; along the midwestern frontier line, prairie and great plains ecosystems lacked standing water and trees. By the mid-1850s it began to cost more to move to the frontier than to remain in a settled area. Fierce sectional competition erupted over the last remaining contiguous area of trans-Appalachian wetlands, in eastern Kansas. Free-soil ideology, which sought to bar the further expansion of slavery, evolved in direct response to the scarcity of wetlands. The restless younger generation, in consequence, was clustered in regions closer to the East, in regions where the expansion of slavery was a core dispute.

The Republican Party justified opposition to the expansion of slavery both on class and racial grounds and on moral grounds. Unchecked slave-state expansion, they argued, would threaten the social mobility of poor whites. As Lincoln had said, in October 1858 in the last of his debates with Stephen Douglas:

> Now irrespective of the moral aspect of this question as to whether there is a right or wrong in enslaving a negro, I am still in favor of our new Territories being in such a condition that white men may find a home—may find some spot where they can better their condition—where they can settle upon new soil and better their condition in life. I am in favor of this not merely, (I must say it here as I have said elsewhere,) for our own people who are born amongst us, but as an outlet for *free white people everywhere,* the world over—in which Hans and Baptiste and Patrick, and all other men from all the world, may find new homes and better their conditions in life.

But, he went on, "The real issue in this controversy—the one pressing upon every mind—is the sentiment on the part of one class that looks upon the institution of slavery *as a wrong,* and of another class that *does not* look upon it as a wrong. The sentiment that contemplates the institution of slavery as a wrong is the sentiment of the Republican party."[7]

In the 1860 presidential election campaign, the North would offer assurances not only of an agrarian frontier for "free white people" to "better their condition" on "new soil" but also of stronger options for upward mobility in an urban, industrial-based, society. The antebellum South, in contrast, could offer few, if any, realistic alternatives to its commercial farming based on slave labor in a period of prosperity in which land and slave prices in already settled areas had doubled. If an entire new generation of younger white Southerners was now forced to abandon aspirations to become slaveholders through frontier migration, they would be consigned, in effect, to the "wage slavery" against which Lincoln himself had spoken so eloquently.

Prophets of a Southern Confederacy, Heirs of Calhoun

Had the seceding South been successful in gaining permanent independence as a nation, its pantheon of honored founders would surely have included three names: South Carolina's Robert Barnwell Rhett, editor of the
Charleston Mercury; Edmund Ruffin, a Virginia planter and noted essayist
and agricultural reformer; and William Lowndes Yancey of Alabama, a
prominent states' rights politician. During long decades of relative obscur-
ity, these early leaders of radical Southern nationalism, self-described as
"Fire Eaters," had kept burning a torch of fealty to John C. Calhoun, the
South Carolinian architect of the states' rights rationale for secession. As
early as the 1820s Calhoun had feared for the safety of slaveholding states in
a Union seemingly destined for permanent domination by free-labor
Northern states heavily influenced by doctrines of social purification, of
which abolitionism seemed the most threatening. During the antebellum
years, these nationalists, isolated from electoral politics, were viewed as con-
tentious outsiders. In 1860 they were transformed into prophets, if not followed as practical, political leaders.

Robert Barnwell Rhett, at a July 7, 1859, rally in rural Grahamville, South
Carolina, six months before the 1860 presidential campaign season was fully
underway, said of nations that "expansion is their law." Thus, the states of the
South must be free to expand if they were to forestall the "insurrections—
Northern intervention and final emancipation" that would surely follow
Republican thwarting of Southern territorial advance. "If our rights are victorious in the next presidential election," Rhett said, "we may consider it as a
kind [of] augury of a more auspicious future. If they are overthrown, let this
election be the last contest between North and South; and the long, weary
night of our dishonor and humiliation be dispersed at last, by the glorious
day-spring of a Southern confederacy."[8]

When Rhett called on South Carolina to imagine itself as a people as "distinct and antagonistic" from the North as Ireland was from England, he and
his nationalist ideologues were laying a foundation for the emergence of Confederate nationalism. During the 1850s, the vanguard of Fire Eaters, observ-
ing the emergence and growth of the Republican Party, noted the fulfillment
of Calhoun's prophesies of sectional strife and of a Southern position of weakness within the Old Union, yet they themselves seemed powerless to convince
a generally Union-loving Southern citizenry of the impending danger to slave

society and to Southern culture. That is, until mid-October 1859, when John Brown, a passionate abolitionist veteran of the struggle in "Bleeding Kansas," corroborated their dire warnings and gloomy predictions.

For several months before Harpers Ferry, John Brown and his band of militant abolitionists had lived quietly on a rented farm in western Maryland as they perfected plans for a slave insurrection armed by federal weapons they planned to capture from the federal arsenal at Harpers Ferry in Virginia. Brown's bold plan failed; members of his band were captured by a federal force under the command of Colonel Robert E. Lee of Virginia, and in the six weeks that followed, Virginia authorities indicted, tried, and convicted them all on charges of conspiracy to incite slave insurrection. On December 2, 1859, Brown, in manacles and hooded, stepped forward calmly as the hangman adjusted the noose.[9]

Southerners in areas far removed from Harpers Ferry seemed transfixed by news of the raid. Near Eufaula, Alabama, local slaveholders reacted with special terror when they learned that some of their own plantations, as one wrote later, "were marked on John Brown's map of blood and massacre as the first spots for the negro uprising for the extermination of southern whites." Fire Eater Edmund Ruffin rushed to Harpers Ferry soon after the raid to gather up some of the spears and pikes Brown's followers had crafted for distribution to slaves, concrete evidence of the danger so narrowly averted. The radical nationalist movement, he said, needed just "such a practical exercise of abolition principles . . . to stir the sluggish blood of the South."[10]

A nation newly linked by telegraphic lines was able to follow closely the unfolding story. Associated Press dispatches carried the tale of attack, capture, trial, conviction, and execution, with stories often filed at three-hour intervals. John Brown's dignity and composure won admiration even in the South, where his "confession" appeared in the press. His final words, written on a scrap of paper he handed to his jailers, resonated across the land: "I John Brown am now quite *certain* that the crimes of this *guilty land: will* never be purged *away; but with Blood. I had as I now think: vainly* flattered myself that without *very much* bloodshed; it might be done." Slaveholder Randal W. McGavock, mayor of Nashville, Tennessee, and a respected man of letters, recorded in his diary: "December 2, 1859—Everything went off quietly and was conducted with perfect military precision. . . . [Brown's] body was given to his wife who carried it off to New York. The abolitionists are holding prayer meetings in the northern states to-day. A great deal of excitement prevails all over the country."[11]

The South, which considered John Brown's trial, conviction, and execution a lawful response to an unlawful plot for mass murder, was astonished by the North's differing reaction. On the day of the execution one Northern newspaper wrote, "There need be no tears for him, for few men die so happily satisfied as did he." A mass meeting convened in Cleveland to coincide with the northward progression of the train bearing Brown's body condemned the execution, resolving that "a conscientious observance of the law of brotherhood as inculcated by Jesus Christ and the law of freedom as taught by Thomas Jefferson" demonstrated that Virginia's governor, Henry Wise, was a "contemptible caricature of the Old Dominion in the days of George Washington." A story in the *Tallahassee Floridian and Journal* headed "Murder Upheld" reprinted a Horace Greeley editorial from the *New York Tribune* which implied that if there were "a clear and rational conviction that the evil [of slavery] we combat could be overthrown," blood and anarchy could be justified. The editors of the Florida paper declared: "There the whole thing is in a nutshell. Brown was wrong only because his means were not proportionate to the end to be accomplished. What in Heaven's name are we coming to? A New York newspaper upholding *the right of the North to shed the blood of their fellow citizens!*"

State governors and legislators in the South now moved swiftly to strengthen their statutory defenses against slave insurrections like that John Brown had plotted. South Carolina took the lead to protect its slave property, to punish slave violence, and to prevent insurrection. On December 21, 1859, its legislature amended its "Act for Better Ordering and Governing Negroes and Slaves" and passed a new "Act to Increase Compensation to Owners of Slaves Executed" and an "Act to Punish Assaults Committed with Concealed Weapons." On December 22 it passed three more: an "Act to Punish Attempts to Poison," an "Act to Require and Regulate Licenses to Itinerant Salesmen and Traveling Agents," and an "Act to Provide for the Peace and Security of the State." Headlines printed over a fortnight in the *Montgomery [AL] Daily Mail* warned Southerners against Northern visitors arriving in the aftermath of Brown's execution. On December 2 a *Mail* editorial, "A Word of Caution," urged the hanging of all abolitionists; on December 6 it carried a "List of Torch Bearers" recounting recent abolitionist incidents. On December 9 a published letter urged the state to arm the volunteer groups that had formed in response to Harpers Ferry. A headline on December 16 captured the militant mood of the South: "Hang 'Em in Time."

A Sectional Election and a "Revolutionary Experiment"

In the presidential election of 1860, one of the most critical elections in American history, four major candidates vied for the presidency: Lincoln, the Republican; Stephen A. Douglas, the Northern Democrat; John C. Breckinridge, the Southern Democrat, and John Bell, candidate for the Constitutional Union Party. The sectional division was an ominous departure from the prevailing political norms and from the warning in George Washington's Farewell Address that political parties organized "by geographical discriminations" might "disturb our union." With the exception of John Bell, all three candidates were sectionally aligned, virtually guaranteeing that no candidate would get a majority of the popular vote. Ironically, the South's earlier insistence, in 1787, on an indirect Electoral College system kept the 1860 election from reverting to the federal Congress for resolution, as it otherwise might have done, since Lincoln won less than 40 percent of the popular vote, although he won a clear majority of the Electoral College.

Had the system of representative democracy functioned as in previous elections, voters in both North and South would have chosen from the same list of candidates. But no electors pledged to Lincoln appeared on ballots in the seven Lower South cotton states, and their citizens afterward felt justified in withholding consent to be governed by the victor. For all practical purposes, the 1860 election devolved into two self-contained contests in which the issues of slavery and the Union held center stage. In the free states, Lincoln battled against Douglas for the mantle of defender of the Union; in the Southern states, Breckinridge sought to persuade voters that he, not Bell, could best defend the South's vital interests. Indeed, campaigning in the South focused on the grave possibility of a disruption of the Union after a Lincoln win.

John Brown's attempt to precipitate a slave revolt at Harpers Ferry the year before had caught Southern citizens off guard; his execution, and the execution of most of his followers, failed to calm the sense of vulnerability among a population that knew in its heart that "their slaves had cause to rise and might find the resources." When public opinion in the North seemed to celebrate Brown's martyrdom, and when numerous abolitionists claimed membership in the Republican Party, Lincoln and his party were demonized in the South as being unconcerned about the safety and security of Southern citizens. To most citizens of the Deep South, their refusal to accept such a president seemed a principled act of self-preservation.

The Dred Scott decision of 1857 and the Lincoln-Douglas debates of 1858 had focused attention pointedly on slavery and on the issue of Union. Lincoln's formulation in those debates, driven by a quest for a constitutional basis for opposing the Supreme Court on Dred Scott, took its inspiration from the Declaration of Independence and the U.S. Constitution, interpreting both as antislavery documents. Jefferson Davis's Portland, Maine, speech in September 1858 may well have given Douglas the basis for his Freeport doctrine, which contained the first clear indication that some in the South believed that the election of a "Black Republican" would lead to secession.[12]

Following John Brown's attack, the Florida House began considering the state of federal relations, prodded by B. F. Perry, an upcountry legislator who had charged that Brown's "villany" was part of Republican Party policy and declared himself in favor of "eternal separation from the Union."[13] By the end of February 1860 the Florida legislature had passed a resolution stating that election of a "Black Republican" would be a cause for secession, and the Alabama legislature had passed one stating that it would trigger a call for a state constitutional convention.

A *New York Herald* editorial of December 1859, "The Presidential Campaign—The Opening of the Great Contest," summarized the bleak election prospects as conservative Democrats saw it:

> Yesterday our state elections, North and South for the present year were concluded, and today we are upon the threshold of the Presidential campaign. How stands the order of the battle? Looking over the instructive schedule of these elections of the present year we find all the powerful Northern sections of the Union in the almost unbroken occupation of the anti-slavery republican party, and the indispensable Southern section in the almost absolute possession of the pro-slavery democracy. Between these two overshadowing sectional parties the conservative elements of the North and the South have struggled in vain, and thus the controlling party managers of the two sections stand as fiercely opposed to each other as the belligerent house of York and Lancaster. For good or evil we are entering upon the most momentous political conflict in the history of the Union; nor can we imagine how this conflict limited to the anti-slavery crusaders of the North and the pro-slavery chivalry of the South can end in anything but the revolutionary experiment of disunion and Southern confederacy.

The single-issue campaign, slavery and Union, would deprive the 1860 election of the capacity to bestow on the victor the mantle of legitimacy.

The Democratic Party fell apart during the national convention, held, with all the best intentions, at the temple of Southern nationalism, in Charleston, South Carolina. The Democrats, North and South, would fail to present a consensus nominee. Stephen Douglas had never found an answer to Lincoln's question in their 1858 debate about congressional enactment of a territorial slave code, and the Alabama state Democratic Party instructed its delegates to the Charleston convention to walk out if the convention refused to bind its nominees to a proslavery platform. After Yancey, the Alabama Fire Eater, led a walkout of delegates from seven other slaveholding states, Douglas's bid to win the presidency was effectively at an end. A follow-up Democratic convention in Baltimore was similar to the first: Douglas gained a resolution of nomination but only from the rump remaining after a second Southern walkout. Most of the seceders went straight to Richmond, where a recessed states' rights convention was reconvened and gave its nomination to John Breckinridge. In Baltimore former Whigs named the final member of the quartet of presidential nominees, John Bell, for the new Constitutional Union Party.[14]

Republicans, meeting in Chicago, bypassed their own better-known candidates in favor of Abraham Lincoln, an Illinois favorite son whose chief asset, in addition to his masterful performance in the debates against Douglas, was his lack of a substantial political record. He seemed the perfect candidate for a party determined to avoid losing a presidential bid at a time when divisions among its rivals put victory so tantalizingly close.

Southern politicians were gradually being converted to the view that immediate secession was the sole way to defend the honored Southern way of life. The Democratic convention in Charleston had failed to support the Fire Eaters' efforts to precipitate the South into secession by splitting Democrats on the issue of a federal territorial slave code, but as the campaign rolled on to become a referendum on slavery and Union, even moderates, especially state governors, became convinced that the South could not risk existence under a Lincoln administration.

By September tension was thick in the South. Since the results of the fall state elections in the North appeared to forecast a Republican presidential victory, citizens in the Lower South began to prepare themselves for a response. Mass meetings, from mid-October through early November, passed resolutions threatening immediate secession should Lincoln be elected president. Local newspapers carried numerous letters to the editor from readers looking to secession as the only means of release. Anxiety was more intense in the Lower than in the Upper South, but concern spread almost everywhere. More state and local legislation was enacted to strengthen statutory control over blacks, both slave and free, beyond earlier efforts in the immediate aftermath of John Brown's raid. Local and state paramilitary preparations increased as well, in a sustained panic about the dire possibility of slave insurrections. There were also fears that a victorious Republican administration would use its powers to introduce into the South John Brown–style outside agitators posing as postmasters and federal marshals among the hundreds of officials who would be appointed after a new Republican administration was in office.

The end of the election campaign itself was anticlimactic. Although the South's national political elite—including Jefferson Davis, soon to be the Confederate president, and Alexander Stephens, soon to be the Confederate vice president—continued throughout the campaign to urge restraint, many in the South had already been persuaded to leave the Union before an elected Republican president could be installed in the White House.

The Hope for a Peaceful Plebiscite

President-elect Lincoln maintained a measured silence in the aftermath of his victory, but his supporters did not; and many of their responses, published in newspapers in the first days of the new administration, revealed a contempt for Southern citizenry. Chicago mayor John Wentworth, editor of the *Chicago Daily Democrat,* in a column entitled "Southern Braggarts," printed two days after the election, loosed a volley of invective that prosecession newspapers of the South widely reprinted. Wentworth dared the South "to try your little game of secession."

> Thus the people of the free North say to the slave oligarchy, We will endure your insolence, suffer your tyranny, bear with your assumption no longer! We have listened to your threats, as insulting as they are cowardly, of what you would do if we dared to carry out our convictions of right at the ballot-box and elect a man who would not bow the knee to you, and who would place your accursed institution of slavery where the public mind would rest in the belief that it would become fully extinct.

You have sworn that if we dared elect such a man you would dissolve the Union. We have elected him, and now we want you to try your little game of secession. Do it, if you dare!

While Wentworth promised protection of the South's "just rights," he warned, "Every man of you who attempts to subvert the Union, which we prize so dearly, will be hung as high as Haman. We will have no fooling about the matter. By the Eternal! The Union must be preserved!" He questioned the courage of the South: "The chivalry will eat dirt. They will back out. They never had any spunk anyhow." It is difficult to imagine words better suited to steel the resolve even of Southern moderates than words like this from a person reputed to have the ear of the president-elect.

A key editorial response in the North offered a test to let the South "go in peace." On November 9 Horace Greeley, editor of the *New York Tribune* and widely renowned as a founder of the Republican Party, wrote an editorial called "Going to Go," which at first seemed to be sanctioning secession. "The telegraph informs us that most of the Cotton States are meditating a withdrawal from the Union because of Lincoln's election. Very well; they have a right to meditate." Greeley himself, he said, held a "chronic invincible disbelief in Disunion as a remedy for either Northern or Southern grievance." "But if someone sees fit to meditate Disunion, let them do so unmolested. . . . If the Cotton States consider the value of Union debateable, we maintain their perfect right to discuss it. Nay: we hold with Jefferson to the inalienable right of communities to alter and to abolish forms of Government that have become oppressive or injurious; and if the Cotton States shall become satisfied that they can do better out of the Union than in it, we insist on letting them go in peace." Greeley stated the test succinctly: "Whenever a considerable section of the Union shall deliberately resolve to go out, we shall resist all coercive measures designed to keep it in. We hope never to live in a republic whereof one section is pinned to the residue by bayonets." But he did not intend a sanction of secession; rather, he claimed to be trying to buy time by encouraging the South to attain the unattainable: objective evidence of majority support for secession, gathered by constitutional means. Only then would the North let the South go in peace. Standard Republican dogma did not believe that a majority of Southern citizens, given a free choice, would vote for a slaveholders' republic.

Greeley's bow to Jeffersonian idealism enabled him to "uphold the practical liberty if not the abstract right of secession" while insisting that "the step be taken, if it ever shall be, with the deliberation and gravity befitting so momentous an issue." Only properly announced elections and open campaigns could make "the act of secession . . . the echo of an unmistakable popular fiat." Should secessionists meet such tests, "A judgment thus rendered, a demand for separation so backed, would either be acquiesced in without the effusion of blood, or those who rushed upon carnage to defy and defeat it would place themselves clearly in the wrong." Most Southern newspapers reprinting Greeley's editorial ended with this ringing reaffirmation of consensual sovereignty, omitting his final paragraph expressing skepticism about the likelihood of Southern compliance with his test. In fact, Greeley concluded with the judgment that reports of presecession activity in the cotton states "bear the unmistakable impress of haste—of passion of distrust of popular judgment. They seem clearly intended to precipitate the South into rebellion before the baselessness of the clamors which have misled and excited her can be ascertained by the great body of her people. We trust that they will be confronted with calmness, with dignity, and with unwavering trust in the inherent strength of the Union and the loyalty of the American people."

In retrospect, it would appear that Confederate nationalists were about to call Greeley's bluff. His widely disseminated challenge no doubt helped persuade many citizens in the Lower South that a bloodless plebiscitary revolution might indeed succeed, perhaps particularly in view of an analogous process unfolding then in Italy. Could secessionists devise, and then execute, a scrupulously democratic mechanism that would demonstrate majority support for the creation of a Confederate nation?

The Momentum toward Secession

South Carolina became the first of eleven slaveholding states to withdraw from the Union. From the nullification crisis of the 1830s on, South Carolinians had proudly claimed right of place, and even before the election the state had positioned itself for an expeditious secession should Lincoln win the presidency. On November 3, three days before ballots were cast, South Carolina's governor, William Gist, an ardent secessionist, requested the state legislature to remain in session pending the electoral results, hinting that an extended session might need to act in case of an emergency. Under the state's constitution, only the legislature had the authority to summon a constitutional convention.

In response to Gist's request, conservative Unionists in the state sought to delay a rush to secession. At the heart of their strategy was an undisclosed plan to force an adjournment of the legislative session as soon as it performed its constitutionally mandated task of designating electors. But their plan did not remain secret, and the governor devised a counterstrategy. An enormous rally in Charleston of advocates of immediate secession, scheduled for the evening before the election, provided the opening for an election-day telegram from Gist to Mississippi governor John Pettus seeking assurance that Pettus would call a special session of his own legislature, thereby blunting the conservative protest against South Carolina's acting first and alone. "If your Legislature gives us the least assurance that you will go with us," Gist wired, "there will not be the slightest difficulty, and I think we will go out at any rate." Two days later Gist sent Pettus a second urgent request. Mississippi conservatives were calling for a "Southern Conference" like that proposed by South Carolina in December 1859, and Gist begged Pettus not to renew his call of the previous winter "for a Southern Council, as the Border and non-acting States would outvote us and thereby defeat action."

Traditional Southern nationalist elders had distrusted party politics and the machinery of popular democracy, but Gist and Pettus represented a new emerging social movement in the Lower South, a protonationalist secessionism that sought to employ politics and constitutional machinery to achieve its ends. Fire Eaters like Edmund Ruffin and Robert Barnwell Rhett were excluded from formal roles in the unfolding secession movement. As the prospects for Lincoln's election loomed larger, the secessionist leaders in the states of the Deep South employed different political strategies from those of the Fire Eaters and appealed to a broader constituent base.

The wires hummed as elected officials and "interstate commissioners" exchanged information and counsel. While South Carolina nationalists would have preferred to act in concert with Mississippi, the arrangements in that state—which involved summoning a special session to call for a convention, then electing delegates, and only then convening the actual convention— would have imposed a month-long delay. If a vote for secession was to follow on the back of a Lincoln electoral victory, South Carolina would have to lead.

The mass meeting of November 5 in Charleston helped squelch the only serious threat to speedy secession. With Unionists unable to mount a countervailing demonstration for delay, the legislature on November 10 called a constitutional convention for December 17, designating December 6 for election of the convention's delegates. Two days before this election, the *Charleston Mercury* printed four lists of candidates' names, designated by degrees of willingness to commit to immediate independent state action. At the mass meeting at Summerville to elect candidates, by unanimous consent candidates were required to pledge themselves to support immediate independent state action on secession.

Few South Carolinians expected their state to remain for long the only one to secede. In an editorial on December 4 the *Charleston Mercury* urged early secession in South Carolina with the intent of influencing other state contests: "There will be no just view of things—no wise action—until South Carolina has seceded from the Union." It went on to point to the Alabama election scheduled for Christmas Eve day. "For the intelligence of our secession to go over that State previous to the day of election, South Carolina must secede from the Union by the 18th day of December—one day after our convention assembles." The numerous state legislative sessions, the procedures underway for electing delegates and for conventions, and secession ordinances—all influenced early secession. The South Carolina movement effectively functioned as a catalyst. Its convention opened on December 17, and although the vote for succession did not occur until December 20, its certain conclusion was widely forecast and overwhelmed opposition forces in other states. There were massive votes for prosecession delegates on December 18 and 20 in Florida and Mississippi, respectively, and on December 24 a secessionist majority of delegates was elected to the Alabama constitutional convention.

During the four-month interval between the election and Lincoln's inauguration, an aroused citizenry in the other Lower South cotton states—Mississippi, Florida, Alabama, Georgia, Louisiana, and Texas—voted to sever their states from the Old Union. Voters in states yet to vote were heartened by the bold action of neighboring states. The secession movement thus began to assume the character of a vortex, with an undertow that drew in reluctant citizens in other states. "Wire workers" like Ruffin telegraphed "glowing reports" from state conventions to elected officials and newspapers throughout the South. The result was a bloodless plebiscite, "surely a wonder on earth."[15] But if on the surface the new generation of secessionist politicians appeared to have engineered a peaceful democratic political revolution, they did so only by removing the issue from the direct choice of the voters, placing it instead in the hands of legislatures or special conventions. Not even their carefully orchestrated propaganda about Northern tyranny could entirely dispel the deep sense of loyalty many Southerners felt toward the American nation or the sense of uneasiness many nonslaveholders felt toward the political motives of their wealthier fellow citizens.

Only reticence to assume a position as advanced as South Carolina's prevented Florida from becoming the second of the Lower South states to secede. Eager young secessionists in Florida had lobbied through the press for swift action. One of the most emphatic polemics, published initially in the *Fernandina East Floridian* and reprinted throughout the state, was drafted by four daughters of a planter from Duval County. Their lengthy missive, with its lengthy title, "ADDRESS of the Ladies of Broward's Neck, through Editors of papers, to Politicians of Florida, as to their present and future protection against abolition emissaries of the N," argued forcefully against adopting too submissive a posture, lest the people of the South "be left to a large and hostile majority in Congress against us and our institutions." The letter closed with a blunt warning "to our aged matrons here and throughout the South, we would recommend to reserve your crinolines to present to Southern Politicians, who have compromised away the Rights of the South."[16]

Similarly bold challenges to reluctant secessionists appeared in other states. Three days after the election, the *Montgomery Daily Mail* carried a letter to the editor from a prominent Alabama politician, James Phelan, soon to serve as the state's governor:

> I am convinced that if the South submits to the rule of this Black Republican administration, slavery is destined to a slow but certain destruction in the Union and under *the ban* of its Government. . . . I think it a solemn duty which I owe to myself and my children, to the common cause of humanity, and to the religious institution of slavery itself, to withdraw it from under the power of a Government thus bent upon its destruction, and with that destruction untold calamities to the white race whose life (so to speak) is bound up with it.

A second, equally vigorous, letter carried the headline "A Voice from a Montgomery Lady":

> A few days ago, we could not be persuaded that the election would terminate as it has—and the wearing of the blue cockade seem rather premature. We could not believe the Northern States would so sin against themselves. We have relatives in the cold North who love, as we do, the Sunny South—but *submission* is out of the question—degradation like that, *they* would blush to witness. We

hear that there are some who still waver seeing no cause for secession—Heaven forbid that there should greater cause be given for an exhibition of self-respect."[17]

A story in the *Montgomery Daily Mail* on November 10, headed "The Flag of Alabama," reported that "the 'maids and matrons' of Montgomery, enthused with the spirit that actuated the women of '76, are making a splendid flag to be presented to the Southern Rights men of this city." At the foot of the cotton stalk that formed the central motif "lies a representation of a rattlesnake with head erect, and fifteen rattles. The motto is *Noli me tangere.*" The blue cockade, that popular emblem of South Carolina secessionism, had made its way to central Alabama, and female patriots crafted cockades and urged men to wear them. As quoted in the *Daily Mail,* the editor of the *Eufaula Express* had reported, "We have received several of these beautiful emblems of resistance from their hands, and feel greatly encouraged in the work of laboring for Southern rights. We never expect to see the South subjugated as long as bravery is encouraged and cowardice detested by the ladies." In a culture of honor like the South, public questioning by women of a man's own social class of his will and ability to protect his family would be hard to resist. It would later prove to be an equally powerful stimulus to volunteering for military service.

In Georgia's hotly contested debate on secession, Fire Eaters Ruffin and Rhett pressed for adoption of a constitutional convention bill. With Georgia vital to the success of a secession movement, a flood of petitions and resolutions on both sides inundated the state capital at Milledgeville. A pro-Union petition, drafted by a Tennessee novelist, L. Virginia French, was presented to the Georgia convention with the signatures of "hundreds of important women, both of the border slave States and of the North." It failed to gain the signature of Augusta J. Evans, herself an Alabama novelist, who wrote that she was "an earnest and uncompromising *secessionist.*"

> As a citizen of Alabama, I am proud to be able to tell you, we have irrevocably linked our destiny with the Carolinas, and if necessary will *drain our veins,* rather than yield to the ignominious rule of Black Republicanism; as a *native of the Empire State of the South,* my heart clings to her soil, and I look forward to the meeting of her convention, with a triumphant assurance that "knowing her rights she dares maintain them," and that in the palmiest days of our coming Confederacy, I shall look back to the 16th day of January 1861 and exclaim exultingly, "*I too am a Georgian.*"[18]

Test votes in January 1861 in the Georgia convention revealed a narrow margin between those for and against immediate secession. In Savannah's municipal election, held January 2, an effort to make the race a trial run on secession failed. In Arkansas and North Carolina, and in Tennessee and Virginia, it would take two rounds of campaigns, plus the surrender of Fort Sumter, to win popular assent for a resort to secession.

In February 1861, a month before Lincoln's inauguration, delegates from six states convened at Montgomery, Alabama, to exercise their "inalienable right" to proclaim the independence of the Confederate States of America. South Carolina's declaration of grievances against the Northern-dominated federal government was the standard on which the claim for independence was grounded. The delegates drafted a provisional constitution, selected a provisional president and a provisional vice president, assumed constituent powers, and enacted legislation that would make the Confederacy a functioning government. The new Founding Fathers were seeking to present the soon-to-be-inaugurated federal president with a fait accompli—a peacefully created, democratically elected, and smoothly functioning sovereign nation.[19]

An "Inalienable Right" to Separate?

The secession of the American South raised a principled question: Do the "people" possess an inherent "inalienable right" to designate themselves as "sovereign"? Can only the international community accord legitimacy? The American Revolution of 1776 had established a government based on the concept that sovereignty derives from "popular consent" rather than from oligarchic or divine "right," but the question of attribution of "sovereignty" to nationality remained unresolved and is still unresolved.

By almost any definition, the Confederate States of America was a viable nation-state during its four-year existence. It broke radical new ground by using the plebiscite to evoke a "constituent power" to make a new nation from the several states. Confederate nationalists had asserted an "inalienable right" of citizens in an administrative subdivision to peacefully claim sovereign independence from an existing nation-state. Had the Lincoln administration accepted such an interpretation of natural rights, plebiscitary secessions might well have replaced wars of national independence over the centuries to come, not only in America but elsewhere, as the primary method for redrawing national boundaries.

Although the Confederate experiment failed in the end, its failure is an insufficient measure of the ingenuity displayed by the slaveholders of the South in creating a Confederacy to ensure the safety, security, and future of the Southern way of life. The means Southerners devised to fashion a republic grounded in chattel slavery were daring and innovative in their resort to the precedent of the revolution that had made a united nation possible and the Declaration of Independence that had given it voice. In the making of Confederate nationalism a large majority of Southern citizenry came to see themselves as a "people" endowed by their Creator with divinely sanctioned institutions. With chattel slavery at the core of those institutions, white Southern intellectuals struggled to persuade their fellow citizens that theirs was not only a people but a race distinct and superior to the Puritan ancestry of the North. But the concept of "American exceptionalism" did not apply to the South's push for a separate governmental identity. The South had made common cause with the streams of ethnic nationalism sweeping through Europe, and it drew solace and inspiration from solidarity with oppressed peoples elsewhere who were struggling for independence.

Partisans of both North and South contended heatedly over the "original intent" of the Founders on questions touching on slavery. Did the Founders intend slavery's "ultimate extinction"? Did they intend that an individual state or group of states could withdraw, peacefully and at will, from the Union if the people in that state or group of states concluded, in an appropriate constitutional forum, that the Union no longer represented them? Had not the New England states threatened such a move toward separation at the Hartford Convention of 1815, when the South appeared likely to dominate the presidency permanently and thus the national government? Had not Massachusetts senator Charles Sumner threatened secession twice during the 1850s, after the Compromise of 1850 and after passage of the Kansas-Nebraska Act? Why could not Southern states do the same when their entire way of life seemed endangered?

Southerners were well aware of the competing nationalisms in Europe during and after the revolutions of 1848. A South Carolina journalist, Edwin De Leon, who first issued the call for formation of the "Young America" movement in an 1845 commencement address at South Carolina College, pointed to the nationalist movements in Europe: Young Italy, Young Germany, Young Hungary, and Young Ireland. Even after the Young America movement had collapsed, literate Southerners continued to follow European developments

closely, noticing, as some Civil War historians have not, that Italian nationalism achieved its long-sought-for goal during the same period, 1860–61, when
American Southerners were considering secession. Benedict Anderson's
investigation of nationalism does not refer to the Confederacy, but it does
suggest, by inference, that American Southerners had as strong a claim to a
"genuine" nationalism as any other contemporaneous movement for independence. Fully one-half of military-age white males in the Confederacy
would present themselves for induction into the military service of the Confederacy in the summer of 1861, and only a genuine popular movement could
produce such a compelling affirmation. This mass mobilization within the
seceding states of the South after 1860 conforms to Hugh Seton-Watson's description of nationalism as the process of becoming a nation: "A nation exists
when a significant number of people in a community consider themselves to
form a nation, or behave as if they have formed one."[20]

Writing in the 1920s, the historian Charles H. Wesley, in *The Collapse of the
Confederacy,* undertook to apply the theory of wars of independence to the
Confederacy. Wesley pointed to the seven-year-long American Revolution
and the eighty-year-long Dutch Revolution as examples of wars of independence that succeeded despite imbalances of population and resources far
greater than those confronting the Confederacy. He cited as the principal failure of the war effort in the American South, the South's inability to hold on
long enough to take real advantage of deep divisions within the wartime
North. He called it "astonishing" that the war did not continue far longer.[21]

Wesley exposed the tautology at the heart of the traditional explanation for
Confederate defeat. If, as a general rule, wars for national independence in-
volve struggles between peoples of inferior population and resources and
their more numerous and better equipped adversaries, it becomes impossible
to accept any analysis of a war for independence that rests solely or chiefly on
an imbalance of resources and population. An analyst must distinguish between successful and unsuccessful applications of similar strategies. To assert, as has the traditional explanation, that the factors that define an entire
category of wars also explain why a particular struggle fails, is to employ a circular logic. It restates its own underlying assumptions.

The experience a century later, of Vietnam in the 1950s–70s, also calls into
question the basic premise of the traditional explanation for the Confederate defeat, the assumption that the war was a "civil war." Civil wars are fought within
the boundaries of a preexisting state, either for control or for redress of re-

gional issues within the preexisting framework. But Southern secessionists did not create the Confederacy in order to inaugurate Jefferson Davis as president as an alternative to Lincoln *within the Union*. Nor did they proclaim independence to reassert a claim to regional power *within the framework of the Union*. The American Civil War was not a civil war at all.

Jefferson Davis, two days before his inauguration in February 1861 as president of an independent Confederacy, announced, "Our separation from the Old Union is complete. NO COMPROMISE; NO RECONSTRUCTION CAN NOW BE ENTERTAINED."[22] With the founders of the Confederacy relying on the American Declaration of Independence itself as a rationale for separation from the Old Union, every action they took after proclaiming independence looked toward establishment of a permanent Confederate nation-state. Independence alone could preserve the Southern way of life. The Confederate government's dispatch of ambassadors was a sure sign that the war was not, to the South, a *"civil"* war. When Southerners drafted a provisional constitution, elected a provisional congress and a provisional president and vice president, they set about perfecting the almost complete infrastructure of a nation. The war that ensued from the North's refusal to accede peacefully to the Confederate establishment of independence ought to be seen as a war by the Confederacy for national independence and by the Union to deny it. The military struggle of 1861 to 1865 was a "most un-civil war."

The Threat to Poorer Whites and Slaves

The Confederacy's claim to be a mass-based movement, a genuine "people's" movement, justifies Confederate nationalism's appeal to popular consent. An eloquent letter to the new president of the Confederacy from Reuben Davis, a prominent Confederate congressman from Mississippi, said that "every man" was involved in this "revolution" and all should join the fight. In the light of subsequent events it was prescient advice:

> We are seeking to establish a government and not to defend one. In a revolution (and this war is in the nature of a revolution) every man puts his neck in the halter and subjects his property to confiscation, therefore every man who is able to bear arms should be required to do it, if the pressure becomes so great as to require it; and this is the opinion of the great body of the people. They naturally ask the question why a certain section of the people should be required to do

all the fighting and endure all the hardships of the camps; and finally conclude
it is better to resume their former allegiance than to fight for others . . . I know
that private interest and to some extent public interest demands that there
should be substitutes and exempts. But when the indulgence of these considerations is endangering the success of the revolution itself, they must yield
upon the ground that it is better that a few interests should perish than that the
Cause fail entirely.[23]

But when the war came, private interests were indeed indulged, and a certain section of the people did bear more than its share of fighting and suffering. Although postwar Southern traditions maintained that the Confederacy
fought for the principle of states' rights rather than for slavery, the evidence
suggests that states' rights had no meaning in nineteenth-century political dis-
course except as the right of citizens of a state to control their own domestic
institutions—for example, the institution of slavery. Southerners who cited
states' rights doctrines did so to defend slavery, sensing the peril in the rise to
national political power of a sectional party that espoused antislavery ideals.
After Lincoln's victory with not a single Southern Electoral College vote, the
Northern Republicans had won control of two of the three branches of the
government, the executive and legislative. Southerners had either to accom-
modate to a possibly enduring subordinate position in a government they had
once dominated or to devise an ideology of a locally based "majority" rule that
would allow preservation of their cherished domestic institutions.

But in that focus on sustaining slavery lay the seeds of the South's eventual
defeat. On the day after John Brown's execution, Edmund Ruffin received a
disturbing report from western Virginia—a region where troops might be stationed if indeed war broke out—that opponents of secession were seeking to
heighten white nonslaveholders' anxieties about the risk to their own political
liberty within a slaveholders' republic; the fear was that "jealousy of the richer,
as well as self-interest would cause them to side with the North, and go for the
abolition of slavery." The *Columbia [TN] Herald* issued a typical nationalist
rebuttal: "In no country and in no States of the Union are the people more
upon an equality, more truly democratic and republican, than they are in a
Southern State, and this is the result of the institution of negro slavery." Georgia's governor, Joseph Brown, arguing that a failure to support secession
would mean abolition of slavery, declared that abolition would strike hardest
at poorer Southerners: "Abolish slavery and you must make the negroes their

equals, legally and socially." J. D. B. DeBow, of *DeBow's Review,* at the behest of the leader of a prosecessionist pamphleteering association, produced an article entitled "The Non-Slaveholders of the South: Their Interests in the Present Sectional Controversy Identical with That of Slaveholders." DeBow wrote, "The non-slaveholding class [is] even more deeply interested than any other in the maintenance of our institutions, and in the success of the movement now inaugurated for the entire social, industrial and political independence of the South." Nationalists promised the nonslaveholding majority that their interests would not suffer by creation of the Confederacy. These were promises they would not be able to keep.

In question also was the reaction of the slave population itself. In state after state in the South, competitive campaigning during referenda on secession focused attention, among voters and nonvoters alike, on the issues of slavery and its future in a federal Union. But nationalists had earlier acknowledged, if indirectly, the threat of a public campaign in the South against Black Republican abolition conducted in full view and hearing of a slave population. DeBow himself believed that Southern independence would calm restive slaves—they "would be under better control because it would no longer be necessary to argue in their presence the question of our relations with the North"—but expressions of fear among other whites about the consequences of slaves' growing political knowledge gathered intensity. From the pen of one prominent South Carolina Fire Eater came this plaintive cry: "I see poison in the wells in Texas—and fire for the houses of Alabama. Our negroes are being enlisted in politics—with poison and fire—how can we stand it?" During the summer of 1861, the spy Allan Pinkerton had been told by a nervous Kentucky slaveholder, "Allan you have no idea of the danger we are apprehending from the blacks. We know that the moment Lincoln sends his abolitionist soldiers among us our niggers will break out and murder all before them."[24]

Dangerous or not, Southern nationalists could not conduct a campaign to confer legitimacy on peaceful secession without revealing to slaves their expectation that Lincoln's election would bring the abolition of slavery. And once the seceding South began to mobilize for war, the precautions considered necessary in the light of this slave awareness exposed the class-based discriminations that would rise to undermine popular support for Confederate nationalism and, in the end, bring the Confederacy down.

Chapter Two   **"Playing Thunder"**

The Impact of Slavery on
Confederate Military Strength

A t the heart of the successful strategy of the founding fathers of the Confederacy to achieve a sovereign nation lay the plan crafted by the Fire Eaters, that group of radical nationalists who had maintained since the 1850s that preservation of the Southern way of life made secession necessary. The Fire Eaters, in effect, had transformed the 1860 presidential campaign into a referendum on Southern independence. These radical nationalists pointed to parallels between the antislavery platform of the Republican Party and the abolitionist movement. Abolitionism, they argued, would necessarily require destruction of slavery, the foundation stone of Southern society.

Could a nation built on the principles of chattel slavery and local sovereignty mobilize its collective resources soon enough and persistently enough to win national independence? Confederate independence would require the organization of a national government strong enough to convince the community of nations that the new republic was real. If Jefferson Davis succeeded, diplomatic recognition would surely follow, and with that recognition would come the confirmation of national independence most Southerners desired so ardently. When Lincoln responded to the loss of Fort Sumter in 1861 by calling for seventy-five thousand Union volunteers to crush the secession movement, few Southerners shrank from the prospect of a trial by combat; they believed the South possessed superior martial valor. But to win, the Confederacy also needed to mobilize a large army and in the shortest possible time. If it could win a few decisive battles, it might persuade the North to abandon efforts to preserve the Union and permit secession of an independent Confederate nation.

Grave danger loomed for the Confederacy, however, if its states' rights philosophy should come to dominate relations between the newly formed central government and the established individual states, and thereby undermine the military struggle. Initially, for example, the states retained the authority to raise troops and control weapons seized by local authorities from the federal arsenals scattered across the South. Thus, as the government in Richmond worked to build an army of its own, its War Department could not avoid almost total dependence on the willingness of individual state governors to provide men and weapons to its central government. And yet, during the spring of 1861 Southern governors in state after state declined to comply fully with requisitions from the War Department in Richmond. These governors were acting, in turn, in response to pressures from slaveholders in their states concerned about the increasing expectations for freedom among their slaves. Seeking to keep control over their slaves, slaveholders urged local political leaders to give top priority to local defense. Emphasis on local defense began to impinge on the efficiency of national mobilization, and the weakening of military strength was a direct consequence of the impact, feared or actual, of slave unrest in the face of the possibility of emancipation.

Efforts to Protect "the Peculiar Institution" amid Growing Slave Unrest

Edmund Ruffin of Virginia, that leading Fire Eater, had expected John Brown's raid at Harpers Ferry "to stir the sluggish blood of the South," and his expectation proved prophetic. Public fervor in the South for secession seemed to reach a peak in Texas, where in September 1860 R. S. Finley, a slaveholder from the town of Rusk, wrote:

> The designs of the abolitionists are no longer matters of doubt—they are lettered in poison, fire, and blood—and visible from Maine to Mexico.... It is no longer safe to tolerate any one, in Southern society, who in any wise affiliates with the abolitionists. Nor should anyone properly make the charge of "lynch law" against Southerners. A people who would lie supinely upon their backs until their enemies burned down their towns and houses, murdered by poison or abolition pikes and spears, their wives and children, and force their fair daughters into the embrace of buck negroes for wives, and plead absence of a *protective law* . . . deserve to be enslaved.[1]

In the Mississippi Valley, due process was now frequently overridden by resort to "lynch law." The *Texas Advocate* for June 21, 1860, reported the hanging of a female household slave after her owner, Alfred Pace, discovered his six-year-old son strangled. A mob accused the child's nurse of the murder and executed sentence on their own after the community voted 64 for hanging and 54 for burning. In Hopkins County, Texas, Dr. Carlos D. Hampton, a Texas physician, on returning from a visit to his Michigan birthplace in the spring, encountered a mob angered by rumors that he had been a delegate at the Republican presidential convention and convinced that he was inciting slaves to revolt. As his wife Cornelia told the story, Dr. Hampton barely escaped lynching. It was dangerous now to be a stranger, white or black, almost anywhere in the slave South. White travelers, peddlers, book agents, schoolteachers, tutors, and traveling salesmen were often accosted and attacked. In Athens, Alabama, so the *Haynesville Chronicle* reported on November 8, 1860, a local vigilance committee rode the doorkeeper of a tavern out of town on a rail after a slaveholder saw him conversing with a slave. The fear went both ways. In northern Mississippi, the Reverend Samuel Andrew Agnew, a slaveholder, had huddled with a group of other slaveholders until Christmas dawn, fearing, as he wrote in his diary of December 24 and 25, "the niggers are playing thunder over at Acock's."[2]

Both Jefferson Davis, who became the Confederacy's president, and Alexander Stephens, the Georgia planter who became its vice president, were among those planters who warned against seceding during the 1860 presidential campaign. "I consider slavery much more secure in the Union than out of it," Stephens wrote in a letter of July 10, 1860. "We have nothing to fear from anything as much as unnecessary changes and revolutions in government. The institution is *based on conservatism*. Everything that weakens this has a tendency to weaken the institution."[3]

Indeed, a number of slaveholders feared that any move toward secession would lead to liberation of the slaves. A campaign pamphlet, "The Destruction of the Union Is Emancipation," written by an Alabama planter under the name Nathaniel Macon, called support for the Fire Eaters and the cause of Southern nationalism "an act of political suicide which I cannot reconcile with the instincts of self-preservation." "*The success of slavery, the successful management of the black race,*" Macon insisted, "*is impossible outside of the Union. It is the Union that gives slavery perfect security, to slaves their present high value, and to slave labor its large measure of success.*" His words were prescient; as the war for national independence for the Confederacy wore on,

the institution of slavery became less secure, and slaves lost their value and labored with increasing resistance. In the end, the leadership of the South
would decide that only emancipation established by the South itself could salvage their cause. It would be too late to save the Confederacy.

In the aftermath of Lincoln's election, Stephens continued to counsel moderation; anarchy, he feared, might erupt within the South. A student of history,
he cited the examples of the English and French revolutions, writing in November 1860, "Revolutions are much easier started than controlled, and the men
who begin them, even for the best purposes and objects, seldom end them. . . .
The wise and good who attempt to control them will themselves most likely become the victims. To tear down and build up again are very different things; and
before tearing down even a bad government we should first see a good prospect
for building up a better." Stephens, like Macon, spoke for many of the "great
planters" of the South in questioning whether the potential benefits of a successful revolution could outweigh the consequences of a military defeat.[4]

Such reservations were to compromise the military efficiency of the Confederacy throughout the coming war. But before the war, ambitious younger
slaveholders, joining forces with the Southern middle classes in the winter of
1860–61, ignored these moderate warnings and carried the Lower South out
of the Union. Mississippi's James Lusk Alcorn, a Whig and the owner of
ninety-three slaves and an estate valued at $250,000, refusing to concede the
inevitability of secession, led the opposition at Mississippi's secession convention. But with the momentum clearly on the side of secession, Alcorn, the
first to vote by alphabetical order, cast his vote for secession: "Mr. President,
the die is cast, the Rubicon is crossed. I follow the army that goes to Rome; I
vote for the ordinance." Other reluctant secessionists, such as Stephens and
Henry S. Foote, who would become prominent leaders of the newborn Confederacy, joined Alcorn.

At the Confederate constitutional convention at Montgomery, Alabama, in
February 1861, the new secessionists shoved aside radical Southern nationalists like Virginia's Edmund Ruffin, Alabama's William Lowndes Yancey, and
South Carolina's Robert Barnwell Rhett to seize control. Their counterrevolution marked a critical point in Confederate history. The Fire Eaters were no
longer the principal ideologues of Southern nationalism; a more conservative
group had taken over. In nominating Davis they showed a preference for less
ideological and more pragmatic politicians, pledged to ensure the stability of
antebellum institutions.[5]

These pragmatic conservatives were aware of an earlier slave revolution in Haiti and recognized the dangers radical Southern nationalists had courted. In 1791 a small group of slaveholders in Haiti, impressed by the success of colonial rebels during the American Revolution, sought to take advantage of turmoil in France, but colonists loyal to France joined colonial officials in resisting a revolution. With the factions fighting among themselves, the slaves were able to exploit white disunity and launch a revolution of their own. They destroyed the island's plantation economy and killed a number of slaveholders and other free persons. Jefferson Davis, in his final speech to the U.S. Senate on January 10, 1861, cited images of the horrors of the Haitian revolution. He urged his Northern colleagues to allow the South to secede in peace, and thus avoid an invasion of the South that might ignite a massive slave insurrection.[6]

The historian Ulrich B. Phillips describes the insecurity endemic to a slave society: "Many men of the South thought of themselves and their neighbors as living above a loaded mine, in which the negro slaves were the powder, the abolitionists the spark, and the free negroes the fuse." "No amount of drumbeating by slaveholding extremists," writes Eugene Genovese, "would have succeeded in whipping up so much panic so often if the whites had not believed the slaves had cause to rise and might find the resources." In Davis, the Confederacy chose a president who, like Vice President Stephens, was committed to protecting the institution of slavery. Speaking before an enthusiastic crowd after his return from the Montgomery convention that voted for secession, Stephens said of slavery: "Its foundations are laid, its cornerstone rests upon the great truth that the negro is not equal to the white man; subordination to the superior race is his natural and moral condition."[7]

The Northern spy Allan Pinkerton, who spent much of the summer after Lincoln's election in the slave states gathering intelligence for President Lincoln, engaged one frightened slaveholder from Bowling Green, Kentucky, in a revealing conversation. The slaveholder told him that the slaves "know too much about him, there has been so much talk about the matter all through the State, that the niggers know as much about it as we do . . . it is too late now; they know as much as we do, and too much for our safety or peace of mind." Mary Woolridge, a slave, reported in her reflections on this time, "My Missus and Massa did not like Mr. Lincoln, but pshaw, all de niggers did." "De Firs' thing dat I 'member hearin' 'bout dat war," Dora Franks, a Mississippi slave, recalled, "was one day when Marse George come in de house an' tell Miss

Emaline dat dey's gwine have a bloody war. He says he feared all de slaves 'ud be took away. She says if dat was true she feels like jumpin' in de well. I hate to hear her say dat, but from dat minute I started praying for freedom. All de res' o' de women done de same."[8]

Slaves listened to conversations among whites, purloined newspapers and letters, and shared what they learned through the slave grapevine. The more loudly their masters and mistresses criticized the federal president for planning to free the slaves, the more they saw him as their best hope for freedom. They saw the secession crisis and trials of the Children of Israel as similar. Like the South's slaves, the Israelites had spent many generations in bondage; blacks saw themselves, too, as descendants of God's "Chosen People," due to win deliverance by divine intervention through an emissary, Moses, who would lead them "way down in Egypt land" to "tell Old Pharaoh, to let my people go." Lincoln seemed a reincarnation of Moses. Dora Franks recalled later, "The children of Israel was in bondage one time, and God sent Moses to 'liver them. Well, I s'pose that God sent Abe Lincoln to 'liver us." "I think Abe Lincoln was next to the Lord. He done all he could for the slaves; he set 'em free. People in the South knowed they'd lose their slaves when he was elected president." The emancipation ideology that had been stirred in slaves' political consciousness was to pose a continuing grave internal threat to the survival of the Confederate nation.[9]

If the Confederate process of trying to make slavery secure unintentionally fostered a countervailing ideology among the slaves, then Southerners indeed needed to exercise caution lest a Haitian-style revolution repeat itself in the American South. On February 24, 1861, a sugar planter named Alexander Pugh of Bayou Lafourche, Louisiana, hearing of seditious rumors in the slave quarters, urged his neighbors to mount intensive patrols. "The negroes have got it into their heads they are going to be free of the 4th of March," he wrote in his diary of the date of Lincoln's inauguration. One group of slaves near Natchez, Mississippi, did choose March 4 for a revolt. Surviving secret testimony from several of the plotters before the Natchez Vigilance Committee suggests how some had taken heart from rumors of immediate emancipation. A "Slave Nelson" said he would fight with the "Abolitionists." John, a trusted driver, told of "Black folks talking of freedom. These boys of Mrs. Dunbars . . . going to raise a company. Simon tells us where they would commence." A slave named Dennis quoted discussions in the slave quarters: "First talk of freedom. Alfred be a soldier. Kill all the damn white people. . . . Simon said he hoped to see the day when he could blow down a damn white man who called him a damn rascal." What alarmed Lemuel Conner, the planter who recorded this testimony, was not the revelation that many slaves wanted to be free, but the way slaves were connecting their desire for freedom to national politics. A slave named Mosely who testified at the Natchez hearing offered explicit evidence of danger: "I said 'Lincoln would set us free.' Alfred and Monroe Harris proposed a company to be raised. Drago has a pistol would shoot master. I got two pistols from Bill Chamberlain. Bill has a five shooter pistol. I heard Harry say Obey would join us. Howard told Margaret he murdered the Dutchman. Harry and Alfred are all for the plan." Natchez planters who heard the terrifying testimony hanged more than forty of the slaves they identified as plotters.[10]

In mid-May 1861, in Jefferson County, Mississippi, and Tensas Parish, Louisiana, word spread of a slave insurrection plot. Aware that "the negroes all know of the war and what it was for," Howard Hines dispatched his family from his Tensas Parish plantation to safety across the Mississippi River, then stayed behind, hiding under his own house, to try to learn about plans for revolt. He claimed to have overheard a sweeping plan: "When Lincoln came down each one was to kill his master and fire houses." In the wake of Hines's report, frightened residents promptly hanged two slaves and jailed five local whites caught accompanying the two blacks, in hopes of learning the identities of additional plotters. The plotters had chosen July 4, "at which time they have been induced to believe—Lincoln's troops would be here for the purpose of freeing them," or so a May 14 letter from Hines to Governor John Pettus of Mississippi reported. Not only was this the date of the traditional celebration of the Declaration of Independence but it was also the date when the so-called Abolition Congress planned to convene.[11]

Near Huntsville, Alabama, Daniel R. Hundley, a planter and the author of an 1860 book, *Social Relations in Our Southern States,* kept a detailed record in his diary for late May of another July 4 plan. A slave captured by a local patrol had apparently blurted out something to the effect that "Lincoln is going to free them all, and they are everywhere making preparations to aid him when he makes his appearance." Alarmed planters formed a Committee of Public Safety and began to visit neighboring plantations to interrogate slaves; those believed to be implicated were executed. Most slaveholders cooperated with the committee, but at least one slaveowner responded to the committee's hunt by spiriting his accused slave, preacher Peter Mud, away from Huntsville via the Memphis and Charleston Railroad. Whereupon committee members telegraphed warnings to communities along the rail line, and police in Memphis captured Mud and returned him to Huntsville. His master was unable to save him this time, according to an entry in Hundley's diary: "We then tried Parson Peter Mud. Peter was proved to be one of the principal conspirators, but the influence of his master's family in his behalf was great—however, he was found guilty by the jury and was hung in about half an hour, after sunset." Mud's execution apparently ended the Huntsville insurrection scare.[12]

Reports from other areas, while somewhat less reliable, suggest that a significant number of slave masters throughout the Mississippi Valley were alarmed at the prospect of insurrection on Lincoln's assumption of the presidency. Nancy Williard, wife of a slaveholder, wrote from Bossier Parish, Louisiana, late in May to a friend about a slave who committed suicide after his capture:

> The negroes are very bold here they have been trying to get up a company to rise six miles above here some of the crowd of runaways they caught one he abused his master to the last and told him that the North was fighting for the negroes now and that he was as free as his master they tied him and went on after the balance and caught some of them and come back to get him an he got lose an taken the cords that he was tied with and hung himself.

Planters cracked down hard whenever evidence or rumor of plots came to their attention. In June 1861, for example, in an unsuccessful attempt at revolt in Monroe County, Arkansas, two black men and one black woman lost their lives.[13]

Most slaves did not take part in insurrectionary plots; the odds against success were prohibitive, and even a hint of involvement would expose innocent and guilty alike to harsh repressive measures. A slave from middle Tennessee left a vivid account of the oppression of blacks: "I was a slave back in 1856, in John Brown's time [he's confused the John Brown panic of 1859 with the 1856 revolt scare]. They were might hard on colored people. They hung two men by the neck right where I was living. That was way before the Civil War. . . . In 1856 they whipped more colored people to death because they thought the colored people were fixing to rise." Slaveholder eavesdropping, interrogation of slave children, and reports from slave informants succeeded in reminding blacks of their vulnerability, and by rewarding slave informants and responding with force to plotting or suspicions of plotting, slaveholders forestalled any large-scale slave insurrection in the spring and summer of 1861.[14]

A number of local governments now tightened the laws that regulated slaves' movements. A police jury in St. Charles Parish, Louisiana, forbade merchants to trade with slaves and tried to compel masters who had allowed armed blacks to hunt for game to confine these slaves to their plantations. In Iberville Parish, Louisiana, a police jury in June 1861 tried to restrict all forms of unsupervised slave movement by passing an ordinance requiring elaborate permission from both masters before slaves on different plantations could consummate a marriage. It also tried to prevent unauthorized slave visits to town: any persons caught without the proper pass were subjected to severe punishment. And in an attempt to put a halt to independent trading, the jury decreed, "No slave could own a boat or a skiff. Those found with boats in their possession were to receive fifteen lashes."[15]

Local versus National Defense

State legislatures, too, assumed a more active role in requiring closer supervision of slaves and of free blacks as well. In March 1861 Louisiana made minor adjustments in its patrol laws, but Alabama and Mississippi passed acts forbidding the common practice of allowing slaves to live without a full-time white supervisor. Both states also strengthened prohibitions against selling "vinous or spiritous liquors" to blacks, slave or free. A special session of the Arkansas legislature enacted a provision requiring that an able-bodied white man reside on every plantation. Texas passed the most comprehensive patrol act of any state in the Mississippi Valley, authorizing patrol captains to call out the patrols "as often as the peace and quiet of the community may require." It ordered every county to mount a regular slave watch; patrol captains were granted broader powers to compel local men to serve on the patrols, and patrols were permitted to inflict up to twenty-five lashes as deemed necessary.[16]

Ironically, the harsh punishments that typically accompanied the discovery of slave "plots" served to heighten slaveholders' feelings of insecurity; the publicity surrounding these incidents served to remind the white population of its continued vulnerability to random violence. With knowledge about the war diffused widely in the slave quarters, with some slaves actively planning insurrection, and with able-bodied white men due to depart to serve in the

Confederate military, a major crisis of confidence was to ensue at home even before large-scale fighting began. The radically altered circumstances of wartime were to make the new rigorous regulations quite difficult to implement, since at the same time that frightened slaveholders were pressing for additional protections at home, the Confederate government was beginning to call up able-bodied white men. Mobilization took away many who would ordinarily have handled patrol duty at home; thus, legislative adjustments to prewar patrol laws could offer little effective relief to slaveholders concerned about control of their slaves. The competition for manpower prefigured what became a chronic and crippling wartime dilemma, the struggle between local and national governments for control over scarce resources.

After conflict with the North began, white Southerners tried to improvise solutions by relying on traditions of local autonomy. The local defense movement, one of the earliest attempts to find an effective method to control slaves, assigned men found unfit for regular military duty to guard duty. In May 1861 a slaveholder, J. B. Mannary, sent a letter to Governor John Pettus of Mississippi warning that reports of slave unrest "have shown us the necessity of organizing ourselves into Home Guards." Many Southerners rushed to offer their services. One slaveholder explained his decision to join an Arkansas home guard unit in these words: "You have no idea of the danger we are apprehending from the blacks. We know that the moment Lincoln sends his abolitionists among our niggers, they will break out and murder all before them. . . . We cannot sleep sound at night for fear of the niggers. . . . We are compelled to mount guards at night ourselves for mutual protection and though there has been no outbreaks as yet, I believe this is the only thing that keeps them in check."[17]

After a trip down the Arkansas River, an Alabama slaveholder named Felts, in a letter of May 24, 1861, reported seeing "companies of home guards all along the River. . . . They are drilling once a week to be ready for any emergency." The enthusiasm of the volunteers waxed and waned in proportion to the perceived threat. The Louisiana sugar planter Alexander Pugh complained that his neighbors soon stopped attending drill sessions. One meeting "was a complete failure," he confided to his diary on May 7, 1861. "There were only two persons present." The inconsistent performance of home guard units was not simply a matter of enthusiasm or the lack thereof. Many of the guardsmen were elderly. A visitor, Elizabeth W. Fox, wrote in a letter that the planter Benjamin L. C. Wailes, who took part in organizing the Natchez home guard unit in May 1861, was almost sixty-four years old, and the commander of Mississippi's militia forces described the Natchez home guard company as the military equivalent of a gaggle of elderly men armed "with broom handles." Many were unable to ride regular patrol for prolonged periods. Still, the pressure was a threat to slaves. After Felts revisited the Arkansas River region, he wrote in a letter of July 28: "As regards the slaves . . . all is quiet, more so than is usual if there be any difference. I never saw them more attentive to their business. . . . Negroes as a general thing have been more dutiful and have given less trouble this season than usual. . . . It is true they are pretty closely watched. The fear of insurrection is nothing like as great now as it was three months ago."[18]

As fear of a great slave revolt receded, masters found other causes for concern, with many slaveholders now noticing subtle and not so subtle changes in slave behavior that threatened to undermine plantation discipline. A number of Deep South slaveholders, for example, reported a disturbing increase in unauthorized slave leave-taking. Kate Stone, the daughter of a plantation owner in the Vicksburg area, complained in her diary for June 19, 1861: "The runaways are numerous and bold." Pugh's diary, in several July entries, told how planters in the Bayou Lafourche region, after a number of slave escapes, mounted a special patrol to round up runaways. Many slaves dodged work during peak labor seasons.[19]

In Mississippi, J. D. L. Davenport, who had learned of an insurrection plot in his neighborhood, demanded to know, in a letter to Governor Pettus: "Where I could be of the most service to my country, *at home or in the army* you see nothing but eternal vigilance will keep down the enemy at home as well as [on] our frontier." Davenport urged the governor not to allow another able-bodied white man to leave the state. Daniel Pratt of Alabama, the most powerful industrialist in the Lower South, sent his governor, A. B. Moore, a request that his company be permitted to remain at home for the foreseeable future; a large number of men from his area were already serving in the Confederate army, and "should the Prattville Grays leave we have verry few men left in our village and vicinity. I scarcely know of a plantation that would have an overseer or owner to attend to it."[20]

Contemporaries certainly felt that Southerners could ill afford to ignore their slaves' desire for freedom. An English observer, in a unsigned letter from New Orleans of May 30, 1862, published in the *London Daily News* and reprinted in the *New York Daily Tribune* in July, posited a clear connection between restive slaves and limited mobilization. The anonymous correspondent wrote that "the agricultural population, which in other countries furnishes the fighting masses, is, here, of course, ineligible for the purpose and ever requires armed power to keep it in order. There have been very alarming disturbances among the blacks; on more than one plantation, the assistance of the authorities has been called in to overcome the open resistance of the slaves." The Arkansas slaveholder Felts, in a letter of May 29, 1861, wrote, "We have but little to fear of negroes unless abolitionists should get among them." Planters nervous about such a prospect moved quickly to inform Richmond of their deep concerns. C. J. Mitchell, for one, warned Davis about the insurrection anxiety in a letter in April. With their sons about to depart for military service, he said, plantation families around Richmond, Louisiana, had begun to worry about slave discipline. Departing soldiers and older men left at home were expressing profound concern about their families' safety "should ever a John Brown raid occur, what with the sparse population and deep seated anxiety in regard to *Negroes*. Such a panic would ensue as would [be] ruinous to our cause."[21]

Mitchell's dire warning reflected the stark political and economic realities. Antebellum slavery had created a "dual economy" that had its core sector in the low country with its slavery-dominated commercial economy, and its peripheral sector in the yeoman-dominated and noncommercial "backcountry." There were significant social consequences of this dual pattern of economic regionalism. Slaves were concentrated, from about 10 percent of the population to more than 75 percent, in the counties within the Mississippi Valley states. The densest concentrations of slaves were in the low country—that is, along the coasts, the fertile river valleys, and the rich black prairies. Thus there was a high correlation between patterns of soil fertility and the centers of plantation slavery. The interests of the commercial sector lay at the heart of the struggle for Southern independence. The noncommercial counties that held white majorities grew only one-third of the nation's cotton in 1860, and yet these same counties contained 83 percent of the white military-age population. This economic, social, and political dichotomy would plague the Confederacy throughout the war.[22]

The disparity in economic fortunes between the core and the periphery might have suggested that disproportionate volunteering for military service would come from the plantation districts, but in general no such pattern occurred in the first year of the war. In the few places where it did exist, plantation slaveholders, ironically, saw a danger in such patriotic response. In April 1861 Governor Pettus of Mississippi received a fevered letter describing conditions in Tippah County: "Owing to the crises of our country," it said, "and the great excitement that now exists and the possibility of an insurrection of the black population as there have been some attempts all ready to poison and also to burn houses over their owners heads while a sleep, and also as you know there has been a good many volunteers taken from this neighborhood, and if there should be another call it will leave our women and children in this section exposed to the black insergeants." Similar warnings came to governors of Texas and Tennessee. Apparently, many older slaveholders especially grew apprehensive during the spring of 1861 about the heavy volunteering among younger slaveholders from the core economic sector. With the ratio of slaves to military-age white men averaging 8.5 to 1 in slave-majority counties, disproportionate volunteering among low-country slaveholders might well have left a vacuum that could abet a slave insurrection.[23]

The Negative Impact of Home-Front Fears on Volunteering

The anxiety of their elders about controlling slaves forced many would-be Confederate soldiers to make painful choices between patriotism and home-front security. Harry McDonald of Winchester, Virginia, was one young man who experienced such frustrations. His father, who had received a commission in an artillery regiment, returned home on furlough in June 1861, but he refused to allow Harry, his eldest son, to accompany him back to camp. (It was the custom for an officer to be permitted to provide an aide for himself.) Cornelia McDonald's diary records her son's reaction: "Poor Harry had fixed his hopes on being the one selected; but [his father] talked with him and told him that though he, being the oldest and stronger would be better able to assist him, he could not think of taking him from home where his presence was necessary, as no man was on the place but negroes." A member of the planter class in Madison Parish, Louisiana, knew of a similar conflict. "He is wild to join the army," wrote Kate Stone of a Mr. Davies in her diary entry for March 1, 1862, "but has his mother and four grown sisters absolutely dependent on him and it seems impossible for him to get off." A sense of responsibility for dependents sometimes forced younger slaveholders who had enlisted to return home to help manage truculent slaves. Private Robert A. Moore, whose regiment had gone all the way from Holly Springs,

Mississippi, to Culpepper, Virginia, wrote in his pocket diary on the day after the Confederate victory at First Bull Run that a Virginia militia held "a court martial to find out who were overseers, they being exempt. A doctor said he was his Pa's overseer and had a fight with a Lieutenant because he would not believe it." Two months later, a number of the commissioned officers in Moore's regiment, almost all of whom were slaveholders, left to return home to Mississippi. With the sound defeat of the Yankees at Bull Run, and with no forward movement in the offing, no doubt it seemed to well-to-do officers safe to give precedence to home-front needs.[24]

In slaveholding regions throughout the Mississippi Valley, young men of slaveholding families frequently hesitated to volunteer. The overseer of Magnolia sugar plantation in Plaquemines Parish, Louisiana, by 1862 was criticizing the men of his parish for failing to respond to a call for volunteers. His journal for March 4, 1862, told of "the military of this parish being called to Geather at point Alahast under special orders of the Governor There was a bout 200 men present when There should of bin 600 Col Wilkinson gave them an opportunity to volunteer but There was but 2 come forth Patriotism is very Low in this parish." By this time Oklahoma Indian slaveholders, who had expressed enthusiastic support for secession, were also holding back when it came time to serve. "Few have enlisted and gone to war," missionary S. Orlando Lee observed in a March 15, 1862, letter to the Indian Commission. Joshua Burns Moore, a lawyer and slaveholder, noted in his diary for April 19 of that year a similar phenomenon among secessionists in northern Alabama: "Our secession friend here first told us there would be no war. They found at last there was no truth in the prediction. They then told us *when the time came,* each one of them would shoulder his *shotgun* and meet the invaders and fight until the death for every inch of the soil of Alabama. Some of them cursed the slow approach of the Northern soldiers and so full of fight were some of them, that they went in squads . . . to get into the army for the fight, as they said, but soon they were seen returning with the excuse they could not get in."[25]

So stinging would public censure of such apparent reluctance become that the Plaquemines Parish *Weekly Rice Planter* felt compelled to acknowledge, in a story headed "Soldiers for the War," that "much has been waistfully said of the greater numbers of volunteers from northern Louisiana and condemnatory of the small numbers from other parishes." In a second article, "Patrols," the editor sought to justify the low rates of volunteering from his parish with an obvious reference to the possibility of slave unrest: "In troublesome times, precautionary measures should not be neglected." Slaveholding families in the plantation districts of southern Louisiana refused to neglect these "precautionary measures" even if attention to local needs worked at cross purposes to the Confederate national interest. Thus, St. Mary's Parish raised one battalion for home defense, but only three companies for national service. If these companies were of normal size, such a pattern would represent a more than 3 to 1 ratio of volunteers for home defense to volunteers for national service. A 1963 history of Civil War Louisiana by John D. Winters concludes that the heavily commercial lower tier of parishes failed to respond as freely to calls for Confederate volunteers as did the noncommercial regions of nonslaveholders. Areas with heavy concentrations of slaves and slaveholders put greater stress on state militia and local defense companies.[26]

The effects of insurrection anxiety on Confederate mobilization can be analyzed by identifying the Mississippi Valley counties where high rates of volunteering might have led to an increase in slave unrest. Out of all free families in the Confederate Mississippi Valley, 28 percent are estimated to have been slaveholders in 1860. The noncommercial counties, which produced only 17 percent of 1860 cotton, had approximately 60 percent of the white men of military age. Furthermore, over 80 percent of the slave population lived in the counties where more than 30 percent of free white families had slaves. In short, the counties with an above average population of slaveholding families were also those that felt heavily menaced by the threat of slave insurrection and, in consequence, provided fewer volunteers. At least initially, then, the majority of whites who were nonslaveholders had to bear a disproportionate share of the military burden. The direct cause of this inequitable allocation of the burden of military service was slaveholders' fear of slave response to the hope of freedom; the eventual result was the end of the Confederacy and the emancipation of the slaves.[27]

State Governors' Undermining of Mobilization

At issue in the conflict between local and national needs was the extent to which nonmilitary concerns of economic and social self-interest among individual planters would be permitted to hobble Confederate mobilization. Local and state officials tended, quite naturally, to be more sensitive to issues affecting local interests and to states' rights over national rights. No elected official could afford, for example, to ignore the pleas for assistance Confederate governors received in the spring of 1861. One impatient citizen, H. A. McPhail, in a letter of April 21 demanded that Texas governor Edward Clark answer a burning question: "If Texas is invaded from Black Republicans, what are we going to do for arms. Will Texas furnish or will each county have to do it?" Shortly thereafter, R. D. Meanelly, in a letter of April 25 to the governor, reported that settlers near Montgomery, Texas, faced a serious threat from hostile local Indians. "Whear is all these companies that has bin raised," demanded Meanelly. "We do not hear a word from any of them if we do not get some assistance soon I fear our settlement will commence giving way." Also, slaveholders accustomed by chattel slavery to the assumption of absolute control over their domains found it difficult to allow officials of the new national government to make decisions for them, particularly if such decisions appeared to run counter to their perceived self-interests.[28]

One thoughtful Texas civilian, R. B. Hubbard, offered an unusually candid rationale for giving priority to local defense. In a letter to the Texas governor of May 13, 1861, he said, in part, "I do not think it will be good *policy* for Texas troops to leave the state. . . . Our exposed Gulf Coast and our long line of border exposed both to Indian despoliation and Mexican forays, as well as our northern frontier threatened by raids from abolitionist Ruffians from Kansas and elsewhere—*all* lead me to the conclusion that Texas will do well to defend herself." Texas governor Clark had complied willingly with the first requisition from the War Department for three thousand fully armed soldiers, but during the six-week interval between his initial response and the second troop requisition of May 1861, Clark received a number of letters from civilians worried about the dangers Texas faced, letters that gave him the distinct impression that his constituents wanted him to exercise caution before agreeing too readily to dispatch any more men and weapons out of the state. When Richmond presented its second major call, this time for five thousand armed soldiers, the governor told the secretary of war, Leroy Pope Walker, on May 20 that he had changed his mind; he believed he had little choice but to respond with a firm and emphatic no. Indeed, each of the other Confederate governors in the Mississippi Valley—Andrew B. Moore of Alabama, Hiram Rector of Arkansas, Thomas O. Moore of Louisiana, John Pettus of Mississippi, and Isham Harris of Tennessee—declined that spring to comply fully with troop and weapons requisitions.[29]

Jefferson Davis did not sit idly by and watch state governors undercut his mobilization policy. He wrote to Louisiana's Thomas Moore to try to impress on him the urgency of turning over all the weapons captured from the U.S. arsenal at Baton Rouge. Only four months before, the Louisiana governor had unhesitatingly dispatched seven thousand weapons to Governor Pettus, yet now, in a letter on May 9 to the Confederate president, Moore rejected his new appeal, writing politely but firmly, "You will bear in mind that self-preservation rendered it necessary to arm the volunteer companies that have sprung up from the exigencies of the times." Confronted by a similar situation, Alabama's Andrew Moore took a similar position, drafting a June 18 letter to his state's senator Clement C. Clay, who happened to be a close friend of Davis's, expressing sorrow at the circumstances that compelled him to deny state arms to a company pledged to Confederate service:

> I deemed it inexpedient to do so. I have determined to issue no more arms for companies unless ordered out for the defense of the State. . . . For the protection and defense of the State against invasion or insurrection, the State has no more than 4000 muskets and rifles. . . . I therefore deem it my duty to retain them in the Armory so that they may be used in an emergency and where most needed. If I issue them they may get out of the State or if they do not they will be scattered over the State and out of place if an invasion or insurrection should occur.

The Alabama governor continued to stand his ground and refused at various times to send weapons either to General Albert Sidney Johnston in Kentucky or to General Braxton Bragg at Pensacola Bay. Indeed, not content merely to refuse to dispatch weapons, several states now embarked on independent efforts to build militia organizations to protect their home fronts. In 1861 the legislatures of Alabama and Texas ordered changes in the arrangements for their state militias, Alabama requiring its county and district militias to muster at more frequent intervals, Texas inaugurating thirty-three new regional militia brigades. By early in 1862, Louisiana, Mississippi, and Tennessee had moved to create statewide militias for service in local emergencies. In Arkansas the legislature passed a similar law, although Governor Rector vetoed it. Such state-sponsored efforts inevitably competed with the Confederate army, both for scarce men and for weapons.[30]

Events in Arkansas showed more clearly than elsewhere, perhaps, the destructive effect of state militia organizations on effective utilization of Confederate resources. Arkansas felt particularly vulnerable to abolitionist raids because of its proximity to John Brown's Kansas; indeed, when a rumor swept through Little Rock in late May 1861 about an impending raid by Kansas "Jayhawkers," residents flew into frenzied preparations to defend their homes. "Such a cleaning of guns and moulding of bullets you never saw," one resident, M. E. Weaver, wrote in a letter. At about the same time, the Confederate War Department dispatched Brigadier General Benjamin McCulloch to Little Rock to assume responsibility for the defense of Arkansas. Conflict erupted very quickly between McCulloch and Governor Rector, and on his own initiative the governor distributed thousands of weapons that had been seized from the federal arsenal at Little Rock to home defense companies. The frustration of losing these resources prompted McCulloch to inform the Confederate War Department, on May 20, that the weapons needed to arm regular Confederate troops were "scattered . . . in every direction, without any method or accountability, and it is impossible to tell what has become of them." The governor, undaunted by the damage his policies had already inflicted, refused to turn over his state militia to the Confederate army, and in a letter to Secretary Walker he insisted that as governor he needed a "permanent state army." Rector would later fail to organize an orderly "state army," and the ragtag assemblage of men disbanded of their own discord in August 1861, taking with them the last of the weapons seized earlier from the Little Rock federal arsenal. The fate of these weapons amply justified McCulloch's concern that the creation of a poorly disciplined state militia would result in the loss of thousands of guns desperately needed by the Confederate army.[31]

Especially during the first six months of the war, the aggressive assertion of states' rights, rooted in anxiety about local defense, especially against possible slave unrest, significantly retarded Confederate mobilization. Walker reported in a letter to Davis on July 24, 1861: "There can be no doubt that if arms were only furnished no less than 200,000 additional volunteers for the war could be found in our ranks in less than two months." And yet the weapons needed to arm these volunteers were available within the Confederacy, since the states, collectively, possessed twice as many guns as the Richmond government. The historian Frank L. Owsley argues that the governors' reluctance to part with these state-controlled weapons crippled the Confederate army; arming two hundred thousand additional volunteers would have increased from four hundred thousand to six hundred thousand the number of soldiers available for combat during the crucial first summer of the war. Such a large-scale augmentation was precisely what the outnumbered Confederate cause needed to take the offensive and win the decisive early victories that might have led the Confederacy to a quick independence during the period when Northern defenses were at their weakest.[32]

The Lack of Volunteers and Weapons

In the immediate aftermath of the first great battle of the Civil War, the Confederacy began to pay a heavy price for the success its local officials had achieved in setting up home defenses to slow a possible slave revolt. On July 21, 1861, Confederate soldiers won a hard-fought victory at First Bull Run, a battlefield fewer than thirty miles from Washington, D.C. President Davis arrived from Richmond just as a badly routed Union army had begun to retreat in disarray, and concerned that his army not lose the momentum of its stunning victory, he suggested that the Southern army push aggressively toward the federal capital. However, General Joseph E. Johnston and General Pierre G. T. Beauregard demurred, citing the exhausted condition of their troops, the poor state of the roads, and uncertainty about the opposition such a pursuit might face. They persuaded Davis that their joint command lacked the resources for an effective pursuit. The home-front defense movement played a decisive role in this decision. Several weeks earlier, after Johnston had requested reinforcements, Davis replied on July 13 that he could do little other than express his regrets; he lacked the weapons to arm all the available volunteers.[33]

The question of what might have happened had the Southern army advanced toward Washington after First Bull Run has been a source of controversy ever since. Bell Irvin Wiley has asked what might have happened had state governors used the weapons under their control to arm thousands of additional volunteers, thereby making reserve forces available to the hard-pressed central government. Wiley concluded that the presence of those tens of thousands of additional soldiers "might well have resulted in an overwhelming movement on Washington instead of in a stalemate." Although some scholars have gone further and insisted that a forward movement would have captured the federal capital, such an outcome was probably unlikely. However, Clement Eaton has made the salient point that "attempting" to capture the federal capital would itself have been extremely beneficial, and B. Franklin Cooling has pointed out that a prolonged siege might well have

sufficiently damaged the Northern cause as to create the impression of
indomitability on which the establishment of Confederate independence
rested. To the extent that anxiety about the safety and security of the home
front deprived the Southern cause of resources, it seems likely that this crisis
significantly retarded the Confederacy's offensive potential. From the very beginning, therefore, the South had to settle into a defensive posture that ensured that the war for Southern independence would become a long war of
attrition.[34]

Nor did such problems end in July 1861. In fact, the Confederate army
called off an offensive planned for the Virginia front in the fall because, even
by then, it lacked the weapons for essential reinforcements. Confederate army
officers were aware of the dangers created by the conflict between local sovereignty and national defense. General Bragg, for example, complained bitterly
about the mania among state governors for local defense. The measured response dispatched to Bragg on November 4, 1861, by Judah P. Benjamin, now
acting secretary of war, caught the essence of the dilemma that confronted the
government at Richmond:

> I fully concur in your strictures on the "local defense" system, but you are mis-
> taken in supposing that the Confederate Government can do anything to pre-
> vent it. The difficulty lies with the Governors of the States who are unwilling to
> trust the common defense to one common head. They therefore refuse arms to
> men who are willing to enlist unconditionally for the war, and put these arms in
> the hands of mere home militia who are not bound to leave the State. It is a very
> untoward condition of things, but as we have no arms and the State authorities
> will not give us control of the matter, we are forced to accept from them just
> what they choose to give. . . . All this is sad, but I know not how to avoid it. Each
> Governor wants to satisfy his own people, and they are not wanting politicians
> in each state to encourage the people to raise the cry that they will not consent
> to be left defenseless at home. The voice of reason which would teach that their
> home defense would be best served by a vigorous attack of the enemy on his
> own frontier is unheeded, and a clamor is raised against us for not attacking the
> enemy in front, by the very men who are depriving us of the possibility of such
> a movement by with-holding the arms necessary for reinforcing our little army
> so fearfully outnumbered that I dare not give you the figures.[35]

As Secretary Benjamin's letter makes clear, anxiety about the stability and
security of the Southern home front was the principal cause of the systematic

diversion of men and weapons toward home defense duty. Although Benjamin expressed considerable skepticism about the need for so much local defense, a 1966 study of politics on the Southern home front by Mary Spencer Ringold concludes that "state authorities had cause to doubt the ability of the Confederacy to deploy strong units for frontier and border defense and to insure safety from slave insurrection." This apparently irreconcilable conflict suggests two tentative conclusions: first, that the slaveholders' crisis of confidence was solidly grounded in awareness of their slaves' potentially aggressive response to the secession movement and the possibility of emancipation; and second, that a justifiable anxiety about the stability of slavery as an institution prompted the slaveholders to pressure state and local officials into giving precedence to local manpower and matériel requirements. In fact, many planters feared, according to James Roark, that "rather than standing astride a perfectly ordered, conservative slave society, they were shakily perched on an unstable social pyramid, with deep fissures only thinly papered over."[36] The institution of slavery clearly played a dominant role in the processes of social change that established the effective limits of the Confederate war-making capacity. And these limitations, in turn, suggest that the wartime South was a society whose whole was less than the sum of its parts.

Chapter Three   "A People's Contest"?

Popular Disaffection
in the Confederacy

The two rival American presidents clearly recognized that the balance of power would swing to whichever cause won the allegiance of Southerners outside the Cotton South. Jefferson Davis worked to bring into the Confederacy four of the Union slaveholding states which had not already seceded—Virginia, Arkansas, North Carolina, and Tennessee; Abraham Lincoln determined to bring all eleven already seceded states back into the shattered Old Union and to hold the loyalty of the others.

Radical nationalists in the South, the Fire Eaters, confidently expected that all fifteen slaveholding states would eventually join the Confederacy. The Lower South cotton states—South Carolina, Mississippi, Texas, Florida, Georgia, Alabama, and Louisiana—had seceded after Lincoln's election. In his inaugural address of February 18, 1861, Davis, who had been elected provisional president of the Confederacy by the constitutional convention at Montgomery, Alabama, on February 9, invited those still in the Union—the eight slave states of the Upper South and the border—into the new republic. Lincoln's promise, at his own inauguration on March 4, not to interfere with the institution of slavery where it already existed was not enough to keep the Upper South states of Virginia, Arkansas, North Carolina, and Tennessee in the Union when the choice came of whether to fight for or against the Confederacy. Lincoln worked frantically to thwart the secession of the border slave states of Delaware, Kentucky, Maryland, and Missouri by purging his administration's policies of any taint of abolitionism. He revoked the limited, and controversial, emancipation proclamation of August 30, 1861—issued by General John C. Frémont and declaring free the slaves of disloyal masters in Missouri—insisting, in a September 22 letter to O. W. Browning, that it would have provoked the secession of Kentucky, which in turn would have led to the secession of Missouri and Maryland: "These all against us and the job on our hands is too large for us. We could as well consent to the separation, including the surrender of the capital."[1]

In a special message on July 4, 1861, Lincoln characterized the war as "essentially a people's contest" and the Union as the best exemplar of the American ideal of popular democracy. He disputed the claim, offered to justify Confederate independence, that the Southern nationalist movement had peacefully created—and democratically elected—a smoothly functioning republic. "The whole class of seceder politicians," Lincoln charged, had engaged in antidemocratic tactics that camouflaged a lack of majority support. "It may well be questioned whether there is to-day a majority of the legally qualified voters of any State, except, perhaps, South Carolina, in favor of disunion." In fact, Lincoln said, "There is reason to believe that the Union men are in the majority in many, if not every other one, of the so-called seceding states." Further, the Union cause afforded the surest guarantee of both political equality and economic opportunity. The North, in stark contrast to the elitist South, was seeking "to afford all an unfettered start and a fair chance in the race of life." Adding an aside Southern nationalists would take as a gross slander, Lincoln said, "I am most happy to believe that the plain people understand and appreciate this."[2] He was appealing over the heads of the aristocratic Confederate leadership to the "plain people" of the South.

"Our Only Chance": Lincoln's Plan for Winning Over the Upper and Border South

The president spent July 21, 1861, the day of the Battle of First Bull Run, at the War Department's telegraph office, anxiously awaiting reports. When, at dusk, the news seemed favorable, he went out for his usual evening carriage ride, only to learn afterward that a battle considered won by the Union had somehow been lost. The next day a long procession of eyewitnesses recounted the sad tale of defeat. That evening Lincoln "lay on a sofa in his office and penciled an outline of what lay ahead to be done, a program for immediate action." He directed that the often-discussed plan for blockading Southern ports now be pushed with dispatch, and ordered a series of troop movements intended to secure the capital itself and provide assistance to pro-Union activists along the mountainous boundary of the Confederate western front.[3] This decision, ignored by many historians, to engage in active promotion of mountain pro-Unionism proved to be a watershed in the evolution of Northern strategy. While it suggests that Lincoln's devotion to Southern Unionism was part of a calculated effort to destabilize the Confederacy, the plan arose out of his long and fervently held conviction that radical nationalists had seduced Union-loving white Southerners into abandoning the nation of their Founding Fathers.

Taking heart from the opposition to secession that had emerged in the Upper South and in the border slave states, Lincoln sought to encourage pro-Union sentiments among the diverse branches of Southern Unionism: slaveholding Unionists in the border states, former Whigs in the commercial core of the South, and the up-country yeomanry. He would capitalize on the political instability in the South, most evident in the resistance of mountain yeomen of western Virginia and eastern Tennessee against incorporation of their up-country homelands into a slaveholders' republic. The vigor of the antisecession movements of the mountain backcountry encouraged his faith in the residual strength of Southern Unionism. That faith was buttressed by the Republican Party's free labor view that slavery's ready source of involuntary labor excluded nonslaveholding farmers and wage earners from full participation in the Southern economy. In May 1861 Lincoln had begun to use Northern military resources to support mountain Unionists; his "Memorandum of Military Policy Suggested by the Bull Run Defeat 23 and 27 July 1861" directed "the forces in Western Virginia" to continue that policy. He proposed that the Northern army try to liberate the Unionist sympathizers of the mountains of "East Tennessee."[4]

The day before Lincoln released his east Tennessee plan, he spent an afternoon with Henry C. Whitney, an old friend from Illinois, and in a candid conversation he explored the catalytic role popular disaffection in the South would need to play for the North to win. The debacle at First Bull Run had apparently convinced him that Northern military power alone could not defeat the Confederacy; rather, the superior Northern resources would be most effective in concert with a divide-and-conquer strategy for fostering unrest inside the Confederacy itself. By providing mountain Unionists with material assistance and ideological encouragement, Lincoln hoped to undermine morale among the most disaffected of the nonslaveholders, who constituted the Confederacy's actual popular majority. "I hope ultimately they will get tired of it and arouse and say to their leaders and to their politicians, 'This thing has got to stop!' That is our only chance. It is plain to me that it's no use of trying to subdue those people if they remain united and bound they won't be subdued."

In Lincoln's judgment, the Confederacy's vulnerability to destabilization was rooted, in part, in contradictions inherent in the earlier ideology of antebellum Southern nationalism. Any argument that American citizens possessed an inalienable right to secede from a government whose policies appeared to threaten what they saw as their vital interests was double-edged. How would a seceding group that had established itself as a new nation founded on respect for local autonomy respond to the inevitable irreconcilable challenges from its own disaffected citizens? How could the Confederacy, for example, logically deny a disaffected group within its own territory an "inalienable right" of its own to secede from a secessionist regime? Any sizable disaffected group could employ secession to demonstrate disagreement with policies that seemed a threat to its interests. Secessionist ideology was, thus, logically inconsistent as well as incompatible with the American tradition of majority rule through representative democracy. Lincoln understood this dilemma. As he had said in a special message on July 4, the inability to sustain democratic government was evidence that "the principle [of secession] itself is one of disintegration, upon which no government can possibly endure."[5]

Southern "Homogeneity" under Threat

For several years before the secession movement began, some Southern nationalists had wondered aloud whether the alienation of mountain yeomen from low-country slaveholders might, in a period of crisis, destroy the structure of Southern society. Edmund Ruffin had feared such a consequence, particularly after a fellow slaveholder's warning to him on the day after John Brown was hanged. A Mr. Thompson, who claimed extensive knowledge of unsettling political developments in western Virginia, had met with Ruffin on December 3, 1859, near the site of Brown's execution, and had pointed with alarm to reports that most of the residents of Harpers Ferry had done nothing whatever to help put down John Brown's raid. Would not secession, therefore, require the South to station troops in western Virginia? Thompson's concern about the loyalty of mountain yeomanry prompted him to wonder whether "their jealousy of the richer, as well as self-interest, would cause them to side with the North, and go for the abolition of slavery." Both Thompson and

Ruffin recognized the danger to the institution of slavery of any spread of such disaffection to the Lower South. Would nonslaveholders within the cotton states follow the lead of mountaineers if they refused to support Southern nationalism? "The dissolution of the union," warned Thompson, "would be the death sentence of Southern negro slavery."[6]

The Confederate leadership itself tended to deny that any such problem existed. In February 1861 Jefferson Davis boasted, indirectly, about the unity of purpose the Confederacy would evoke as long as its conduct of affairs conformed to the traditions of Southern political culture. Speaking of his fervent conviction that the attainment of national independence would carry the South "to the safe harbor of constitutional liberty," he said in a February 16 speech shortly before his inauguration as provisional president, "Thus we shall have nothing to fear at home, because at home we shall have homogeneity."[7]

Nor was Davis alone in assuming an ideological consensus about the relationship between the justification of slavery and the survival of Southern popular democracy. A month before the 1860 election, the Alabama Fire Eater William Lowndes Yancey articulated a basic axiom of Southern political culture: "The white race is the citizen, and the master race, and the white man is the equal of every other white man." The Confederate leadership clearly hoped that a commonly held racial ideology would sustain nonslaveholders as well as slaveholders in "homogeneity" in the face of any threat to the Southern way of life.[8]

Davis did not respond directly to Lincoln's challenge to the South on the ideology of democracy but chose to emphasize instead the broad base of popular support he believed the Confederacy enjoyed. In a July 20, 1861, message to the provisional Confederate Congress, he argued that strong popular support for the Confederacy made defeat unthinkable: "To speak of subjugating such a people, so united and determined, is to speak a language incomprehensible to them." Still, he sought to discredit Lincoln's view by attacking the ethical basis of the Union claim that it was the sole fit defender of American idealism. In a paragraph on Northern "outrages" against "the sacred claims of humanity," Davis included a sentence on the "horror" of the Northern embargo on medical shipments to the South: "But who shall depict the horror with which they [will] regard the cool and deliberate malignity which, under the pretext of suppressing an insurrection, said by themselves to be upheld by a minority only of our people, makes special war on the sick, including the women and children, by carefully devised measures to prevent their obtaining the medicines necessary for the care."[9]

As the secession movement evolved, however, the range of popular responses in the Confederacy to Southern nationalism revealed weaknesses within its social foundations. Southern nationalists had carried the seven Lower South cotton states out of the Union with ease, but in the eight states of the Upper South and the border, secessionists had encountered resistance, failing to persuade a majority of the voters that the 1860 electoral results constituted a sufficiently grave threat to justify secession before Lincoln's inauguration. Indeed, during the winter of 1860–61, an overwhelming majority of the yeomanry of the Upper South decided against it, playing a decisive role in the series of referenda on immediate secession held in February 1861 in Arkansas, Missouri, North Carolina, Tennessee, and Virginia. They frequently employed the ideological vocabulary of antebellum politics to support their contention that creation of a slaveholders' republic threatened political liberties Southern yeomen cherished.

At the heart of Southern political culture in general lay an obsessive anxiety about such a loss of freedom. In a society where the term "political slavery" meant subjugation to "arbitrary control," politics tended to emphasize equality before the law for all free men of any social position. If any group of outsiders, particularly low-country slaveholders, seemed poised to threaten this tradition of equality of all white men before the law, yeomen could mount a spirited defense of their traditional right to control their own destiny, citing the values of the culture of Southern honor. And in the years when radical nationalists had carried on their campaign for revolution, the South was struggling to adapt to a new, and relatively untried, single-party electoral system with no political party within the South committed to the special interests of the common people. Although, from the 1820s until the 1850s, a two-party alignment had cast the Democratic Party as defender of the interests of the "common man" against the self-styled "aristocrats" represented by the Southern wing of the American Whig party, in 1854–55, after the Kansas-Nebraska Act led to conflict between the Whig Party's Northern and Southern wings, that party disintegrated. The Know-Nothing Party attempted to fill the void but failed to shed the stigma of abolitionism sufficiently to assume the regional and national roles of the displaced Southern Whigs. Thus the Democrats were left, during the secession crisis of 1860 and 1861, as the only effective national political party represented in all of the Southern states. Because Southern Whigs had no remaining formal political organization of their own, the Southern wing of the Democratic party absorbed the very "aristocrats" who had been its most bitter antagonists. This awkward alliance of convenience, in turn, transformed the Southern tradition of vigorous interparty competition into a new kind of intraparty factionalism.[10]

Watchful yeomen could hardly help noticing the antidemocratic rhetoric employed by many proslavery ideologues who now joined the Democrats. Fire Eater Robert Barnwell Rhett, who distrusted majority rule, and the proslavery theorist George Fitzhugh spoke for a good many other leading Southerners in asserting that some form of slavery was the only solution to the antagonism between capital and labor regardless of race. The South Carolina Fire Eater L. W. Spratt declared, "Slavery cannot share a government with democracy—it cannot bear a brand upon it." It would take only a few such utterances to heighten the deeply ingrained anxiety of yeomen about domination by slaveholding "aristocrats." Confederate conservatives had used such apprehension in the Upper South as the basis for a principled justification for a counterrevolution to seize control from radical nationalists at the Montgomery constitutional convention, held a month before Lincoln entered the White House.[11]

Yeoman Fears of "Military Despotism" in the Upper South

In the campaign that preceded Arkansas's February referendum, many yeomen wondered whether nonslaveholders like themselves could enjoy political equality in a slaveholders' republic. A campaign circular asked a pointed question: "Do you *know* that in the Confederacy your rights will be respected, that you will be *allowed to vote* unless you are the *owner of a negro*?" In Arkansas, where fewer than one free family out of five owned any slaves, an appeal of this sort could be extremely telling, and partly in response to such appeals, yeomen voters sent enough Unionist delegates to the state's secession convention to stall secession there. An Arkansas Southern nationalist who felt that he understood the social origins of the resistance of the mountain yeomanry suggested a radical method of forging a popular majority for secession: transformation of nonslaveholders into slaveholders by the gift of one slave to each household that had none. Even in South Carolina, Judge Robert S. Hudson confessed to frustration over the weakness of up-country support for Southern nationalism. Concluding that Southern nationalism was most attractive to those with a material stake in a slaveholding society, Hudson urged the sale of one-tenth of the slaves to nonslaveholders: "By that means, you might make interest supply the deficiency of patriotism."[12] Such a rationale assumed that if all Southerners had an economic interest in slavery they would support secession.

Considering the fervor of the yeomanry's guarding of its political liberties, it is hardly surprising that Southern nationalists found secession quite difficult to attain in the four slaveholding states of the Upper South until after Lincoln's call in April 1861 for seventy-five thousand volunteers to suppress the "insurrection" in South Carolina. Lincoln's call, in response to the Union's loss of Fort Sumter, altered popular attitudes in the Upper South. On April 20, one week after the surrender of the fort, the Reverend John Berrien Lindsley, a minister, educator, and slaveholder in Nashville, wrote in his diary, "All this week the city intensely excited. waves of revolution tempestuous." Virginia was the first to secede, then Arkansas, North Carolina, and Tennessee voted to join the Confederacy. Although in counties with a nonslaveholder majority the February referendum votes went against secession when this was the only issue at stake, and in western Virginia and eastern Tennessee yeomen overwhelmingly vetoed immediate secession, by April the issue was no longer only self-interest but also the Union's demand for troops to fight the Confederacy. Governor John Letcher of Virginia and Governor Isham Harris of Tennessee led their states out of the Union rather than supply troops to the North against the South.[13]

In Virginia, Letcher felt sufficiently pressed by the urgency of the crisis after Fort Sumter to engage in a secession strategy that would unwittingly, two years later, lead to a new pro-Union state of West Virginia. One month before the April date set for his state's second referendum on secession, Letcher entered into a military alliance that would bind Virginia to the Confederacy. To mountain Unionists, this maneuver, coming just before the referendum to determine the public will, seemed an open betrayal of democratic rule. The *Morgantown Star* spoke for majority opinion in the trans-Allegheny region in its editorial of April 20, 1862, which called secession "repulsive" and warned that if "*secession* is the only remedy offered by [eastern Virginia] for all our wrongs, the day is near when Western Virginia will rise up in the majesty of her strength, and, repudiating her oppressors, will dissolve all her civil and political connexion with them, and remain firmly under the time-honored stars and stripes." As the *Star* predicted, Virginia's secession prompted a convening of a pro-Union meeting, at Wheeling, where the delegates concluded that the Old Union offered the only hope for preserving political freedom. They resolved "to secede from secession" and to seek the admission of western Virginia to the Union as a separate state.[14]

The West Virginia separatist movement inspired eastern Tennessee yeomen, who likewise felt aggrieved by a similar preemptive action of their state's governor. With June 8 set for a second secession referendum, Tennessee governor Harris, with the acquiescence of key members of the General Assembly, on May 7 consummated a secret military alliance between his state and the Confederacy. Secessionists, conceding the coming defeat of the referendum in eastern Tennessee, chose to focus instead on voters in middle and western Tennessee with tactics the Reverend Lindsley, himself a slaveholder, described in his diary for June 8: "Regarding the whole matter as null from illegality, I did not vote. In Middle & West Tennessee no canvass was allowed the speaking and printing being all on one side. It is said that in East Tennessee a full and free canvass took place."[15]

The Reverend William Brownlow, a Unionist from eastern Tennessee, the editor of the *Knoxville Whig*, and the most prominent Methodist leader in east Tennessee, wrote an editorial in the *Whig* urging east Tennesseans to vote in the June referendum, lest "military despotism" swallow them up: "Let every man, young and old, halt and blind, contrive to be at the polls on that day. If we lose then our liberties are gone and we are swallowed up by a military despotism more odious than any now existing in any monarchy in Europe." Brownlow invoked the legacy of the American Revolution as justifying resistance to the destruction of political liberty he believed certain to follow the creation of a national government in which slaveholders wielded final authority. And despite the Tennessee governor's secret pact committing his state to a military alliance with the Confederacy, most east Tennessee yeomen would refuse to be bound by that pact. Angry Unionists at a convention at Greenville adopted a "Declaration of Grievances," accusing Tennessee secessionists of subverting the will of the popular majority. The convention proposed a separate state for east Tennessee, like the new state proposed for western Virginia. Immediate statehood eluded the mountain Unionists in both western Virginia and eastern Tennessee, but their fervent commitment to seceding from secession suggests that Lincoln chose wisely in designating both regions as primary targets for a destabilization strategy.[16]

The secession movement's entanglement in intrastate sectionalism had its roots in the settlement patterns that produced the Southern "dual economy." Throughout the antebellum period, when highlanders in Virginia and Tennessee and their low-country rivals belonged to separate political parties, Democrats and Whigs had contested over issues like representation, taxation, and internal improvements. During the secession crisis, the enthusiasm of many slaveholders for secession persuaded their traditional up-country antagonists to oppose any measure intended to increase the power of the low-country slaveholders. Secessionists made much of the issue of home rule for the states; the yeomanry also was concerned about the question of who would rule at home. With sovereignty conveyed from the Union to a Southern republic, recourse to a power greater than that of slaveholders would be gone, particularly in a Confederacy with a single organized political party. A highland yeomanry devoted to preserving its own autonomy saw a national government dominated by the well-to-do as no longer providing an ultimate restraint on slaveholders' power. Their anxiety over subjugation to "political slavery" encouraged a preservationist ideology to counter the revolutionary ideology of Southern nationalism by protecting the vital interests of yeoman dissenters.[17]

Violence now broke out in the mountains of eastern Tennessee between rival state militia groups, those armed by the Union and those armed by the Confederate government. A similar pattern of violence occurred in western Virginia, where Letcher's strategy of preemptive secession played very badly in a region long noted for strident hostility to the more affluent eastern region. In both states, armed partisans of the rival causes organized themselves into self-defense groups. Frightened Unionists and others described the local militia groups, in the words of one, as "marauding parties," and in western Virginia a letter from an A. I. Boreman to Francis H. Pierpont, governor of the Union-occupied area of Virginia, reported that militias drove "hundreds of men . . . away from their homes . . . and their property—horses, cattle, etc.— carried off or destroyed." Lincoln saw this epidemic of political violence as providing a compelling rationale for offering weapons and training to mountain Unionists.[18]

Nonslaveholder Reluctance to Secede in the Border States

While Arkansas, Tennessee, and Virginia eventually joined the Confederacy, the mountainous enclaves within each of these states, with fewer slaveholding families, remained sources of festering disaffection against Confederate authority for the balance of the war. So too in other regions there was a strong relationship between the proportion of slaveholders in an area and the depth of its support for secession. In the Mississippi Valley, for example, nonslaveholder counties were clustered together in the highlands, among the Appalachian Mountains east of the Mississippi River and among the Ozark and Ouachita Mountains west of the Mississippi—up-country areas far removed from the commercialized low country dominated by slaveholders.

The border slave states proved even more resistant to secession than the northern tier states. In Missouri, counties with fewer than 10 percent slaveholders dominated the political geography. In Kentucky, slaveholding tended to be much more evenly dispersed than in Missouri, and so Southern nationalism might have been expected to have more appeal there. And yet secession was unlikely to win majority support in either state, both of which had yeoman enclaves.[19]

Although agitation for and against secession reached a fever pitch in Kentucky in the months after the firing on Fort Sumter, the state escaped much of the political violence that swept across the disputed boundary between the Union and the Confederacy after the legislature adopted a posture of "armed neutrality" as a means of exempting the state from the consequences of choosing between the two sides. That neutrality worked to the advantage of both the Union and the state. Lincoln abstained from sending federal troops into Kentucky, concerned that a provocative approach might lead to its secession. With no Northern military encounters, a relative calm prevailed in the state during the summer of 1861. Partisans of both causes busied themselves with organizing "state" and "home" guard units that would later become competitive vehicles for recruiting white Kentuckians into both Northern and Southern armies.

In Missouri, agitation for and against secession produced a more violent political crisis in the aftermath of its February secession referendum than it did in Kentucky. Despite Missouri voters' rejection of secession in the referendum, the pro-secessionist governor, Claiborne Jackson, tried to lead his state out of the Union. In response, Union partisans summoned assistance, and Lincoln assigned General Nathaniel Lyon to keep Missouri in the Union. After Lyon's Northern troops attempted to defend key points—the St. Louis arsenal and the Hannibal and St. Joseph Railroad—pro-secessionists were aroused and clashes escalated, from a disarming of secessionist militiamen in

St. Louis to guerrilla ambushes, and from spirited skirmishes to the climactic Battle of Wilson's Creek on August 10, 1861. "Free-soil" veterans of the 1850s struggle in "Bleeding Kansas," seeing an opportunity for vengeance against Missouri "Border Ruffians," launched a John Brown–style abolitionist foray with ragtag Kansas "Jayhawkers," and by August 1861 Missouri was engulfed in a multifront civil war. General John C. Frémont, replacing as Union commander the martyred Nathaniel Lyon, who had been killed at Wilson's Creek, declared martial law and on August 30, 1861, freed the slaves of disloyal masters. He cited as justification Missouri's "disorganized condition, the helplessness of the civil authority, the total insecurity of life, and the devastation of property by bands of murderers and marauders, who infest nearly every county of the State." The violence gradually subsided, and Missouri was saved for the Union, in large measure because Southern nationalists failed to mobilize a popular majority in support of secession.

In both Kentucky and Missouri, much as inside the Cotton South itself, secessionist ideology appealed to many younger slaveholders and to Democrats disillusioned by their party's equivocation on the expansion of slavery. But when the majority of voters in these two states weighed secession against attachment to the Old Union, the expansion of slavery did not seem important enough to warrant disruption of the Union.

Abetting the move toward moderation in both Kentucky and Missouri were the efforts of affluent former Whigs, many of them older slaveholders who shared the anxieties about secession expressed by great planters in the Deep South and the Upper South. These former Whigs were much more numerous in the border states, and their views proved more influential there in blocking secession, in part thanks to the relatively low percentage of families in these states owning slaves, and to the hostility of most up-country yeomen and urban workers to a slaveholders' republic. The attempts to incorporate into the Confederacy regions with relatively low proportions of slaveholders had generated partisan conflict, and Lincoln's destabilization policy provoked it further. The stakes in manpower were high. While there were 666,203 military-age white males (fifteen- to forty-year-olds) in the seceding states of the Mississippi Valley, there were 431,841 in Kentucky and Missouri alone. The Unionist majority in the border slave states kept them tied to the Union, but tens of thousands of white men from Kentucky and Missouri served in the Confederate army with devotion over the four years of war. But even greater numbers of white and black Missourians and Kentuckians served on the

Union side. The Confederacy's failure to appeal to popular majorities in the border slave states forced it to comb its manpower resources much more closely than might otherwise have been the case.[20]

The floodtide of violence that hit Missouri spilled over into the Indian territory in the spring of 1861 after Jefferson Davis sent an emissary to negotiate diplomatic recognition between the Confederacy and leaders of the "Five Civilized Tribes," Cherokees, Chickasaws, Choctaws, Creeks, and Seminoles. Within each of these Native American nations, the social cleavage between slaveholders and nonslaveholders tended to separate more affluent "half-breeds" from impoverished "full-bloods." Albert Pike successfully negotiated Confederate treaties with the slaveholding "half-breed" leadership, but fierce fighting erupted in consequence with groups of their heavily armed "full-blood" rivals. Nonslaveholding Cherokee "full-bloods" organized the Pins, a self-defense group, prompting "half-breed" slaveholders to organize a militia of their own. The Pins attacked the property of "half-breed" slaveholders. One slave, Morris Sheppard, recalled later: "Dey taken it out on de slave owners a lot before de War and during it too. Dey would come in de night and hamstring de horses and maybe set fire to de barn." For example, in the Upper Creek Nation of the Indian territory, the attempt to negotiate with Pike sparked violence. A "full-blood" faction, led by Chief Opoethleyohola, took refuge in Kansas, but before these Upper Creeks abandoned their homes, they sought vengeance against their slaveholding antagonists and took three hundred slave families off to the sanctuary of abolitionist Kansas. Almost two thousand black slaves were liberated in the process. "Half-breed" slaveholders responded to this and similar attacks by abandoning the Indian territory altogether, taking their slaves with them to the safety of Confederate Texas. Thus, long before Lincoln proclaimed emancipation, chattel slavery had ceased to function as an effective labor system throughout most of the Indian territory. Segments of the five tribes located in Virginia, Tennessee, Arkansas, Kentucky, and Missouri experienced outbreaks of politically motivated violence as well.[21]

The tide of violence across the Confederate western front illustrates the dimensions of the struggle over the allegiance of Southerners outside the cotton states. Highland yeomanry placed a higher priority on the survival of political liberty than on the sustaining of racial "homogeneity" by preserving slavery; this fracturing of the antebellum consensus widened further the field of action for Lincoln's divide-and-conquer strategy. Indeed, Lincoln's strategy of ap-

pealing to the pro-Union interests of yeomen in the Upper South comple-
mented his attempts to forestall secession in the border slave states by appealing to the interests of slave masters in Kentucky, Maryland, and Missouri,
arguing that investments in slave property would be far safer inside the Old
Union than outside it.[22] The two prongs of Lincoln's strategy used explicitly
contradictory means, one addressed to yeomen's suspicions about slaveholders, the other seeking to cultivate Unionism among slaveholders themselves.
Confusion and contradiction in the Confederacy were inevitable as a result,
elevating preexisting tensions within Southern society and escalating political
and social conflict in the highlands of the western front. The conflicts chipped
away at the unity the Confederacy assumed would bind all free Southerners
to the movement for national independence. The resulting politicization of
popular democracy did precisely what Lincoln had hoped it would do—prevent a consolidation of Confederate nationalism.

Expansion of Slaveholding Territory: The Balance of Power between North and South

Although political violence on the western front seemed to follow the expansion of the Confederacy, the government in Richmond dared not deviate from
that line of policy, since expansion in the Mississippi Valley was as politically
necessary as it was strategically vital. The government was aided in this plan
by a decisive Confederate victory at First Bull Run, which sparked a confidence that encouraged Southerners to demand aggressive forward movement. Thomas R. R. Cobb, a judicial scholar respected in both the North and
the South and a prominent secessionist from Georgia, wrote to his wife on
July 24, 1861, about the soaring optimism among Confederate loyalists:
"[First Bull Run] *has* secured our Independence." Davis inadvertently added
fuel to this bonfire. Speaking to a cheering throng the day after First Bull Run,
he let slip a remark, recorded afterward in the diary of John B. Jones, the chief
clerk at the Confederate War Department, that seemed to promise imminent
capture of Washington, D.C., and the state of Maryland: If the invincible Confederate army was on the march north, he said, "a peace would soon be consummated on the banks of the Susquehanna or the Schuylkill."[23]

   In the light of the military history of U.S. expansion, with its established
precedent of aggressive acquisition of disputed land to gain the most favorable
position for postwar negotiations of national boundaries, the Davis adminis-

tration had little choice but to move as forcefully as it could to gain control over slaveholding territory. The Confederate secretary of state, Robert M. T. Hunter, outlined the territorial framework from which the Richmond government preferred to bargain when the time came to negotiate the peace that would confirm Confederate independence. The Confederacy would then claim the territories of Oklahoma, New Mexico, and Arizona and incorporate all the slaveholding states except for tiny, and isolated, Delaware. In a letter to James W. Mason on February 8, 1862, Hunter insisted that the South could never live at peace without such territory, otherwise "all hope of balance of power between [North and South] would be gone and the Confederate State would be in constant danger of aggression from its northern neighbors."[24] Hunter's awareness of the need for a balance of power offers a cogent justification for the expansionist policy of a government that seemed to recognize that an independent Confederacy that incorporated virtually all slaveholding states could expect to continue to function as a viable nation.

"A Low Treacherous Set of Men": Pacification Efforts in the Highlands

Unfortunately for the Confederacy, the attempt to achieve strategic expansionist goals for the future forced it to grapple in the present with the antisecessionist insurgency in the highlands of the Mississippi Valley. Davis himself would doubtless have preferred to leave pacification of highland enclaves for the postwar period, had not the need to complete the making of the Confederacy before peace negotiations began imposed considerable pressure to act. Further, these enclaves were of such political and strategic importance that they could not be left alone. For one thing, the virulence of the highland insurgency supported Lincoln's argument about the antidemocratic character of the slaveholders' regime. Then, too, the uncontrolled partisan violence stood as an embarrassing refutation of the claim that the new government exercised firm control over its entire domain.

Even more important, the centers of this insurgency commanded strategic access to river and railroad transportation networks coveted by the War Departments of both North and South. The slender peninsula of western Virginia jutting out between eastern Ohio and western Pennsylvania controlled commerce and communication between the Middle West and Washington, D.C. The headwaters of the Potomac River rose in western Virginia, and the

Baltimore and Ohio Railroad ran through this small but important region. Control of eastern Tennessee was equally vital to the Confederacy, since the Tennessee and Virginia Railroad, running through eastern Tennessee, formed the principal interior connection between Richmond and the Gulf Coast states. In addition, the mountainous terrain of these western highlands seemed to offer an ideal venue for defense of the Lower South against a Northern invasion. Its high ground offered a time-honored military advantage, one that could compensate for the South's relatively inferior resources of manpower and arms. Thus, the fate of the Confederate nation would rest, to a significant extent, on its ability to consolidate its position among the disaffected yeomanry of the western highlands.

Davis understood all this. Initially, the Confederacy asked for little direct sacrifice from its highland yeomanry, and the government sought to deploy Confederate military power so as to induce disaffected yeomen to acquiesce in the Confederacy's sovereignty. In the first year of the war, Southern forces maneuvered extensively in yeoman enclaves of the Mississippi Valley. A number of general officers served in this pacification campaign, among them Robert E. Lee and Henry Wise in western Virginia, Leonidas Polk and Edmund Kirby Smith in eastern Tennessee, Albert Sidney Johnston and Felix Zollicoffer in southern and eastern Kentucky, Benjamin McCulloch in northwestern Arkansas, Sterling Price in southwestern Missouri, and Albert Pike in the Indian territory.

The organized and gentlemanly style of more traditional battlefield warfare, which Davis might have preferred, did not prove adequate for long. In response not only to the general demands of war but also to yeomen sensitivity to even the mildest military occupation, the Southern army resorted to more-aggressive measures after some Confederate troops sent to occupy highland enclaves encountered organized local opposition. During the fall of 1861, Confederate troops stationed in Arkansas encountered an anti-Confederate organization called the Peace and Constitutional Society, centered in the highland counties of Van Buren, Newton, and Izzard. With a claimed membership of 1,700, the society had sworn to resist the Confederacy in every way possible and to assist the Northern army wherever it appeared. Typical was a declaration by residents of Izzard County: "They would never muster under the d——d nigger flag, but if any one would just come along with the stars and stripes they would fight for it too when they got here." In up-country areas of Virginia outside the western mountains, the intense social pressure generated by the flocking of thousands of young men to the Southern army in the summer and fall reinforced some yeomen's determination not to fight for the Confederacy. Resistance to volunteering grew so vociferous in Bedford County that a group of prominent citizens who were Confederate loyalists told Davis, in a letter of July 12, that "a low treacherous set of men positively and absolutely refuse to muster." Local dissenters were insisting "they would not serve unless drafted."[25]

Thus it soon became apparent that pacification would require far sterner measures by the Richmond government. Shortly after reaching eastern Tennessee, Polk discovered that local Unionists, among them leaders like William Brownlow, Representative Horace Maynard, and Senator Andrew Johnson, had no intention of acquiescing peacefully in the attempt to secure their homeland for the Confederacy. With rival militias employing terror and intimidation to gain control over the east Tennessee highlands, Confederate officials concluded that only imprisonment or exile seemed likely to still the loud and discordant voices. In July, Polk dispatched an urgent warning to Richmond: "No time is to be lost in East Tennessee."[26]

With the Lincoln administration now providing weapons to Unionist militia in eastern Tennessee, and with certain Unionists helping Northern spies, the Confederate leaders could not sit back. They moved to break up an espionage network linking Unionists in eastern Tennessee with compatriots in western Virginia. Davis faced demands for harsh reprisals but at first demurred, trusting that leniency would be a more effective response than reprisals. Unionists then struck an embarrassing blow against the Southern war effort on the night of November 8, 1861, less than a week after voters had ratified Davis's selection as provisional president. They burned five of nine bridges along the vital stretch of the Tennessee and Virginia Railroad between Stephenson, Alabama, and Bristol, Virginia. Their act of sabotage sent shock waves all the way to Richmond. John Jones, the War Department's chief clerk, assessed the situation in his diary entry for November 11, 1861: "Bad News. The Unionists in East Tennessee have burnt several of the railroad bridges between this and Chattanooga. This is one of the effects of the discharge of spies captured in Western Virginia and East Tennessee. . . . Until the avenues by which the enemy derives information from our country are closed, I shall look for a series of disasters."[27]

Davis, moving decisively now, ordered the arrest of as many suspected bridge burners as the Southern army could apprehend. Army courts-martial tried those who were accused on a charge of treason, convicted them, and sentenced them to death by hanging. Most of the sentences were carried out on the ruins of the burned bridges. When a Confederate officer inquired whether the president concurred in these sentences, Secretary of War Judah Benjamin, on December 10, 1861, replied curtly, "He entirely approves of my order to hang every bridge burner you can catch and convict." But these executions, instead of dissuading mountain Unionists, seemed to arouse them more, and a prolonged, violent, and ultimately futile struggle to assert Confederate sovereignty over the Appalachian highlands ensued. The persistence of insurgency frustrated Confederate plans to consolidate control over territory they considered vital to the survival of the new nation.[28]

The failure to gain the allegiance of Southerners along the disputed western boundary cost the hard-pressed Southern cause dearly. Had popular majorities in Missouri and Kentucky, for example, become enthusiastic converts to Southern nationalism, the pool of military-age men on which Confederate forces in the Mississippi Valley drew could have been as much as 65 percent larger than it actually was. Then, too, if there was any area where the terrain offered a force inferior in numbers and weapons the chance to fight effectively against a much larger number of invaders, the highland regions of the western front was certainly one. Yet these mountains, as it became clear, would be no safe haven for outnumbered Southern troops; indeed, the Confederacy had to detach large numbers of soldiers to take on the thankless task of pacification duty in the mountains of Virginia and Tennessee. This meant that the Southern war effort lacked the resources to mount a major offensive in the trans-Mississippi region of Arkansas, Louisiana, Missouri, Oklahoma, and Texas. Some later critics of Confederate strategy have argued, correctly, that the Confederacy's failure to maintain an effective military presence in the trans-Mississippi west was critical. It allowed the North to concentrate its own forces in two rather than three major combat theaters.[29]

Lincoln was keeping a watchful eye on events in the western highlands. His destabilization policy had helped to support the anti-Confederate insurgency in western Virginia, and he had a special interest in the activities of these mountain Unionists. Until Nashville, Tennessee, fell to Union forces in February 1862, western Virginia remained the only place in the South where Lincoln could implement his plan of relying on Southern Unionism as the basis for a wartime reconstruction. His first annual message as president on December 3, 1861, showed his satisfaction at the Confederate failure to pacify mountain Unionists: "After a somewhat bloody struggle of months, winter closes on the Union people of western Virginia, leaving them masters of their own country." He believed that the North could not win the war without controlling western Virginia and therefore allowed local Unionists to push forward with plans for a new state. The effort would be rewarded, in the spring of 1863, with the admission of a new state of West Virginia into the Union.[30]

Although Unionists in eastern Tennessee failed to win admission for their own proposed state of Franklin (named for Benjamin Franklin), they did manage, for more than two years, to sustain an active resistance to Confederate authority. In consequence, large numbers of Southern troops were diverted from active field service elsewhere. The presence of the Army of Tennessee did not prevent thousands of Confederate deserters from using the inaccessible backcountry of eastern Tennessee as a refuge; the mountains also served as a sanctuary for tens of thousands of draft evaders and resisters. The insurgency in these mountains was to contribute significantly to the military loss of eastern Tennessee, for not only did the Northern army that liberated Knoxville in September 1863 receive a hero's welcome from local citizens, but mountain Unionists abetted the spies and guides. In the course of the war more than thirty thousand east Tennesseans enlisted in, and fought with, the Union army.[31]

Much as the Fire Eater Ruffin had earlier feared, the antisecessionist ideology fashioned by mountain Unionists rapidly made its presence felt in backcountry enclaves in the Lower South as well. Nonslaveholders there began to view the debate over Southern nationalism as a precursor to a debate over the survival of their own political liberties. Nor did the creation of the Confederate States of America do much to relieve such anxieties and reduce the activities of antisecessionists. Southern nationalists could no longer avoid the challenge of coping stringently with popular disaffection within their territory. It remains one of the unresolved riddles of the Confederate experience how half or more of the military-age white men of the South could be preparing to fight for the cause of Southern independence while thousands of others were swearing continued fealty to the Union cause.

In July 1861 John M. Daniel and Edward A. Pollard, editors of the *Richmond Examiner,* decided to bring the problem of yeoman Unionism out into the open. An unexpected setback at Rich's Mountain compelled Daniel and Pollard, two of the South's most penetrating social critics, to break with the practice of concealing Southern weaknesses from the prying eyes of Northern spies. While freely acknowledging the pivotal role "faulty generalship" had played in the skirmish in western Virginia, they insisted that the defeat at Rich's Mountain "was chiefly due to treachery on the part of those natives of the country who guided the march of the invaders." Mountain Unionists were "a bitter, secret and malignant enemy." In a prescient observation, Daniel and Pollard wrote, "This is indeed the distinguishing feature of the war we are engaged in." Their language was strikingly similar to the vocabulary often used to describe insurrectionary slaves: "The enemy at home is as troublesome to manage as the enemy in the field." And their prescription for coping resembled that proposed for dealing with insurrection anxiety: "Nothing but the most determined bravery and the most sleepless vigilance can work out success and triumph amidst unknown opponents like these." "Loyal as the great mass of our people are to the cause in which they have so zealously enlisted, there is yet no doubt that the South is more rife with treason to her own independence and honour than any community that ever engaged before in a struggle with an adversary." By invoking the sacrosanct canons of loyalty, duty, and honor, Daniel and Pollard left little doubt that they viewed Unionist disaffection as a grave internal threat to the Confederate revolution.[32]

In their editorial Daniel and Pollard admitted that "a large class of people" believed that "the allegiance of the people was due primarily, if not exclusively to that power [the federal government]." "Unionism has been taught as a sort of religion, and the conscience of the susceptible and superstitious has been enslaved to the idea of the supremacy of the central power." Even more disturbing, this "sentiment of treachery to the cause of . . . [the] South is more general than was ever known before in any country engaged in a great revolutionary convulsion." Then came a more shocking confession: "There is also lurking in the Southern Community a deep-seated feeling of aversion to slavery." Daniel and Pollard located this "aversion" among persons "not themselves to the manor born." While antislavery attitudes of yeomen Unionists were "partly religious," "*all this class of people in our community persist in looking on our struggle with the North as nothing but a struggle between the slaveholder and non-slaveholder upon the issue of the righteousness of the slave institution*" (emphasis mine). This penetrating critique of Southern secular religion accurately forecast the decisive role that conflicts within Southern society would play in the outcome of the war.[33]

Growing Yeoman Disaffection in the Lower South: The "Dual Economy" Leads to "Dual Politics"

By this time, yeoman dissenters had already begun to behave in a fashion that hinted at what Daniel and Pollard dreaded most—the existence, even in the South's commercial slaveholding core, of strident disaffection. Indeed, later evidence from slaves shows that some white dissidents were in touch with slaves. One such slave, Harry Smith, described the nocturnal activities of white dissidents in the neighborhood of his master's plantation: "Some of the lower classes of whites who could, would steal away to the cabins among the slaves, and with a person watching to see if Massa was coming, would read about the coming war." Slaves at work in the fields of a plantation in St. Bernard Parish, Louisiana, learned about the war and the possibility for freedom from a mysterious stranger who walked up, talked about Lincoln, and quickly disappeared. William Walters, the son of a freedom-hungry slave woman, later told of their experience as runaway slaves: "The slipper offers [i.e., runaway slaves] were often captured, but Mammy Ann and her little boy William (that's me) escaped the sharp eyes of the patrollers and found refuge with a family of northern sympatizers living in Nashville." White dissidents who stole away to slave cabins to read slaves the war news, who stopped slaves in the fields to tell them about Lincoln, or who sheltered runaway slaves had already breached the intraclass racial homogeneity on which Southern slaveholders depended for the security of their chattel property.[34]

There were also reports of more-open pro-Union activity among the disaffected. In early May 1861 the Committee of Constables in Hair River, Mississippi, asked their governor for permission to arrest a self-professed Free-Soiler who had publicly proclaimed his belief that Lincoln would soon free the slaves. And a resident of Mobile, Alabama, John Woodcock, overheard a disturbing conversation among dissident yeomen in Greene County, Mississippi, which he summarized for Governor John Pettus in a letter of May 5, 1861: "They will fight for Lincoln when an opportunity offers. . . . They defy your power and say should it become necessary they will poison the wells with strychnine." The governors of Texas and Louisiana received similar warnings; dissidents there were threatening to attack civilians if attempts were made to force them into the Southern army. In April Governor Edward Clark of Texas received a letter of warning from a James Harrison stating that foreign-born residents of northeastern Texas not only opposed secession but were threatening abolitionist activity as a defense against being compelled to serve. Unionism among yeomen in the Lower South seems to have occurred in a widely dispersed pattern that paralleled the antebellum Southern dual economy.[35]

Because of the high incidence of illiteracy, and hence the lack of written records, it is difficult to discover retroactively the reasons why yeomen sided with the Union. However, evidence from west-central Alabama suggests that Daniel and Pollard had correctly grasped the essential features of preservationist ideology. Even in the Lower South, up-country yeomen had developed a philosophy based on the values of a production-for-use economy and were disposed to view the war for Southern independence as a struggle in which the Old Union, not the Confederacy, seemed to offer the surest means of protecting their liberty.[36]

In light of the fervent patriotism through most of the Lower South, yeomen Unionists could scarcely expect to escape public notice of their rejection of Southern nationalism. Writing on July 16, 1861, one Southern loyalist, W. L. C. Musgrove, informed the governor of Alabama, A. B. Moore, of his distress over the activities of a group of men who intended "to sustain the Old Government of the United States." "I am informed by very reliable sources," Musgrove wrote, that "a very considerable no. of the inhabitants of the Counties of Winston, Marion, Fayette and some of Walker and Morgan, are disaffected towards the Confederate Government and are actually raising and equipping themselves to fight against the same." Apparently, these Alabama Unionists suited their actions to their words. Six months later, P. C. Winn, another alarmed citizen, told the new governor of Alabama, John G. Shorter, of "armed companies" in Winston County "which drill regularly with the avowed purpose of defending the Union." What most disturbed him were the sentiments expressed during a series of conversations with some of the Unionists; when he told them he would enroll them in the Southern army, they responded that, "frankly, if they [had] to fight for anybody they would fight for Lincoln." Both reports confirmed the impression left by the results of the earlier secession referendum in Winston County, where local voters had rejected secession by better than a 3-to-1 margin.[37]

It obviously required a great deal of nerve for a young man from Winston County to cast his lot with the Confederacy, as a yeoman farmer named Henry Bell did. His correspondence with his Alabama family provides a poignant instance of a young yeoman who found it necessary to defend his Confederate patriotism against friends and family. Bell had moved westward to Choctaw County, Mississippi, from his family's home in Winston County. When he decided to support the Confederate cause, his relations in Alabama found the news so disturbing that virtually the entire family—two brothers, a sister, and his father—wrote separate letters to him urging that he cling to the Union. Shortly before Fort Sumter, brother John expressed the family's position: "We are for linkern [Lincoln]. We are willing to be governed by a man who will do as linkern ses he will do." At the time Henry apparently simply reaffirmed his Southern loyalties. Ten days after John's letter, on April 21, their father, James B. Bell, sent Henry a forceful explanation of reasons why nonslaveholders ought to hold fast to the Old Union. He reacted heatedly to the suggestion that the Alabama Bells would think differently if only they lived in "an enlightened country." He distrusted slaveholders: "All they want is to git you pupt up and go fight for there infurnal negroes and after you do there fighting, you may kiss there hine parts for o [all] they care." Six weeks later, on June 10, Henry's brother Robert made a determined effort to deter him from siding with the South; responding to Henry's contention that Unionists were traitors, he wrote that the accusation was "a ly" and insisted: "I am a heap freader [more afraid] of the disunions with their helish principals than I am of lincon." "I was bornd and Raised in the union and I expect to dy with a union principal in me. I will Dy before I will take an oath to support the Southern confedersa when ever lincoln dus eny thing Contrary to the Constitution I am then redy and willing to help put him a way from their so I ad No More." Rejecting this impassioned family advice, Henry decided to follow his own dictates, and as a signal of his patriotism, he apparently had the local postmaster forward the letters to Governor Moore of Alabama, along with a note suggesting that his family's letters revealed the strength of treasonous sentiments in Winston County. Enclosed were two affidavits testifying to Henry's own patriotism.[38]

The Bell family in Alabama obviously felt strongly that Henry's prosecessionist sentiments reflected badly on the clan's reputation. His sister Elissay, with the approval of her family, had made plans to have brother Henry "pick me out a Sooter" from among the eligible bachelors in his new neighborhood in Mississippi, but in an April 21 letter to Henry she added to her original list of forbidden character traits, "If there is none but disunion men there for God Sake let them alone for I would disdain to Keep Company with a disunionist for if he will Cede [secede] from the government that had allways sustaned his Rights he would Cede from his family."[39] Her comment that the federal government "had allways sustaned" their rights confirms Daniel and Pollard's suggestion that yeomen Unionists saw the central government as the final guarantor of their freedom. The connection Elissay Bell made between loyalty to the central government and loyalty to the family reflects the link of yeoman Unionism with the everyday household economy. The Bell family saw Henry as a prodigal son who could not consider himself in good standing with them until he conformed his views to their own. His individualism, probably his ambition and upward mobility as well, had triumphed over the communalism that had been the dominant social characteristic of the non-commercial South.

The Bells' profound distrust of slaveholders was based on their conviction that the well-to-do of the South did not respect the equality of their poorer brethren. Yeomen from the Lower South were as fearful as their Upper South brethren that a triumphant slaveholders' republic might pose a threat to the survival of popular democracy. Perhaps more surprising is the fervor of their professed loyalty to Lincoln; even after months of secessionist propaganda, they saw him as the legitimately elected president of the United States and thus entitled to presumptive loyalty and respect. So long as Lincoln respected the sacred U.S. Constitution, the Bells seemed willing to abstain from the struggle for Southern independence. In Alabama opponents of Southern nationalism rebounded from their failed attempt to prevent the secession of their state by proposing a separate state of Nicajack in the northern highlands. Unionist pockets continued to flourish in enclaves in northwestern and southwestern Louisiana and in northeastern and western Texas. Disaffection was strongest in the regions where the commercial economy was the least well developed; concern about the survival of their "household economy" seems to have haunted the up-country yeomen every bit as much as insurrection anxiety haunted the slaveholders.

And yet, nonslaveholders by the scores of thousands did enlist and serve proudly in the Confederate army. For such soldiers, Lincoln's initial call for troops seems to have raised the specter of an unprovoked invasion of their homeland by hordes of hostile Yankees. For most nonslaveholders in the antebellum South, the institution of slavery defined the standards against which the entire population, slave and free, formed its views of the culture of Southern honor; all free white men, slaveholder or not, could feel proud of their equality with all other free men. Indeed, this value system of equalitarian honor predisposed many yeomen to fear Lincoln the "abolitionist" and the unknown consequences of the emancipation he would surely proclaim. When one landless yeoman named Jim Jeffcoat, forced by poverty to work in the fields alongside slaves, was taunted by them, his shame turned to rage that these blacks "instead of looking up to him called him 'pore white trash.'" With the call for Confederate volunteers he found a way to overcome his sense of unbearable affront, and hurried to become "one of the first in the county to volunteer." "I'd rather git killed," he explained to his family, "than have all these niggers freed and claimin' they's as good as I is."[40]

The division between communal and individual interests stimulated by the secession movement split the Lower South yeomanry in two; the antebellum "dual economy" now led to a "dual politics." Communally oriented yeomen might fail to see Lincoln's election as a sufficient pretext for revolution; individualistically oriented and upwardly mobile yeomen might support the slaveholders' republic. Both viewed themselves as fighting to defend the sacred altars of Southern civilization but differed on how best to protect what they held most dear. For while the upwardly mobile saw their future prospects as riding on the outcome of the struggle for Southern independence, the communally oriented concentrated their attention on the networks of extended kin groups that made up their household economy. As Daniel and Pollard warned, yeomen Unionists rejected the argument that they bore a sacred obligation as white men to fight in defense of the South's "peculiar institution." The secession movement disrupted the antebellum racial consensus by forcing yeomen to choose between political alternatives that laid bare long obscured strains in Southern society.

During the first year of the war, Lincoln and Davis both gambled heavily on their ability to gain the allegiance of the Southern yeomanry. Neither president could predict with certainty how yeomen would align themselves along the ideological continuum. While Lincoln underestimated the degree of popular enthusiasm in the South evoked by the secession crisis, Davis overestimated the persistence of this enthusiasm in the face of popular alienation from the cause. Experience would reveal that levels of support for Southern nationalism were linked to differing circumstances within the diverse regions of the Confederacy. As the war progressed, perceptions of these circumstances would continue to evolve, even as the circumstances themselves continued to change. Because these competing ideologies relied on parallel symbolic systems, yeomen could call on whichever ideology seemed most suited to their own interests. Support for Southern nationalism would continue to rest on the degree of congruence between a yeoman's perceptions of his interests and the Confederate government's conduct of the war. Yeomen soldiers who walked the line between patriotism and disaffection might turn toward disaffection if the war to protect the South from a Yankee invasion was managed in a fashion that diminished their own sense of equality.

The secession crisis had helped transform popular democracy from a means of political consensus into a cause of political divisiveness. Since the fate of the Confederacy rested on the success of its appeal to the majority of white Southerners outside the Lower South's commercial core, the outcome of this ideological struggle for the allegiance of these "other" Southerners did much to determine whether the Confederacy would emerge triumphant from the war of attrition Lincoln shrewdly characterized as "essentially a people's contest."

Chapter Four **"This War Is Our War, the Cause Is Our Cause"**

Aristocrats and Common
Soldiers in Confederate Camps

Had the Confederacy been in a position to follow up aggressively after its victory at First Bull Run, or had Southern nationalism won majority support along the South's troublesome northern boundary, then the new-born republic might well have won recognition for its independence long before the North could intervene effectively to mobilize its superior resources. But neither occurred, and it grew increasingly clear that final victory would go to the cause whose social system could best sustain full mobilization.

Southerners responded to these challenges in a rather paradoxical fashion. While the agrarian Confederacy reconfigured its weak industrial sector for wartime with surprising facility, the regime in Richmond had to struggle to find a politically palatable method of allocating labor between the home front and the military. Thus, at the same time that munitions production expanded dramatically to meet the army's needs, a faltering Southern agriculture failed to uphold the war effort. Much of this paradox was the result of a population imbalance between North and South; the South had to draw down its military-age population far more severely than did the North. Still, a national system of labor allocation within the Confederacy would have eased the strain on agriculture had states' rights ideology not thwarted such a resolution. Even so, if the Confederacy could accomplish its remarkable state-run industrial revolution, then states' right ideology need not have presented an impassable barrier for centralized control over the allocation of labor. Yet, with the increasingly discriminatory Confederate enlistment policy and military encampment, perceptions of unequal treatment of yeomen with preference to planters would determine the outcome of the war at least as much as the imbalance of resources between the North and the South.[1]

Jefferson Davis deserves much of the credit for the rapid, and successful, initial phase of Confederate mobilization. His training at West Point, his combat experience in the war with Mexico, and his tenure as secretary of war in the Franklin Pierce administration, all prepared him for leadership in defending the Southern claim to national independence. Davis apparently never shared the hope, sincerely held by many radical Southern nationalists, that no war would need to be waged. He was convinced that the North would not let the South go in peace, and thus he labored, between his inauguration and the firing on Fort Sumter, to put the Confederacy on a full-scale war footing as expeditiously as possible. To do this, he fashioned a political administration that was in striking parallel to the established government of the Old Union, with a cabinet headed by secretaries of state, treasury, war, and navy; an attorney general; and a postmaster. He personally assumed virtually direct control of the war effort, dividing the work of the War Department among staff bureaus assigned to handle manpower questions, procurement, production, transportation, and distribution of munitions and supplies. Despite inevitable confusion and frequent mistakes, this fledgling Confederate government, at first, mobilized its resources more effectively than did the less experienced administration of the federal president, Abraham Lincoln, who was new to Washington's ways.

In the battle at First Bull Run, a battle neither side was fully prepared for, the Confederacy turned back the Union army's single-pronged overland attack against its national capital at Richmond. Lincoln's hand had been forced by the impending discharge of the first group of Northern volunteers and by a public outcry for a trial of arms, and he pressed General-in-Chief Winfield Scott for a decisive forward movement. Although Scott knew the army lacked the training and discipline for a major campaign, he consented to a plan of battle in which Brigadier General Irvin McDowell would attack the newly constructed Southern position near Manassas Junction, Virginia, where the Orange and Alexandria Railroad met the Manassas Gap Railroad. McDowell was worried that the Southern army opposite his colleague, Major General Robert Patterson, a force commanded by Confederate Brigadier General Joseph E. Johnston, would use the Manassas railroad to reinforce Manassas Junction. Patterson was ordered to observe Johnston and report his movements, but he failed in that task and Johnston slipped away unnoticed by the Yankee forces. It turned the tide of First Bull Run, transforming a promising Northern attack into a glorious Southern victory.

"To Repel the Threatened Invasion": Raising a Standing Army

First Bull Run's triumph vindicated Davis's preoccupation with mobilization. When in response to the fall of Fort Sumter back in April 1861, Abraham Lincoln had requisitioned seventy-five thousand ninety-day Union volunteers, Davis was prepared to respond decisively. With the provisional Confederate Congress already summoned into emergency session, Davis, in an April 17 proclamation, called Lincoln's summoning of volunteers a declaration of war and proclaimed the Confederate government's solemn duty "to repel the threatened invasion . . . by all the means which the laws of nations and the usages of civilized warfare place at its disposal." When the Congress arrived twelve days later, Davis urged its members "to devise the measures necessary for the defense of the country." Central to such measures was the organization of an army strong enough to defeat an invading force. He requested permission "to organize and hold in readiness for instant action, in view of the present exigencies of the country, an army of 100,000 men." Although Davis's message was unambiguous, crosscurrents within the provisional Congress prevented its prompt implementation. Committed to states' rights ideology, the Congress recognized its president's request as one that had been anathema since the Revolutionary War: creation of a large standing army to act at the discretion of an appointed head of state. In a message to the Congress on April 29, Davis sought to silence such critics with an appeal to public sacrifice in defense of "their birthright of freedom and equality." "A people thus united and resolved," he said, "cannot shrink from any sacrifice which they may be called on to make, nor can there be reasonable doubt of their final success, however long and severe may be the test of their determination to maintain their birthright of freedom and equality as a trust which it is their first duty to transmit undiminished to their posterity." Congress responded to this eloquent plea and granted authority to raise a standing army of a hundred thousand men, but it balked at setting three years, or the duration of the war, as the standard term of service. Confident that the war would be short and fearful of granting too much power to the executive, it proposed instead a term of service of sixty days. Davis objected to this, for he knew how difficult it would be to assemble, muster, equip, and train large numbers of raw recruits and expect them to engage in combat effectively in so short a period. Congress agreed that his reasoning was sound, but compromised by extending the term of service to a mere twelve months. It recognized, in addition, the traditional authority of state governors to call out their own militia volunteers.[2]

The conservative nationalist struggle for control of the allocation of Southern labor against more radical demands of states' right ideologues would persist throughout the war. Whenever the Davis administration sought additional authority to centralize labor resources between the war front and the home front, Congress insisted on preserving a significant degree of decentralized control over such allocation. Decentralization was, in itself, consistent with the system of checks and balances built into American democracy, but in the wartime South the separation of powers did not sustain democratic rule, and without a national Supreme Court, judicial review faltered. In the executive branch, Davis ran for president without opposition in the only Confederate presidential election; and in the legislative branch, senators in the Confederate Congress (like their counterparts in the U.S. Congress) were chosen by the state legislatures, not by the voters directly. Thus, only elections for the House offered a full and unmediated voter voice on issues of national concern, and even here democratic balances were missing, since there was no organized opposition party. Partly in consequence, all three elected Confederate congresses, senate and house, were dominated by slaveholders, hence by a minority of the free population of the South. About 90 percent of elected members, apparently, were slaveholders; and slaveholder dominance, in turn, caused the government to tend to respond with greater sensitivity to the perspectives and interests of factions within that minority than they displayed to those of the nonslaveholding yeoman majority.[3] Persistent complaints about bias in favor of the wealthy were to haunt the Confederacy throughout the war.

Other political problems appeared almost as soon as the Southern army began to accept volunteers under the new legislation. State governors refused to turn over to Richmond all the federal weapons captured from arsenals in their states, and the Confederate War Department was forced to conclude, during the spring of 1861, that it had too few rifles to issue weapons to all the twelve months' volunteers who had turned out in the fervor of patriotism. Davis had to devise a policy to conform to the letter of the new law yet evade its intent: the army would accept twelve months' volunteers who brought arms with them, but volunteers who brought no arms would be required to enlist for three years or "for the war." The wisdom of requiring long-term enlistments for raw recruits seems unassailable, but this two-track enlistment plan ran counter to the antebellum taboo in the South against statutory distinctions made on the basis of social position. For privately armed volunteers—obviously those with greater means—to have the option of enlisting for one year while volunteers who could not provide their own weapons were compelled to serve for three years seemed a clear act of discrimination.

Davis may have justified this dual enlistment scheme to himself as an indirect means of forcing recalcitrant governors to arm state militias pledged to Confederate service with their hoarded weapons from the federal arsenals. But whatever Davis's rationale may have been, he failed to hear a stern warning about the dangers of dual enlistment from an authoritative source, Judge William M. Brooks, the Perry County planter who had presided over the Alabama secession convention. Brooks investigated the causes of discontent among soldiers in his own county, and in May 1861 he wrote to urge his president to rescind the two-track enlistment policy, citing as his reason discontent among the troops fostered by a combination of factors—the boredom of camp life, concern about the welfare of their families at home, and agitation by persons ill disposed toward the Confederate cause. Brooks wrote that "but few of the non-slave-holding working class" had been in the initial group of two hundred volunteers from his own low-country county. When a group of loyal slaveholders managed to persuade three hundred yeoman farmers to join up, these new recruits, after several weeks in camp, tried to enlist for the same twelve-month term available to privately armed volunteers only to discover that they must enlist "for the war" because they had come unarmed. "It is traiterously whispered into their ears," Brooks cautioned Davis in his letter, "that the slave-holders can enter the Army and quit it at the end of twelve months, but if they enter it, it must be for the war, however long its duration. I leave you to imagine the consequences." The dual enlistment policy reinforced preexisting "jealousies" among the yeomanry and seemed to confirm the allegation that "nothing is now in peril in the prevailing war but the title of the master to his slaves." The yeomen soldiers from Perry County had declared that they would "fight for no rich man's slaves." Brooks urged Davis to accept unarmed volunteers for twelve months' service so that yeomen, too, could be convinced that "this war is our war, the cause is our cause."[4] Concrete evidence of discrimination against the poor would tend to contradict Southern claims to revolutionary egalitarianism.

Brooks's letter to Davis echoed Edmund Ruffin's earlier worries, expressed before the war began, about the diffusion of disaffected and antislavery sentiments from the Southern highlands into the low country. Such concerns would be forcefully expressed again, in July, by the editors of the *Richmond Examiner.* Thus, as early as May 1861, preservationist ideology had already been seeded within the Southern army.

Related social tensions emerged as soon as Confederate soldiers began to come together in military rendezvous. With up-country yeomen tending to live in isolation from low-country slaveholders, few of either group had previously encountered many of their social opposites before they arrived at the training camps to which the army routinely sent all new volunteers. An egalitarianism of mass mobilization could have leveled potentially disruptive social distinctions, but the Confederate army camp experience instead seemed to nourish unusually strong resentments among the volunteers. Although not all officers were slaveholders, the close correlation between privilege in civilian society and higher rank in the army could hardly go unnoticed by those who had neither rank nor privilege.

In large measure, the correlation between military rank and civilian privilege was a consequence of the manner in which most states chose to raise their initial troop allotments, allowing influential citizens to recruit locally; company-grade officers were elected, as had been traditional. As a result, most commissioned and noncommissioned officers came from the more affluent social strata, and their attempts to impose military discipline offended individualistic Southerners of every social stratum, including members of the slaveholding class not themselves chosen as officers. Resentments cut both ways. Most officers were from the planter class, but some were of lesser social station than the men they commanded. One son of a planter, Harry St. John Dixon, wrote in his diary on May 18, 1863, after the war had been underway for two years, "It is galling for a gentleman to be absolutely and entirely subject to the orders of men who in private life were so far his inferior and who when they met him felt rather like taking off their hats than giving him law and gospel." The differences between the privileges granted to officers and the hardships imposed on others were deeply irritating to everyone who failed to benefit from them. The slaveholder Edwin Hedge Fay, who was only a private, resented regulations that forced him to request permission to leave camp, while "the officers can go to town at option, stay as long as they please, and get gloriously drunk in and out of camp when it suits them to do so." Fay wrote home angrily, on April 21, 1862, about the comfortable tents provided for officers and his own overcrowded tent. "There is too much difference made between officers and privates in the army as regards conveniences."[5]

Only careful displays within the military establishment of recognition of the equality of all white men could have affirmed the cardinal principle of Southern antebellum culture, that the institution of slavery made nonslaveholders equal in rights to any free man. Frank Richardson, the son of a prominent Louisiana planter, found, to the contrary, that ordinary soldiers were living below the lot of slaves while officers lived in a style equivalent to that of slaveholders. As he wrote to his father, "The life of a common soldier is a most hard and rough one. It is a great deal worse than that of a common field negro, but these commissioned officers they are just like the owners of slaves on plantations they have nothing to do but strut around dress fine and enjoy themselves. But in fact the most of the common soldiers have to be treated like negroes or they will not obey and beside they are a very low set of men being composed of these low Irish and the scum of creation." If there was anything the Southern yeomanry would resent more deeply than slurs about its Celtic origins it would be that they needed to be "treated like negroes." A prominent east Tennessee Unionist and Southern-born slaveholder, Oliver Perry Temple, in a later account of the war protested that mountaineers were not "the waste of the white population of the slave states."[6]

When Theodore Mandeville, the scion of a Natchez planting family, discovered that common folk made up the bulk of the company in which he had intended to enlist, he searched for another company better suited to his taste. He found one with a higher proportion of the well-to-do, but encounters with commoners were still necessary and he found them distasteful. He wrote to his family in 1861 and 1862 of the differences between himself and his peers and other volunteers in his new company: "We are distinct parties: the Aristocrats and the Democrats." An equation of traditional Whigs with aristocrats, and Democrats with the common folk reflects the political and economic distance between slaveholding planters and poorer nonslaveholding yeomen that was to haunt the Confederacy throughout the war.[7]

But not all "aristocrats" shared this sense of social contempt. Captain Nathaniel Dawson, whose own instincts were egalitarian, complained in a letter to his wife from Harpers Ferry, Virginia, on May 10, 1861, that "I am sorry to say that there are some men in the co. too nice for many of the duties required of them, and I have frequently to be an example. . . . I am subjected to much inconvenience in consequence. But I desire to share all the hardships and dangers of my men." At a camp near Corinth, Mississippi, L. D. Poe, an officer from a slaveholding family, was disgusted by the arrogance of many of his fellow officers. He wrote to a friend on April 1, 1862: "Could you drop there a few moments and see how they do things up, I think you would be disgusted. It seems that every jackass you meet sports brass buttons and stripes (I have a mind to throw mine away) Ye Gods! They go with hereditary trees—but this pleases some."[8]

Servants for Aristocrats, Hardship for Commoners

No single feature of Confederate camp life demonstrated the gulf between "aristocrats" and "commoners" more glaringly than the army's practice of permitting body servants to accompany their masters to the camps. Private Frank Richardson found camp life without a personal slave more onerous than he cared to endure, and on December 14, 1861, begged his mother to dispatch one. He asked that the slave tote a variety of "the little things, which you may wish a son [to have], your poor son at Columbus, who is suffering for the good of his country." Another well-to-do Louisiana volunteer had an elderly slave who was "in the habit of putting on his master's shoes and stockings for him every morning," so Maria Southgates Hawes, wife of a commanding general, wrote in her reminiscences. She begged her husband to help the unfortunate volunteer escape the ridicule that resulted from the ministrations of his benevolent but "tyrant" slave. The captain of a Mississippi company, Robert Moore, attempted to respond to complaints about the unfairness of some volunteers' having slaves to perform camp chores. On October 18, 1861, he noted in his diary that he had ordered these slaves to cook for the entire company, only to encounter strenuous protests from the masters: "The boys say they will send their negroes home first. The Co. had a meeting and drew up a resolution asking the Capt. to let the cooking go on as before." They would do without such service rather than share a cook or a table with their social inferiors. In June 1862 Robert M. Gill, a slaveholder from Mississippi, accepted an invitation to dine with the officers' mess of his regiment; having arrived after the officers had eaten, he had to eat with the clerk. Gill insisted on seeing the colonel and told him, "I considered myself a gentleman, treated everybody gentlemanly, and demanded the Same of everybody, and that I eat at Nobody's Second table, not even Gen'l Beauregard's."[9]

The elegant and lavish accoutrements brought to camp by some "aristocrats" dramatically showed up the more plebeian possessions of yeomen "dem-

ocrats." For example, each member of the Washington artillery of New Orleans "furnished his own uniform and equipment, officers their own horses";
"the whole command was put on a war footing without expense to the State
or Government," and the regiment departed for Richmond aboard a "special
train." William Miller Owen, who served with the Washington artillery from
Bull Run to Appomattox, writing in a memoir after the war, said that this special train carried a chest filled with gold coin donated by doting relatives and
"a French Creole, Edouard, from Victor's, a New Orleans restaurant. Ah! He
was *magnifique*. . . . his dishes were superb, the object of the adoration of all
the visitors who did not enjoy the luxury of French *cuisine* in their own
camps." Some soldiers from slaveholding families even joined a special squad
mess that had body servants to prepare meals from ingredients paid for by
members of the mess. In addition, enterprising slave servants hired themselves out, for a fee, to perform other personal chores for affluent soldiers,
such as laundry and repair of clothing. Soldiers who had no slaves of their
own sometimes hired free blacks "to serve in the menial services essential to
the camp," so James W. McHenry reported in August 1861 to Tennessee governor Isham Harris. But for most common soldiers, contributing to a mess
fund or hiring a camp servant was, of course, prohibitive. And they had to
rustle up their own meals. James Lusk Alcorn, a Whig, assuming his own
newly mustered command in Corinth in June 1861, wrote home to lament the
presence of "five thousand men, *fresh* volunteerd, poorly clad, rather poorly
fit, without a sufficient supply of anything."[10]

So galling was the inequality within the Confederate army that some
groups of resentful yeomen soldiers passing through a community seized
slaves from plantations to perform camp services for themselves or for those
of their officers who lacked the accoutrements of the gentleman officers. After
the victory at Wilson's Creek in August 1861, Confederate soldiers on their
way through one county in Missouri, so a slave, Gus Smith, recalled later,
"stole all de niggers dey could." Perry McGee, who had been a slave in Missouri, told how the soldiers involved in one such theft said to him: "Hey, little
nigger, we want you to go with us and wait on de Captain." They put McGee
on a horse and took him to a nearby town. "I had to clean off de horse, and
played marbles and turned handsprings and dey had me for a monkey." Three
days later a relative of his master found him and "begged de soldiers to let me
come back" home. The custom of respect for the property rights of civilians
had given way to what yeomen saw as a higher law, invoked by angry soldiers

determined not to live like or to feel like inferiors while defending a Southern cause that rested on a principle of equality of all free men.[11]

The Davis government could halt the spread of such resentments only by demonstrating to patriotic yeomen that the cause of Southern nationalism was their cause as well. In May 1861 John Sale, of Aberdeen, Mississippi, a lawyer of modest means, complained about the unequal economic burdens imposed by the dual enlistment policy. Volunteers who were not well-to-do, Sale asserted, could not afford to surrender three years' income in exchange for an infantry private's salary of eleven dollars a month and ought, therefore, to be asked to serve only a single year term. The chief of the bureau of war, Albert Taylor Bledsoe, a political theorist, theologian, and mathematician, replying to Sale, defended the existing policy and praised the patriotism of these privately armed volunteers, especially those who would not accept even the usual modest pay: "A still nobler example has been set by those who have not only armed and equipped themselves, but also refused to take pay as privates for the twelve months for which they enlisted."[12]

Thus, long before 1864, when the Confederate government eventually found it necessary to resort to universal conscription to achieve adequate military manpower, the process of mobilization had already begun to expose raw conflicts between the perspectives and interests of divergent social groups within Confederate society. But victory in a war of attrition—which the war had become—would demand broadly based popular support, and therefore Davis would need to reconcile all such conflicts if he was to sustain martial ardor among the yeomanry in particular. But rather than test states' righters, who he knew would resist any efforts to equalize conditions among the volunteers, Davis simply sought to explain the logic of dual enlistments to the resentful yeomen. It was a lame response and an ineffective one, and as a result in a yeoman-dominated state like Arkansas the War Department could not raise soldiers for a three-year army stint. By deferring to the sensibilities of the states' rights faction, Richmond had caused the pace of mobilization to be slowed during the crucial first months of the war.

War Department policies also placed additional inequitable burdens on the yeomanry by failing to provide prompt payment to newly mustered groups. Amid the confusion that reigned in the spring of 1861, departmental auditors attempted to define the conditions under which the Confederacy would assume responsibility for paying members of state militia units that were turned over to the national army. They adopted an inflexible position.

"All payments to troops," read the War Department's regulations, "shall commence from the time they were received into service and ordered to proceed to their destinations." Yet the precise date when troops were "received into service" was hard to determine, since most units had originally pledged their services to their state, and only after a state unit had achieved the minimum authorized strength did the transfer to national service begin. Some units reached that minimum strength quickly, others had to spend extended periods in camp before the requisite number were on hand. Because many units did not know the precise date of their transfers, the schedule of payments from unit to unit was inequitable. The War Department, inept at dealing with this muddle, stuck to the letter of its own regulations: departmental auditors would certify payroll vouchers for recruits only when local paymasters supplied definitive evidence of the exact date when the governor of the state completed the transfer of each unit to national service.[13]

Initially, the problem of payment to soldiers was not a result of lack of money in the treasury; the Confederate War Department, during the first nine months of the war, apparently had sufficient funds to discharge all its assumed obligations. Nonetheless, many units, particularly those from the trans-Mississippi west, never could provide satisfactory evidence of their transfer dates and so never received the money due them for their first few months of service. Payless periods were often prolonged even further when the War Department encountered difficulties in distributing the money to far-flung units in the field. For months at a time, large numbers of soldiers received no income at all to send home, leading to acute hardships for those whose families' food and shelter depended on the eleven dollars per month military pay of their absent fathers, brothers, and sons. In a bitter letter written to Governor Pettus of Mississippi in the fall of 1861, Mollie Shoemaker complained of the destitution her family was suffering. Her husband had not been paid for his service, and she and her children were hungry: "No provisions except a few potatoes and some rice My rent is due and my landlady urgent for her money What in the name of mercy are we to do? I am very feeble and sick most of the time."[14] Local paymasters informed their superiors in Richmond about the hardships such policies were imposing on poorer soldiers, but War Department officials persisted along an unswerving path of established rules.

Davis apparently spent considerable time reading such citizen correspondence, responding to it as best he could. Historians, like the contemporaries who criticized Davis after the war was lost, have blamed him for excessive involvement in War Department affairs. Implicit in this criticism is an accusation that the Confederate president was wasting his energy and attention in overadministering War Department minutiae rather than focusing on grand strategies. It is undeniably true that the Confederacy did flounder at a number of critical moments because its leadership failed to devise decisive and comprehensive conceptions of strategic purpose, but those failures had little to do with the time Davis invested in trying to ease his soldiers' hardships. Indeed, his activities on behalf of aggrieved individuals no doubt did more good than harm, and to the extent that his personal intervention helped to put a human face on a war effort beset by charges about insensitivity to the hardships and inequities suffered by the yeomanry, his response to civilian complaints would have been time well spent.

Awareness of these troubling crosscurrents did not prevent Davis from expressing a sense of pride about his successes during the first nine months of Confederate independence. His new nation, in turning back the initial Northern invasion at First Bull Run, had gained time to prepare. Davis's November 18 message to the provisional Confederate Congress summarized these considerable achievements; it was, no doubt, the high-water mark of his personal tide of optimism. The bountiful 1861 harvests and the vastly boosted production of munitions and supplies encouraged him to proclaim: "Upon a fair comparison between the two belligerents as to men, military means, and financial condition, the Confederate States are relatively much stronger now than when the struggle commenced." There were, naturally, areas that called for improvement, Davis said in this message, railroads being the most urgent. Yet he felt sufficiently secure to predict: "If we husband our means and make a judicious use of our resources, it would be difficult to fix a limit on the period during which we could conduct a war against the adversary whom we now encounter." "For the rest we shall depend on ourselves. Liberty is always won where there exists the unconquerable will to be free." So long as the central government could sustain public belief that "this war is our war, the cause is our cause," as William Brooks had put it, the Confederacy would survive.[15]

Northern and Southern Strategies for Victory

The Lincoln administration launched its second major offensive at the same moment that Davis was expressing guarded confidence in Confederate mobilization. Lincoln seemed determined to give Southern defenses a rigorous test; in addition to increasing the level of activity at the numerous points of friction along the thousand-mile border between the Confederacy and the Union, the North now tightened its naval blockade, at the same time dispatching large seaborne expeditions in the direction of the most important Southern port cities: Charleston, New Orleans, and Norfolk. At the end of October 1861, the expedition for Charleston left Hampton Roads, Virginia, with seventy-seven ships and twelve thousand men under the command of Brigadier General Thomas W. Sherman; it easily captured the lightly defended island of Port Royal, one of the chain of sea islands near the entrance to the South Carolina port of Charleston. Major General Benjamin Butler, with a ten-thousand-man force at his side, set sail for Ship Island, Mississippi, in later November and quickly overran its defenses. There would now be ready access to the two forts that provided primary protection to the port of New Orleans. And during the first week of January 1862, the Union navy transported General Ambrose Burnside, with his fifteen thousand troops, to Fort Hatteras, North Carolina, to prepare for an attack against the Confederate fort on Roanoke Island, which guarded the back door to Norfolk. By combining an effective naval blockade with a simultaneous menacing of pivotal sites throughout the South, Lincoln probably intended to stretch the Confederate defensive perimeter beyond the limits of its military resources.

Lincoln's sophisticated and comprehensive strategy for warfare on land and on sea bore scant resemblance to the simplistic plan that had led to the earlier Union debacle at First Bull Run. The initial Northern hopes had rested on a single decisive military campaign to end the war by seizing the Confederate capital at Richmond. But after First Bull Run, Lincoln concluded that saving the Union would require full mobilization of Northern industrial might to provide for an army of at least half a million men serving "for the war." With a war of attrition now more likely, Lincoln also took account of the complex sets of problems presented by the additional task of restoring federal authority to occupied seceded states. The sheer size of the Confederate nation would play a major role in his analysis. In the first place, the eleven seceded states encompassed almost seven hundred thousand square miles and held a population of nine million. In the second place, this wide expanse of territory had a continuous land boundary with Northern states that stretched from tidewater Virginia to western Texas. And third, the Confederate seacoast extended over a long transverse from the Virginia capes around the Florida peninsula all the way to the Texas-Mexico border at the Texas port of

Brownsville. Against so large and dispersed an enemy, the conduct of a successful war would demand not only unprecedented degrees of coordination within and between the general staffs of the Union army and navy but also full industrial mobilization with the vast augmentation of armed forces.

Lincoln encountered resistance when he attempted to induce his senior officers to put his comprehensive strategy into practice. Lincoln shared this problem of resistance to centralized authority with Davis, whose own multi-faceted scheme had been resisted by his Congress. Balking within the Union leadership ranks was particularly vigorous in the case of General Don Carlos Buell, the Union commander in central Kentucky, who offered all manner of excuses for his refusal either to take the offensive or to cooperate with adjacent military departments. Lincoln, exasperated by behavior that seemed more and more like willful dalliance, nonetheless wrote to Buell with great circumspection on January 13, 1862, offering a succinct explanation of his reasoning:

> I state my general idea of the war to be that we have the *greater* numbers, and the enemy has the *greater* facility of concentrating forces upon points of collision; that we must fail, unless we can find some way of making *our* advantage an over-match for *his;* and that this can only be done by menacing him with superior forces at *different* points, at the *same* time; so that we can safely attack one, or both, if he makes no changes; and if he *weakens* one to strengthen the other, forbear to attack the strengthened one, but seize, and hold the weakened one, gaining so much.

A concluding reference to First Bull Run suggests that the memory of a Yankee victory snatched away by the unexpected arrival of Confederate reinforcements had made an indelible impression on the president.[16]

The flurry of redeployments required by the new Northern strategy could not long remain hidden from an observant Davis. After all, the Confederate War Department was receiving regular intelligence from spies in the Northern states, just as the North was from spies in the South, and a large number of reports, if often exaggerated and inaccurate, came to Davis from civilian and military sources alike about the strength and movements of Northern forces. Throughout the fall of 1861, the Confederate president carefully sifted all available intelligence to try to anticipate the Northern thrust and to assess the adequacy of his Southern deployments, as established in late September in line with the geographically based departmental command system favored by the prewar federal army. Defense of the vast expanse of Southern territory was immensely difficult, and in September 1861 Davis had divided his army into fourteen departments, ranging in size from Department No. 2, which encompassed the Tennessee, Cumberland, and Mississippi River Valleys, to the much more compact Department of Fredericksburg. The Union's land and sea movements, he concluded, probably heralded a positioning of invasion forces in forward staging areas, and his previous deployment the best deployment he could devise until a spring 1862 offensive could get underway.

Problems of Southern Readiness: Two-track Enlistment, Furloughs, Election of Officers

Of far greater immediate concern to Davis was the crisis still smoldering after congressional rejection of his recommendation that three-year not twelve-month enlistments be set as the standard term of service. Individual state governors, bowing to yeoman resistance, had on their own given most volunteers the preferred term of twelve months; as a result, only 115 of the 390 regiments in service in mid-December 1861 listed themselves as volunteers "for the war," leaving the Southern army with 275 regiments of twelve months' men. All these enlistments were set to expire during the spring and summer of 1862, at virtually the same time when a Northern offensive could be expected. The urgency of preventing the discharge of these seasoned troops at a crucial time forced Davis to seek to induce twelve-month volunteers to add two years to their original enlistments, even without congressional backing.

Secretary of War Judah Benjamin told his president at the end of November that the impending expiration of the twelve-month enlistments was "the most important of all the subjects that can engage the attention of Congress." Training and seasoning had already consumed up to half of the twelve months of duty. Benjamin urged the provisional Congress to grant "a liberal bounty, together with a moderate furlough" to get the twelve months' men to reenlist for the war. To members of the Congress uneasy about the military risks furloughs would bring, he offered calming reassurances that his staff would manage the schedule of leaves carefully so as "not to endanger the safety of the Army." On December 11, 1861, the Congress granted the War Department the authority to end the two-track enlistment policy altogether.[17]

The December 11 legislation generally followed Confederate War Department recommendations; it gave volunteers who reenlisted before the expiration of their original commitments a fifty-dollar bonus and a two-month furlough, with transportation home and back provided at government expense. The record of the army's procrastination in disbursements compelled field commanders to offer unusually generous leave policies to encourage reenlistment.

The army could not hope to conceal such massive leavetaking from its watchful enemy, thus providing an opportunity to attack the weakened Confederate positions. The logic of using the three winter months to provide the two-month furloughs to three-quarters of the army made it virtually inevitable that Confederate military safety would be endangered in that period, no matter how carefully the War Department managed schedules. It was a risk it seemed necessary to take.

The danger of a reduced army was multiplied by two eccentricities in the Confederate reenlistment process. Acting on its own, the provisional Congress went beyond Davis's request for concessions to prospective reenlistees and offered them both the right to reorganize into new companies and the right to elect their own new company, regimental, and battalion officers. It is true that in peacetime state militias did traditionally have the right to organize themselves into small units and select their own officers, but such rights were generally exercised before incorporation of the state militias into a national army, and they certainly were not intended for outnumbered forces in the active presence of an enemy. Indeed, to combine an eased reenlistment process with a bottom-up reorganization of an army in the field seemed a rash way to compensate for the damage inflicted by the Congress's earlier refusal to accept Davis's proposal for a three-year enlistment period. Within ten days of passage of the December 1861 reenlistment act, General Braxton Bragg reported that his command at Pensacola, Florida, had already begun to unravel. "Men who were perfectly willing to accept good and competent field officers," Bragg complained, "are now torn and tossed about by the intrigues of designing men, seeking their own advancement or revenge upon those who have made them do their duty." In fact, "Discord now reigns where all was harmony, and our very best field officers are sure to be sacrificed to this fell spirit." The provision permitting the election of new officers had brought "demagogues" to the fore who were "misleading [the troops] from anything but pure motives." The electioneering accompanying such contests for rank was, he said, an "evil, greater than all others combined."[18]

Bragg did hope to retain most of his troops, but he could not help railing against the additional burdens of the new law. "In one month," he wrote in a letter of December 20, "we should have secured 5,000 of the 6,000 twelve months men here. Now, if we get 2,000 we shall do well." And most damaging of all, "Our best field officers are certainly sacrificed; a poor reward for past faithful service. They would have cheerfully met this fate at the hands of the enemy, but from their own government it is hard to bear."[19] If for no other reason than lost morale among seasoned field officers, campaigning for officers inevitably reduced combat readiness.

In retrospect, it appears that the provisional Congress chose very nearly the worst possible moment for its risky experiment in military reform. By December 1861 the prolonged period of military inactivity after First Bull Run had led to a monotony of camp life that, along with the continuing daily doses of unaccustomed discipline, dulled the ebullient spirits of many patriotic Southern volunteers. Demoralization had followed, too, from the inequitable dual enlistment policy, the chronic delays in receipt of military pay, and the elitist behavior of more-affluent soldiers. With the sudden bottom-up reorganization, disgruntled common soldiers could use a ballot to protest the lack of respect accorded them as free white men. They could form their own new companies and elect officers of their own choosing, effectively striking back at an officer corps that had been dominated by often haughty and contemptuous officers from slaveholding families. Reports that electioneering by the candidates for military commissions "filled the men with liquor and demoralized them" lent credence to Bragg's judgment that the new reenlistment process, as Wilfred Buck Yearns has written, "tended to unstabilize" the entire Confederate army.[20]

Two of the Confederacy's most prominent generals, Joseph E. Johnston in Virginia and Robert E. Lee in South Carolina, employed official and unofficial channels to express grave concern that combat readiness would fall to a dangerously low level during the winter months. Johnston pointed out in a letter to Secretary of War Benjamin on January 18, 1862, that, with the enlistment of virtually every twelve months' soldier on the Virginia front expiring "at no distant day, it would be necessary to grant furloughs in very great numbers during the next few months in order to obtain many re-enlistments for the two years following." "To grant them in such numbers," Johnston warned, "I deem incompatible with the safety of this command." Lee had remonstrated to a delegate to a South Carolina state convention several weeks earlier, with his customary eloquence, that the traditional pattern of military self-organization was dangerous even in peacetime. "What must it be in time of war, when it may occur at periods that might otherwise prove highly disastrous?" He raised a question that must also have been in his president's mind: if the Southern army was risking disaster during the winter of 1862 in a failed attempt to encourage voluntary reenlistment, "I tremble to think of the consequences that may befall us next spring when all our twelve-months' men may claim their discharge."[21]

Benjamin replied in mid-January to the sensitive and often overcautious Johnston. Legitimate concern for "the safety of your command," he admitted, would prevent the immediate approval of large numbers of furloughs. But, he predicted, "The eager desire for a furlough during the unclement season will form the strongest inducement for your men." A healthy reenlistment rate would "afford the best guarantee of your having under your orders a large force of veteran troops when active operations recommence." Much of Benjamin's argument turned on the unlikelihood of a winter offensive from the North. Since "the present condition of the roads" was an obstacle to a military venture, "It is surely better to run a little risk now than to meet the certain danger of finding a large body of your men abandoning you at the expiration of their terms." "There is danger on both sides," he said, advising the general "very urgently [to] go to the extreme verge of prudence in tempting your twelve months' men by liberal furloughs, and thus secure for yourself a fine body of men for the spring operations."[22]

In an earlier response to Bragg, Benjamin had used a similar line of argument about the effects of a winter hiatus on military defense, but in that letter he expressed, much more directly than he did to Johnston, his displeasure with the burdens imposed by the provisional Congress. Nonetheless, Benjamin saw Davis and the War Department staff as engaged in a determined effort "to execute the law as to prevent the disorganization of the Army." "No one can deprecate more sincerely than I do the obvious consequences of what you well denominate the system of universal suffrage in the Army; but the lawgivers have spoken, and we must do the best we can." Benjamin went a step further and shared with Bragg the War Department's best case for the new reenlistment process. As he wrote in this January 5 letter, "If the winter closes upon the campaign without serious disaster all will be well, for it is impossible, with the varied efforts already made, with the large supplies already purchased, and with the numerous expedients now in progress, that some successful venture shall fail to occur, and thus put into our hands all that is wanted to wrest from the foe the admission that our subjugation is impossible."[23] Official confidence in Southern defenses thus rested on two assumptions: first, that the usual winter suspension of offensive activity would leave the existing defensive perimeter secure until the spring, and second, that all unarmed soldiers would have weapons before the Northern offensive got underway.

That Davis had allowed an obviously flawed enlistment bill to become law was ironic in light of comments he was said to have made at dinner the same day he submitted to Congress the plan to abolish dual enlistment. The Confederate attorney general reported that Davis had expressed concern about the "discontent" created by the "mismanagement" of the original twelve months' enlistment. Davis worried openly, as had Lee, that most of the discontented twelve months' volunteers would decline the inducements for reenlistment and leave the Southern army vulnerable in the spring of 1862. But he rejected the option of vetoing the entire bill lest it delay reenlistment even further, and he chose not to use his constitutionally granted line-item veto. (He had previously vetoed four other bills, the first, on February 28, 1861, banning the further importing of African slaves, but none of these involved an item veto.) He apparently decided to make do with the flawed law because its passage represented a significant victory for the nationalists' persistent contention that an effective army required long-term enlistments. Besides, an outcry would certainly have arisen had he vetoed the two congressional amendments to his own request for a reenlistment bill.[24]

Had Congress accepted Davis's initial recommendation for a three-year reenlistment period, it might then have been possible to capitalize on the first rush of patriotism and create, from the beginning, a large army of volunteers willing to serve for a longer term. But it did not do so, and an entire year would pass before it acceded to a further extension of a centralized allocation of labor. In April 1862 Congress would draft soldiers for the same three-year term for which many Southerners might well have volunteered willingly the previous spring. By the loss of that year, however, states' rights ideologues had unwittingly undermined the drive for Southern independence. Many other battles between the Confederate Congress and the president would have to be waged, on such issues as habeas corpus, impressment, finances, and the railroads, before a Confederacy weaned on local sovereignty would face the demands of an effective war of attrition. That the government eventually did find the will to achieve such a revolution explains why the Confederacy was able to fight as long and as well as it did, and yet the tortuous process of ideological adaptation of Southern society to military and political exigencies may well have set outer limits of Southern endurance that were insufficient for victory.

Secretary Benjamin put the matter well when he acknowledged that there was danger on either side of the dilemma. Although failure to attempt reenlistment would make virtually certain a total military collapse the following spring, the process devised by Congress to avoid this danger put its armies in an extremely vulnerable position. Davis and the War Department knew full well that the Confederacy needed a winter respite to repair the damage of the struggle over labor allocation. If by some stroke of good fortune the outnumbered Southern army could hold off its massively reinforced enemy until most of its twelve months' volunteers had reenlisted, by spring the Confederacy would be prepared to turn back a Yankee offensive. But good fortune was not on the Confederate side in the gamble.

Chapter Five   The Failure of Southern
Voluntarism and the Collapse
of the Upper South Frontier

O n Christmas Day 1861 General Albert Sidney Johnston, with premonitions of disaster, repeated his familiar refrain that his Department No. 2, commonly referred to as the Western Department, lacked the resources to defend a six-hundred-mile front along the Tennessee and Kentucky border of the Upper South frontier. Inclement weather was no assurance of a lull in fighting; indeed, it increased the likelihood of an attack. "The contest here," Johnston said, "must be relinquished for the winter by the enemy or a decisive blow soon struck." His intuition and his assessment of his Northern foe convinced him that to "make the latter is their true policy." He made a flat prediction in a letter to Secretary of War Benjamin: "A decisive battle must probably be fought here for the freedom of the South."[1]

The Upper South frontier protected the Northern gateway to "The Heartland of the Confederacy," a rough triangle centered in Tennessee with an apex in central Kentucky and a baseline across the middle of Georgia, Alabama, and Mississippi. Here was the South's most highly concentrated aggregation of mineral, agricultural, and industrial production; its geographic core; and the transportation lifelines of the Confederacy. The city of Nashville, at the center of this triangle on the southern bank of the Cumberland River, was as important in this crucial area as Richmond was in the east, so it was not coincidental that command of the Western Department had been entrusted to the highest ranking field officer in the Confederate army, a man who had been Davis's friend from their West Point days. But Johnston's overland trek from his duty station in California to his new post in Nashville took more than three months, from June to late August 1861, and in the meantime Governor Isham Harris of Tennessee filled the manpower vacuum with his Provisional State Army, a large and well-supplied force, as the Congress had authorized governors to do by enlisting men for a twelve months' tour.

Harris made several critical mistakes that were to hobble the Southern cause throughout Johnston's tenure as commander. With no federal arsenal within its border, Tennessee had no captured federal weapons to distribute to militia units, and Harris had therefore ignored the War Department mandate for three-year terms for unarmed volunteers. Although public fear had subsided when no massive slave revolt occurred, slaveholders wanted to hold on to their weapons, and an incumbent running for reelection as governor could not ignore their troubled concern that a Union invasion might ignite a slave rebellion. As a result, on his arrival Johnston found an army largely of unarmed volunteers, to be trained and to serve for a period of no more than a year.

In addition, Harris's concentration on building a series of forts along the Mississippi, one of six principal north-south invasion routes, left much of Tennessee virtually defenseless, especially the state capital at Nashville. Governor Harris had appointed as senior officer of the Tennessee militia Gideon Pillow, a man with a controversial record in the war with Mexico. A riverine planter himself, Pillow shared Harris's belief in the importance of river defense: "If the enemy should succeed in opening the river," Pillow said, in a May 15, 1861, letter to Secretary of War Walker, "he will reach New Orleans, devastating the whole country as he goes . . . and thus isolate Arkansas, Louisiana and Texas." Pillow, following the governor's example, had decided not to delay military preparations until Tennessee seceded officially and, with two weeks left before the second secession referendum, ordered western Tennessee slaveholders to send their slaves to help fell trees and clear brush at the site of what would become Fort Randolph. A number of Tennessee slaveholders responded with great enthusiasm to calls for laborers, and masters from Mississippi and Arkansas also sent slaves to speed the completion of Fort Pillow.[2]

Kate Stone, in her diary entry for January 22, 1862, captured this spirit of cooperation in north Louisiana: "Gen. Polk has called on the planters from Memphis to the lower part of Carroll Parish for hands to complete the fortifications at Fort Pillow, forty miles above Memphis. A great many Negroes," Stone wrote, "have been sent from Arkansas, Tennessee, and north Mississippi, and now it comes Louisiana's time to shoulder her part of the common burden. . . . Nearly everyone has promised to send, some half of the force of men, some more, some less." These black laborers enabled the Confederacy to put in the field a greater number of white soldiers than would otherwise have been possible.[3]

Slaveholders' Resistance to Military Appeals for Slave Labor

Had the Confederacy been able to sustain a similar synergy of black and white labor throughout the war, the forces in the Western Department might have fought on nearly equal terms against their numerically superior and better-equipped Northern adversaries. Soldiers protected by well-constructed battlements would have held an enormous advantage over troops maneuvering in the open field. But growing friction between slaveholders and the Confederate government, and between slaves and yeomen soldiers working on building defenses, undermined the effectiveness of both black and white labor and inhibited construction of essential installations. Slaveholders grew more and more reluctant to send slaves to the fortifications, depriving Johnston of the labor he needed to correct the imbalance in defensive alignment he had inherited from Harris and Pillow.

Slaveholders chafed against requisitions for military laborers for a number of reasons. The army had naturally requisitioned able-bodied male slaves, but these men were the plantations' prime field hands and their masters' most valuable assets. In addition, opportunities for self-emancipation abounded in army camps. As early as June 15, 1861, Daniel S. Donelson wrote to the Fort Randolph commander to ask him to keep a sharp watch for his runaway "negro boy Joe," who, he was sure, would seek work as a body servant in one of the camps. And many masters worried lest borrowed slaves exposed to the drinking, gambling, rough language, personal violence, and political discussions in military encampments would share seditious notions with other slaves on their return home.[4]

In October, John Houston Bills, owner of more than eighty slaves, answered a military requisition with a bitter soliloquy on the loss of his own political liberty: "Start 4 of my men at the call of General Polk to work on fortifications at Fort Pillow. A most villainous call, one he has no right to make and is the beginning of a despotism worse than any European Monarchy. We talk of 'fighting for liberty' when we had more 'liberty' and prosperity twelve months ago than we shall ever see again, I apprehend." Although one slaveholder in northeastern Mississippi, Francis Terry Leak Jr., organized a planters' central committee to induce dawdling masters to send their blacks to the forts, his committee requisitioned a mere forty-six hands. Many other masters, too, made gallant efforts to support the war effort, but a significant number of others decided, like Bills, to protect their own interests first.[5]

The sudden expansion of the war zone in the fall of 1861 made the construction of defense works more important than ever. On September 2 Major General Leonidas Polk, who had been appointed Episcopal bishop of Louisiana in 1841, invaded Kentucky without seeking clearance from Richmond and, as interim departmental commander, seized Columbus, Kentucky, in response to activity that seemed to presage the long-feared Mississippi River invasion by the Union forces. In itself this seizure of the first defensible point south of Cairo made good sense, even if it was a flagrant violation of Kentucky's "armed neutrality." But Polk failed to recognize that his decision had transformed an unfortified Paducah into a point of commanding significance at the terminus of the Mobile and Ohio Railroad with control of the mouths of both the Tennessee and the Cumberland Rivers. Had Polk managed to seize and fortify Paducah as well, it would have been possible to defend four of the six invasion routes into Tennessee. But he did not do so, and the alert Union commander at Cairo, General Ulysses S. Grant, only recently promoted, moved quickly and decisively to secure Paducah for the Union. Without Paducah, Columbus became more of a liability than an asset, and the attractiveness of a waterborne attack made Nashville itself, temptingly close to the Kentucky border, more vulnerable than ever.

Johnston needed to seal the cavity along the inland rivers quickly, both because of the importance of securing the water routes into the Upper South and because of the coming inclement weather, limiting the period when major construction would be feasible. Nothing perhaps showed the distortion of priorities more clearly than the discovery, by a Lieutenant Joseph Dixon, that the civilian who surveyed Fort Henry had not only placed it on the wrong side of the river but also selected a site several feet below the mean high-water mark, with the winter rainfall threatening to submerge much of the fort. Fort Donelson, too, approximately eleven miles due east of Fort Henry, had been placed in a less than ideal site. But the lateness of the season and the work already done made relocation of either fort impractical.[6]

Since it was politically impossible to withdraw from Kentucky once the Stars and Bars flew above Columbus, Johnston tried to meet the threat he considered most pressing, a Union invasion down the Louisville and Nashville Railroad. He moved departmental headquarters seventy miles north, to the central Kentucky town of Bowling Green, on the banks of the Barren River and straddling the railroad to Nashville, and sent an experienced engineer, General Lloyd Tilghman, to command Forts Henry and Donelson and to complete their defenses "with the utmost activity." A group of community leaders, most of them slaveholders from the Tennessee River Valley town of Tuscumbia, Alabama, went to Fort Henry to see what civilian volunteers could do and met with Generals Polk and Pillow. With their own homes threatened by attacks against the unfinished fort, the committee offered, in a November 22 letter, to organize a privately armed corps of five thousand older men to work for forty days. The desire to protect their slave property interest probably prompted this offer to risk the lives of older whites rather than send their own slaves to do the job.[7]

Military engineers at other sites now began to complain about acute labor shortages. Engineers at Fort Polk on Island No. 10 had warned in October that, with only sixty slaves there, the completion of defenses would be retarded. The chief engineer at Fort Pillow, Montgomery Lynch, told Polk on December 1, "We have but forty two negroes here and I hear of no more coming." Johnston complained that he could never get more than a tenth of the slaves required to build essential fortifications, and ordered Major Jeremy Gilmer, chief engineer in the Western Department, to select a position near Nashville for departmental headquarters to "fall back" to should an attack come from the rear. Major Gilmer did everything in his power to induce slaveholders to send their blacks to complete work on the river forts and to start construction on the Nashville defenses, but received only weak excuses for his pains. "The number of hands is insignificant," Gilmer said in a report to General Johnston, "and the agents report that it will be impracticable to procure them at this time." "The negroes in the vicinity of the city are hired out until the end of the year and not under the control of their masters." With local slaveholders reluctant to break profitable annual hire contracts, Gilmer doubted that "any material progress" could be made on the Nashville defenses at that time.[8]

At a meeting with Secretary of War Benjamin in mid-December, Nashville's mayor, R. B. Cheatham, brought along a letter bluntly warning that Nashville, "with all of its public stores, is in imminent peril." General Tilghman took the unusual step of requesting Jefferson Davis to send artillery for Forts Henry and Donelson, circumventing the chain of command. Johnston shared his own sense of foreboding with Governor Harris, to whom he turned for assistance, but although Harris assured him in a December 31 letter that he could obtain the needed slaves, only a fraction of the required five hundred appeared. "The response to my appeal for laborers," the governor confessed, "has not thus far been as flattering as I had wanted and expected." Not even an emergency request from a governor closely associated with slaveholding interests had overcome the firm reluctance of slaveholders to send their slaves. According to the 1860 census, more than one million slaves lived in Tennessee, Alabama, and Mississippi, almost a hundred thousand of them within a hundred miles of Nashville. Yet the army could not get the loan of five hundred to begin construction of the Nashville defenses.[9]

Lieutenant Dixon, who supervised the work at Donelson, urged that supplying labor be mandatory: "I wish you would get the general to give an order to press labor, for it cannot be obtained here in any other way." But Johnston understood the grave political implications of military seizures of private property in a nation committed to states' rights ideology, and his personal preference was for persuasion. Major Gilmer, in a circular of December 11 to "The Citizens of Nashville," appealed for slaves "to fortify the approaches to the city . . . the better to protect your capital and State against the contingency of an invasion by our relentless enemy" and suggested that owners could send their own overseers to protect their property, promising lodging in "tents or in frame huts." Yet Johnston's inducements swayed "very, very few," despite his offer of premium wages of a dollar per hand per day, almost three times the eleven dollars per month pay of infantry privates. Only after five months of failure to get slave workers did he authorize the impressment of a limited number of laborers. His order of January 27 came too late to fend off a Northern winter offensive.[10]

"We Cannot Work the Negro and Our Kind of Soldiers at the Same Time"

In addition to the grave shortage of slave workers, in the tension-filled atmosphere of Southern military camps it became clear that yeomen soldiers refused to work side by side with slaves. "I would suggest," Gilmer reported to departmental headquarters in November, "that the batteries at Fort Donelson can be completed sooner by the troops, perhaps, than if an effort were made to collect negroes from the surrounding country." "Fatigue parties" could do the work. "In imminent danger, the Brigadier General commanding Fort Donelson might be authorized to press all neighborhood negro labor into service, but under other circumstances I do not think the labor of the troops and slaves can be combined to any advantage." At Fort Polk on Island No. 10 tension arose between black and white laborers. The commander, General M. Jeff Thompson, wrote to General Polk in a letter of December 16, "I have discovered by experience that we cannot work the negro and our kind of soldiers at the same time." "As the number of negroes which I have been able to collect in this country is so small, I have ordered them all sent home this evening."[11]

But if white laborers resented working on similar tasks, and presumably at a similar status, with slave laborers, white yeomen soldiers could compensate to some extent by procuring a slave body servant for themselves or their nonslaveholding officers, thereby regaining diminished status. In January 1862 "a parcel of drunken rowdies"—four yeomen soldiers from the Western Department— tried to bully Hinson McVay, a middle Tennessee slaveholder, into turning one of his slaves over to them. But McVay, who owned eleven blacks but only one prime field hand and who was himself afflicted with "shaking palsy," would have been unable to support his own dependents without "my only man servant" that "is of any consequence." "Now they say they have a wright to take a negro man to cook and wash for every soldier." McVay called this "equal to highway robbery" in a January 15 letter. In the end, he staved off seizure but feared that the armed "rowdies" would return to "take our meat and bread too." "I should not think that we should be worse off if the Lincolnites were among us."[12]

Southern yeomen volunteers who brandished their guns "to take a negro man to cook and wash for every soldier" were breaking dramatically with the ethical style of antebellum Southern culture, for any appeal to popular democracy to justify such a seizure raised a profound challenge to the fundamental right of owners to retain their slave property. If military service gave a yeoman the right to seize a body servant, masters had either to surrender such property or prepare for a struggle. The alternative was for officers who were slaveholders to respect the yeomen's sense of their equality as free white men and release them from the "nigger work" of personal service.

The Dual Threat of Insurrection, from Slaves and from White Yeomen

General Johnston had discovered on his muster rolls thirty thousand soldiers he could not deploy because they had no weapons. The arms-starved Upper South frontier once again had to rely on civilian volunteers to supply matériel.

Both Johnston and Governor Harris urged civilians to provide serviceable muskets and rifles to the Army of Tennessee. Some did, and several regiments were equipped with reconditioned private weapons, but by and large slaveholders responded even less enthusiastically to this call than to the appeal for fortification laborers, no doubt because of the need for arms on the plantations to control and discipline slaves now imbued with a new hope of freedom.[13]

While stopping short of organized resistance by groups of slaves, the unrest appeared to permeate large and small slaveholdings alike and in areas remote from no less than proximate to likely arenas of military conflict. One Yazoo Delta mistress, watching her overseer depart for the war, said anxiously, "I hope the Negroes will not give me unnecessary trouble." "A Planter's Wife," in Warren County, Mississippi, reported to Governor John Pettus that the departure of her overseer for military service had aggravated hunger in the slave quarters and she feared a revolt.

Even household domestics, ordinarily regarded as the most loyal of the slaves, began to display a growing militancy. Kate Stone noted, in her diary for June and July 1861, that before the July 4 meeting of the special session of the U.S. Congress summoned by President Lincoln, "The house servants have been giving a lot of trouble lately—lazy and disobedient. . . . I suppose the excitement in the air has infected them." Even "Aunt Jane, head of them all," was not immune; she "ran away this morning but was back by dinner." "Mama did not have her punished" because "all of them are demoralized." An August accusation of poisoning at the hands of a slave cook induced panic in Amite County, Mississippi, and Mary Wilkerson, a soldier's wife, wrote to her husband Micajah, "You remember that Joe Day was crazy about when you went off well they come to find out what ailed him. Old Terry had put gypsum seed in his coffee it had liked to killed him. They whipped Old Terry and put her off in the field." In Louisiana a man's "negro woman was tried and convicted today of killing his only child," Alexander Pugh recorded in his diary on August 26. "She is suspected of having killed his two other children, one being drowned and the other supposed to have been killed by a dog." With fear of arson, too, spreading in Kentucky and Mississippi, slaveholders felt more vulnerable than ever.[14]

War undermined slaveholders' property rights in other ways as well. In July in Arkansas County, Arkansas, an overseer named Higgins got into a drunken brawl with a slave and threatened to shoot him. The slave, whose owner was away in the army, ran to a local judge, who kept him overnight. The next morning Higgins did gain custody, but in a dispute and struggle on the way back to the plantation, the overseer was killed. "When the news got here a number of overseers and some others collected and went down and got possession of the boy and brought him to Redford and hung him publicly." In prewar times such a summary execution of a slave accused but not convicted of a capital crime would have been grounds for prosecuting members of the mob, but not in wartime, and the owner's official complaint about the lack of due process and the haste with which the mob destroyed his valuable property was ignored by officers.[15]

In late November the same citizens' committee of Tuscumbia, Alabama, that proposed sending five thousand elderly white men in place of slaves to work on fortifications urged citizens to donate their best private weapons to the national army. Their circular, addressed to "Fellow Citizens of North Alabama and North Mississippi," met slaveholders' counterarguments. "The impression that many men have that they will be more secure by retaining their arms for their personal defense is a great error." The conflict between local self-reliance and the willingness to accept centralization of authority and risk the security of slaveholders' property was to be an enduring dilemma of a Confederate society in wartime.[16]

If the demands of national independence seemed to slaveholders like a distant abstraction or an unacceptable burden, it is scarcely surprising that many nonslaveholders in the highlands of the Mississippi Valley, farther removed from the commercial economy and society, found even less reason to support the Southern cause by private sacrifice. To begin with, a number opposed secession and the war, and emissaries of the Southern government who sought to assert national authority in the highlands soon encountered determined resistance from pockets of yeomen Unionists. Colonel Robert Blount, commander of a muster camp in Greene County, Alabama, informed Secretary Benjamin that Unionist insurgency had spread to an "adjoining county"; not only had "Union men . . . secretely organiz[ed] and . . . elected officers," but they apparently intended to "act in concert" with an organized group of three hundred or so armed "avowed Union men." Blount appealed to Benjamin, in a January 1862 letter, for help in dealing with this armed insurgency, but Benjamin could offer little aid. Attempts to crush east Tennessee Unionism by executing convicted arsonists and detaining suspected leaders achieved only partial success. Soon after the November 1861 bridge burnings, North Carolina governor Henry T. Clark, while grateful for the relative peace in the western part of his own state, acknowledged that "a border warfare must ensue." Governor Joseph E. Brown of Georgia, in a letter the next day, seconded Clark's request that "troops be thrown upon the frontier of Georgia at once, to assist in suppressing the rebellion"; but Benjamin had no troops to send, and Brigadier General W. H. Carroll, commander of the district of Knoxville, transferred responsibility to Johnston in early December. "The insurrection in this part of Tennessee," he wrote, "demands a prompt and vigorous policy. I have the men but not the arms." Johnston, too, was short of weapons and, as the winter of 1862 approached, faced Northern armies in Kentucky, Missouri, and Illinois, all seemingly poised to attack weak points along his six-hundred-mile front.[17]

"The Magnitude of the Danger": The Fall of Nashville and the Upper South Frontier

To both Lincoln and Davis, control over the Tennessee-Kentucky border was second in importance only to the defense of their respective capitals. Lincoln lobbied actively to ensure that the Northern army moved with due regard to that priority. He pressed the War Department to undertake a winter offensive on the vulnerable western front to deny the South the respite it needed to gather its forces and fortify its frontier. With General George B. McClellan, who had restored esprit de corps to the battered Army of the Potomac after the defeat at First Bull Run, now seriously ill with typhoid fever and not eager for an immediate offensive in the east, Lincoln urged western commanders Don Carlos Buell and Henry W. Halleck to launch a coordinated campaign on New Year's Day 1862 to relieve Confederate pressure against east Tennessee Unionists. Hearing disturbing reports of civilian executions by the Southern military to deter attacks on Confederate rail lines, Lincoln wrote to Buell: "My distress is that our friends in East Tennessee are being hanged and driven to despair, and even now I fear, are thinking of taking rebel arms for the sake of personal protection." "In this we lose the most valuable stake we have in the South."[18]

In the late fall of 1861 the North was also coping with a series of setbacks that threatened to halt military progress. One such setback was an episode of diplomatic embarrassment. In what became known as "the *Trent* affair," Lincoln reluctantly agreed to release two captured Confederate diplomats rather than risk a war with Great Britain over freedom of the seas. Another was the fiscal paralysis of the North after its reserves of gold and silver dropped to dangerously low levels. And with General McClellan too sick to lead his army, Lincoln was despondent: "What shall I do? The people are impatient; [Treasury Secretary Salmon P.] Chase has no money and he tells me he can raise no more, the General of the Army has typhoid fever. The bottom is out of the tub. What shall I do?" What he did do was issue General War Order #1 of January 27, commanding all land and sea forces to prepare for "a general movement . . . against the insurgent forces" scheduled for February 22.[19]

Halleck had told Lincoln, in a January 6 letter, that an attack like that contemplated for east Tennessee "will fail as it always has failed, in ninety-nine cases out of a hundred. It is condemned by every military authority I have ever read." Halleck gave command of his share of the western offensive to Grant, who undertook diversionary expeditions near Columbus, Kentucky, and Fort Henry. On January 29 an unreinforced element of the Army of Tennessee engaged in the battle of Mill Springs, Kentucky, the first in the series of Northern victories that were to culminate in the collapse of Confederate defenses along the Upper South frontier. Both before and after the defeat at Mill Springs, General Johnston tried repeatedly to persuade his superiors to dispatch additional men and weapons to the Confederacy's Western Department. On Christmas Eve he complained in a letter to Mississippi governor John Pettus about the excessive length of his defensive line; he had to guard the Mississippi at all costs while also keeping a large force at Cumberland Gap at the entrance into the upper Tennessee River Valley to prevent "the invasion and possible revolt of East Tennessee." He could not continue to control the Tennessee and Kentucky border in the face of the Northern forces at so many points along his front. Further, he said, civilians were deaf to his urgent pleas for volunteers. "Our people do not comprehend the magnitude of the danger that threatens." He warned Benjamin in a January 22 letter, "All the resources of the Confederacy are now needed for the defense of Tennessee."[20]

It was not a moment to request assistance from Richmond. As a consequence of the reenlistment process devised by the provisional Congress, Johnston's request coincided with the period of the Southern armies' greatest weakness. The War Department had given unit commanders discretion to grant furloughs only "in such numbers as may be deemed compatible with the safety of their commands," and the department interpreted the standard furlough period as narrowly as possible, not the sixty days specified by Congress but a "full thirty days at home," with travel time to and from counted against the sixty-day maximum. Nonetheless, the department could do little about the almost certain turmoil that would follow the new law's provision for the re-election of field officers by their men, except to limit elections to units where a majority had reenlisted. The large turnover among experienced officers predicted by General Bragg apparently did occur. According to a series of War Department special orders issued between mid-December 1861 and mid-April 1862, Davis accepted a large number of resignations from field officers. Three thousand or more of thirteen thousand officers left the Confederate army during this four-month period; along with massive leavetaking among the common soldiers, the loss of a quarter of the experienced field officers damaged Southern combat readiness during that 1862 winter.[21]

Without seasoned reinforcements, Johnston now began to badger the War Department for permission to accept unarmed twelve months' recruits, this at a time when Benjamin was doing everything possible to persuade veteran volunteers to reenlist for three years. Polk joined Johnston in this campaign, noting the presence in Columbus of ten regiments of twelve months' veterans and pointing out that not a single regiment was enlisted "for the war." "Cannot the exigency authorize the suspension of your rule?" In early January, Johnston maintained that the Yankees have "justly comprehended that the seat of the vitality of the Confederacy, if to be reached at all, is by this route." He needed reinforcements. When all else failed, Johnston forwarded a lengthy report defending his request for permission to muster unarmed twelve months' recruits on the grounds that because of the weak household economy of up-country Tennessee he had been unable to induce highland yeomen to enlist for three years. Reenlistment of Johnston's own twelve months' veterans got underway, but the chronic delays in payment of military salaries were no help. As Polk noted in a Christmas Eve letter to Benjamin, "A number of regiments have never received a dollar since entering the service," and the soldiers were "getting very sore under this state of affairs." The offer of a large bonus for reenlistment was no inducement to soldiers who had yet to receive any money at all. Polk asked to be "immediately so pecuniarily placed as to enable me to secure for the war the services of those who are now ready to re-enlist, as well as those who are daily manifesting a desire to do so."[22]

All this maneuvering around obstacles took a toll on combat readiness along the western front. Little more than a month before, Grant had launched a Union attack on the inland river forts. Tilghman reported on a high rate of absenteeism at Fort Donelson and blamed the reorganization of two regiments at the fort. Tilghman himself thought that electing field officers would reduce absenteeism, since winning office would free successful candidates "from feeling themselves bound to court the good will of their men to secure their election." If this could be done quickly, he hoped "to be able to restore matters to a more wholesome status"—and none too soon. With "still near 2,000 unarmed men in my command," Tilghman said, "I have not men enough armed at this post to man one-half the lines within the fortifications, much less to effect anything at points commanding my whole works." His anxiety at "this unvarnished state of things" led Tilghman to complain about other concerns as well, including his uncertainty about how to use five hundred black laborers due to arrive "in a few days." Major Gilmer had discouraged the use of such slave workers, and Tilghman sought guidance on how best to deploy this unexpected resource.[23] Also, for months before the winter offensive, "suspicious persons" from eastern Tennessee with passports issued by the Confederate secretary of war for travel along the Tennessee River Valley had proceeded on to Washington, D.C., and supplied information about vulnerable Confederate defenses. Slaves, too, were aiding the Union cause. A spy in the Tennessee Valley reported, "I found that my best source of information was the colored men, who were employed in various capacities of a military nature."[24]

With Fort Henry still lacking a full complement of heavy artillery, Johnston dispatched an emergency request for long-range cannon only ten days before the date Grant had chosen for his attack. Two new regiments of armed recruits had come, but Johnston lamented in a letter to Benjamin, "These men are reaching us too late for instruction. . . . They are as likely to be an element of weakness as of strength."[25] The weather was also a matter of concern. Tilghman, commanding at Henry, was contending with one of the wettest winters on record. Civilian observers along the watersheds of the Southern heartland reported that rainfall during January measured 30 to 114 percent above normal; in February precipitation was 43 to 92 percent above normal. Both of the inland rivers rose to near record levels, and a large part of Fort Henry disappeared beneath the Tennessee River. Flooding along the Cumberland was also hampering the defenders of Fort Donelson. By the time Grant began boarding the transports at Cairo to move up the Ohio to the staging area at Paducah and from there into the Tennessee River, Fort Henry may well have been ripe to fall into his hands.

Tilghman telegraphed Polk for reinforcements, but Polk feared the attack was part of a plan to encircle the city of Columbus and refused. Tilghman got a similarly negative response from Johnston, and with three thousand soldiers in a water-logged fort unable to effectively resist a Yankee force of seventeen thousand backed by ironclad gunboats, Tilghman ordered his troops to abandon both Fort Heiman and Fort Henry and to march immediately to the safety of Fort Donelson. With a group of eighty volunteers, he shelled the Northern flotilla and reached temporary safety at Fort Donelson, but on the afternoon of February 6, his command now safe, Tilghman surrendered himself and his volunteers to the uncertain fate of a Northern prisoner-of-war camp. He was exchanged in the fall of 1862 and would later fall with great valor during the Vicksburg campaign.

The command of Fort Donelson, which went to the highest ranking officer, changed hands five times during the week between February 5 and 12, as new units arrived in rapid succession. Brigadier Generals John B. Floyd, Simon Bolivar Buckner, and Gideon Pillow badly mismanaged the fort's defense, declining to try to stall Grant's advance although there were good reasons to believe they held a potentially decisive advantage. They refused to attack any of Grant's isolated columns, stayed in the fort, and allowed Union steamers to land fresh troops. Once a siege was underway, despite their surprising victory in an exchange with the supposedly invincible gunboats, this trio of generals made hasty plans to abandon the fort. Floyd and Pillow were determined to avoid capture, considering themselves especially vulnerable to Yankee vengeance, so Buckner, the lowest ranking general, was selected to capitulate while the other two beat a hasty retreat. Many troops were taken prisoner, and Buckner surrendered Fort Donelson to Grant, unconditionally, on February 16.[26]

The fall of Donelson sealed the fate of Nashville. Johnston could do nothing to slow the pace of the Northern advance without a fortified position, and now no such position existed. The installation along the Cumberland at Clarksville, Tennessee, "still in an unfinished state" because of a shortage of slave laborers, was, according to a letter from a G. A. Henry, "no more effective for defense than . . . before a spade of dirt was removed." Until he was actually at Nashville, center of the quartermaster, commissary, and ordnance depots for the Western Department, Johnston apparently did not realize that almost nothing had been done to construct the fallback position he had requested in November. A heavily outnumbered Confederate army fighting in the open stood little chance of successful resistance, and Johnston, with great reluctance, ordered his army to abandon Nashville. Officers in charge of the various depots, without adequate transportation, left behind copious quantities of food, clothing, camp equipage, ordnance, and irreplaceable machinery, although Colonel Nathan Bedford Forrest, who escaped from Donelson with his entire command, salvaged some of these desperately needed supplies. Nashville's poor scrambled to gather what they could from the mountains of soon-to-be-abandoned supplies. Many of the most prominent secessionists fled the city in fear of Northern vengeance, and thousands of civilians escaped alongside the retreating soldiers. As Johnston's soldiers retreated through the streets of a city many had sworn to defend to the last, John Berrien Lindsley, a leading educator assisting as a physician, captured in his journal the emotions of anger, frustration, and humiliation:

> February 16—Johnston's army passing the university from 10:00 A. M. until after dark—camped out at Mill Creek. Light of camp fires very bright at night. The army was in rapid *retreat*—the men disliked bitterly giving up Nashville without a struggle. The Southern army however was too small to make a stand against the overwhelmingly superior numbers of Union troops.

> February 17—What I saw of Johnston's army today and yesterday fully equalled any description I have ever read of an army in hurried retreat before a superior force, whose fangs they must avoid. There was hurry, confusion, alarm, and on the part of many a sullen dissatisfaction at not being able to fight.[27]

On February 25, 1862, the Northern army marched into an undefended city, and within four months virtually the entire Upper South frontier had fallen to the Union army. Polk had no choice but to abandon Columbus, and did so on March 2. The loss of the anchor position so weakened Confederate defenses along the Tennessee, Missouri, and Arkansas borders that Halleck was emboldened to order a Yankee advance. The first Union victory came on March 8 at the Battle of Pea Ridge, Arkansas; a second, on March 14, with Yankee occupation of New Madrid, Missouri. Johnston tried to concentrate his forces at Corinth, Mississippi, but failed to regain the initiative. On April 6, 1862, he was shot in the leg and bled to death at Shiloh. Stalemate was followed by the Confederate surrender of Island No. 10 on April 8, surrender of New Orleans on April 24, evacuation of Corinth on May 30, and surrender of Memphis on June 6. The defensive line Johnston had inherited from Harris,

Pillow, and Polk, and which he gave his life to defend, was overrun. Ironically, only in the Unionist hot bed of eastern Tennessee could Confederates hold the ground staked out so aggressively during the previous summer.

"Our Army . . . on the Eve of Dissolution": Union Victory and Assignment of Blame

The disaster provoked a furious round of scapegoating in the Confederacy. Jefferson Davis refused to hold Johnston accountable for a series of defeats rooted in flaws in Confederate nationalism too deep and too grave to blame on any single individual. To be sure, General Johnston had made a number of mistakes; yet his primary responsibility probably lay less in strategic failures than in his honest belief that the antebellum ethics of noblesse oblige would induce slaveholders to donate the essential private arms and slave laborers. His prolonged delay in acknowledging the failure of slaveholder voluntarism led to delay in employing military fatigue details or undertaking the round of emergency fortifications that might have fended off the Yankee winter offensive.

Instead of sacrificing an old friend to the ravenous critics, Davis accepted responsibility himself, as commander in chief, for devising too ambitious a defensive system. He worked diligently to recoup Southern losses. His personal analysis of the debacle is revealed in a March letter replying to stinging criticisms from Judge William M. Brooks, the same Alabama planter who had earlier scorned the dual enlistment. Davis wrote more candidly here perhaps than anywhere else in acknowledging "the error of my attempt to defend all the frontier, seaboard and inland." But, "If we had received the arms and munitions we had good reason to expect, that attempt would have been successful and the battlefields would have been on the enemy's soil." Brooks had complained of his "purely defensive" system; Davis pointed to the imbalance of resources between North and South as justification for the decision to fortify strong positions rather than attack. In a subtle but powerfully revealing aside, he laid responsibility for failure where it belonged: "The first duty now is to increase our forces by raising troops for the war, and bringing out all the private arms of the country for the public defence."[28]

Davis had thought as carefully as Lincoln had about how to maximize the effectiveness of mobilization. His was a carefully considered strategy to capitalize on what seemed to him the unique features of the Southern social system. His aristocratic, and peculiarly Southern, plan assumed that slaveholders' selfless donations of slave laborers would enable the Confederacy to construct fortifications strong enough to resist Northern attacks until military reinforcements could arrive. Similarly generous provision of private weapons would outfit soldiers with serviceable rifles and muskets until the Confederacy could reach a self-sufficient munitions production. But Davis's reliance on slaveholders' voluntarism miscarried badly. Fears of slave unrest and disaffection prevented many slaveholders from donating the necessary labor and weapons. And while it is true that Lincoln himself committed mistakes in the organization and deployment of free Northern labor resources, the conspicuous failure of Southern civilian voluntarism seems to have fatally compromised the Confederate defense of its western front.

Davis's unusual candor about the limitations imposed by conflicts within Southern society was echoed in an early January 1863 report to Davis by then Secretary of War James Seddon. His was possibly the bluntest public analysis of the winter 1862 collapse by a Confederate cabinet officer. In November 1862 Seddon had succeeded as secretary George W. Randolph, who had succeeded Judah P. Benjamin in March 1862, and he could speak with greater frankness than an incumbent who had been responsible to any degree for that disastrous winter. Seddon's report blamed resentment within the ranks about the call for "inequitable" sacrifice that extended tours of duty for some while others "equally interested and capable" refused to serve the Cause. Seddon summed up the full range of that 1862 debacle:

> Our Army was in incipient disorganization and on the eve of dissolution. The natural consequences ensued in a series of grave reverses. Reverse succeeded reverse. In the east, Roanoke Island, the key to the inland waters of North Carolina, was captured. We had to fall back from Manassas, abandon our defenses at Yorktown, and yield Norfolk with all the advantages of its contiguous navy-yard and dock. In the west, Forts Henry and Donelson fell, with the loss at the latter of the gallant force who had victoriously repelled till exhaustion disabled them to meet overwhelming numbers. All defenses on the Upper Mississippi had to be yielded or abandoned, and Nashville, the capital, and Memphis, the leading city, of Tennessee became the unresisting prey of the victors. Finally, as the crowning stroke of adverse fortune, New Orleans, the commercial emporium of the South, with the forts that guarded the outlet of the great artery of trade in the West, after resistance so feeble as to arouse not less of shame and indignation, passed into the occupancy of our foes.[29]

"Thinking More of Cotton and the Dollar Than of Our Country"

Voluntarism failed the South in yet another respect: in the greater priority given to making a profit in cotton and other staple goods over providing needed food. The draft act of April 1862 assumed that since the Confederacy had a large supply of unskilled slave labor that could be used to relieve the demand for labor in essential industries, slaveholders and other skilled citizens could remain at home, making it possible for the South to feed and supply both military and civilian populations while freeing enough men to win the war. Key to this assumption was an aristocratic belief that commercial farmers would recognize their duty to the new nation by curtailing the production of nonedible staples and increasing food production. Slaveholders would arrange for substitutes to fight in their stead so they could direct their slave labor toward food production. But noblesse oblige did not overcome selfish individualism among the planters; the fabulous prices offered for cotton in the wake of embargo and the blockade induced a number to plant more cotton and less food.

At the same time, the torrential rains of the winter of 1861/62 ruined the winter wheat crop, and in a dramatic shift in weather patterns, a hard drought stunted the next summer's corn. Excessive production of staple crops like cotton and underproduction of food crops combined to produce a subsistence crisis, the very sort of disaster that the congressional provision of draft substitution and exemption for plantation managers was intended to prevent. When news about the lack of food at home reached the camps, many yeomen soldiers went home, with or without official leavetaking. M. M. Fortinberry, a Mississippi soldier, wrote his governor in December 1862 to explain why many yeomen had deserted: "We have failed to make a crop. Poor men have been compelled to leave the army and come home to provide for their families we have corn for bread and hogs for meat but no salt to save it some of us is paroled prisoners got home and found our families without anything at all has been out fifteen months come home without a dollar and now pay $1.25 per barrel for corn that would make about three pecks to a barrel." Neither public nor private relief agencies provided adequate support to the families of such poorer soldiers.[30]

So widespread was public awareness of the urgent need for corn that patriotic Southerners, many of them slaveholders, took the lead in exposing planters who cultivated cotton instead of food. In February 1862 R. C. Parker, a slaveholding cotton farmer who saw his neighbors preparing to plant full cotton crops, reported to Governor John Shorter of Alabama, "It appears to me we are thinking more of cotton and the dollar than of our country." In March the *Tuscaloosa Observer* wrote that slaveholders responsible for widespread cotton planting had committed "treason" and ought to be "hung as high as Haman." "Talk about Lincolnites among us," thundered the *Observer,* "the man who can deliberately resolve to do such a thing is meaner than the meanest Yankee that was ever born." Susanna Clay, mother of Alabama senator Clement Clay, in a March letter to her son wrote that "the small planters intend to plant cotton, on the plea they were following the example of the larger planters, who would make a sufficient quantity of corn for their negroes and after peace sell cotton, and that they would have no market for corn and no means to get money."[31]

While slaveholders were struggling to sustain the antebellum society, many nonslaveholders were fighting against starvation. Confederate officials, painfully aware of the need for record food crops, joined private citizens and newspapers in a campaign to persuade commercial farmers to substitute corn for cotton. Had the small and medium-sized slave-run farms widely dispersed throughout the Mississippi Valley actually focused on food production, yeoman families might have been able to endure the unusual crop failures of 1862 without extreme privation and the consequent desertions of yeomen soldiers. But they did not, and home-front dependents of many poorer soldiers found it impossible to manage. "The lands in the poor section is now destitute of labor to cultivate it," wrote Jonathan F. Bailey, a slaveholder from Marion County, Alabama, to General H. P. Watson on March 31, "while in the rich section there is not now an average of one white man to a plantation."[32]

If slaveholders had great difficulty finding competent overseers in wartime, many families without slaves and with their male members in military service were often unable to harvest even minimal food. Edward H. Moran, a Confederate officer serving in the piney woods region of southeastern Alabama, wrote to his wife Fannie in June 1862 about the burdens endured by soldiers' wives in "the poorest country you ever saw or could imagine," though he blamed the backcountry more than the war.

The men have gone to the war and the few women that are left have to plow and sow and reap and mow on the principle of "root hog or die. . . ." I don't blame the men for going to the army. They could damage their condition and perhaps help somebody else take care of their country for certainly they can't care to have their own saved. Any country in the world would be damaged by the possession of it. I tell you Fannie, if it had not been that providence had a surplus of material, this part of the world would never have been made.

In March 1862 the Plaquemines Parish *Weekly Rice Planter* ridiculed poorer Louisiana soldiers who enlisted for the duration in order "to be furnished bread, or stay home and starve," and offered a sardonic prayer: "Thank God, we have something to eat for ourselves, our wives and children. And when we go to war it is from a spirit of patriotic feeling and not to live off the government or starve at home."[33]

Despite the desperation of poorer soldiers, the Confederate government refused to moderate its demands for manpower, and by the spring of 1862 in many backcountry regions calls for militia drills were threatening early spring plowing and sowing. In response to an order mandating weekly militia drill, Lawrence M. Jones, the commander of a militia regiment in Shelby County, Alabama, asked Governor Shorter to leave a few men on the farms to help the three hundred women who had to take up the plows.

Shelby County is a poor county. In two weeks from this date there will be three hundred females at the handle of the plow. They are patriotic ladies and will stand between the handles of the plow with great bravery. Our voting population formally was sixteen hundred, We have thirteen hundred men in the field. . . . Thus leaving few men behind—Therefore I suggest to you that I think the few that are left behind should not be called out oftener than once a month. . . . It is now crop time. Let those who remain at home make all the corn they can, for their little ones.[34]

The April 1862 universal enlistment law froze the enlistments of all volunteers and prevented yeomen from returning home to assist in planting food crops for their families. The May 31 *Selma Morning Register* carried an angry letter from a "country woman" who wrote that the widows and wives of soldiers put responsibility for the soldiers' plight squarely on the shoulders of speculators and extortioners. Another anonymous woman writing to the *Register* blamed both the state and central government for refusing to impose strict controls on wartime prices. The families of hundreds of poorer soldiers, she said, were compelled to subsist, children and adults alike, on corn bread and water. In early July 1862 Governor Shorter received a detailed accounting of the suffering from S. K. Rayburn, a railroad official and a prominent Alabama citizen active in county relief activities:

There are many of the families of the soldiers in this county that are actually in a suffering condition and unless there can be some relief given by you or the State Department there will surely be starvation amongst them before the new crop can be gathered. . . . Corn's now worth in this county one dollar and twenty five cents per bushel. The means now used by the county for their support is exhausted and the poor women and children crying for bread. . . . There are but five wealthy persons in our county and the burden of supporting so large a number of families has been a heavy draw on them.[35]

As early as May 1861, the president of the Memphis and Charleston Railroad, Samuel Tate, had sought to turn Davis's attention to the urgency of securing a vote for secession from Missouri because it had an "abundant supply of provisions," but the Confederacy had failed to persuade either Missouri or Kentucky to secede. Writing to Governor A. B. Moore in November that same year, a concerned Alabamian had recommended: "Should the blockade not be raised by the first of March next, I think the Governors of the different states ought to advise the planters to plant but little or no cotton and all grain crops—with two crops of cotton on hand the price could hardly be remunerating. Besides we cannot look to Kentucky and Missouri for supplies." The governors of Alabama, Missouri, Mississippi, Virginia, and Tennessee appointed delegates to a planters' convention scheduled for Memphis in mid-February 1862. As the delegates convened, news came of the loss of Fort Donelson and the evacuation of Nashville, yet two days of heated debate ensued over cotton versus corn, as the *Memphis Daily Appeal* reported. Colonel J. F. Simmons proposed a twenty-dollar per bale tax on all cotton produced that year, especially needed since "in Kentucky, the James River country and a portion of Tennessee and Alabama, the enemy were cutting off the supply of grain, pork, etc. we have been relying upon, and the remaining portion of the country will have therefore to grow an increased quantity of produce." The planters' convention, nonetheless, could not bring itself to urge confiscatory taxes on cotton, and it rejected Simmons's resolution, instead issuing a mild appeal to patriotism: "It is the opinion of this convention that every planter throughout the Confederacy in determining the character and extent of his crops to be planted, should bear in mind that it is reduced almost to a certainty that the armies of the Confederacy are to be supplied almost exclusively with provisions from the cotton states."[36]

In mid-March proponents of stringent controls carried their battle to the Confederate Congress, where Senator Albert Gallatin Brown, of Mississippi, a large slaveholder but often a spokesman for the interests of poorer Southerners—the only antebellum politician in Mississippi never to lose an election—offered a resolution requiring a forfeit for producing excess cotton: "That it shall not be lawful for any head of a family to produce more than three bales of cotton, of four hundred pounds each, and one additional bale, of like weight, for each hand employed in the cultivation of the same. . . . For every additional bale to the number prescribed above thereof, the grower shall forfeit forty dollars." Texas senator Louis Wigfall objected strenuously that Brown's resolution was "unconstitutional, inasmuch as it *created* a crime, by imposing a fine of forty dollars upon a citizen for doing a thing which he had every right to do." Wigfall compared the proposal to "the Blue Laws of New England"; Congress "might as well pass a law to fine a man for kissing his wife on Sunday." His point of view carried the day.[37]

State governments sought to address the problem after the central government found it too hot to handle. In April 1862 Governor Hiram Rector of Arkansas pushed Governor Francis W. Pickens of South Carolina to ban cotton cultivation altogether: "Cereals should be grown exclusively. Cotton *abolished.*" But despite the stringent restraints on Arkansas products, the state's principal newspaper, the *Arkansas True Democrat,* reported that planters were producing as much cotton as they pleased. The following year, in a March 1863 proclamation to the "Planters of Alabama," Governor Shorter would blame cotton producers for the state government's inability to relieve distress among soldiers' families.[38]

Francis Leak dispatched a stinging letter to his congressman in February 1862 after discovering that his neighbors intended to plant at least as much cotton as usual. Voluntary agreement would be futile, the Mississippi planter wrote to John W. Clapp. "The whole country sees that in the event of the continuance of the war and of the blockade, the agricultural labor of the South ought to be chiefly devoted to the production of bread stuffs and provisions of all kinds; it also sees that it is impossible to bring about such a result by mere voluntary agreement among the planters. . . . There are hundreds and probably thousands of planters, who will plant more cotton, sugar or tobacco, because their neighbors plant less." In May he complained bitterly to Governor Pettus about the failure of voluntary conversion to corn production in Mississippi and urged stern action against slaveholders who planted large cotton crops: "If they will not do their share in raising corn for the army, and for the families of the thousands of poor but gallant men fighting the battles of the country, they ought to be made to do their share by heavy taxes." Confiscatory taxes on wartime cotton production would be "exceedingly popular." Planters were giving priority to cash for the future over food for the present.[39]

James Lusk Alcorn, who had accepted an appointment as a general with the Mississippi volunteers, left in disgust in December 1861 after Davis denied him a commission in the regular Confederate army. Davis, Alcorn wrote to his wife Amelia, was "a corrupt tyrant" and "a cold sickly dyspeptic" who had forgotten "the nature of Southern[ers]" and thereby threatened to "loose the jewel entrusted to his charge." Alcorn proceeded to produce as much cotton as he felt he needed, and spent much of fall 1862 smuggling it into Northern hands, writing to his wife that "the smuggling business has become popular and people are beginning openly to trade. . . . The authorities out in the hills, I am told, are furious." Alcorn was harvesting greenbacks and gold and expected, if his crop was not burned by Confederate soldiers, to harvest a lot more of them. "I have been very busy," he said, "hiding & selling my cotton. I have sold in all 'one hundred & eleven' bales, I have now here ten thousand Dollars in paper (Green Backs) and one thousand Dollars in Gold. I have still some fifty bales of old cotton and about forty bales of new cotton picked out and ginned. If I escape the burners, I will be able to realize $20,000.00 more. I am busy I assure you and am making my time count."[40]

Yet despite the self-interested behavior of many Mississippi planters, cotton production throughout the South as a whole fell almost two-thirds between 1861 and 1862. A study of the planter class by James L. Roark argues that declining cotton output paved the way for rising grain supplies.[41] But if so much additional food was produced, how can we explain the widespread complaints of food shortages during and after the 1862 growing season? The best estimates of Southern cotton production during the Civil War era do show a sharp decline from 1861 to 1862, and an even larger percentage change between 1862 and 1863:

Year	Cotton Production in Bales
1859	5,387,000
1860	3,841,000
1861	4,491,000
1862	1,597,000
1863	449,000
1864	299,000
1865	2,094,000

But close examination shows that a two-thirds reduction in output of cotton might not reflect a sharp decline in the actual number of acres planted in cotton as much as the unusually adverse weather conditions of 1862 and the erosion in control of slave workers. A network of Smithsonian Institution volunteer weather observers, armed with thermometers and rain gauges, recorded conditions at their stations three times daily during the 1862 growing season. Data for a belt from central Alabama through Columbus and Natchez, Mississippi, to Austin, Texas, documented a pattern that would certainly have resulted in a significant drop in the yields of both cotton and grains. The January–February 1862 rainfall totals in wheat-growing regions were 46 percent over normal levels, but during May, the time of most germinations, rainfall in the eastern two-thirds of the Mississippi Valley fell 53 percent, and in June to July, the month that determines corn yields, rainfall was an astonishing 74 percent below normal throughout the entire Mississippi Valley.[42]

Judge Brooks, who had written to Davis sharply criticizing Confederate mistakes, wrote to Alabama's Governor Shorter in March 1862: "The Spring has been very backward, and but little grain or any other thing has been planted." So, too, Rayburn, the railroad official active in Alabama relief efforts, wrote to the governor in July that rains had delayed spring plowing and planting and made the winter wheat crop in central Alabama "an entire failure." In southern Louisiana the Magnolia plantation journal noted plaintively, "Nearly all our corn has turned yellow in the last days and it is actually burning up for want of rain." And a Perry County, Alabama, owner of two thousand acres and ninety slaves, Philip Henry Pitts, wrote in his plantation book for June 12 that "we are a good deal behind. . . . We need rain down here." Mrs. Mae Coleman, of Arkadelphia, Arkansas, told her brother in August, "I am afraid we will hardly make bread owing to the severe drought in June and July. The spring was so wet that the farmers were late getting their corn planted—the dry weather set in the latter part of May and continued until the latter part of July." In addition, epidemics of colic, mule cholera, and "Charbon disease" among the work animals on farms in Mississippi and Louisiana led to the loss of irreplaceable stock in the breeding regions in the Lower South.[43]

The declining discipline among slave labor affected cotton and grain production at least as much as environmental factors did. John Bills, the western Tennessee planter, recounted a tale of drought and disorder in his plantation journal over the summer of 1862.

June 2, 1862—Hicks, my overseer at Cornucopia not over his corn the first time. He is greatly behind and will make a failure I think.

June 12—Crops backward and fould. Negroes do not work well.

June 18—My corn crop South of cabins much improved. Bottoms foul and grassy.

June 21—My crops are not good at either place.

July 7—The weather hot and dry. This is the warmest day yet. Corn twisting much. Early planting must be badly injured soon.

July 9—Crops not doing well. Failing.

July 11—Some rain this morning. None at Hickory Valley. Not a season here for anything.[44]

Nonslaveholders' noncommercial cotton production probably accounted for about a 10 percent reduction from the 1861 levels, voluntary conversion by commercial planters for another 15 percent. Deteriorating control of slave labor and bad growing weather taken together, not planter sacrifice, may well have been responsible for the remaining reduction of cotton output from the 4,491,000 bales of 1861 to the 1,556,132 bales of 1862. This could explain, at least in part, the otherwise contradictory testimony about planter reduction in cotton production and yeoman anger at planters for failing to produce enough food for home front and war front. If commercial farmers undertook adjustment in the corn/cotton ratio sufficient only to compensate for their own shortfalls in food production, the widespread suffering so clearly evident during 1862 becomes more readily comprehensible. (See maps 5.1 and 5.2.)[45]

The more planters in a county, the greater the degree of food independence. Particularly striking is the correlation between the percentage of families in a county who belonged to the planter class and that county's ratio of self-sufficiency. The commercial region had both the slave labor and the land to shift into food-producing activities. Poorer families had neither. In areas where the most arable land was devoted to food, the combination of labor lost to mobilization and the adverse growing weather created a food crisis local resources could not overcome. No matter what the big planters did with their land, the Confederate transportation system could not have moved surplus grain long distances, but what mattered most about the behavior of "great" planters like Alcorn was the selfish example they set for the medium- and smaller-sized slaveholders who could have provided substantial help to hungry yeoman families.

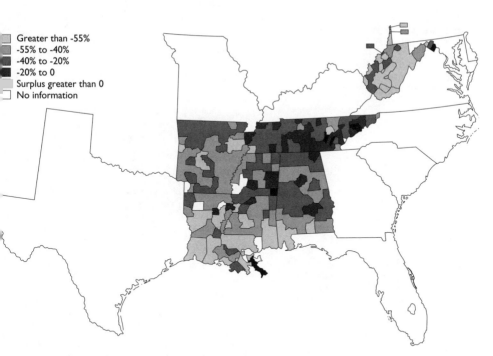

Map 5.1. Estimated 1862 food deficit without corn/cotton shift

Home-Front Profiteering, Reduced Camp Rations, and Incipient Class "Rebellion"

Once the full extent of the 1862 crop failures became evident, and with army rations getting shorter, it was inevitable that soldiers would wonder how their families were faring. As a soldier in the 37th Mississippi Infantry saw it, home-front destitution was worse than privation in camp. "I would not mind living hard," wrote Private Andrew Patrick to his wife, "if I node you was not suffering but you are there and I am here and cant tend to you." Later, when word of the new bill exempting overseers in plantations with twenty or more slaves spread throughout the army, many yeomen changed their minds about sticking it out. "I am uneasy about you and the children getting something to eat," confessed Patrick. "There is already a heap of men gone home and a heap says if their familys gets to suffering that they will go if they have to suffer." In mid-October 1862 Colonel Lucius B. Northrop, commissary general of subsistence, received a report about "the scarcity that now threatens the army." The

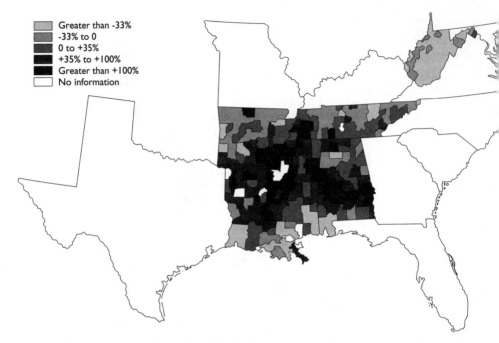

Map 5.2. Estimated 1862 food deficit with maximum corn/cotton conversion

supply depots of the Southern army were "completely exhausted," with meat for rations for no more than "300,000 men for 25 days."[46]

The state of supplies was truly "alarming," said Frank Ruffin, son of Edmund Ruffin, who brought the matter directly to the attention of then Secretary of War Randolph. Loss of access to Kentucky and Tennessee had cost the Commissary Department 85 percent of the meat supplies on which it had been depending. With shortages of salt in some areas and food "short in others from drought," Ruffin saw no alternative but to smuggle supplies through the blockade or through the Northern lines. Randolph agreed, but Davis was concerned about sanctioning smuggling. From the field came disturbing reports of predation within the Southern army, and a worried Major J. F. Cummings wrote to Northrop in early November that Bragg had seized supplies purchased for the Army of Northern Virginia. In response, Northrop explained that shortage of subsistence in Tennessee prevented the export of supplies "absolutely necessary for subsisting the forces in the field." The feuding commissaries exchanged feuding letters, Bragg's officer stoutly maintaining that the seizure was "a *military necessity* rendered unavoidable by the fact that you had so thoroughly stripped the country as to leave nothing for the subsistence of our army," Cummings denying that charge.[47]

Few options remained except to slash soldiers' rations. Frank Ruffin reported to Colonel Northrop in early November 1862 that "the very severe drought of the past summer and early fall" made it impossible to get enough meat for Lee's army from suppliers in Virginia. Northrop's bold plan more than a year earlier to drive a herd of longhorn cattle from Texas was foiled by the 1862 drought, and Northrop acknowledged that the short rations, begun in the fall of 1862, must continue. Soldiers were complaining freely about gnawing hunger. From Bragg's Army of Tennessee, in December, came the frank statement, "We have had not anything to eat since yesterday at dinner." Private Edwin Hedge Fay told his wife Sarah of a similar situation in a Mississippi encampment: "I still think this war will close next spring for I dont see how we are to carry it on." "I have fears myself," Fay confessed, "of a growing spirit throughout the South in favor of *reconstruction*. John Carter said yesterday that he for one was very willing to go back." Defeatism sharpened by hunger and rage against inequities led to an outburst of desertion. Fay sought to reassure Sarah about his own continued devotion to the cause: "When I despair of the Republic I shall come home and lose my life trying to protect you from insult. Desertions are multiplying so fast in this army that almost one-third of it is gone."[48]

In July 1862 a delegation of volunteer soldiers from the 33rd Mississippi Infantry wrote to Governor Pettus to complain about a Mrs. Amanda Scott who lay sick and alone while the children of her absent husband went about hungry. From Coffee County, Alabama, Governor Shorter heard from a Lucresy Simmons. "This is to inform you," she wrote,

> of the treatment of Some of the Soldiers wives in this settlement Some of them is living on bread alone without salt we have underSoud here that thare was Some appropriations made for the releaf of them if it is so its not attended to here instance one Marion Rudd has been in the war 12 months his wife was left quite destitute of the means to live on and She has never received but 12 buoshels of corn and 30 lbs of meat. . . . information wanted I have lost 2 Sons in the war I wish to know how to proseade to draw their money.

Another impoverished woman, Nancy Brazwell, wrote to Shorter in desperation in August, "I am a sickly woman and if I don't get help my children must starve. I hear my husband is dead."[49]

Slaveholders' pursuit of wartime profits was one of the principal sources of class resentment in the Confederacy. But despite the yeomen's destitution and despair, many planters, caught by the wartime financial squeeze, continued to plant cash crops instead of food; they felt so tightly squeezed that they refused to purchase Confederate bonds. On November 11, 1862, Governor Thomas O. Moore of Louisiana tried to explain the situation to an angry President Davis: "Planters will not sell cotton for *Bonds*—not because they distrust the bonds but because it is money they need now and not an investment. They cannot pay taxes with the bonds, nor can they buy shoes or beef for their negroes with them. Our richest people are in bad condition for the coming winter. They are literally without money to purchase those necessaries which the owners of large plantations must have."[50]

Brigadier General Richard Winter, concerned about sagging morale in his own state militia brigade in Mississippi, dispatched an account to Governor Pettus, comparing problems faced by men "in the poorer section of the Brigade" with those faced by men "in the richer portion of the Brigade." Among the poorer group, the primary issue was "what is to become of my little crops, & wherewithin shall we feed not only our own family but the families of the volunteers (and they are numerous) which have been left on our hands & under our protection"; for the richer group, it was, rather, "what is to become of my wife & children when left in a land swarming with negroes without a single white man on many plantations to restrain their licentiousness by a little wholesome fear or visit with condign punishment any act of wrong or insubordination." Both rich and poor wondered whether "the crops of corn will be made." Increasing numbers of yeomen soldiers were deserting, angered and alienated by reports of profiteering by affluent Southerners, and by inequity and conscription.[51]

The rebuff the failure of civilian voluntarism in the Confederacy offered to Southern antebellum assumptions about the equality of all free white men helped to transform reenlistment in the field into an inequitable exercise of arbitrary authority. Only by reviving faith in the equity of sacrifice could the planter leadership rekindle the faded aura of revolutionary egalitarianism. Common soldiers resentful of elitist behavior were even more disheartened by the string of embarrassing military defeats caused at least in part by slaveholders' refusal to sacrifice equally for the Southern cause. Elitism on the war front and selfishness on the home front were poor omens for the future of the slaveholders' rebellion. A war effort dependent on the nonslaveholding majority for the bulk of its manpower could not afford to conduct a war for independence in a fashion that gave yeomen soldiers grounds for questioning the commitment of slaveholders. As the Richmond regime struggled to move beyond the disastrous winter of 1861/62, it could no longer avoid taking stock of the conflict between slaveholders' anxieties about the security of slavery and the diffusion of preservationist ideology among white nonslaveholders within the Southern army. When poorer men in the ranks could identify individual wealthy slackers by name, it became difficult for many to justify the loss of their personal autonomy that compulsory military service entailed.

Seddon's 1863 characterization of the army as "in incipient disorganization and on the eve of dissolution" suggests that the reenlistment act of December 1861 had backfired. Rather than evoking devotion to the cause, that attempt to induce twelve months' volunteers to add two years more to duty tours deeply offended many veterans already angry at the elitism of slaveholding soldiers. These veterans, in turn, began to resent the grudging support of many affluent civilians. In light of their reluctance to join in common sacrifice, the forceful attempts to encourage reenlistment raised the specter of subjugation to "political slavery" in the minds of those who served while others refused. These objections caused such dissension during the critical winter of 1861/62 that it retarded battlefield performance along the Upper South frontier, and elsewhere as well.

Chapter Six   Invasion of the Heartland
and the Failure to Achieve
Universal Conscription

With the collapse of its Western Department the Confederacy experienced a sense of defeatism from which popular morale was never able to recover. "These calamities may be a wholesome chastening for us," wrote John B. Jones, chief clerk at the Confederate War Department, at the end of February 1862. But the loss of the defensive installations guarding the inland rivers and the Northern occupation of the Upper South borderland meant the end of easy access to supplies of livestock, meat, and grain from central Kentucky and middle Tennessee. The Northern blockade became more effective than ever. No longer could Southerners hold Union forces at bay along their frontiers. Any victory for Confederate independence would require expulsion of a massive army of occupation from its multiple footholds in middle and western Tennessee.[1]

At the same time, social tension within the army and on the home front continued to complicate attempts at expanded Confederate mobilization. Slaveholders continued to pursue interests at cross-purposes to the revolution, and without leadership from the slaveholders, government policy, in effect, would tempt the yeomanry to resist Jefferson Davis's efforts to centralize control over labor allocation. Yeomanry would continue to resist national labor demands in the guise of universal conscription, while states' righters found grounds for complaint against any radical expansion of the central government. In this new politics a third element, Southern slaves, were to play a decisive role. Slave masters had to contend with a huge population who saw their own interests as opposed to those of the Confederacy.

The Inauguration of Permanent Government

The inauguration of the permanent government for the Confederate States of America in February 1862 was staged at a gloomy time of diminished military prospects. With a permanent government replacing the provisional government, revolutionary Southern nationalism had become mature. Unlike its predecessor, which held assumed constitutional powers, the permanent government would rest on a direct electoral mandate. The inaugural ceremony was held purposely on February 22, the birthday of George Washington, whose towering statue provided a dramatic backdrop for the occasion. President Davis observed that "the day, the memory, and the purpose seem fitly associated," although, he admitted, "after a series of successes and victories, . . . we have recently met with serious disasters." A cold downpour chilled and dampened the mood of a somber assemblage that could barely hear its president read his stirring inaugural address, challenging the South: "to show ourselves worthy of the inheritance bequeathed to us by the patriots of the Revolution, we must emulate that heroic devotion which made reverse to them but the crucible in which their patriotism was refined."[2] Southern whites could prove their love of liberty, Davis said, by accepting willingly an indefinitely prolonged struggle.

Catherine Devereux Edmondston, that articulate plantation mistress in Halifax County, North Carolina, reflected on the concurrence of Washington's birthday, the inauguration of the Confederacy, and the defeats in the field:

> February 15, 1862—I heard, alaas! that it was too true that Fort Donaldson had indeed fallen on the 15th & that Gen Johnston was in retreat from Nashville! Heavy news, but we have no particulars.
>
> February 22, 1862—Today was Inaugated, amidst rain & clouds, at Richmond our first President Jefferson Davis! God grant him a prosperous & *peaceful* Administration! . . . May the mantle of Washington, whose birthday we have chosen for the natal day of our nation, fall upon you. May his spirit imate you!

This self-described "Secesh Lady" was expressing the fond hope that both the rulers and the ruled would discover the spiritual resources to rebound. But despite their fervent patriotism, the Edmondstons had seriously considered leaving their plantation after hearing that a February 8 attack had established a Northern beachhead on Roanoke Island. Parts of Elizabeth City had been burned, and many household slaves had cast their lot with the Union. After a week of agonizing indecision, the Edmondstons decided to stay on their remote plantation, assuming that General Ambrose Burnside was unlikely to come that far.[3]

A similar calculus of familial versus national interests may well have defined the limits of many other slaveholders' support for the Southern revolution. White Southerners had to learn how to deal with an enemy garrison on the home front. Some residents of Nashville, particularly the "Secesh Ladies," adopted a stance like the Edmondstons' of "refusing to hold any communication" with the invaders, but only the privileged few could remain in the occupied city while enjoying the luxury of noncommunication; most citizens had no choice other than to flee. But hasty exodus could be costly, with assets left behind abandoned to pillage and looting. No one could predict with certainty how long their home region would remain under Northern control; those with the resources to manage a hasty move and a powerful compulsion to avoid life under Yankee occupation were those most likely to go. Fire Eater Edmund Ruffin had left his beloved home state of Virginia rather than remain under Yankee domination "even for an hour."[4]

A "Terrible Gloom" and Panic: The Surrender of Nashville

Back in November 1861, General Albert Sidney Johnston had issued a stern warning to complacent slaveholders. The effects of an occupation, he explained to Governor Isham Harris of Tennessee, were so uncertain that sacrifices alone could shield their beloved way of life. And three months later Mary Jones, a plantation mistress in Liberty County, Georgia, wrote to her husband, Lieutenant Charles C. Jones, of the "terrible gloom" caused by news of the recent military disasters. "The hour has arrived," she said in a letter, "when men and women too in the Southern Confederacy must seek to know and to do their duty with fearless hearts and hands. Our recent disasters are appalling. The thought of Nashville, the heart of the country and I may say the granary of the Confederacy, falling into the hands of those robbers and murderers casts a terrible gloom over us all. That point in their possession, it really appeared that they might touch every other in North Alabama and Georgia."[5] News of Nashville's impending loss fomented panic throughout the heartland. Since it was the first major Southern city to fall, no one knew how the Yankees would treat local residents, particularly those active as secessionists or as functionaries in the Confederate government.

The breadth of the territory left vulnerable by the fall of Fort Henry enhanced the anxiety. From its point of origin below Knoxville, the Tennessee River flows in a large U southwest past Chattanooga, then west across Alabama, and then north through Tennessee and Kentucky to join the Ohio River near Paducah. The fall of Fort Henry meant that Union gunboats could roam unimpeded to the falls in the river at Muscle Shoals, Alabama. The ten days of uncertainty between the fall of Fort Henry and the surrender of Fort Donelson frightened civilians in northeastern Mississippi. As a minister, the Reverend Samuel Andrew Agnew, himself a slaveholder, put it in February 1862, "There is a panic at Corinth and people are leaving there as fast as they can. . . . A thousand rumors are flying." The historian Stanley F. Horn described a similar frantic atmosphere at Nashville the day after Fort Donelson capitulated:

> All through that terrible, turbulent sabbath the terror-stricken men, women and children surged through the city's streets. Some just wandered aimlessly from place to place, eagerly catching the latest rumors and excitedly passing them on—with additions. Others more practical minded loaded their possessions onto wagons and carriages for a hasty departure. Those who had no private vehicles crowded the railroad stations and jammed departing trains; men even clung to the tops of the coaches as they pulled out.[6]

Some Nashvillians took matters into their own hands. Lizzie Hardin told how "stalwart women commenced rolling flour barrels, shouldering sides of bacon and gathering up clothing until they had sufficient supplies." Poorer residents apparently joined the general onslaught on the soon-to-be-abandoned commissary stores of Johnston's army. John Berrien Lindsley wrote in his diary for February 17 of "all sorts of vehicles in use—stout men walking off with sides and hams—Irish women tottering under the same."[7]

In the countryside, too, many people fled. A Yankee colonel, John Beatty, who entered the Green River Valley while passing through Kentucky, noted on February 13, "We passed many fine houses and extensive, well-improved farms. But few white people were seen. The negroes appeared to have entire possession." Mary A. Newcomb, a nurse who was riding a steamer up the Tennessee River, saw a similar scene: "The boat stopped at several large plantations, and we were permitted to go ashore and take a look at the grand houses once occupied by wealthy slaveholders, but now left to the tender mercies of the soldiers of either party." When Colonel Beatty's unit neared Murfreesboro, Tennessee, he learned of the slave reaction to the exodus of their masters: "To a colored boy who stole into our lines last night, with his little bundle under his arm, the major said: 'Doesn't it make you feel bad to run away from your masters?' 'Oh, no, Massa; dey is gone, too.'"[8]

Exodus from the Plantation Belt

Runaway slaves had been seeking freedom in Northern encampments ever since the beginning of the war and wherever the Yankees went they attracted a large number of younger slaves, most of them men determined to claim the freedom they believed Union armies had brought with them. Official Northern policies had sought to discourage slave escapees, on the pragmatic grounds that sympathetic treatment of fugitive blacks would forfeit support from loyal slaveholders in the border slave states. A few Union officers, however, explored the limits of the fugitive slave policy, and emancipation eventually forced its way onto the Union war agenda with the slaves' own persistence and the immanent logic of war against a slaveholding power. But not until September 1862, when Lincoln issued the Preliminary Emancipation Proclamation, did War Department policy allow Northern soldiers to assist in the slaves' quest for freedom. The blacks who flocked toward the Union army as it approached Nashville were part of an advance guard of others who would flee their masters' revolution.

Folklore provides graphic and contrasting demonstrations of the perspectives of masters and slaves. A freed slave from Pulaski, Tennessee, vividly recalled the day when his freedom came with "de Lincum soldiers":

> Old Massa come down de road dis mornin',
> Wif de muffstash on he face;
> He grab he hat and he lef' very sudden,
> Like he gwine to leave de place;
> Ole massa runned away,
> And de darkey stayed at home;
> It must be very confiscatin';
> De Lincum Soldiers come;
> Dere's wine and cider in de cellar,
> And de niggers must hab some.

Blacks who had seen their masters run from "de Lincum soldiers" were unlikely to accept antebellum ways or a sense of slaveholder omnipotence ever again. At Memphis, the master who owned Louis Hughes had boasted loudly about the invincibility of Southern valor, but after the fall of Nashville, he began to prepare to move his family and slaves "to a place of safety." "Our folks became alarmed right away," Hughes wrote later in his autobiography, "and commenced talking of moving and running the servants away from the Yankees, to a place of safety. . . . They never thought that slavery would be abolished, and so hoped to come back again. . . . The vaunted courage of this man seems to have early disappeared, and his thought was chiefly devoted to getting his family and his slaves to some obscure place, as far away as possible from the Yankees that were to be so easily whipped."[9]

Some white Southerners who fled had good reason to fear Northern reprisals. Former presidential candidate John Bell and the former Confederate secretary of war Leroy Pope Walker, both of whom lived in Huntsville, a Tennessee River town in northwestern Alabama, were quick to flee. After the fall of Fort Henry, gunboats were able to cruise up the Tennessee, and after the April 6–7 battle at Shiloh, neighbors spotted a cluster of Yankee troopships steaming toward Huntsville. Bell and Walker, convinced that their roles in the birth of the Confederacy made them especially vulnerable to retribution, gathered up what possessions they could and left, barely avoiding capture. One of Bell's slaves celebrated his master's hurried departure by thanking divine power:

> O Praise and Tanks!
> De Lord he Come
> To set de people free
> An' massa think it day ob gloom
> Ab' we ob jubilee
> O neber you fear if neber you hear
> De driver blow his horn.

Just as God was said to have rescued the Children of Israel by putting Pharaoh and his army to flight, so did many slaves believe that the Yankees had liberated them by causing their masters to flee.[10]

Bell and Walker were part of a massive and hurried exodus away from the Northern army of occupation in the Tennessee River Valley; a number of the refugees were prominent in state and national politics. (Bell's industrial slaves in Tennessee, incidentally, were at the heart of the alleged—and brutally suppressed—slave insurrection scare of 1856.) Many who remained behind criticized Bell and Walker's flight. Walker's advance preparations for flight suggested that he had used his governmental position to gain information unavailable to others. He had resigned his cabinet position in September amid charges of incompetence and had accepted the command of an unarmed Alabama regiment shortly before Shiloh, too much of a coincidence to some. To Alabama senator Clement Clay, who had earlier recommended Walker for his post in the cabinet, Clay's brother John wrote on March 30 from Huntsville: "[Leroy] Pope Walker has resigned his Brigadiership (because he felt slighted by Bragg I learn) and returned here a few days ago, took his family South of the [Tennessee] river . . . and arranged to move his plantation negroes." If a friendly planter found a fellow planter's conduct worthy of censure it is hardly surprising that many yeomen, without the resources to move their own families, let alone their property, from danger found the planters' abandonment of their plantations deeply disturbing.[11]

In the wake of these bold federal advances, the threat of invasion aroused fear and weakened feelings of patriotism throughout the Upper South. Two months earlier, after Christmas, John Park, an Irishman newly elected mayor of Memphis, wrote a harsh polemic in the *Memphis Daily Appeal* castigating "the real estate owners of the City of Memphis" for their lack of "interest in the proceedings of the PLEBIANS, who are the rulers." Park directed his special ire at the refusal of Memphis aristocrats to assume their share of guard duty; the elite had tried to inveigle poorer men "into the service of standing guard, which you should have done, and which you refused to do." Park doubtless spoke for many nonslaveholders in responding to this subversion of popular democracy and abdication of noblesse oblige; he challenged Memphis aristocrats to "come out and show the community where you stand, whether neutral, Lincoln or Davis." And in the final hours before Union troops entered Nashville, Mayor R. B. Cheatham and a committee drawn from the "Nashville Gods," the social and political elite, rowed across the Cumberland to extend to the enemy commander a warm official welcome.[12]

Joshua Burns Moore, a slaveholder and lawyer from the Tennessee River town of Tuscumbia, Alabama, analyzing the effects of slack patriotism on home-front morale, noted a direct connection between the defeatism that swept over his hometown of Tuscumbia and the behavior of local politicians prominent in the secession movement. Moore wrote in his diary for February 17, "I never saw a set of men more completely whipped out at our reverses than the citizens of Tuscumbia. They are completely panic-stricken." A large number of the most prominent local secessionists decided to flee rather than risk Yankee reprisals. Moore himself, who had opposed immediate secession, found it difficult to forget that "when Ala. seceded, this county voted 1100 majority against it—the secessionists polled about 350." These men "were at that time rampant for a fight, wanted the contest to come—Swore that 1 Southern man could whip 5 Northern ones. Now where are they?" Near Tuscumbia "some of them are packing up preparing to run off and leave the poor and moderate men to do the fighting. W. L. B. Cooper and Norman fixing to skulk the issue; instead by their example attempting to restore confidence, they are adding to the panic." The link between the cooling of secessionist ardor and the growth of popular disaffection led Moore into this penetrating critique of the role of the well-to-do in the diffusion of preservationist ideology:

> Now do they expect the poor people are fools not to draw their own conclusions from their actions. Do they suppose the poor men of these counties have forgotten their promises that there would be "No War" at the time they were hastening the State into the attitude of rebellion? That when the contest came, if in the course of events it did arrive (which they affirmed it would not), they would be the first to shoulder their guns and fight? My opinion is that they are about played out. Let them go. The worst of it is they leave the rest of us in a deadly contest, in pursuing which we had not the slightest agency—and at a time when retreat and submission leads us, seems to me, to a certain destruction.[13]

Moore wrote this critique on February 22, Jefferson Davis's inaugural day, when Davis challenged Southerners to make their reverses be "but the crucible in which their patriotism was refined."

Many slaveholders seem to have concluded that the crucible of occupation was too hot to bear. When slaveholders in southern Louisiana learned of the sudden collapse of resistance at the supposedly impregnable forts guarding New Orleans, they reacted much as had the planters in the Tennessee Valley. A sugar planter from Bayou Lafourche, learning of the attack on Forts St. Phillip and Jackson, kept the boilers on his two river steamers near full pressure. "The fires are kept up day and night ready to start as soon as [we receive] the dreaded news that the Federal gunboats have passed the forts." When the "dreaded news" finally came, he loaded his family, white and black, and about half his processed sugar aboard and headed upstream away from New Orleans: "When we entered the Mississippi, it had become a seething mass of crafts of all kinds that could be made into possible conveyances to carry away the terror-stricken people who were flying from their homes with their loved ones and their treasures, all making a mad dash for the mouth of the Red River." He failed to find the hoped-for serenity at the Red River town of

Alexandria, Louisiana, and moved on to Texas after less than a year. His family eventually spent much of the war in Europe.

In late May in reprisal for Southern guerrilla raids against Yankee outposts, General Benjamin Butler dispatched to Baton Rouge a gunboat fleet that shelled the Louisiana capital at dawn: "These were not sheep but human beings running pell-mell," wrote Eliza McHatton-Ripley, " . . . panting and rushing tumultuously down the hot dusty roads, hatless and bonnetless, some with slippers and no stockings, some with wrappers hastily thrown over nightgowns. . . . they ran as though demons pursued them, never turning back or branching off . . . through yards and over fences and down narrow dusty lanes—anywhere to get from the clash of steel and the bursting of countless bombs!" Unprovoked Northern attacks on civilian targets were rare; still, it took only a few such episodes to convince nervous slaveholders that the safest recourse was to remove themselves and their slave property from danger.[14]

Some of the migrations from threatened zones covered great distances. Jane Simpson recalled that her master moved his slaves to Texas from Burkersville, Kentucky: "Dey started running de slaves to Texas 'cause dey thought de Yankees couldn't make it plum to Texas, but dey did." The reminiscence of a slave, Priscilla Gray, who lived in Williamson County, Tennessee, almost certainly refers to the fall of Nashville: "During' de wah, de masrter sent 100 ob us down in Georgia to keep de Yankees fum getti' us en we camped out durin' de three y'ars." A slave named Wiley Childress recalled later, "During de war Missus tuk mah mammy en-us chilluns wid her ter de mount-ins 'till de war wuz gone. Did'nt see no soldiers." While no definitive count of the numbers of slaves transported away exists, the best estimate suggests that planters moved approximately 250,000 into Texas alone during the war. Migration east of the Mississippi probably did not exceed the number who reached Texas.[15]

The sheer magnitude led to an instability that necessarily complicated the conversion of Southern agriculture to a war footing and signaled the opening of an irreparable cleavage between the slaveholders and their revolution. When planters in the Tennessee, Cumberland, and Mississippi Valleys reacted to the threat of pending Northern occupation by fleeing to safety, they broke faith with the traditional noblesse oblige that was understood to guide their public behavior. Few planters wished to subject themselves to the opprobrium that befell Leroy Pope Walker in Alabama, but if they did not go, they reasoned, they could not prevent their prime field hands from escaping to the Yankees, especially young male slaves without spouses who would be the most likely to take great risks for freedom. Confederate independence would seem a hollow victory if its attainment cost Confederate slaveholders their most valuable assets, and increasing the physical distance between slaves and the Yankees seemed the only countermeasure likely to staunch the flood of runaways. Their moves to counteract the hope of emancipation left slaveholders vulnerable—on grounds of avoidance of conscription and so on—to public censure about their own slack patriotism; open criticism, in turn, reinforced a principal concern of preservationists: that slaveholders would compel yeomen to carry a disproportionate share of the burden of fighting for Southern independence. The disasters along the Upper South frontier further widened the cleavage between slaveholders and the yeomanry.

As the war continued, Joshua Burns Moore pondered the implications with increasing alarm, and shortly after the Northern army began its occupation of Huntsville in April 1862, he demanded to know, "Where is the boasted chivalry of North Ala? Alas, it is fled to the hills and mountains." The sight of secessionists escaping from the Yankees reminded Moore of their prewar boasts: "*When the time came,* each one of them would shoulder his *shot gun* and meet the invaders and fight to the death for every inch of the soil of Alabama." "Now anyone would have supposed that when an enemy approached this valley an army of men standing as a wall, bristling with shot guns, old flint locks and every conceivable weapon would have been found to resist the approach." No such shoulder-to-shoulder phalanx appeared; instead, a "spectacle presents itself today. When the Northern soldiers landed at Decatur, every one [illegible] warriors took to their heels, and have concealed themselves wherever their friends let them and [we] can't find them." Worse still than this spectacle, Moore continued, were the effects of public misconduct on control over the slaves. So many overseers and slaveholders joined the crowd of absconding secessionists that they left many "defenceless families of females without protection." Many slaves seized this opportunity to assert their freedom from customary constraints: "The negroes, having no master to look to, quit work and go idling about the country, hundreds of them I learn at and around the camps. Nothing, or but little, will be made in the valley. The negroes through idleness will become demoralized and it will be a wonder if they do not commence commission of crimes of deepest dye—I apprehend great danger from the above cause. We have staid at home, our negroes have so far kept at work, but if other negroes become demoralized, they will corrupt others."[16]

The president of the Confederacy himself had learned firsthand about the disintegration of control over slaves that followed from the presence of the invading Yankee army. Davis and his older brother Joseph owned adjacent riverfront plantations, Hurricane and Brierfield, on an exposed peninsula, called Palmyra Bend, in the Mississippi River about twenty miles south of Vicksburg. War came to Palmyra Bend with explosive suddenness in the spring of 1862, when the Union navy tried to capitalize on its victory at New Orleans by moving upriver as rapidly as possible, hoping to force cities along the Mississippi to surrender before defenses could be built. Baton Rouge and Natchez capitulated quickly, but the residents at Vicksburg refused to surrender to a small naval flotilla, and an abortive two-month siege began.

A combined land-sea force tried at first to bombard Vicksburg into submission and then to dig a canal around it. (On Vicksburg, see also chap. 8.) As scouting parties scoured the riverfront for slaves willing to donate their labor to the invaders, a neighbor of the Davises, James Allen, recorded the results: "Mr. Joe E. Davis here—moving some of his negroes; with him Joe Mitchell, Dr. Hamilton and Mr. Cox—his negroes have destroyed all his house, furniture, wine cellar, etc." Davis's brother acted decisively and, recognizing the untenability of his situation, moved as many slaves as possible to safety. The refuge he found at O. B. Cox's plantation near Jackson, Mississippi, gave Joseph time to send a letter of explanation to his younger brother: "I had been to the plantation and brought off some of the negroes. The measles at Brierfield prevented me from bringing more. The river was falling rapidly and I directed those remaining should plant corn as the water fell but I have little confidence in the overseers. They are accountable for the robbery and pillage that occurred." Before the war, the Davis brothers had experienced recurrent problems with a series of overseers unhappy about limitations on the freedom granted them to punish slaves. The Davis slaves may have pillaged the plantation when an inexperienced overseer trampled on customary slave privileges there. Whatever the reason, this violent outbreak among blacks whom neighbors used to describe as "Joe Davis's free negroes" because of the supposedly benevolent treatment accorded them was a measure of the depth of the labor crisis in the Mississippi River plantation belt, once Northern vessels passed New Orleans and Memphis.[17]

Slave violence intensified the insecurity that prompted slaveholders to abandon their plantations. Mississippi governor John Pettus begged Davis for authority to raise local defense groups for the river counties to counteract the influence of Northern naval vessels on the Mississippi. Even before slaves destroyed the Davis home, Davis agreed "entirely with you as to the existence of the necessity for such bands in the section of the country specified." Governor Thomas O. Moore of Louisiana dispatched a similar expression of concern to Davis about the vulnerability of plantation counties in his own state, requesting decisive action to restore public confidence.[18] The loss of confidence that flowed from the collapse of the defenses guarding the Mississippi Valley plantation belt had disastrous consequences as many planters put self-interest above the interest of the Confederate revolution. Slaveholders might have been well advised to heed General Johnston's injunction that the fight for independence was best prosecuted along the frontiers not in the heartland of the Confederacy.

The Failure of Fiscal and Conscription Policies in the Face of Rising Union Morale

On the other side, Union morale soared as a direct result of military success on the western front, and General Ulysses S. Grant became a national hero. With stunning victories at Forts Henry and Donelson, the way had been opened into the Southern heartland. When confronted at Fort Donelson by Brigadier General Buckner's request for a gentlemanly armistice to negotiate the "terms of capitulation," Grant had replied bluntly the same day: "No terms except an unconditional and immediate surrender can be accepted. I propose to move immediately upon your works." Grant fought his campaigns with "a new, grim, and determined character" that caught the essence of the cultural divergence between North and South. A bustling Northern free-labor society felt little empathy with a slow-paced aristocratic slave-labor society. By proving on the field of battle that Northern men could humble Southern chivalry, Grant had provided a dramatic boost to public confidence in the North that probably affected the ultimate outcome of the war. With the rising public confidence, Lincoln could more readily acquire the resources to continue the war.[19]

Grant's victories along the Upper South frontier overlapped with final federal legislative action on the measures that helped overcome a Northern fiscal crisis. In the wake of a December 30, 1861, suspension of specie payment, the

Northern Congress debated a revolutionary step: creation of a national fiat currency, that is, paper money not backed by silver or gold but legal tender to meet any public or private debt. It was a radical departure from the hard-money policies the nation had inherited from the Jacksonian era. Many Republicans, including Secretary of the Treasury Salmon P. Chase, had balked at the legal tender question, fearing the attraction of highly inflationary methods of emergency financing, but the Northern treasury was almost bankrupt and new direct taxes would not generate sufficient revenue for many months. After six weeks of debate, the bill authorizing "greenbacks" came up for final vote in the House on February 6, the same day Grant accepted the surrender of Fort Henry; in a vote that followed strict party lines, Republicans closed ranks to ensure passage by a vote of 93 to 59; on February 13 Senate Republicans, too, enacted the measure, 30 to 7. A Senate-House conference committee resolved differences between House and Senate versions of the bill during the period when Donelson fell and Johnston evacuated Nashville, and the Legal Tender Act passed on February 25, the day General Buell entered Nashville. Although the mere issuance of fiat money could not in itself resolve the North's fiscal crisis, so buoyed was Northern morale by the dramatic victories of early 1862 that the new greenbacks gained ready public acceptance. This, in turn, ensured that the army would continue to exert relentless pressure; the Legal Tender Act dashed Southern hopes that fiscal woes might cause the Northern war machine to come to a grinding halt.

Realizing that Lincoln now had the means to continue to prosecute the war, and that the South must therefore sharply escalate its mobilization, Davis wasted little time in outlining the dramatically deeper sacrifices a lengthy struggle would require. Only three days after taking his second oath of office, on February 25, 1862, he sent the new Confederate Congress a message that began with an apology for the failed "effort to protect by our arms the whole of the territory of the Confederate States," then moved quickly on to the cause of the crisis at hand: "The policy of enlistment for short terms, against which I have steadily contended from the commencement of the war, has, in my judgment, contributed in no immaterial degree to the recent reverses which we have suffered." Lest the newly convened permanent Congress forget the eccentric role its provisional predecessor had played in the February disasters, Davis argued that "the process of furloughs and reënlistment in progress for the past month [has] so far disorganized and weakened our forces as to impair our ability for successful defense." An apparently high rate of voluntary reenlistment gave Davis heart, and he insisted, "We shall not again during the war be exposed to seeing our strength diminished by this fruitful cause of disaster—short enlistments." Still, implicit in his remarks was the option of a resort to compulsory service if too few Southerners responded to pleas for long-term volunteers. Davis gave himself comparable room for maneuver on another issue certain to provoke heated debate, paying the cost of the war. He expressed satisfaction that the fiscal system in place "has proved adequate to supplying all the wants of the Government," but alerted Congress to his firm conviction that the Southern economy could provide additional resources if necessary.[20]

The new Congress tried to force Davis's hand. Several days of impassioned speech making about the disasters at Roanoke Island, Forts Henry and Donelson, and Nashville led to a resolution of March 3 asking Davis to specify "what additional means in money, men, arms or other munitions of war are in his judgment necessary." Davis knew political maneuvering when he saw it and responded the next day with a wish list derived from estimates hastily prepared by the secretaries of war and navy: another three hundred thousand men in the army, fifty additional coastal and ten oceangoing vessels, 750,000 small arms of all calibers, five thousand cannon, and five thousand tons of gunpowder. Davis ended with an impolitic slap at congressional posturing: "The amount of money which will be required will depend upon the extent to which the articles needed may be obtained, and as I cannot hope to get more than a small part of that which a reply to the resolution required me to enumerate, I have not attempted to convert the articles into their probable money value." Rebuking those in the House who wished to blame his administration alone for the February military disasters, he promised to submit, in due course, requests for "the appropriations which it is deemed proper to ask, in view of the public wants and the possibility to supply them." He also promised to report "on the condition of the finances of the Confederate States."[21]

There was bad news about the campaign to reenlist the twelve months' volunteers "for the war"; it had failed, despite or perhaps because of the intensive effort to induce these volunteers to add two years to their initial one-year enlistments. At the end of December regiments with twelve months' volunteers constituted three-quarters of the army; on March 1 the War Department reported that, of the 340,250 names on Confederate muster rolls, only 92,775 were serving on enlistments "for the war." The two months of disorganization and disaster consumed by the reenlistment process had boosted the proportion of three-year volunteers by only a fraction—from 25 percent to 27 percent. For several more weeks, the War Department kept up pretenses about a last-minute surge in longer-term enlistments and, while acknowledging that a "very meager" number of Virginia troops had reenlisted, continued to insist, "It is known unofficially that a large number of men have re-enlisted and many new companies have been organized who have not yet been reported to this office." Pretense could only go so far. Davis was sarcastic about his "hope" for 300,000 additional soldiers; the prospect of losing more than 240,000 of the soldiers already under arms could not avoid worsening an already tense situation.[22]

A trying financial crisis proceeded in tandem with manpower problems. In a report of March 14 Secretary of the Treasury Christopher Memminger hinted, for the first time, at fiscal paralysis. Memminger estimated that $175 million of the $200 million needed for the balance of 1862 would have to be raised either by new direct taxes or by bonds and fiat currency. While Congress refused to levy any new taxes, it did authorize, on April 17, issuance of the necessary volume of bonds and currency. Indeed, throughout the war the Confederate Congress showed a marked preference for monetary solutions— that is, bonds and currency—rather than fiscal reform measures like direct taxation, a preference that was to impose devastating limitations on wartime endurance. Because states' rights ideology canonized limited government and hard money, the 1861 Confederate Constitutional Convention in Montgomery, in Article 1 of its provisional Constitution, had authorized coinage of silver and gold and banned direct taxation without the taking of a new census. Limited government and hard money might have sufficed for peacetime, but in war such policies would prove woefully inadequate, and the stage was set for wartime financial crisis.[23]

Much of this fiscal quandary stemmed from the nature of antebellum society as a debtor economy. Its commercial agriculture had depended on externally supplied credit to underwrite the growth of cash crops; in 1861 citizens and institutions held a total of less than $30 million in specie. With Southern patriots demanding their own national currency, the new government had rushed to create a circulating paper medium to replace the hated Yankee dollar. While the Confederate Constitution did not prohibit making fiat money into legal tender, it did not authorize such a step either; thus, the government printed paper money it refused to recognize as legal tender. When the war got underway, ambiguity about whether fiat money should become legal tender worked expediently in combination with the prohibition on direct taxes; the Treasury, on constitutional grounds, justified the payment of military expenses with fiat money and explained the avoidance of direct taxation. This subterfuge produced predictable results: a 300 percent inflation rate during the first year of the war. While proposing to issue millions of dollars of new fiat currency, Memminger privately admitted, "Experience has established that this is the most dangerous of the methods of raising money."[24]

Given its prewar debtor status, its lack of hard money, its own embargo policy, and the Northern blockade, the South simply could not have avoided this initial recourse to the "most dangerous" means of financing the war. Davis employed all available means to acquire the necessary resources. But fiat financing need not have continued until it created, as it did, an ocean of inflated currency. Had the regime chosen to tax slaveholders on the slaves and the slave-grown products that were their principal assets, it could have imposed a tax-in-kind of, perhaps, 5 percent on slaves, livestock, and crops. Instead, it imposed a 10 percent tax-in-kind on agricultural produce alone, further alienating yeoman farmers. By transforming the government into both a national granary and, in effect, the largest slaveholder, the Confederacy would have acquired the resources to resolve some of its most critical problems, including the chronic dilemma of how to feed yeomen's families and how to obtain military laborers. But the Richmond regime avoided those financial realities and turned to the minority of bond holders for fiscal guidance for the balance of the war. As a result, it created two distinctive types of financial instruments: fiat money, issued in small denominations to serve as a circulating medium—it was not convertible, was not a legal tender, and paid no interest—and bonds, issued in large denominations, intended as an investment not as a circulating medium. The Confederacy pledged its full faith and credit to bond redemption at the end of the war, in specie with interest; and initially bond sales enabled the government to tap the resources of its aristocracy without igniting the political firestorm that would have erupted in response to direct taxation. But so limited were Southern specie reserves that bond sales quickly absorbed most of the hard money. Instead of halting the sale of bonds, the government issued new ones to restrain inflation, on the disingenuous theory that fiat money used to purchase bonds represented paper currency withdrawn from circulation. Thus, bond purchasers were allowed to use unbacked fiat money to acquire redeemable bonds, an apparently innocent step that in fact prepared the way for a postwar windfall for those in a position to purchase bonds.[25]

By the end of the war the Confederate treasury would have issued $1.5 billion dollars in fiat money for which it assumed no liability and more than $700 million dollars of bonds it was obligated to redeem, in specie with interest. In effect, allowing bond purchases with fiat money protected bond holders from the ravages of wartime inflation. Had the South won the war, generations of taxpayers would have been forced to repay the foreign loans required to provide bond holders with the nominal value of bonds purchased with inflated fiat money. During the war, the calculated reliance on unbacked paper currency meant that the South discharged, Raimondo Luraghi writes, "the cost of forced industrialization upon the people at large, the usual result of inflation."[26] Common folk did not understand the intricacies of a financial manipulation whose full consequences would not reveal themselves until long after the war ended, but yeomen soldiers did feel the direct effects of the inflationary spiral that was the surface manifestation of fiat financing. A 300 percent inflation rate meant that the eleven dollars a month salary of an infantry private as measured in constant prewar dollars was by the spring of 1862 worth less than two dollars a month. Considering also the chronic problems of the slow payment and distribution of military salaries, it seems likely that the low real value of army pay helped to deter many yeomen from reenlisting "for the war." Thus, the most common rationale for draft resistance was a wave of wartime family crises, and the resulting disinclination of many soldiers to extend twelve months' enlistments forced a resort to universal national conscription.

During the interval between his first message to the new Congress and his request for a national draft, Davis reacted to the disasters on the western front by ordering widely dispersed elements of the Confederate army into a massive concentration at Corinth, Mississippi. He tried to assemble an army powerful enough to expel Grant from his foothold along the Tennessee River near Shiloh, summoning troops from the whole of the western theater, from Arkansas, from Columbus, Kentucky, from New Orleans, and from Mobile. Adroit use of the railroads allowed the assembling of a force of more than forty thousand combat-ready troops under Johnston's command at Corinth. When the Union army learned about this massive concentration, a race of sorts ensued. Confederates won this contest, and Davis informed Johnston on March 26, "I breathe easier in the assurance that you will be able to make a junction of your two armies." He urged Johnston to attack before Grant could make "a junction with [the force] advancing from Nashville."[27]

On March 24 Davis's newly appointed chief of staff, Robert E. Lee, learned that a convoy of Northern troop ships had passed Norfolk the previous evening; subsequent reports indicated substantial reinforcements to the enemy force opposite the Confederate position at Yorktown. Lee surmised that a major offensive was underway. Simultaneous concentrations on the eastern and western fronts would place a heavy burden on Southern manpower reserves, and Davis quickly realized that sustaining the multiple concentrations Lee proposed would require a radical reformulation of Confederate mobilization policy. Even if the army succeeded in turning back the invading columns, it seemed clear that large armies would have to remain in the field after the initial twelve months' enlistments expired. Davis waited as long as was prudent, then on March 28, when it was obvious that more than two-thirds of the troops would probably leave service at the expiration of their voluntary enlistments, he asked Congress for a system of universal conscription. With McClellan on the move toward Richmond, Butler menacing New Orleans, and Buell holding Nashville, the Confederacy simply could not survive the discharge of more than 140 regiments of seasoned veterans. A national draft was essential to overcome related catastrophes: a series of defeats on the battlefield and a low rate of voluntary reenlistment.[28]

Never before in American history had a war required national conscription. States' rights ideologues in the Confederacy would discover that disasters in battle and the imbalance of resources of North and South made compulsory service essential. With Lincoln's plan for mobilizing Northern resources making a Northern multifront offensive more feasible, the South either had to fight a modern mass war or give up its struggle for independence. The imposition of a national draft would assist the cause, but only if conscription lifted popular morale, for success in modern warfare rests on popular morale. Given Southern traditions of egalitarianism, acquiescence to a draft would require that the South subject all its citizens to the discomforts and dislocation of compulsory service. Had the Confederacy indeed created a truly egalitarian *levée en masse,* it might still have been possible to forge the necessary revolutionary social consensus, much as egalitarian nationalism had animated the armies of Napoleon.[29]

"The Burden Should Not Fall Exclusively on the Most Ardent and Patriotic": Universal Conscription, with Exemptions for the Privileged

Jefferson Davis recognized that conscription had to be truly universal if proudly individualistic Southerners were to be induced to accept it. Indeed, his March 28 message offered Congress encouragement to create "some simple and general system for exercising the power of raising armies." Davis cited the "vast preparations made by the enemy for a combined assault at numerous points on our frontier and seacoast" as one of two justifications for requesting authority to compel "all persons of intermediate age not legally exempt for good cause [to] pay their debt of military service to the country." Equity formed the other argument. Concerned that "the burden should not fall exclusively on the most ardent and patriotic," Davis asked for a law to put "all persons residing within the Confederate States between the ages of eighteen and thirty-five years, and rightfully subject to military duty . . . in the military service of the Confederate States." The exemptions for "youths under the age of eighteen years" and for men "of matured experience" were intended to retain a home-front labor reserve "for maintaining order and good government at home and in supervising preparations for rendering efficient the armies in the field." His request for "some plain and simple method" of drawing upon the manpower reserves of the Confederacy amounted to an appeal for centralized labor allocation.[30]

When the First Confederate Senate met on March 29 to receive Davis's message, the two senators from Texas, Louis Wigfall and Williamson Oldham, joined in a spirited debate. Senator Wigfall, after reaffirming his credentials as a lifelong states' rights man, took a nationalist position on the necessity and constitutionality of conscription. In response to Oldham's fervent states' rights counterargument, Wigfall retorted, "Cease this child's play." Objecting heatedly that he "didn't come here to be lectured," Oldham offered the hope that subsequent debates "would be conducted with that gentlemanly mildness which characterize[s] senators," to which Wigfall rejoined, "I don't know about the mildness." An even angrier exchange erupted in the House between states' righters and nationalists.[31] Once ideological passions emerged with such force, both houses closed their doors and referred the volatile issue to their respective military committees for discussion in closed sessions. Although the text of Davis's March 28 message had appeared in some newspapers, the veil of secrecy around the debate over conscription meant that passage of the draft act on April 16 would come as a demoralizing surprise to soldiers eagerly awaiting their spring discharges only to get the news that they had been drafted "for the war."

The preamble of the new draft law invoked defense of the homeland against unprovoked invasion as the justification for universal conscription:

> In view of the exigencies of the country, and the absolute necessity of keeping in the service our gallant army, and of placing in the field a large additional force to meet the advancing columns of the enemy now invading our soil: Therefore, *The Congress of the Confederate States do enact,* That the President be, and is hereby authorized to call out and place in the military service of the Confederate States, for three years, unless the war shall have sooner ended, all white men who are residents of the Confederate States, between the ages of eighteen and thirty five years.

But tucked away near the end of the legislation was this proviso: "That persons not liable for duty may be received as substitutes for those who are." To compromise the clarion call to defend the sacred homeland by allowing a few of those liable for duty to send a substitute seemed a blatant concession to wealth and privilege, since substitutes usually had to be bought for cash from among unnaturalized foreigners or those too young or too old to be drafted or who were otherwise exempted. The draft act paid homage to the tradition of civic egalitarianism while simultaneously allowing discrimination based on social position. Angry nonslaveholders coined a slogan to express the bitterness they felt toward Richmond. The disaffected would thereafter characterize the slaveholders' revolution as "a rich man's war and a poor man's fight."[32]

Compulsion to do one's duty also seemed to insult the honor and reputation of Southern men, and Alabama governor John Gill Shorter labeled conscription a grave assault on the traditional civic voluntarism that undergirded Southern honor: "If our liberties are to be won by *conscripts* or *Draftedmen,* the Contest is to become one much more dubious that I have ever, yet been inclined to admit." From Thomas R. R. Cobb, a Georgia planter serving on the Virginia front, came the blunt warning that passage of the bill would mean that "all patriotism is dead, and the Confederacy will be dead sooner or later." When Cobb learned about the enactment of conscription, he wrote hurriedly to his wife on April 24 from his post near Yorktown to say that the law was "an infamous outrage."[33]

Just how substitution as a means of avoiding the draft found its way into this first Confederate draft act remains a mystery cloaked in the secrecy of the congressional deliberations. Substitution was certainly not part of the plan submitted by the president; indeed, his War Department, on March 5, had revoked regulations that had hitherto allowed informal substitution among the volunteers. Albert B. Moore, who has studied the Confederate draft more carefully than anyone, maintains that substitution "was intended to mollify the harshness of the conscript law, but more particularly to reserve skill and talent for service in the essential industries." The credibility of this plausible hypothesis is severely undercut, however, by the passage on April 21 of "An Act to Exempt Certain Persons from Enrollment in the Armies of the Confederate States." This April 21 amendment to the law of April 16 established a system of occupational exemptions of "certain persons," clearly intending this to mean those performing essential religious, medical, educational, and industrial functions; it also specifically exempted the physically unfit, as well as persons serving in either the national or the separate state governments. With the draft law and the amendment to it passed only five days apart, Congress had doubtless considered them simultaneously. Had substitution been part and parcel of the attempt to protect essential industrial pursuits, as Moore believes, the substitution clause would more logically have been attached to the April 21 law, not the April 16 one. It seems probable, therefore, that Congress did view substitution as separate and distinct from occupational exemptions, and perhaps gave priority to anyone with the means to pay someone to go in his stead.[34]

States' righters no doubt saw the substitution clause as insulating individual freedom from the centralizing tendencies of a national system of labor allocation. Under this interpretation, substitution would be a quid pro quo for citizen consent to a presumably universal conscription law. Wigfall's speech in the Senate provides insight into the nature of the compromise probably struck during the secret debates that followed. While warmly endorsing the draft, Wigfall had openly criticized one of the principal states' rights features of the December 1861 reenlistment bill, the election of officers. "No troops can be carried effectively into the field," asserted Wigfall, "who elect their officers."[35] Yet the April 16, 1862, draft bill not only continued this practice, which conservative nationalists viewed as inimical to combat readiness, but also carried over into the new law the previous arrangement for sixty-day furloughs, bounties for reenlistment, and reorganization of units in the field. Substitution probably formed part of a package of compromises to secure states' rights support and some yeoman backing of the draft measure.

Had secrecy not shrouded the debate over conscription, Congress would have been less isolated from alternative points of view and objections like Wigfall's. Newspapers would have carried the news and editorial comment; concerned citizens would have written to local newspapers or to Congress. Congressional leaders might well have discovered that yeomen concerned about "political slavery" would reject a draft that managed to allow certain slaveholders to stay safely at home. There had already been rumblings in several states that might have alerted the Congress to pending trouble. Texas governor Edward Clark had attempted to use a newly enacted state militia law to aid slaveholders terrified by black militancy. Men enrolled in the active companies served at the pleasure of the governor "to repel invasions or to put down insurrections"; reserve companies were set aside for men "unable to leave their immediate neighborhoods." "Unable" could mean "unwilling" to risk slave unrest on plantations. Resulting resentment within the ranks of draftees led General William G. Webb, commander of the Lagrange County brigade, to plead with the governor to abolish the reserve companies; he pointed to widely known examples of able-bodied wealthy men who dodged active service by enrolling illegally as reserves.[36]

Louisiana governor Thomas Moore had embarked on a similar course to ease concern about slave insurrection. On January 23, 1862, the Louisiana legislature ordered all able-bodied white males between the ages of eighteen and forty-five to enroll in parish-based militias; units might be called out for duty anywhere in the state for periods of up to six months. Much like the April 21 amendment enacted by the Confederate Congress, the Louisiana measure provided statutory exemptions for civil officials, druggists, preachers, and Confederate functionaries. But in addition, acting on his own authority, Governor Moore, concluding that low-country plantation discipline could not withstand the loss of every able-bodied white man, had issued an executive order exempting one able-bodied white man per plantation. Brigadier General R. H. Todd, of the state militia, wrote in March to protest the plantation exemption scheme: "In some parishes of the brigade, I doubt whether a single company could be raised of persons not entitled to the exemption." Todd agreed with the Texan Webb that the state had a duty "to secure the slave-holding communities from the dangers arising from insubordination among the negroes," but the extra exemptions seemed to throw the burden of compulsory service almost exclusively on the yeomanry. "Should such be the effect of it," Todd cautioned, "this class might be impressed with the inequality, if not the injustice of its operation, and this might tend to defeat that harmony and cordial co-operation for the public defense among all classes so very necessary in the present great emergency."[37]

From her plantation home in Madison Parish, Louisiana, Kate Stone had taken note of the rancorous muttering prompted by the suspicion that local aristocrats had refused to bear their fair share of the common military burden. Referring to one such aristocrat, she wrote that he was

> wild to join the army but has his mother and four grown sisters absolutely dependent on him, and it seems impossible for him to get off. He says it is much harder to stay at home than to go. Joe Carson is crazy to join the army. He cannot study, cannot think of anything else, but his parents will not consent. He is most wretched. The overseers and that class of men are abusing him roundly among themselves—a rich man's son too good to fight the battles of the rich— let the rich men go who are the most interested—they will stay at home. Such craven spirits. So few overseers have gone.[38]

To describe yeoman critics of planter patriotism ("that class of men") as "craven spirits" was to miss entirely the significance of their rhetoric.

Resentment of an Unequal Law

Purposeful creation of an inequitable draft seemed a gross violation of the civic egalitarianism that had made it possible for yeomen to fight in a slaveholders' revolution in the first place. Motivated both by anger at the draft and by a pragmatic response to the arrival of the Union army in the Tennessee River Valley, yeomen in northern Alabama embarked on antidraft activity as soon as they learned about the new law. Bushrod Rust Johnson, an ardent Confederate loyalist from Columbus, Mississippi, then recovering from a wound sustained at Shiloh, pointed out to Colonel Thomas Jordan on April 21, "The northern counties of Alabama, you know, are full of Tories." "There has been a convention held recently in the corner of Winston, Fayette, and Marion Counties Alabama, in which the people resolved to remain neutral." Johnson understood this resolution to mean, in fact, that "they will join the enemy when they occupy the country."[39]

Such disaffected yeomen saw the Yankees as potential allies in their struggle to resist a government insensitive to their interests. In a June 21 letter to his wife Lila, a deeply concerned Major William H. Mott wrote, "I have said nothing about the desertion in our regiment, which of late has become quite popular among the cowardly devils that are in the army." Yet he understood the ideological origins of antidraft sentiment: "I do not think they go because they want to renounce the Confederacy as the Federals would like to believe. The conscript law altho having done a great deal of good has likewise done a great deal of harm, causing many to desert who perhaps would have acted otherwise had it not been for the act." "An idea exists in the army to some extent," he observed, "that the soldiers are the mere cat's paw of the wealthy, and ignored by them as men and equals. This idea is talked over very materially by the most ignorant." Deserters left camp "crying that they are free men and unwilling to be forced into measures of any kind without their consent at least." The South was reaping a harvest of disaffection from the underrepresentation of the yeoman majority in Congress; yeomen felt no compulsion to obey discriminatory laws enacted by a minority, almost all of them slaveholders. Desertion became for some a form of honorable and principled protest against unjust laws.[40]

The members of at least one regiment refused, as a body, to accept compulsory reenlistment. When, in the wake of the April stalemate at Shiloh, the Army of Tennessee retreated to its base camp at Corinth, the Union army laid siege to this northern Mississippi town. The besieged soldiers, learning that they had been drafted "for the war," were so displeased that the 2nd Tennessee, a regiment "composed entirely of Irishmen," rose up "in a state of rebellion" against serving beyond the end of their soon-to-expire twelve months' term. Officers tried gentle persuasion, but the soldiers maintained "a sullen and determined air." When resistance assumed the "air" of a mutiny, the officers called on an artillery unit for support, and its commander, Captain William Creagh, received orders "to put my battery in position to command their camp." The pointing of loaded cannon at Southern soldiers, the captain told his wife on May 13, was "a most unpleasant duty," but he kept his cannon "bearing on them until they came to terms."[41] Soldiers intimidated into reenlisting by the threat of Confederate artillery were surely unlikely to serve with either loyalty or enthusiasm.

By and large, the army did accept the argument that a draft was the only way to stall the Yankees' forward march. Volunteers already under arms, among the most loyal of Confederate citizens, could be expected to give the

benefit of the doubt to their government on whether substitution was an acceptable breach of the Southern social contract. Yet many yeomen quickly
concluded that the draft acts provided the wealthy with opportunities for
evading compulsory service. In mid-July 1862 one nonslaveholder sent Mississippi's governor, John Pettus, an angry complaint:

> It appeares hard that som of us have to gow off to wor and others stay bak home
> swearing the will not go and there is not Jeff Davises nor Bourgardes a nuff to
> get them to ware heare is . . . a young stout man got moor than a most eney of
> us to defend thinkes himself a bove the comon solgers that we poor ones that
> have to go and leive our famelis who is as dear to us as his think very hard of it
> heare is . . . who is also a stout able young man at home bragging how he is beet-
> ing the Confedrecy when wee think that wee have a mutch to tend to as ether of
> the a bove naimed wee hope that if you have eney authority to have thes men in
> the feel you will not neglect it.

Opportunities for abuse abounded in both the exemption and the substitution systems. Many civilians who could afford legal counsel retained lawyers
who exploited ambiguities in War Department regulations in order to successfully shield their clients from compulsory service. Persons intent on evasion could create scripts to suit the rules. Since the law exempted one druggist
for "each apothecary store now established and doing business," certain art-
ful schemers ignored the obvious meaning of "now established" and busied
themselves "setting up a *drug store* . . . with a few bottles of castor oil, some
boxes of pills and a soft-bottomed chair."[42]

The North, too, would experience intense—and more violent—antidraft
activism, especially during the spring and summer of 1863, shortly after the
federal Congress enacted conscription. Substitution was allowed in the North
as well as in the South, and it became a focus for popular resentment there too.
But for several reasons the middling classes in the Union did not become as
involved in antidraft activism. The Northern draft was selective not universal,
and its provision for "commutation"—a release from service on payment of
three hundred dollars—was low enough that the inability to pay was mostly
confined to the urban poor. Perhaps the more closely a democratic society approaches truly universal service, the more important it becomes that the conscription be truly democratic.[43]

The South's substitution clause appears to have led to particularly egregious frauds and evasions. During the period up to November 1863, the Con-

federate secretary of war estimated that at least fifty thousand men otherwise eligible for the draft escaped service by providing substitutes. A brisk brokerage business devoted to procuring substitutes for a fee emerged; and the price of a substitute rose above three thousand dollars. Unscrupulous brokers discovered that they could multiply their earnings by using the same substitute again and again; poor and desperate men could also profit by accepting money as a substitute, enrolling in the army, and then deserting to seek another situation for another stipend.

Those unwilling or unable to pay the hefty broker fee tried to find substitutes on their own. Witness an advertisement that appeared in the *Vicksburg Whig* of August 6, 1862:

WANTED

Anyone wishing to act as a substitute for a man subject to the conscript act, will receive the following compensation: a likely negro boy and five hundred dollars, Address B., Appeal Office.[44]

The poor had no "likely negro boy" or five hundred dollars to offer, and public displays of the advantages of wealth could hardly avoid doing great damage to the morale of men subject to conscription—and thus possible injury or death—who could not afford to issue such lifesaving tenders.

Less obvious but more damaging consequences were to follow once rapidly escalating prices for substitutes began to threaten morale among the middling classes as well as the poor. Edwin Hedge Fay may have been typical of middling farmers who agonized over whether to make use of the substitution clause. Fay, a schoolteacher, owned five slaves and lived near Minden, Louisiana. He did not join the initial surge of volunteers but waited until April 4, 1862, to enlist as a private in a cavalry company—as it turned out, only about three weeks before the new exemption for teachers would have freed him from the army altogether. When Fay heard about national conscription, he called the new law "tyrannical but [I] am satisfied that it is the speediest way to put an end to the war." Writing to his wife, he expressed concern that with so many commissioned officers in his regiment making plans to find substitutes, "we will have no officers." By the end of May he had decided, "I will give any sound man over the age of 35 years of age my horse, saddle and bridle and 400 a year for 3 yrs, if the war lasts so long, to take my place. . . . so many are going home that they have got me into the notion." "There is nothing dishonorable about it that I can see. I will simply be saving my life for my family for I feel assured that I can not stand it three years . . . if I can hire a substitute I shall do it." But when the captain of Fay's company, a Captain Wimberly, decided to take advantage of the exemption for men over thirty-five, he heard from the women of his hometown. "Capt.," one soldier told him, "all the women about Minden say you should not desert your Co. in the hour of extremity and they are all down on you." Such public censure prompted Fay to careful reconsideration of his own intentions. "About this 'substitute business' I hardly know what to say," he wrote home. "I hear of so much having been said about returned or returning volunteers that I do not know whether to brave the stings and taunts of outraged women who do not desire to see any return home because forsooth their husbands are not among the number." His agonizing was to no avail, for Fay could neither discover a way to qualify retroactively for the teacher's exemption nor locate a substitute at a price he could afford.[45]

In the five hundred counties in the Mississippi Valley, the average per family worth ranged all the way from a low of $414 to a startling high of $130,000 (equivalent in 1995 dollars to approximately $2 million). Decisions about whether to seek a substitute were probably most rending in counties where family worth ranged between $4,000 and $10,000—below $4,000 it was out of the question and above $10,000, financially possible. Most counties in this category were adjacent to the rich-soil areas dominated by the larger slaveholders and could readily see the difference in family circumstances; 30 percent of all free families in the Mississippi Valley lived in this middle zone, and 40 percent of the 30 percent—or 12 percent of the total—owned slaves in this zone, where one-third of all Mississippi Valley cotton was produced. The number of men who could afford a substitute was even smaller. Fay's family with five slaves could not afford the luxury of a substitute. (See map 6.1 for regional distribution of families by financial worth.)[46] The letters sent home by Fay, an articulate and thoughtful Harvard graduate, provide a rare glimpse into the range of responses among soldiers to the April 1862 draft act. The fifty thousand affluent Southerners from the slaveholding minority who sent high-priced substitutes to war in their stead were delivering an unintended message to the yeoman majority about the limits of patriotic sacrifice. Ironically, those who could escape service had the most at stake in military victory. Those with slaves had material interest in the war, those who did not had no material stake in it yet they were required to give the most—their service and, often, their lives.

Joshua Moore, in the Tennessee River Valley, saw every episode of Union

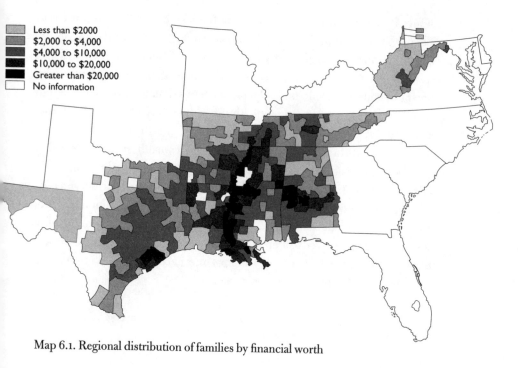

Map 6.1. Regional distribution of families by financial worth

occupation as rousing slaves' expectations of imminent freedom, and concluded that "the Federal Army—the negroes and Southern white people cannot inhabit the same country." He grew so pessimistic that he considered leaving his home. On April 30 he wrote in his diary a prescient assessment of how conflicting ideologies were establishing the limits of Confederate endurance; those with no vested interest in slaveholding would not "fight through a long war" to save it. "The object of the war says Mr. Lincoln is the restoration of the Union as it was," Moore wrote.

> He may think so, and doubtless does. But from the very nature of the contest, so sure as the war continues, it is the death blow to negro slavery. There are but some or a little over 300,000 men taking all the slave states, that are interested in it (that is owners of slaves), now men who have no interest in it are not going to fight through a long war to save it—never. They will tire of it and quit. If the Southern states return to the Union by some kind of compromise, this may save it. If the North puts forth their whole strength, it is gone forever.[47]

Once it became clear that the Army of Tennessee lacked the resources to expel the Yankees from the valley, Moore arrived at an appropriate hypothesis: both the institution of slavery and the cause of Southern independence were doomed. When the military situation became urgent enough for the government to compel all able-bodied white men to serve, the private interest in controlling slaves came in conflict with the public duty of national defense. The possibility of substitution for men of means, plus the frauds and abuses of the system that further enhanced the power of wealth, made it clear that compulsory service was obligatory only for the yeomanry and the middling classes. In addition, when the Southern political system tried to reserve a portion of its stretched labor supply to serve in counterinsurrectionary duty against possible organized slave revolts, many yeomen reacted with hostility to a system they perceived as betraying their own interest, invoking a preservationist ideology that became the principal internal threat to the conservative nationalism of Jefferson Davis's government.

Chapter Seven **In the Wake of Military Occupation**

Disaffection, Profiteering, Slave Unrest,
and Curbs on Civil Liberties

ew crises test national character as remorselessly as the failure to repel
an invasion. The capacity to endure a hostile and prolonged occupation can provide the decisive test; emerging nations like the Confederacy have to forge a spirit of nationalism that can encourage unyielding
resistance to an invader. An army of occupation provides restive elements with overt and covert opportunities to strike out at the revolutionary
party. During the American Revolution, not only did the British succeed in encouraging many slaves to seek their freedom but their presence precipitated
conflict between patriot and Tory factions of the free population. Should nationalists fail to hold collaboration to manageable levels, an army of occupation
may foment internal unrest intense enough to undermine popular support for
the revolution itself. Such a time of testing came to the Confederacy.

Despite often heroic efforts, the Confederate army had been unable to turn
back closely spaced Yankee attacks along its Tennessee, North Carolina, Louisiana, and Virginia fronts. It was compelled to employ partisan warfare to maintain an effective military presence within its occupied zones. But partisan
fighters rely on noncombatants, and a society like the Confederate South, composed of slaves, states' righters, and disaffected yeomen, in the end found it a formidable task to summon the necessary unified support. Nor was the North, any
more than the South, prepared for a modern "total" war, that is, a war of attrition
in which civilian resolve is as critical a factor as industrial resources or military
strategy. In the occupied Southern capitals of Tennessee and Louisiana, where
Unionist governments were restored, conventional warfare and occupation
could not compel restored allegiance to the Union, and by the summer of 1862 a
war that had begun as a relatively gentlemanly contest between traditionally organized armies had become a struggle to the death between rival societies.

Guerrilla Warfare and Internal Resistance to the War

Lincoln had done his best to exploit the North's superior resources in countering the advantages defensive warfare gave to the South. Union armies won decisive victories in the west; Confederate forces gained the advantage in the east. Simultaneous Union advances worked well in the vast expanse of the Mississippi Valley, with the parallel alignments of the Tennessee, Cumberland, and Mississippi Rivers easing coordination of offensives, but in the east geography favored the Southern defenders. The river systems in northern Virginia obstructed the path of overland invasions, and the Blue Ridge Mountains impeded coordination between offensive Union operations in the Shenandoah Valley and eastern Virginia. Then, too, the North discovered that its eastern front commanders were less effective than those in the west; for the South the reverse was true.

During the first half of 1862, when Northern armies seemed to sweep all before them, the Southern will to continue the fight despite reverses burned on, especially among women in slaveholding families. In the weeks following Shiloh, Cordelia Scales, a volunteer at a local hospital who lived on a plantation in northern Mississippi, found her loyalty stronger as military prospects grew bleaker. When word came of the fall of New Orleans, Baton Rouge, and Natchez, she wrote to a friend: "I think Vicksburg will be taken soon but if it does fall we are farther from subjugation than *ever.* Never until the pulse of every *man, woman* and *child* ceases to *beat* need our enemies *think* to conquer us; but I fear *no such result* and though we may pass through a *severe* ordeal and many of us find a *bloody grave,* yet God is for us and He will lead us to *inevitable* victory." Kate Stone, too, felt her "blood boil" when she read the proclamation issued by General Butler on entering New Orleans in May. Butler's proclamation required that residents of the occupied area take an oath of allegiance to the United States. It was "most tyrannical and insulting." "Let us hope this will arouse the spirit of the people who still linger at home and send them to the battlefield. How can anyone in the South ever fall so low as to take such an oath of allegiance?" Such strong-willed young slaveholding women exerted a powerful moral influence on young Southern men trying to decide whether to enlist; they lionized those who enlisted and scorned those who remained at home, especially after enactment of universal conscription in the spring of 1862. At least one teacher felt he had to enlist, even though he was foreign-born and therefore exempt. Mr. Stenckrath complained, "Mees Kate is driving me to war. She talk so much about men going and I so sensitive it move me silent for half and hour." Stone repented that Stenckrath took her remarks "as personal to him," but she and a group of friends "are all on fire with the subject, we cannot bridle our tongues all the time."[1]

When first approached about sanctioning guerrilla raids in the South, Confederate Secretary of War Judah Benjamin refused on the grounds that it violated the rules of civilized combat. General Albert Sidney Johnston, too, on receiving a request from Captain E. J. Launders for authority to muster independent guerrilla companies in the frantic preparation before the battle at Shiloh, rejected it out of hand. To Launders, Johnston wrote curtly, "*You have been wholly misinformed.* No independent companies will be received into the service. . . . There is no branch of the army under any general order of the character indicated in your letter nor will any such order be given. . . . All the troops must be subject to the articles of war." This adherence to the rules of gentlemanly contest died with Johnston at Shiloh. Johnston's immediate successors in the Western Department—General Beauregard, later to be relieved by Davis, and General Bragg—embarked on a guerrilla campaign, and loyalty on the home front also manifested itself in guerrilla activities against the occupying invaders. Mark Valentine, a planter's son who had resisted all entreaties to join the fighting, was caught up in the fervor and agreed to help organize a company of partisans. Seventeen-year-old Walter Stone, Kate Stone's young brother was, his sister wrote, "riding around nearly every day ostensibly hunting, but we think he is trying to organize a secret guerrilla company to harass the enemy should they land troops near here." Such partisan activity eventually compelled the Northern army to deploy tens of thousands of combat soldiers to defend against hit-and-run attacks in occupied zones.[2]

A decentralized and elusive host of militant civilian Southern loyalists could have crippled almost any force Lincoln could have kept in the field to fight and occupy captured Southern territory while at the same time protecting the Northern army and its supply lines from sabotage and continuing a military advance. A unified occupied nation of nine million persons, proud of their independence and determined to throw off the yoke of oppressive rule, would have been difficult to occupy even temporarily with success, and impossible to subdue permanently. But the presence of antisecessionist enclaves within Confederate territory meant that guerrilla warfare could cut two ways.

After several months of occupation duty in 1862, Captain L. Guy Wollard, from the low-country commercial South—who had nothing but contempt for the "ignorant and superstitious" highland yeomanry—wrote in his diary that they spied for the Union and ambushed Confederate scouts: "These men who are satisfied with any government which does not disturb their slothful mode of life as a general thing refused to enlist in the service of the Confederacy but skulked among the mountains, acted as spies to the Yankees, and as bush-wackers to fall upon small parties of our scouts from their ambush and slay them as brutishly as they do their hogs." A counterinsurgency campaign to cope with such treacherous people would require the posting of thousands of Southern troops at home at the same time that response to Northern invasions required every combat-ready soldier at the front. The Davis government found itself in the paradoxical position of resisting Northern occupation in some areas of the South while imposing a Southern occupation among its own people in others.[3]

Pacifying highland enclaves became harder after the Confederate Congress enacted compulsory conscription in April 1862. One worried loyalist, H. W. Sholar, had written Arkansas governor Hiram Rector the previous fall that yeoman farmers in Montgomery County "dont intend to go fite till they are drafted and if they get tuck prisoners they will tell the North they would note of fought against them they was compelde to do so." When Rector attempted to enforce a state militia draft in mid-March, he received a pointed warning from Sholar that yeomen from Green County saw the militia draft as a "mob action" their political principles required them to oppose. "Discord in our ranks" had been aroused by the state militia draft, Sholar said. "Men will not suffer to be driven against their wills like a beast." If state authorities persisted in this unpopular measure, "We will soon have two parties here. This will not do. 'United We Stand, Divided We Fall.'" An observer in northeastern Texas described the reaction there to the draft as "a spark lighting on powder." In eight Red River Valley counties that had voted against immediate secession during Texas's February 1861 referendum, a region heavily populated by antislavery German Americans, some had proposed seceding from the Confederacy itself when Texas seceded from the Union, but they opted instead to sit out the war. The 1862 congressional vote for universal conscription changed their strategy from a passive to an active response; they formed an antiwar Union League, armed themselves, and devised plans for resistance.[4]

The Demand for Martial Law and Suspension of Habeas Corpus

Antiwar organizations similar to that in Texas appeared in Alabama, prompting Governor Shorter to tell Secretary of War Randolph, "There are several counties in this State in which much disaffection exists. In these counties there will be great difficulty in enforcing the conscript act." General Edmund Kirby Smith, the hard-pressed commander of the Department of East Tennessee, who had witnessed enough violence there to recognize the need for sterner measures, had already decided that martial law would be a useful weapon. He crafted a dispatch to Davis that offered ample grounds. "I find East Tennessee an enemy's country and the people removed from the immediate presence of the Confederate troops, in open rebellion." In response to such requests, Davis, on April 8, suspended the writ of habeas corpus and declared martial law in almost all of eastern Tennessee's civil jurisdictions. Once it became clear that the Confederate army could not expel the Northern invaders from eastern North Carolina and middle Tennessee, Davis asked the Congress for authority to impose martial law there as well. The Confederate Congress moved with celerity to suspension of the writ of habeas corpus. Senator Louis Wigfall urged speedy passage: "The condition of the country [makes it] necessary to declare martial law in certain places." On February 27, 1862, Congress cited "the present invasion of the Confederate States" as justifying presidential power to suspend civil liberties "in such cities, towns, and military districts as shall, in his [Davis's] judgment, be in such danger of attack by the enemy as to require the declaration of martial law for their effective defense." Davis declared martial law immediately in four Virginia cities, Norfolk, Portsmouth, Richmond, and Petersburg and two months later, on April 18, suspended civil liberties in occupied western Virginia, coastal South Carolina, and in eastern Tennessee, now threatened by Yankee invasion.[5]

The government's struggle to constrict traditional civil liberties to prevent collusion with the enemy in strategically vital territory aroused some states' rights critics—Robert Toombs, Edward Pollard, and Robert Barnwell Rhett among them—who saw the suspension of habeas corpus, and in secret session, as indisputable proof of the president's secret intention to impose a military despotism. Indeed, imposition of martial law opened such deep ideological wounds that Vice President Stephens assumed the leadership of a powerful states' rights faction that was to make life miserable for Davis. For his part, Edmund Ruffin recognized the distinctions between free speech in peacetime, on the one hand, and sedition in wartime, on the other: "This measure, I trust, will permit & induce the arresting & punishing of disloyal residents, spies & traitors, who have heretofore escaped all punishment, & almost all constraint." Still, it did not help matters when General John Winder, the Richmond provost marshal, administered martial law so harshly that the Confederate Congress had to amend authority for martial law on April 19, 1862, fewer than two months after the authority had been granted; the new amendment restricted presidential powers chiefly by setting a limit on the duration of the authority to declare martial law.[6]

Resistance of Wealthy Planters to the Patriotic Call to Burn Crops

Just as disaffected yeomen were met by a draft, martial law, and suspension of civil liberties, so affluent slaveholders now also encountered government ultimata to ensure their loyalty to the Cause. The primary economic issue for slaveholders was slavery and the value of their staple crops. Now, with Union forces drawing near the plantation heartland, the Confederate Congress, on March 4, 1862, ordered planters in invaded areas to destroy their unsold staple crops to prevent Yankee seizure of raw materials badly needed by Northern industry.

On the eve of the war the South had been growing more than 80 percent of the cotton used for the mechanized production of cotton textiles in the North, a massive output that provided the driving force behind industrialization in Europe as well as in America. The Confederacy withheld its 1861 staple crops from the world market as part of its policy of "King Cotton diplomacy," imposing acute hardship on Northern industries and countries abroad, especially Britain, which was heavily dependent on cotton. When, during an 1858 debate in the U.S. Senate, William Seward, than a senator from New York, argued that the North could not allow the South to secede in peace, Senator James H. Hammond of South Carolina had replied: "What would happen if no cotton was furnished for three years? I will not stop to depict what everyone can imagine, but this is certain: England would topple headlong and carry the whole civilized world with her, save the South. No, you dare not make war on cotton. No power on earth dares to make war on it. Cotton is King."[7] Such a sense of its economic power had helped steel Southern nerves for war from the beginning, and persuaded the South that a prolonged war against the North was a struggle it could not lose. Thus, Southern planters' destruction of accumulated crops to prevent their falling into Yankee hands was the ultimate weapon in the Southern arsenal.

A letter to Jefferson Davis from a Mr. Alexander of Memphis, was an ominous harbinger, however. If the Yankees continued to advance, the local provost marshal was preparing to destroy the "large quantities of sugar and cotton . . . stored away in this city," but the economic consequences to local planters would be grave: "To destroy this sugar and cotton without compensation will reduce to poverty a number of good and loyal men." But compensation was not intended for "good and loyal men" or any others. Alexander pointed out the obvious: cash-poor planters burdened by war taxes would be ruined unless the government paid the fair market value of their unsold staples "in Confederate notes"; failure to pay for property destroyed at government behest would "throw a damper on the Confederate cause, because the burden is not equal." Farmers who supplied meat and grain to the army were receiving payment in Confederate notes; the "cotton planter" who had "suffered most" believed he, too, "ought to be relieved where his cotton is burned for the public good." Yet, its fiscal resources already strained, the South could not afford to implement Alexander's sensible proposal.[8]

As it turned out, most planters tried to save as much of their property as they could despite their government's instructions. Besides, the sheer volume of unsold cotton, approximately four and a half million 400-pound bales, made any rapid destruction of more than a fraction of the 1861 crop unfeasible. The heavy rains that accompanied the 1862 invasion had contributed to a high moisture content in the cotton bales that would make igniting self-sustaining fires in hastily jumbled piles of bales immensely difficult.

In its debate the Confederate Congress considered how to ensure voluntary compliance in the destruction of unsold staple crops in invaded areas. The day after the Senate military committee proposed such an act, on March 1, Gustavus Henry of Tennessee offered an amendment to "encourage the burning of cotton, tobacco, &c . . . by proposing to indemnify . . . fully for all products destroyed." William Porcher Miles of South Carolina, speaking for the House military committee, replied on March 15 that the collapse of western front defenses dictated "energetic action. The destruction of cotton [is] the first consideration, and the compensation a matter of detail." Henry Foote of Tennessee, taking keen exception, warned that uncompensated destruction would "paralyze the arms of the people of the South." Tennesseans were "as patriotic as could be found anywhere," but he knew of "but very few who would thus reduce themselves and families to beggary for the sake of the country." Jabez L. M. Curry of Alabama was deeply offended by this; the Yankees should "burn" any citizen of Alabama "so avaricious that he would not, with his own hands, put the torch to every lock of cotton rather than that the Lincoln government should get it." Roger Pryor of Virginia agreed: Foote's warning was an "exhibition of flinching"; by "its very daring and desperation" uncompensated destruction "would commend it[self] to all patriots." It was this argument that carried the day. The final vote on March 15 was for immediate destruction of staple crops; indemnity for lost property was to wait until after war was over.[9]

Brave patriots would surely, as Foote had argued, put the torch to their own property as soon as the situation grew grave enough to demand such a sacrifice, so Edmund Ruffin thought. He had gleaned from Northern newspapers information that seemed to confirm that the embargo had already crippled the cotton textile industry, and he eagerly looked forward to the stinging rebuff Union invaders would receive when they tried to purchase staples from Southern patriots. There would be no Yankee-style profiteering among Southern planters, Ruffin said, but "very different results. The cotton & tobacco, which would be the most eagerly sought booty where available, will mostly be burnt. The more safe portion . . . will be held back, if not destroyed by the patriotic owners." As soon as their staple crops were destroyed, patriots would be expected to turn to guerrilla attacks against Northern military outposts and civilian shipping. Many patriotic planters throughout the heartland did, indeed, try to comply. The Northern armies that entered Nashville, New Orleans, Natchez, and Memphis found that planters had cooperated with the Confederate military in burning large quantities of unsold staples. Captain E. E. Porter reported to General Beauregard, "I have caused to be burned in Fayette, Shelby, and Tipton Counties, Tennessee and Marshall, and De Soto Counties, Mississippi upwards of 30,000 bales of cotton." "My men" he said, "have met with but little opposition"; "150 men, almost all large planters" had taken part in the task of destruction.[10]

The prolific Kate Stone wrote in her diary from her plantation home in Louisiana that planters near Vicksburg had agreed among themselves that, with the fall of New Orleans, burning their own cotton was "the only thing to do." "As far as we can see are the ascending wreaths of smoke, and we hear that all the cotton of the Mississippi Valley from Memphis to New Orleans is going up in smoke." Nor was it an easy job. "It is hard to burn bales of cotton.

They will smoulder for days. So the huge bales are cut open before they are lighted and the old cotton burns slowly. It has to be stirred and turned over." But loyal planters regretted "the necessity of destroying the cotton," and it cast "a gloom over the country that nothing but news of a great victory could lighten." Amid loud prayers for such a victory could be heard deep sighs of despair: "The planters look upon the burning of the cotton as almost ruin to their fortunes, but all realize its stern necessity." Stone ended on a proud note: "We have not heard of one trying to evade it."[11]

Many other affluent Southerners, however, refused to heed the call to sacrifice and lost confidence in the goal of the Confederacy. From his post near Clinton, Louisiana, an agitated recruiting officer, Warren Cole, dispatched a hurried note to General Polk almost three weeks after the fall of New Orleans: "We have traitors amongst us. . . . We have been sadly betrayed in this State. Hundreds of men . . . have already made secret arrangements for a heavy sugar and cotton speculation; therefore will sell our country to save their property." Most of the cotton "immediately on the river bayous has already been burned. But little sugar has been destroyed." The invaders offered to protect "all private property," and Cole concluded, "We have many in our midst that will bite at this bait, specie being paid for cotton and sugar." When General Beauregard learned of widespread cotton selling among prominent citizens of Natchez, and also of Southerners taking the oath demanded by occupying forces, he complained bitterly: "In the very heart of the Confederacy, with an immense slave population, it ill behooves the citizens of Mississippi at this trying juncture to quail or quiver before our insidious foe." A loyal citizen near Iuka, Mississippi, scorned the brisk business between local residents and the Yankees. Southerners were selling provisions and cotton in addition to hiring out their wagons and teams at premium prices: "The enemy is doing us great harm . . . by making friends of nearly all the citizens."[12]

In the town of Bolivar, a west Tennessee Whig, John Houston Bills, owner of four plantations and eighty slaves, was confessing by the summer of 1862, "I am so worn down by the War. My feelings are all for peace. . . . Our people seem bent on fighting it out, which must be a desperate game and of doubtful issue." Bills refused to burn his unsold cotton, and even worse, he decided to sell some of it to the Yankees. On August 21 he sold thirty-two bales for $11,431 at 90 cents per pound, a handsome boost over the 11-cent price of 1860. "The high price of cotton in some degree helps us in our losses by the War, yet I have no doubt I am now injured in my estate *one hundred thousand dollars* with a good prospect of losing much more of the balance."[13] The desire to protect his possessions eventually led Bills to betray a revolution he had never supported enthusiastically. On December 12, 1862, he joined forty or fifty of the most influential men in Bolivar in taking the oath of allegiance to the Union, hoping thereby to escape the effects of the coming Emancipation Proclamation, which applied only to areas under Confederate control. Taking the oath of allegiance had become a common form of accommodation among affluent planters in the Mississippi Valley.

The question of how to deal with cotton hoarders arose whenever the Yankees entered a new region. Near Memphis, Confederate army squads sent to burn Confederate cotton encountered armed resistance. General Sherman sent a message that "much excitement exists in West Tennessee about the burning of cotton. One riot in which four soldiers were killed. Talk in Pocahontas of an organization to protect cotton against the order to burn." In northern Mississippi, immediately south of Memphis, Colonel B. B. Harman concluded that the region "as a theater of defensive military operations is untenable." Land in the Delta was too flat and too thoroughly bisected by good roads to enable "a small force operating against a large force" to prevent commerce between planters and Yankees. "Doubtless large quantities of cotton remain in the hands of the planters, and with the advantages which the enemy possesses, will be secured." Harman could see no way to prevent "the necessities of some and the lukewarmness of others in the cause" from inducing holders of cotton to dispose "of their staples to the enemy rather than resort to the course which both law and patriotism direct."

The patriotism of Davis himself was called into question as a result of his brother Joseph's hurried flight from the family plantation near Palmyra, when he took time to seek an advantageous interpretation of the law to try to save nine hundred hidden bales of cotton. Joseph did not inform his brother that family property was involved and that he had arranged for two hundred bales to be carted to a concealed location; he simply asked Jefferson to overrule the local officer, who was insisting that he destroy all cotton whether or not it was in danger of falling "into the hands of the enemy." Citizens who heard of the surreptitious movement of the Davis cotton away from the river took matters into their own hands before Joseph's letter reached Jefferson in Richmond, and so Joseph wrote, "The two hundred bales of cotton I had taken 30 miles up big black [Big Black River] has been hunted up and burned I do not know by whom, and I see by the papers that yours and mine have been burned at home." A Mississippi paper, the *Raymond Gazette,* reported the incident, whereupon Jefferson Davis fired off a letter of complaint to the paper. The story, he said, was "circulated to create the impression that I have preserved my cotton when that of my neighbors was burned." He denied any knowledge of what had actually occurred, and asserted that any suggestion that "I have sought to preserve my cotton or given the ordinary attention to my private affairs" was "basely false." A president compelled to disassociate himself from a sibling's misbehavior was clearly at risk of losing public confidence.[14]

The issue of planters' betrayal of the revolution arose during the most trying moments of the Peninsula Campaign, just when it seemed that General George McClellan was ready to march into the Confederate capital at Richmond. Davis recognized that public confidence had been badly shaken by slaveholders' seeking windfall profits on embargo diplomacy or abandoning their plantations and carting away property, including slaves, to prevent seizure by Yankee soldiers. Many of the South's most affluent citizens had failed to join selflessly in measures deemed essential to the war effort. The Yankee occupation, far from inciting unyielding resistance to the invading enemy, was exacerbating the social tensions between planter and yeoman traditionally restrained by the Southern political culture.

Urgent Demand for Manpower in the North and the Push for Emancipation

By 1862 war weariness had become a factor in the North much as it had in the South when the Confederate Congress pressed twelve months' veterans to volunteer for a longer term. Steadily rising Union casualties, from camp diseases and from combat and capture, did little to encourage those not yet in service to volunteer. A rising crescendo of criticism from Northern Democrats, and even from Republicans, about Lincoln's conduct of the war was undermining popular morale. Northern Democrats were worried that this first Republican administration would promote a legislative program only peripherally related, or so it seemed to them, to saving the Union. In particular, their fire was aimed at the likelihood of Republican adventuring in emancipation. The Democrats were concerned with good reason. Since the war began, the radical wing of the Republican Party had been eager to transform the war to save the Union into a war against slavery. But if there was one policy issue on which most Northern whites agreed—Republican as well as Democrat—it was the principle that slavery ought to be allowed within the traditional slave-holding states. The success of appeals to such Northern racialism had put Lincoln in a very difficult position.[15]

The failure of the Peninsula Campaign could not have occurred at a more unpropitious moment for the North. At the end of May 1862, while McClellan was arguing with his superiors over the need for reinforcements, Davis and Lee had mapped plans to shove the invaders back from their capital. With Burnside menacing Norfolk from his base in North Carolina, and with large Union armies positioned in the Shenandoah Valley and near Washington, D.C., it seemed clear that Lincoln's strategy had made it possible for sheer weight of Northern numbers to overwhelm Southern resources. But Davis and Lee, gambling that excessive caution would prevent McClellan from a bold response, divided their outnumbered army to make simultaneous drives against enemy positions and relieve the pressure on the Confederate capital. With brilliant planning by Lee and Davis and courageous execution by General Stonewall Jackson preventing full concentration of Northern power and making possible full use of Southern strength against the massive Northern army, victory was achieved. The proximity of Washington to Richmond had worked to the disadvantage of the Northern army, since Lincoln, determined to avoid a repetition of the sacking of Washington in the War of 1812, ordered some forces left in northern Virginia to block a direct assault on the city. Davis and Lee dispatched Jackson on a daring raid that demoralized Union forces in the Shenandoah Valley by repeated strikes at isolated Northern units.

In June 1862 Lincoln dispatched his secretary of state, William Seward, to an emergency meeting of Union governors to assist in raising new volunteers and drafted a confidential letter that minced few words. The Confederate forces now held the strategic option once enjoyed by the Yankees: a choice among several targets. "If we send all the force from here to McClellan, the enemy will, before we can know of it," said Lincoln, "send a force from Richmond and take Washington. Or, if a large part of the Western Army be brought here to McClellan, they will let us have Richmond, and retake Tennessee, Kentucky, Missouri, &c." The president urged the governors to help raise a hundred thousand infantry to capture Richmond "without endangering any other place which we now hold—and will substantially end the war." Lest anyone doubt his determination to continue the fight, Lincoln assured them: "I expect to maintain this contest until successful, or till I die, or am conquered, or my term expires, or Congress and or the country forsakes me; and

I would publicly appeal to the country for this new force, were it not that I fear a general panic and stampede would follow—so hard is it to have a thing understood as it really is." To call for new troops at a time when Northern public opinion looked toward an early end to the war was a blow, and the governors balked at first but did agree to draft a memorial that would ask the president to call on the states for two hundred thousand new volunteers. By July 2 it seemed clear that the Army of the Potomac had abandoned the Peninsula Campaign, and Lincoln raised the goal to three hundred thousand "to bring this unnecessary and injurious civil war to a speedy and satisfactory conclusion."[16]

Lincoln had struggled to keep the slavery issue separate from the war, hoping that submerged Unionism in the Upper South especially would make it possible to restore loyal regimes when those states were occupied. Davis, for his part, was less concerned about Unionism in the South than about unrest among slaves in the event of an invasion of the plantation belts along the Mississippi River. But neither Lincoln nor Davis could prevent slavery from emerging as the dominant issue in a prolonged war. The slaves did not rise as a body or in insurrections, but Confederate measures to forestall revolt had taken a heavy toll on Southern resources, and in the end the survival of slavery, the nub of friction between the antebellum North and South, would become the most critical issue shaping the outcome of the war itself. Along with white yeoman disaffection and planters' determination to protect their property, and the resulting erosion of a will to sacrifice for a war of long duration, it was slavery that made the crucial difference.

The activities of congressional Republicans continued to politicize the issue of emancipation in the North. In August 1861, with lukewarm support from Lincoln, the federal Congress had passed the First Confiscation Act, directing invading Union field commanders to seize slaves along with other Confederate property. As the Union army moved southward, and with more and more slaves seeking refuge within Union lines, it grew increasingly difficult to distinguish between those slaves the army was required to seize and those it was required by the Fugitive Slave Law to return to their masters. On March 13, 1862, Congress sought to resolve this dilemma by forbidding officers, under threat of court-martial, to return forcibly any fugitive slave, whether or not the owner was loyal to the Confederacy. On April 16 another law was passed, to provide for gradual—and compensated—emancipation of slaves in the national capital of Washington, D.C. On July 17 Congress passed the Second Confiscation Act, defining slave property as a particular object of military confiscation and declaring that confiscated slaves "shall be forever free."[17]

Lincoln, while not an abolitionist, did abhor slavery, and once it became clear that Southerners would not readily abandon their quest for independence, he had tried, in numerous ways, to lead the border slave states toward some form of voluntary emancipation. But the efforts failed, and on July 12 he summoned to the White House congressional delegates from the border states of Delaware, Maryland, Kentucky, and Missouri to urge them to accept compensated emancipation while they still had the option. He acknowledged their wish to save both slavery and the Union, but warned: "If the war continues long, as it must, if the object be not sooner attained, the institution in your states will be extinguished by mere friction and abrasion—by the mere incidents of war. It will be gone, and you will have nothing valuable in lieu of it." Lincoln had already reconciled himself to what most of the delegations from the border slave states refused to accept: the longer and harder Southerners fought for independence, the more intense would the pressures for emancipation become.[18]

Although the border slave states' delegations were unaware of it, Lincoln's July 12 offer was to be their last chance to gain compensation for their endangered human property. The tenor of this meeting had already told Lincoln what he needed to know; the border states could not summon the will to accept his offer. Accordingly, he privately informed two of his cabinet members on July 13 of his decision to strike a blow against slavery. When, the next day, a majority of the delegates rejected Lincoln's offer of gradual, and compensated, emancipation, that rejection led to an immediate radicalization of the Union war effort. The Northern Congress, like the Southern Congress, had been debating a national draft, but so intense was opposition to it in the North that Congress chose, instead, to require each state to mount a state militia draft if it could not meet its share of the three hundred thousand volunteers Lincoln had called for. The Second Confiscation Act had granted the president the authority to employ emancipated blacks in any capacity required by the military struggle, and Congress added a clause to the Militia Act permitting the War Department to enroll blacks for "any military or naval service for which they may be found competent." Within a fortnight of the end of the lost Peninsula Campaign, both Lincoln and his Congress came to the same conclusion: emancipation and arming of blacks were both essential to saving the Union.

Lincoln summoned his cabinet members on July 22, 1862, and read to them the preliminary draft of an emancipation proclamation. It cited the Second Confiscation Act as justification for extinguishing, via presidential decree and without compensation, property rights in slaves in the seceded states. Two cabinet members objected: The postmaster general, Maryland's Montgomery Blair, was concerned that the move would cost Republicans heavily in the fall congressional by-elections and in numerous state and local contests. Secretary of State Seward asked whether the emancipation of slaves behind Confederate lines would not appear to be "the last measure of an exhausted Government, a cry for help, the government stretching forth its hand to Ethiopia, instead of Ethiopia's stretching forth her hands to the government." Seward urged the president to delay announcing such a decision until "you can give it to the country supported by military success." Lincoln took their strictures seriously and withheld the public proclamation until the next Northern victory. Lincoln's delay had the consequence of requiring him to pretend, for two months, that he had not decided to do what he had, in fact, already decided.[19]

At the same time, Lincoln was moving quickly on other measures to push the momentum of the Northern war effort. In July he put Major General Henry W. Halleck in command of "the whole land forces of the United States, as General-in-Chief," thereby removing McClellan from a potentially disruptive position at the top of the chain of command. The move also made possible Grant's return to active field command. Halleck now had to rescind orders he himself had put in place in November 1861, when Lincoln made him commander of the Department of the Missouri. General John C. Frémont, Halleck's predecessor in Missouri, had fallen from grace when he refused to countermand an emancipation proclamation to which Lincoln took exception. On taking over from Frémont, Halleck had directed Northern forces to keep fugitive slaves from coming within their lines, demanding that Grant, and all other general officers under his command, hew to Lincoln's expressed policy of respecting slaveholders' property rights. But now Halleck told Grant the time had come for an altered course: "It is very desirable that you should clean out West Tennessee and North Mississippi of all organized enemies. If necessary take up all active sympathizers, and either hold them as prisoners or put them beyond our lines. Handle that class without gloves, and take their property for public use. As soon as the corn gets fit for forage get all the supplies you can from the rebels of Mississippi. It is time they

should begin to feel the presence of war on our side." The order to handle secessionists "without gloves" by seizing "their property for public use" signaled that slaveholders' slave property was now at risk.[20]

"Deliver Us from Under This Bondage": Growing Slave Resistance on the Plantations

Booker T. Washington, who lived as a slave in western Virginia, would capture the mood of many in the slave quarters in his autobiography *Up from
Slavery*. "When war began between the North and the South," he wrote,
"every slave on our plantation felt and knew that, though other issues were
discussed, the primal one was slavery. Even the most ignorant members of my
race on the remote plantations felt in their hearts, with a certainty that admitted no doubt, that the freedom of the slaves would be the one great result of
the war, if the Northern armies conquered." Mary Woolridge, a former slave
in Kentucky, said after the war, "My Missus and Massa did not like Mr. Lincoln, but pshaw, all de niggers did." "My master used to ask us chillun, 'do
your folks pray at night?'" recalled Talitha Lewis, an Arkansas slave. "We
said 'no', 'cause our folks had told us what to say. But Lawd have mercy, there
was plenty of that going on. They pray 'Lawd deliver us from under this
bondage.'"[21]

Traditionally assumed by owners to be loyal, or at least passive in acceptance of their condition, many slaves showed signs of unrest that led their masters to seek to limit their contacts with outsiders. One Louisiana sugar planter
ordered his overseer not to allow "preaching of any sort . . . in that plantation
and Negroes not to be granted passes to attend exhortations elsewhere." In
Arkansas, Mrs. Mary B. Eskeridge denied a slave his accustomed right to be
hired out in another town, explaining to a correspondent, "I am fully alive at
this time to the anxieties and increased vigilance and precautions for the general safety of our families—against loose indulgences and free contact with
mean spies and abolitionists." A number of slaves did not take the increasing
restraints passively. Lizzie Neblett, less than three weeks after her husband left
Texas for Confederate service in the summer of 1863, complained of a recalcitrant slave named Sam: "Sam has been out. He started to see his wife last Sat.
after dinner and returned late Monday evening. He is determined not to clear
up trash land, and no doubt expects to be a free man before another year." She
protested, "The negroes are doing nothing, but ours are not doing that job

alone; nearly all the negroes around here are at it. Some of them are getting so high on anticipation of their glorious freedom by the Yankees I suppose, that they resist a whipping." The *Montgomery Weekly Mail,* as early as March 1861, reported that Robert Wicker, an overseer at A. H. Chappel's Macon County plantation, had caught a slave from another plantation leaving a Chappel cabin early one morning. Wicker ordered the slave to take off his coat and prepare for a whipping. "The boy refused, drew a knife and made for the door. Mr. Wicker seized him and both fell to the ground together, the boy inflicting a mortal wound on the left side just below the diaphragm.... The negro made his escape but we learn has since been arrested."[22]

Northern forces had steadily gained access to the heartland of the Mississippi Valley's plantation belt, beginning in January 1862 with the South's defeat at Big Sandy River in eastern Kentucky and continuing to June after their loss of Forts Henry and Donelson; the surrenders at New Madrid, Missouri, and Island No. 10 and Nashville in Tennessee; the withdrawals from Columbus and Bowling Green, Kentucky, and from Forts Randolph, Pillow, and Pickering, Tennessee; the stalemate at Shiloh; the surrender of New Orleans; and the early June withdrawals from Corinth, Mississippi, and from Memphis. The Mississippi River was now open from New Orleans north to Port Hudson and south from Memphis to Vicksburg; both the Tennessee and Cumberland Rivers lay at the mercy of Northern gunboats and steam-powered transports. Almost three-quarters of plantation-sized slaveholdings in the Mississippi Valley were now within fifty miles of a waterway accessible to Northern vessels, and only in central Alabama and in east central Mississippi and Texas, and in the east, were plantations isolated enough to be relatively invulnerable to slave escapes to freedom.

An increasing number of slaveholders felt justified in separating themselves from the general war effort. Why should they support a government that seemed unable to defend the interests that formed the cornerstone of the Southern republic? Was it not the planters' business to ensure that slavery survived the struggle? With the advance of the disastrous 1862 growing season, the Southern revolution began to reap the whirlwind of its commitment to local autonomy as many slaveholders took the preservation of slavery into their own hands. But slaves themselves were increasingly emboldened by the promise of emancipation. A Texas slave, Ida Henry, told of an overseer known for his "meaness over the slaves." "One day," she recalled later, "de slaves caught him and one held him whilst another knocked him in de head and killed him." After an overseer whipped a slave during the summer of 1862, a group of slaves devised a hangman's noose from their cotton suspenders and stalked, captured, and killed him. After Jim Rankin, who owned a farm in Marion County, Mississippi, returned from the war "meaner than before," a slave "sneaked up in the darkness an' shot him three times. Oh My Lord! He died the nex' mornin'. He never knowed who done it. I was glad they shot him down," remembered a former slave.[23]

After the fall of New Orleans at the end of April 1862, many southern Louisiana slaves fled their plantations. A shocked resident of Bossier Parish wrote in a letter, "There is a great many Negroes in the woods they think old Lincoln is a fighting for them." The advancing Yankee troops were accelerating the loss of slaves from Southern plantations. General Pillow wrote to Jefferson Davis in July 1862, "The Federals are sweeping the country of everything. They have taken over one thousand negroes from Phelps City, Arkansas. They have taken all of my negroes—men, women, and children, near 400 in number and everything else I had." On the Bowman family estate in West Feliciana Parish, Louisiana, "very near 450 negroes were liberated by the Yankees." Within a year after Northern troops arrived near James McCutcheon's sugar plantation, 233 of his 250 slaves had run away. James Gillespie, a planter in the Natchez area, counted 118 slaves among his property in January 1862; by December, only 33 remained.[24]

Commercial counties with higher proportions of planter families contained larger farms with many more slaves than plantations in the less affluent backcountry. Markedly wealthier, they had suffered less from labor and crop yields diverted to Confederate mobilization, but slaves provided the labor from which flowed all their wealth, and any significant loss in slaves would produce strong political pressure for a remedy. Staunching that flow and regaining control over slave laborers became a priority for these planters in the Mississippi Valley heartland. In response, Mississippi governor John Pettus requested permission, in May 1862, to organize partisan ranger companies, needed "to create a sense of security among the people and keep down any disorders among the slaves." Pettus also sought assurance that conscription would not drain his state of men needed to oversee slaves. So, too, Louisiana governor Thomas Moore, after the fall of New Orleans, asked that conscription be suspended so sufficient men and weapons could be kept at home to overcome "the stupendous calamity" war had brought to his state. Davis replied that he understood, but that planters must find overseers among men not subject to the draft because "there is no power to exempt them." He did acknowledge "the necessity of the employment of Partisan Rangers in the River counties," but refused them draft exemption.

Finding able-bodied substitutes to replace badly needed overseers off in military service was often impossible, and soon state officials were receiving a deluge of complaints. Typical of such complaints was a July 1862 letter to Alabama's governor from a Mrs. Bart Smith: "I have had great trouble to get overseers for my own and my children's plantations." "Where there are so many negroes upon places as ours, it is quite necessary that there should be men who can and will control them, especially at this time. Unaccustomed as I am to the control and management of a plantation, I am now in charge of one hundred negroes upon this place which I find is quite as much as I am capacitated to do in that peculiar line of business." After a bitter summer of struggling to supervise her slaves, an Alabama woman, Mrs. J. W. Lajlue, begged Governor Shorter to get her overseer back: "I have no brother *no one* on whom I can call for aid. I am living *alone* now, with only my child a little girl of 2 years old. I am now surrounded on all sides by plantations of negroes— many of them have not a white person on them. I am now begging you will you not in kindness to a poor unprotected woman and child give me the power of having my overseer recalled." A desperate letter from Addie Harris said, "My place needs a man to overlook things." "Only think Governor of the situation your wife would be in was she placed as we are. I have but one son and he is only four years old. . . . I have not a white soul on the place but my two little children, and if the Negroes get to fighting or anything of the kind in daytime or night I send for a white man and they will not come." Shorter did grant individual draft exemptions, whether or not the conscription act allowed them.[25]

The wife of a Texas planter, Mrs. W. J. Whatley, wrote her husband in great despair in November 1862, urging him to hire all his slaves out for the 1863 season: "I do not think it is worth while for me to try to stay here without someone to stay here with me for the negroes will not work." A Perry County, Alabama, slaveholder, James F. Bailey, faced with the prospect that conscription would cause "mis-rule," pleaded in March with General H. P. Watson not to take more men from his area. "In the negro population in some places there is manifested a disposition to mis-rule and insubordination, occasioned no doubt from the removal of our male population from their midst." Concerned citizens from Washington County, Alabama, petitioned Shorter not to enforce the state militia law in their county because "we are defenseless—there is not sufficient men left in the county for patrol duty." Nor was the problem confined to the Mississippi Valley. An April letter from his wife to W. W. Boyce, congressional representative of the 6th South Carolina district, spoke for probably thousands of plantation mistresses who were trying to manage blacks who no longer considered themselves slaves. "I can give orders first-rate," she wrote, "but when I am not obeyed, I can't keep my temper."[26]

Something had to be done. With Lincoln's Emancipation Proclamation scheduled to apply to states remaining in rebellion on January 1, 1863, Confederate officials pressed their superiors in Richmond to enact some measure to cope with the growing threat to the institution of slavery. Brigadier General Daniel Ruggles, in the District of Mississippi, brought the matter to the attention of the secretary of war:

> Voluntary enlistment and the conscription have taken into the military service of the country such a large proportion of the active freemen of this district, including the owners of slaves and other persons engaged in their management, that many plantations with numerous slaves are being left without the ordinary and necessary control of the white man, and daily applications are made to me to detail or to authorize the retention of proper persons to superintend them. Pernicious influences have already been manifested upon many of these plantations, and it is perhaps not without reason that fears are entertained of some serious disturbance in the sections most densely populated by the servile race, which are in most cases approachable by navigable streams.

Most alarming of all, Ruggles said, was the possibility that there could arise an "opportunity for the execution to any extent of the recently enunciated purpose of the Federal Government with reference to our slaves."[27]

Nothing in the previous experience of most slaveholders had prepared them for the speed with which the slaves were now asserting their right to freedom. As Northern armies plunged farther into the Southern heartland, many slaves believed emancipation imminent. With hiring of competent slave managers virtually impossible on many plantations, planters begged Richmond to exempt experienced overseers from compulsory military service.

Class Legislation: The Debate over Keeping Exemptions for Slave Overseers

On August 18, 1862, the Confederate Congress convened an extra session that turned out to be one of the most critical sessions of the entire war. Many members at home after the mid-May recess had learned a great deal about the crises on the home front: in the backcountry, many saw the draft law that exempted certain persons and certain occupations as class legislation; in the low country, urgent help was needed to regain, and maintain, control over the slaves. The Congress delayed efforts to reconcile these competing perspectives and interests, apparently in the hope that Lee's Maryland campaign might finish the war in victory. Antietam was to end such hopes.

An extended congressional debate ensued on how best to care for the poor. South Carolina's representative William Miles introduced a bill to extend the conscript age from thirty-five to forty-five, and Franklin Barlow Sexton of Texas urged Congress to raise the pay of privates and noncommissioned officers from eleven to fourteen dollars per month. William Chilton of Alabama doubted the Confederacy could afford such an increase, and besides, Southern soldiers "were not fighting for money but for freedom and glory." Henry Cousins Chambers of Mississippi said that Sexton's bill would cost the Confederacy $33 million. The House resolved the question, for the moment, by noting that raising military pay would increase inflation and thus rob the soldiers of any real benefit. On the question of raising the age of conscription, the House was sharply divided. It might cause "bad feeling in certain sections of the Confederacy," Henry Foote said, and Caleb Herbert of Texas warned that it might provoke Texans into "raising . . . the Lone Star Flag." The new draft acts of spring 1862 had indeed produced "bad feeling" in the backcountry and even led to several unsuccessful attempts at county secession.[28]

Should substitution and exemption continue to be allowed? On the issue of substitution, Thomas Semmes of Louisiana insisted, in the Senate debate, that "every man, high or low, rich or poor, should be forced to go into the army for the defense of the country." "All citizens should be put on the same footing." Governor Moore of Louisiana asked that the draft be suspended in the trans-Mississippi west because "dormant disloyalty had been awakened with the disaster that brings our enemies so near, and the murmurs of the suffering mingle with the complaints of the mercenary, the taunts of the disorganizers, and the whispered treason of tories." Secretary of War Randolph cautioned,

"It is unwise to injure the public service for the benefit of individuals, and therefore no substitution founded merely on consideration of private interest should be tolerated." Substitution should be authorized, for example, only for "experts in trades necessary for the prosecution of the war, overseers in districts having few whites and large numbers of slaves, and generally in such callings as are essential for the public welfare." Senator Edward Sparrow of Louisiana proposed that substitution be allowed for anyone who was "the only white male adult on a farm or plantation having thereon not less than fifty slaves," suggesting that field commanders be authorized to detail a soldier "to act as a special police" on plantations already stripped of their male superintendents.[29]

James Phelan of Mississippi asked, "Why not let the poor man stay at home to protect his own family against the slaves of the rich man." "If we are to have class legislation," he said, "let's legislate in favor of the poor. The rich will take care of themselves." Texas's Louis Wigfall was tired of hearing criticism of class legislation and had hoped never to hear of the subject again, but he confessed that "as the law now stands there is class legislation. None but the rich men can procure substitutes." Still, he could see no alternative to aiding the plantations. Congress "had excepted one white man on plantations where there were large numbers of slaves, not because he might be a rich man, but because it was deemed imprudent for the public service to leave the slaves without someone to keep them in subjection." Robert Barnwell of South Carolina regretted the necessity for substitution but thought it essential for a large slaveholder, "because it was more important to the prosperity of the country that he should remain on his plantation and keep his slaves in subjection." Several senators from the Upper South opposed detailing of soldiers to plantation duty. Walter Preston of Virginia insisted that "the conscript army should not be prostituted into a police guard for the slaves." William Simms of Kentucky noted the extremely high price of substitutes that had burdened the army with recalcitrant soldiers, since "substitutes composed nine-tenths of the deserters."[30]

The bill that eventually passed closely resembled the proposal Secretary of War Randolph had made originally. No longer could any individual escape compulsory service simply by procuring a substitute, and persons supplying substitutes had to be engaged in a skilled trade or to "have the charge and active management" of a farm or plantation with fifty or more slaves.

On September 19-20, 1862, in the aftermath of Lee's retreat from the stalemate at Antietam, the collapse of the Maryland campaign, and expectations of capture of the railroad junction at Harrisburg, the Confederate Congress turned quickly to consider the issue of exemption and how best to insulate the institution of slavery. To withdraw able-bodied white men up to forty-five years of age from restive plantation districts would be tantamount to conceding slavery's demise. But to legislate relief would be to impose the burden of fighting even more harshly on backcountry yeomen. On September 19 Senator Semmes proposed to discharge from draft liability "one overseer on each plantation cultivated by negro labor and owned by any person absent in the service of the Confederate or state Governments, or by any minor, widow or unmarried woman or person not of sound mind." He did not define how many slaves it took to make up a plantation. An amendment such as Semmes's, as it stood, would have removed almost every slaveholder from the Southern army. By exempting overseers, asked several senators, did Congress intend to legislate in favor of slave labor against white labor? Alabama's William Lowndes Yancey, one of the fathers of the Confederacy, said he "eschewed class legislation" but proceeded to support exemption of overseers as an absolute necessity.[31] Albert Gallatin Brown of Mississippi opposed exempting college students: "It was wrong to pass general laws and then make particular class exemptions. It savoured of favoritism." James Phelan called the state officials who qualified for exemptions "the great blood suckers of the State Treasuries."[32]

In the end, the Senate did exempt overseers "and such other persons as the president shall be satisfied on account of equity or necessity ought to be exempted." That compromise gave low-country planters what they desired while passing on to Davis the responsibility for equalizing the effects of expanded conscription on poorer nonslaveholding Southerners. Senator Wigfall urged the Senate to set the minimum number of slaves required for exemption at twenty, largely because most states used twenty in laws that mandated minimum levels for white supervision. Only plantations that had employed an overseer before the draft act would be eligible. Wigfall supported "the employment of overseers not for police purposes, to keep down insurrections, but to make the negroes work, which the experience of ages had proved they would not do except under compulsion." A majority of senators voted yes.[33]

During a critical six-week period in the fall of 1862, the South came closer to victory than it would ever come again, but the fortunes of war abruptly turned. Between the exhilarating victory at Second Manassas on August

29–30 and the adjournment of the Southern Congress on October 13 came the bitter stalemate at Antietam, Lincoln's Preliminary Emancipation Proclamation, and the passage of the highly unpopular Confederate conscription and exemption laws. Some planters patriotically refused to take advantage of the "Twenty Nigger" exemption. J. T. Terrell of Aberdeen, Mississippi, rejected a personal exemption. "I can say I do not want any," insisted this wealthy young aristocrat to his parents, "as I think it is the duty of every man to bear an equal part in this struggle. . . . I think all men that own property to any extent and especially negro property Should take a part in this war as it has a tendency to encourage the poorer classes." Other planters, however, scrambled at the chance to escape compulsory service.[34]

With many nonslaveholders resenting the granting of privilege to an upper-class group that represented no more than 5 percent of the white population, an increasing number of yeomen deserted, resisted the draft, or even joined the Northern army. In December the novelist Augusta Evans sent to her confidante Jabez L. M. Curry, a criticism of "the Exemption Bill" for provoking "the spirit of insubordination and disaffection which is rife in our armies." Senior officers in the army were confessing "great uneasiness at the rapidly spreading spirit of defection in their commands," she said. "The number of desertions in Genl Pemberton's army, and even among troops stationed in Alabama, is appalling and fears are entertained of painful and disastrous consequences, unless the evil can be promptly remedied." With courts martial "everywhere in session" dispensing harsh punishment to captured deserters, men pleaded, Evans wrote, "in palliation of desertion, the cries of hungry wives and starving children." Some of the officer corps themselves sympathized with men who received letters from home urging them to "come home *at every hazard.*" Exempting overseers "has resulted most unhappily," Evans admitted, "in the creation of an antislavery element among our soldiers who openly complain that they are torn from their homes and their families consigned to starvation, solely in order that they may now protect the property of slave holders; who are allowed by the *'Bill'* to remain in quiet enjoyment of luxurious ease." "A band of 300 *furloughed* soldiers had organized themselves and sworn never to return to their regiments and to sternly *resist* all enrolling and arresting officers." Evans entreated Curry to urge Congress to move quickly at its next session to amend the overseer bill and purge any taint of class bias. Otherwise, the rapid spread of popular "insubordination . . . may prove . . . potent in completely dividing our people."[35]

In December 1862, in a long and passionate letter to his close friend Jefferson Davis, Senator Phelan painted a dismal picture. "Instead of being, as it ought to be, a measure that saved the country," the new exemption bill "threatens to be the cause of its subjugation."

> Never did a law meet with more universal odium than the exemption of slave owners. Its injustice, gross injustice, is denounced even by men whose position enables them to take advantage of its privileges. Its influence upon the poor is calamitous, and has wakened a spirit and elicited a discussion of which we may safely predicate the most unfortunate results. . . . It has aroused a spirit of rebellion in some places, I am informed, and bodies of men have banded together to resist; whilst in the army it is said it only needs some daring men to raise the standard to develop a revolt.[36]

Economic regionalism lay at the base of Confederate class conflict that erupted in the wake of the overseers' exemption. Of plantations with slaves in the Mississippi Valley backcountry, only 22 percent of the more than twenty thousand were in the noncommercial regions out of which the yeomanry came. On average, only 1 percent of the military-age white men in counties practicing a "family economy" would have qualified for an overseers' exemption, while in the commercial sector, 10 percent of the white men eligible for the draft could have claimed such an exemption, and in one Louisiana parish 50 percent of the draftable men could have availed themselves of it.

Popular resistance to conscription ought properly to be viewed as a continuation of antebellum class consciousness. Eugene Genovese has pointed out that planter hegemony over backcountry yeomen had rested on the planters' willingness to respect the regional autonomy of the yeomanry by refraining from explicit economic exploitation.[37] When the planter-dominated war regime in Richmond enacted a conscription system that strongly favored the economically advantaged, yeomen had little difficulty concluding that planters had violated that antebellum consensus. And yet, planters could not ease such yeoman class consciousness without surrendering their control over plantation slaves.

The period between enactment of the "Twenty Nigger Law" and the January 1, 1863, Northern implementation of the Emancipation Proclamation marked the most critical challenge of Davis's presidency. From wide areas of the Mississippi Valley came dire warnings about yeoman resistance to the amended conscription system, and no amount of propagandizing about the beneficence of slavery seemed likely to dissuade most slaves from longing for and seeking emancipation. If Davis was to salvage the Confederate Revolution, he had to counter popular resistance to the planters' government among a skeptical yeomanry while maintaining control of the slaves. The slaveholders' revolution had become an explicit defense of slaveholders' interests. Scores of thousands of nonslaveholders now renounced allegiance to the cause. The war would drag on for two more years, but class conflict in the South virtually ensured that superior Northern resources would eventually overcome Confederate valor. The War for Southern Independence was, in consequence, effectively lost.

Were the interests of social groups within the South sufficiently congruent to provide a foundation for a mature nationalism that could weather a prolonged and hostile occupation? The knowledge among many nonslaveholders that the well-to-do were unwilling to bear a fair share of the burden of national defense made any such confidence unrealistic. Unless enough slaveholders in occupied areas could, by example, meet the distrust at the heart of preservationist ideology, the belief that secession was a strategy by slaveholders to save slavery and, thereby, to protect their self-interest at the cost of nonslaveholders' lives, the Confederate government would have to punish slaveholders who evaded the military service as it punished yeomen dissenters. This it did not do. In the aftermath, at least fifty thousand white men from the seceding states took up arms on behalf of the Northern cause before the war's end, the cutting edge of a lower-class antiwar movement. Among the slaves, the desire to fight for freedom impelled more than two hundred thousand, including free persons of African descent, some from the North, to join in the service of the Union cause. Class disaffection, black and white, was in the end to cost the Confederacy at least half a million men; it was a loss that made the vital difference.

Chapter Eight "The Carefully Fostered
Hostility of Class against Class"

Demoralization and the Fall
of Vicksburg

N o war for national independence can long survive if its leading
classes are, or are perceived to be, brutally insensitive to the interests
of the common folk, or if its leadership elite, in the conduct of the
war, seems more determined to protect its own property interest than
to share in the sacrifices essential for victory. The use of force by
Confederate commanders to counter antiwar sentiments among Southern
yeomen diverted scarce manpower from the front and intensified civilian resistance to conscription, impressment, and taxation. This self-perpetuating
downward spiral had particular impact on the campaign to defend Vicksburg.
Not long before Grant's final assault on the city, the Reverend Henry C. Lay,
Episcopalian bishop for the state of Arkansas, expressing dismay about the
desperate state of military affairs, wrote in a letter of February 23, 1863: "As for
Arkansas, I can only cry Alas! Alas! The enemy can take possession whenever
he feels it worthwhile to send a respectable force." "Our hills are filled with
Tories who resist the conscription law and plunder loyal men. . . . Our army
has melted like a snow wreath and chiefly by desertion . . . we are chewing
the bitter fruit of that American upas, the carefully fostered hostility of class
against class."[1] As the Vicksburg campaign unfolded, Southerners in the war
zone increasingly lost control over slaves, who now saw freedom as an imminent possibility, and planters sought to save what they could from the double
maelstrom of war and emancipation, while less affluent, nonslaveholding
whites watched as many in the aristocracy pursued self-interest first.

Defenses at Vicksburg Weakened by Planters' Reluctance to Provide Slave Labor

Vicksburg occupied a commanding position high on a chain of bluffs overlooking the huge horseshoe-shaped bend in the Mississippi River midway between New Orleans and Memphis. Waterlogged swamps, for a radius of thirty miles, completely encircled the bluffs and hills on which the city sat. The Mississippi had meandered across this alluvial floodplain for millennia, leaving a series of old channels interlocked with the main channel through a maze of lakes, bayous, creeks, and rivers. Control over Vicksburg meant dominance over access to the national heartland—the cotton plantations along the river. Jefferson Davis, whose Brierfield plantation lay approximately twenty miles below the city, understood full well the strategic importance of holding Vicksburg. So did Abraham Lincoln. In November 1861 he called the Mississippi "the backbone of the Rebellion," "the key to the whole situation." "If the Confederates once fortify the neighboring hills," Lincoln warned, "they will be able to hold that point for an indefinite time, and it will require a large force to dislodge them."[2]

After New Orleans fell in late April, Admiral David Glasgow Farragut made a dash upriver to capture Vicksburg before the Confederates could fortify it. Along his route, the terrified civilians in both Baton Rouge and Natchez surrendered, but Farragut stalled at Vicksburg and then retreated back down river. Following the additional Union victories of the spring, Farragut again moved against Vicksburg in June, this time joined by naval and army units from above. Deciding to bypass the obstacle by digging a canal across the narrow neck of the Vicksburg peninsula, the Northern commanders sought to open up the Mississippi to Northern shipping without compelling the city to surrender. About 1,200 slaves offered their services and worked beside Northern canal diggers, no doubt anticipating that this would earn them freedom more speedily. But the canal failed, and with the summer dry season approaching and water levels dropping precipitously, Farragut's flotilla had to withdraw, so suddenly that the slave volunteers were left behind. "The abandoned Negroes gathered on the levee," writes John Winters; "their shrieks of woe rang out over the water as the boats moved away."[3]

Kate Stone, on her plantation near Vicksburg on the Louisiana side of the Mississippi, wrote vividly in her diary about the impact of the Northern advance on slave discipline. The Northern "vandals" had promised freedom to blacks along the river:

June 29, 1862—We hear today that the Yankees are impressing all the Negro men on the river places and putting them to work on a ditch which they are cutting across the point opposite Vicksburg above De Soto.

June 30, 1862—The excitement is very great. The Yankees have taken the Negroes off all the places below Omega, the Negroes generally going willingly, being promised their freedom by the Vandals.

July 24, 1862— . . . several Negroes returning from their Yankee pleasure trip, weary and footsore and eager to get home. Numbers of them pass here going home, bending their necks to the yoke again, preferring the old allegiance to the new. But numbers are still running to the gunboats. We would not be surprised to hear that all of ours have left in a body any day.

Stone reported that "a good many planters are leaving the river and many are sending their Negroes to the back country. . . . Dr. Nutt and Mr. Mallett are said to be already on their way to Texas with the best of their hands." A letter to the governor of Mississippi from A. K. Farrar, the Confederate provost marshal for the Natchez district, reflected a rapid erosion in the control masters exerted over their slaves, with many runaways having gone to join the Union army:

There is a general disposition among the negroes to be insubordinate, and to run away, and go off to the federals. Within the last twelve months we have had to hang some forty for plotting an insurrection, and there has been about that many put in irons. . . . I would like your instructions as to the manner of proceeding against persons who will keep no overseer, and make but little provision for their negroes, rendering it necessary for them to steal, starve or go naked. There are some few cases of this kind here, when negroes seemingly are permitted to forage upon the community. The owners will not look after them, will not provide for them, nor will they employ an overseer. The negroes having such liberties, they are enabled to harbor runaways who have fire arms and traverse the whole country, kill stock and steal generally, supplying those who harbor them, and send to market by negro market men.

Within eighteen months, owner abandonment of plantations had fundamentally altered the demography of the Mississippi Valley, weakening the war effort of Confederate forces by denying ready access to labor and supplies.[4]

Almost as soon as they learned of the fall of New Orleans, Vicksburg's merchants raised prices to unheard of levels. The editor of the *Vicksburg Whig,*

Marmaduke Shannon, excoriated the profiteers: "All men think all men extortioners but themselves. They forget that in the Holy Book . . . extortioners are classed as murderers, adulterers, and liars and not with common sinners." "Think of this, ye church members, who are selling articles at one hundred times their true value and are thus preying upon the lifeblood of the people, and seriously jeopardizing the lifeblood of the country."[5]

In addition, by the time Grant launched his 1862 fall offensive many Confederate merchants were rejecting Confederate paper currency, since the government had again refused to make it a legal tender, and yeomen found this kind of sharp dealing outrageous. A letter from one Arkansas soldier, A. O. McCollom, to "Dear Friends" on Christmas Day, said, "When it comes to that I think it is time to quit." An Alabama slaveholder, David Hubbard, wrote to Senator Clement C. Clay about the absolute necessity for halting the merchants' practice. Merchants "are refusing Confederate Treasury Notes in payment of debts due first of January." He implored Senator Clay to act: "Have you no way to compel men? . . . You cannot maintain your army any longer. Don't be guilty of creating a Rebellion and involving our people in it and then by timid policy or folly put it out of the people's minds to succeed. It you dont make your currency good, you cannot keep your army in the field."[6]

The principle of noblesse oblige espoused by antebellum planters had carried with it the moral obligation to assume a leading role in periods of social and political crisis, but activities such as those engaged in by many planters and merchants now broke with that article of faith. The resistance to impressment of a number of planters, their wartime profiteering, and abandonment of plantations further eroded antebellum paternalism. The planter James Allen, for example, although he considered himself a staunch Southern patriot, found it impossible to comply with an emergency requisition for workers. "Declined sending any," Allen noted in his diary for May 15, 1862. "Cant send negroes 25 miles to work 1 night and no overseer to work them when they get there." Less than a week later, he turned down another emergency requisition, this time for a driver and a team. "A Mr. Tucker sends me word if I do not send my team and negro he'll send a posse after me and the team; who the hell *he* is I dont know," retorted the obviously annoyed planter. "I have paid no attention to their requisitions, think half are by scoundrels to get planters teams to haul private property."[7]

"The crux of the difficulty between the Confederate government and the planters," writes James Roark, "lay in the difference between their ultimate goals." Roark sees members of the planter class as "primarily committed to the preservation of the plantation system."[8] Even during the first high wave of enthusiasm for the Southern cause, some planters had already expressed reservations about the propriety of complying with military requisitions for slave laborers for building fortifications. Indeed, the reluctance of many planters to offer their slave laborers had led to fatal delays in building the much needed forts along the Mississippi and in constructing defensive works at Nashville. (See chap. 5.)

"Acting under your orders to impress negroes to work on the public defense of this place," the provost marshal reported in November to General John Pemberton, the new Confederate commander, "I gave directions to arrest any planters who refused to obey the orders of impressment." One planter tried to resist the impressment gang: "The guard sent to impress negro labor brought a Mr. Trumbell, who not only refused to furnish such a proportion of his force but is charged with secreting the negroes in the woods." A number of planters employed tactics of evasion, most commonly, ironically, conniving with slaves themselves, who were even less willing to be sent off to work on the fort than the owners were for them to go. Many slave managers looked the other way while able-bodied male slaves fled to the woods. When word reached the Fonsylvania plantation of Benjamin Wailes about the imminent arrival of an impressment gang from Vicksburg, the overseer Alfred Quine recorded this sequence in his diary:

February 20, 1863—All them rundway to keep the solgers from getting them.

February 21, 1863—Five men rundway.

February 22, 1863—Five men in the woods all the rest home and well.

February 23, 1863—Elie came in out of the woods. . . . Six men in the woods.

March 1, 1863—Pleasant Days All hands at home and well but Winburn sick.[9]

A January 1863 editorial in the *Clarksville Standard* chastised planters severely for resisting military impressments of slaves: "The idea that a white man can be taken away from his wife and children, and put into the field, not only to fight but to do menial service, while a sleek negro cannot be reached but stays at home in comfort, is monstrous." The paper called on the legislature to enact stringent laws to compel recalcitrant slaveholders to release slaves for military labor; able-bodied slaves should "take the place of white men now kept out of the line of battle to do . . . occupations of drudgery."[10]

Certain planters continued to resort to bribery and corruption on behalf of their special interests, and less affluent slaveholders began to notice that the number of slaves taken from some owners differed considerably from the number taken from others. Governor Pettus received a bitter complaint of such practices from James Garner, a self-described "poor man," owner of a single slave family, who tried to distance himself from those who refused to send any slaves. "I am willing to bear my part as far as I am able," he wrote, but he was irate that other slaveholders "who are a good deal abler than I am have not sent." "It seems to me that the work should be more evenly divided so as not to injure one man more than another."[11]

One group with small slaveholdings protested to Pettus that in Copiah County a planter whose cotton production averaged four hundred bales a year sent only one hand, while a second planter who produced three hundred bales a year also received a requisition for a single slave. "We dont complain at sending our negroes to Vicksburg," said the protesting slaveholders, "but we look to our Governor to have the impressments equalized." A Houston journalist wrote, "Those planters that [have] a good stock of fat fowls, and plenty of good liquor stored away in their cellars were always the favored parties. That was all the protection they needed." As the conviction spread that planters were conniving with the army to ensure favored treatment, some unable or unwilling to offer bribes took more-direct steps to protect their possessions. Colonel H. B. Lyons, confronted by civilians prepared to resist his impressment gang, dispatched an urgent telegram to Governor Pettus, saying, "State law interferes with impressment of negroes by force of arms. How shall I procure them? Armed mobs in Holmes County have resisted my impressment detachment."[12]

Even when slaves were turned over to the military, the Confederate army had to detail soldiers to compel the impressed slave laborers to work during the day and to prevent them escaping at night. But as pressure on Vicksburg grew, so did the number of slave escapes. "You can keep the negroes spoken of this morning in your employ during the day," said an aide in an exchange in June with the departmental quartermaster, "but they must be returned to jail at night." The officer in charge of constructing fortifications at Jackson, Colonel Benjamin S. Ewell, Johnston's assistant adjutant general, wrote to General Buckner on June 6: "There seems to be some difficulty in getting and keeping negroes for the fortifications here. After they are collected and delivered to the Engineer Department, they ought to be . . . guarded and apprehended if they run away by the military power."[13]

General Grant had sought to profit from the mistakes of the failed attempt against Vicksburg in the summer of 1862 by ordering a two-pronged pincer assault from his bases in western Tennessee. He gave his trusted second, General William Tecumseh Sherman, command of the waterborne prong, taking charge of the overland march from the northeast himself. His goal was to place General Pemberton in a position where a significant mistake might lead to the capture of Vicksburg. The second Northern offensive started just before January 1, 1863, the date Lincoln had set for the inauguration of emancipation, and a time in the war when planters were even less willing than before to supply slave laborers for work on Southern fortifications.

The proximity of Grant's army also proved a powerful lure to slave runaways, who continued to flee toward the Yankee camps. The Southern army lacked the cavalry resources to interdict them, and the number increased in inverse proportion to slaveholders' ability to continue to pay white yeomen the customary fees for captured fugitives. An irate patrol captain, T. W. Ham, of northern Mississippi, demanded of Governor John Pettus clarification of the increasing muddle: "What are we allowed for capturing runaway negroes if we are allowed anything? I would like to know, for we captured eleven the other day and I sent them to their owners and Colonel Bantean told the young man that took them we are bound to take them up and send them to their respective owners without paying us the expenses. The trip cost us forty dollars and we got nothing for it if that is the law the rest may go for me waiting for an answer."[14]

Renegade Bands, Desertions, and Bushwhacking

The counterinsurgency campaign against draft resisters, evaders, and deserters simply worsened the disaffection it was supposed to control. Many now moved the short step from armed disaffection to social banditry. J. F. H. Claiborne, a planter refugee from Natchez to the backcountry regions along the southern Mississippi Gulf Coast, took it upon himself to inspect the camp of a new cavalry company and discovered that Hancock County yeomen were joining up with the intention of evading active service. "Two-thirds of these men have, heretofore, *refused* to volunteer," he wrote to Major M. B. Clarke, chief enrolling officer for the department, in mid-August 1862. "Several of them are of suspicious loyalty and the majority of them decided to join [Captain James] Miller with the hope and belief that they will never smell gunpowder." These yeomen had neither battle-fit cavalry mounts nor the resources to furnish them. "The joining of Miller's Co. is a mere *evasion* to avoid obeying *your* order," he informed Clarke. Two weeks later, Claiborne uncovered an even more egregious example. "In defiance of your orders No. 1 and No. 2, a company composed exclusively of conscripts had been organized and mustered into what is called Steed's Battalion of Cavalry." "The moment they were mustered in and promised a bounty of $50," he reported, "they were furloughed for an indefinite term, and every one of them are now at home pursuing their usual avocations." "Many of these men have often publicly declared that they would not and could not be made to leave this county. They are now organizing another company *called* an artillery company, composed of conscripts."[15]

Claiborne told influential family friends, including Mississippi senator Albert Gallatin Brown, about this state of affairs, whereupon back down through the Southern chain of command came an order to investigate the allegations. Captain T. J. Hart, who led the detachment dispatched to investigate, venturing further west to the sandy parishes of southeastern Louisiana, was astonished and shocked by what he found. "It is impossible to believe," he reported to Major Clarke in November, "hundreds of young men, young and healthy, that are down in these barren parishes, all doing nothing but trying to avoid the conscript law." Back in Hancock County, Hart, confirming Claiborne's account, learned that the signature of Major Steed of the "Battalion of Cavalry" on an enlistment certificate could grant a man virtual exemption from active field service. Steed extracted from each yeoman he helped a gratuity—cords of firewood—which he then sold in Mobile "for a big price, the citizens say the Major has made a big thing by it." "A Soldier's Sister" had written to Governor Moore in early August from Bayou Chicot, Louisiana, to complain about renegade partisan units who were preying on the families of absent soldiers. "Our homes are entered and pillaged of everything they see fit to appropriate to themselves." The partisans claimed to be foraging under orders: "They do not as much respect private rooms, but enter inspite of tears and entreaties and turn up beds and rip open closets, break open whatever happens to be locked, in fact they leave no corner untouched."[16]

Pemberton, a West Pointer who had served as commander of the Department of South Carolina and Georgia, knowing full well that incidents like these could not be tolerated, launched an all-out campaign of counterinsurgency. General Earl Van Dorn, responding to a series of complaints from northern Mississippi, suggested in December that Pemberton send a "sufficient force to Tatum Station where they will apprehend a great number of deserters." That same month a loyal citizen, James M. Porter, expressed regret that his patriotic duty compelled him to report on armed bands of disloyal persons, draft evaders, and deserters: "There is a very strong Union party in some neighborhoods on the North East portion of Itawamba and the South East Tishomingo, which is said to extend to west Ala. There are also men in these sections subject to conscription and some deserters skulking about." The superintendent of conscription for Texas, Major J. F. Llewellen, warned that reports of yeoman resistance to the "Twenty Nigger Law" were widespread in the region from which Pemberton needed to draw troops to defend Vicksburg. "In certain German settlements resistance to conscription is seriously contemplated." A deputy dispatched to check it out reported back, "The Germans of my District and the adjoining counties are in a state of open rebellion to our Government." The Union League, which claimed more than five hundred members across Austin, Washington, Fayette, Lavaca, and Colorado Counties, was swearing to resist conscription. One enrolling officer "was assaulted and driven from the place . . . also a friend was actually mobbed, by being beaten with sticks, iron bars, etc."[17]

Other organized antiwar groups existed in wide areas of northeastern Texas, with German-American draft evaders apparently planning to "assemble and resist to the death." The commander of the district of Texas, Brigadier General William Webb, took the same course of action as Pemberton and dispatched a regiment "to disarm the disloyal Germans and enforce the draft and conscript act." One officer in northeastern Texas found resisters "remarkably stubborn, and I am satisfied [they] do not intend to submit to enrollment"; he requested detailing a regular army unit "to bring them in and as the militia nearly all sympathize with them I cannot rely upon them." In the Alabama backcountry counties of Coffee, Dale, and Henry, the social banditry of antiwar groups rivaled that of groups in Arkansas, Mississippi, and Louisiana.[18]

But deployment of regular army troops for counterinsurgency risked further inflaming what counterinsurgency sought to control. Escalation by the government begat escalation by the disaffected, as draft evaders and resisters made common cause with deserters against the government. Once the Southern army decided to attack antiwar groups, the Confederacy began to experience a war within its war. Backcountry skirmishes strikingly resembled the violence that had occurred between patriot and Tory factions in the Southern colonies during the American Revolution, but in that earlier revolution

Southern elite groups had eventually accommodated to yeoman class consciousness. In the Civil War, the Confederacy seemed unable to respond in any effective way to accusations of inequitable wartime burdens.

There was also the problem of guerrilla warfare. On November 17, 1862, Clarke dispatched a file to Pemberton with a report of an investigation on renegade partisan rangers. Return orders were delivered in early December: "Major Clarke, enrolling officer, will disband all corps of Partisan Rangers whose commanders have not shown the proper authority for raising the same. . . . You will render any assistance that may be necessary, employing a competent force if necessary."[19]

When random violence associated with the loss of social order erupted in their home regions, soldiers at the front expressed anxiety for the safety of their dependents at home. The commander of the 26th Mississippi Infantry, Colonel A. E. Reynolds, wrote a passionate letter in January 1863 to Jefferson Davis about poor morale: "The Counties of Tishomingo, Tippah and Marshall are now being laid waste, not only by the Yankees but more destructively by the Tories and Southern thieves. . . . They are not only robbing women and children of their property but they have also taken from them everything to eat, even men of wealth have actual starvation staring them in the face. . . . most of these women and children, at least in Tishomingo, are the wives and children of my soldiers." These soldiers did what they felt they had to do. "Many of my men hearing of the insults and wrongs offered their wives and children have left camp without leave; many have returned and a good many have gone to bush-wacking." Reynolds challenged his commander in chief, "Should not something be done for their relief?"[20] When otherwise loyal soldiers took unauthorized leaves to protect dependents at home, as Reynolds pointed out, soldiers often became brigands.

Alex Fitzpatrick, a sixty-three-year-old slaveholder, wrote directly to Davis in November 1862 to advise him how to cope with Lincoln's impending Emancipation Proclamation. In the light of white racial unity, the prospect of emancipation ought to afford the South a magnetic rallying point, and Fitzpatrick suggested that Davis issue a counterproclamation for a truly egalitarian *levée en masse*. "Lincolns Emancipation Proclamation indicates," he warned, "that the North dont intend to stop short of our subjugation or extermination and it behooves us to decide whether we will submit, be free, or die if necessary in a mighty and just struggle for liberty." Conversations with local yeomen had persuaded him that the class biases inherent in Confederate conscription were at the root of popular disaffection: "While I am no demagog, allow me to say that nothing has gone so far to demoralize our army as the substitute sistem. The wealthy alone are able to hire substitutes and the poor (whose families are much neglected) have to do the principal part of the fighting." Slaveholders "have no alternative left but to fight for the defense of our property as well as our liberty and he that would not in the most bold manner die in the last ditch if need be in defense of his property is not worthy to be free." "I am opposed to the black flag," Fitzpatrick wrote, referring to the giving and expecting of no mercy, "unless the property owners that have furnished substitutes are compelled to stand in the breech side by side with the brave soldiers that are fighting for liberty."[21]

Emancipation as a Military Weapon:
Class and Racial Concerns, North and South

When his second offensive near Vicksburg failed, Grant moved his headquarters from Memphis to the immediate vicinity of Vicksburg, acknowledging, in effect, that capture would require a prolonged campaign. His new base enabled Northern forces to maintain constant pressure on the Vicksburg garrison and would make it easier to enforce the new policy of emancipation. So heavy did the Union pressure become that local slaveholders faced a stark choice—abandon their plantations or watch their fortunes evaporate—and many struggled to salvage what they could. By the time of Grant's final Northern offensive in mid-April 1863, he would face an isolated and dispirited force of Southern defenders.

Lincoln's issuance of the Preliminary Emancipation Proclamation proved so controversial in the North itself that Republicans suffered devastating by-election losses in the fall of 1862, and currents of Northern home-front disaffection reached Grant's army as well. Private Cyrus Boyd wrote in his diary in August 1862 that "a good many of the soldiers and people are *bitterly* opposed to having 'niggers' take any hand in the war." Some Union soldiers began to desert to the Southerners. "It is currently reported among the prisoners," said one Confederate colonel, Wirt Adams, in a letter of January 1863, "that unless Vicksburg is taken within 30 days, the West will secede. Their friends in the West are now writing the soldiers to desert and come home and they will not be returned to the army." Northern morale would begin to lift toward the end of March 1863, when the changing of the seasons worked an almost magical transformation on the cold, weary, and rain-drenched Union soldiers, but no factor seemed to exert a greater impact than Lincoln's December 1862 annual message speaking directly to concerns about the impact of emancipation in the North. "It is dreaded," he acknowledged, "that the freedpeople will swarm forth and cover the whole land." He supported a plan to house freed slaves on plantations abandoned by slaveholders in their flight from emancipation. With black refugees resettled on abandoned plantations, none would need to move to the Northern states.[22]

Lincoln, unlike his Southern counterpart, was coping directly with class- and race-based concerns. The resulting positive effects on Union morale are apparent in an open letter from a Northern soldier, James K. Wells, to his hometown Indiana newspaper:

> Now I want to ask you if negroe equality is established in Indiana yet. Some of you tried to make the soldiers wives believe that their husbands were fighting to free the slaves and send them into Indiana by the 1st of April. I want some of you smart educated Knights of the Golden Circle to let me know when you see the first squad of negroes coming from the south to become citizens in owen county. . . . The majority of the union soldiers are in favor of restoreing the Union and the Constitution if it frees every slave in the south. . . . You know as well as I do that the rebels have had a chance to save their slaves and property too by coming back to the Union in due time but they did not so who is to blame but themselves.[23]

With an abatement of Yankee anxieties, Grant's army could transform emancipation from a mere proclamation into a military weapon of immense effectiveness.

If the abandoning of plantations helped to reduce disaffection in the North by offering the possibility of housing in the South for former slaves, it had precisely the opposite effect on Southern morale. Planters who fled could not avoid reinforcing the impression that the affluent were abandoning the national cause in its extremity. Slaves transported away were unavailable to work to strengthen Vicksburg fortifications or to produce desperately needed food. Emancipation, in effect, virtually sealed the doom of the Confederate garrison at Vicksburg.

P. A. Willis, in Holly Springs, wrote a vivid account, castigating the Yankees for "making war on women and children, stealing and destroying every species of property, running off two-thirds of the negroes in the county, and burning houses." In a letter to Samuel E. Carey on February 3, 1863, Willis enumerated the blacks freed by the "fiends in blue coats." He himself had "lost every negro" and "every negro of Mr. Walter's left, even Harry." "But, Oh God, Carey, the poor suffering planters makes my heart bleed—in this whole county, all is gone—corn, fodder, flour, all their provisions, all their stock, wagons, teams, vehicles of every description—Fences and Negroes." R. L. Dixon, a planter from Greenville, Mississippi, wrote in March of the thoroughly efficient foraging by Northern soldiers on his own plantation: "They stole all the fowls, about 100 hogs and shoats, all my mules . . . drove off all my stock of every kind and sheep. They did not leave a hoof on my place, not even a milk cow." On the Louisiana side of the river, Kate Stone wrote in her diary, "The negroes on Mrs. Stevens', Mr. Conlet's, Mr. Catlin's and Mr. Evans' place ran off the camp, and returned with squads of soldiers and wagons and moved off every portable thing—furniture, provisions, etc." Although Sherman's attempt to lead a mixed naval and infantry force around Vicksburg proved unworkable, in April Grant proclaimed Sherman's Deer Creek expedition a signal success because it "carried our troops into the heart of the granary from which the Vicksburg forces are fed. . . . The citizens fled from their plantations. . . . Much of their beef, bacon and poultry was consumed by our troops. . . . Several hundred negroes also returned with the troops." "At least three of my army corps commanders take hold of the new policy of arming the negroes and using them against the enemy with a will." Slavery could not survive such losses for long.[24]

Some bold slaves, under the stimulus of emancipation, sought vengeance on their former owners. Kate Stone visited a neighbor's plantation to find the owner spread-eagled on the ground and cowering beneath loaded guns wielded by three blacks. They spared his life but broke into his home, "ranging all through his house, cursing, laughing and breaking open things." After a two-hour siege, the slaves allowed the terrified Stone family to go home, but there they stumbled on a similar scene; their home too was occupied by armed black strangers. "They had gathered from the neighboring places. They did not say anything, but they looked at us and grinned and that terrified us more and more. It held such promise of evil." Shortly after midnight the next day, the Stone family stole away from their plantation and fled to the temporary safety of the swamps. "All the servants behaved well enough except Webster, but you could see it was only because they knew we would soon be gone. We were only on sufferance."[25]

With planters fleeing precipitously, the burden of supplying laborers for fortifications work fell even more heavily on less affluent slaveholders. John Taylor, who described himself as a small slaveholder with only three able-bodied field hands, told Pettus bitterly, "There are a great many who has their negroes idle or running away from the enemy who could furnish some for the good of the country." A. S. Moyers, the head of the militia in Brandon, Mississippi, answering Governor Pettus's call for an emergency muster, responded on July 12 with a stark warning that "the country is in great commotion. Large numbers are leaving with their negroes, etc. Impossible to assemble militia. . . . Shall I make the call anyway?" In August the editor of the *Shreveport Semi-Weekly News* wrote bluntly what many poorer Southerners felt as they watched affluent neighbors flee: "Already we hear of persons making preparations to leave this place with their negroes. This is patriotism—with a vengeance."[26]

Residents of the areas toward which slaveholder refugees headed with their slave labor often hesitated to receive the newcomers. The Reverend Samuel Agnew wrote from northeastern Mississippi, "The neighbors South are holding meetings and passing petitions declaring they will not permit the swarms of negroes now going South to settle among them and impoverish their country." The Stone family itself encountered significant hostility when they took up refuge later near Tyler, Texas. "They call us all *renegades* in Tyler. It is strange the prejudice that exists all through the State against refugees. We think it envy, just pure envy." Charles Ramsdell is certainly correct in arguing that emancipation "had the effect of making the war, which on the Southern side began as a effort to save the people from invasion, now appear as one to save the property of the slaveholder."[27]

"Sacrificing Their Country for Lucre": Cash Crops versus Food Crops

In February 1863, when Northern troops pillaged James Alcorn's Yazoo River plantation, Alcorn wrote to his wife Amelia that he was using Confederate currency to purchase land in Greene County, Alabama, and his wife should do the same in paying off debts to her neighbors. He had little faith in the security of Southern money; "real money" was a different matter. Said Alcorn to his wife, "Hold on to your Gold as you cling to dear life." "In relation to your farming, you had best put in as much cotton as possible. You need not listen to what others say, plant corn to do you and the balance in cotton." "The war can't last twelve months longer and cotton at the close of the war will be worth a dollar a pound in good money." In the end, Alcorn's refusal to heed the dictates of patriotism reaped substantial fruits, for he survived the war with enough "good money" on hand to stave off a postwar tax sale of his father-in-law's Alabama plantation.[28]

As rumors spread about the large numbers of slaveholders like Alcorn who were planning to plant cash crops not food crops, the *Milledgeville Confederate Union* published a stinging editorial on January 20, 1863: "The planters of Alabama, Georgia, Florida and the Carolinas hold the fate of their country in their hands. To them much is given, and of them much is required." "If they do not plant very heavy crops of corn the present year, we can only see starvation and subjugation ahead." Patriotic duty required planters in relatively safe areas of the interior to "furnish supplies not only for the armies in the field but for the people of all of the Confederacy." Once it became clear that planters intended to repeat their performance during the 1862 subsistence crisis and plant cotton instead of corn, Alabama governor Shorter responded, "The enemy cannot conquer us in battle—but famine would disband our armies. . . . Here is our greatest danger." "The Army must be fed. . . . The slave labor of the country must be devoted to the reproduction of essential provisions." Four days later, Shorter issued a ringing "proclamation to the planters of Alabama," urging planters in the strongest possible terms to forswear cotton production for the patriotic duty of growing food to feed the army and the civilian population.[29]

General Pemberton informed Secretary of War James Seddon in January that "experience has proven to me the impracticability of preventing the illicit trade [selling cotton to the North]. . . . It is a matter of deep regret, it is nonetheless true, that pecuniary interest has shown itself to be the very first consideration of a large proportion of those to whom the fortunes of war has given the opportunity to dispose of the great staple." Another letter from Pemberton to Seddon, in April, told the sad tale of his frustrating struggle: "There is great difficulty in suppressing the illicit trade in this Department. The enemy is in possession of the country on three sides of us and the citizens for the most part do not seem to see the wrong that is done in obtaining from the enemy articles which they think they greatly need." Also, in early January 1863 General Joseph E. Johnston said in a letter to Davis, "We have not *food enough* here if the *enemy* is *vigorous.*" A note to Alabama's Senator Clay from an Edward D. Tracy said of arrangements at the Vicksburg post: "The meat ration has already been virtually discontinued, the quality being such that the men utterly refuse to eat it." "Morally speaking, of course, a man is under an imperative obligation to be as patriotic and valiant when he is empty as full, but practically considered your lean and hungry soldiers are no more to be depended on than Julius Caesar thought Cassius." In an aside, Tracy concluded, "No matter how reliable they might be, after a few days fast, they would cease to be valuable."[30]

To the editor of the *Arkansas True Democrat,* planters were the chief offenders among speculators fattening themselves on the blood of poorer Southerners. He accused planters of "sacrificing their country for lucre"; he had received incontrovertible proof that planters seeking to maximize profits had withheld foodstuffs from the market at the same time that they were refusing to provide subsistence to the families of poorer soldiers. A group of Confederate commissary officers accused selfish slaveholders of bringing the Confederacy to the very brink of defeat. "We are about to be conquered, not by Lincoln's troops, but by far more dangerous domestic enemies." The *Milledgeville Confederate Union,* an influential voice in the Lower South, said in a piercing editorial, "The cry for bread is heard from every section." With the effects of the 1862 subsistence crisis still evident, the paper warned that slaveholders' selfish behavior courted vengeance by the poor: "The war is fought for the rich by the poor and the poor must be fed. If the law making power will not protect the families of the soldiers, may we not fear the soldiers will come home and supply themselves from the barns and the smoke houses of the rich?" Brigadier General Stephen D. Lee wrote to Major J. J. Reeve: "The planters and negroes are much demoralized along the Mississippi River, and from what I can learn large cotton crops are being planted by men who are regarded as above suspicion. On some of the places the negroes are almost in a state of insurrection." "It is very difficult," Lee said, "to get reliable information from the river, owning to the demoralization and the fear of property."[31]

President Davis delayed as long as he dared before focusing the glare of public condemnation on slaveholders who gave priority to cash crops. "If through a confidence in early peace, which may prove delusive, our fields should be now devoted to the production of cotton and tobacco instead of grain and livestock, and other articles necessary for the subsistence of the people and the Army," Davis warned in an address "to the Southern people" on April 10, 1863, "the consequences may prove serious, if not disastrous, especially should the present season prove as unfavorable as the last." He urged planters to "lay aside all thought of gain," and he condemned "the attempt of groveling speculators to forestall the market and make money out of the lifeblood of our defenders." "Even if the surplus be less than is believed," he said, "is it not a bitter and humiliating reflection that those who remain at home, secure from hardship and protected from danger, should be in the enjoyment of abundance, and that their slaves also should have a full supply of food, while their sons, brothers, husbands, and fathers are stinted in the rations on which their health and efficiency depend?"[32] The juxtaposition of a reference to abundant diets for slaves and stinted rations for the army was the sharpest possible rebuke of avaricious planters.

Executions of Conscript Deserters and Erosion of Discipline in Military Ranks

In the district of Arkansas, in the summer of 1862, General Thomas Hindman executed scores of conscript deserters in a vain attempt to salvage decaying discipline. Later, in December, Hindman ordered unarmed draftees to charge Northern positions, with their unloaded guns and their bodies as their only weapons; he had heard that these soldiers had refused "to fight the national flag." During the battle some soldiers, in Robert L. Kerby's words, "charged and died with empty muskets in the hands"; others deserted rather than participate in suicidal combat, and "a regiment of Arkansas Confederates went over to the enemy." By the time General Edmund Kirby Smith assumed command of the Trans-Mississippi Department in February 1863, more than half of Hindman's Arkansans had deserted. In eastern Louisiana, in mid-May, Kirby Smith disbanded Lieutenant Colonel Joseph Warren Speight's Texas brigade because "the command is an undisciplined mob, the officers are as worthless as the men, and without material in the ranks for supplying their places." Speight himself described his men as "worthless, unreliable, and to some extent disloyal." Kirby Smith distributed the least disloyal remnants of Speight's brigade among other commands. Major General Richard Taylor received some of these tainted reinforcements, and although Kirby Smith had taken pains to send him the best of what remained from the brigade, Taylor had difficulty getting his troops to join the effort to raise the siege at Vicksburg.[33]

Pemberton, finding a vigorous system to get deserters back increasingly necessary, asked Brigadier General Wirt Adams to dispatch a cavalry company to the area around Jackson to round up a group of deserters. From

Brigadier General James Chalmers came a report that he had "collected a company of General Van Dorn's command, near the area around Panola." In northeast Georgia the numbers of deserters and resisters grew so large that a company of state militia was dispatched, so Captain W. W. Porter wrote to Pemberton, to "scour the mountains for the arrest of deserters and other persons . . . inciting rebellion." A local newspaper reported that "the deserters have nearly, if not all, returned to the army, whilst the disloyalists, if there are any left find it best to keep still." The presence of armed state militia did prompt several hundred men to volunteer rather than face conscription, but J. F. White, an officer from the inspector general's office in Richmond who visited Mississippi in mid-April 1863, protested that such men "will not be of any service to the Confederacy for these companies were raised near the Enemy's lines and will desert if they have an opportunity." A distressing message came to the Vicksburg quartermaster from the superintendent of the Southern Railroad, Major L. Morris: "The troops sent from here yesterday to Big Black Bridge refused to leave the train on their arrival there compelling the Engineer and Conductor to move on to Vicksburg so as to get a siding to allow other trains to pass on." An overnight stay in Vicksburg failed to mollify these recalcitrant transfers. "They leave Vicksburg for Big Black Bridge but I am informed they occasion the greatest delay by a general determination not to leave the train."[34]

On April 3, 1863, a mass desertion occurred among a regiment of Mississippi state troops that was being moved toward the combat zone. "The Lt. in charge of the guard policing the camp and also said guard have been placed under arrest," reported Brigadier General J. V. Harris: "Charges will be preferred." Word of this incident reached Pemberton quickly when Brigadier General Daniel Ruggles sent a message that "some eighty men . . . deserted here last night, carrying arms and equipment, seizing a ferry boat some distance above the town and crossing the Tombigbee River about one o'clock A. M." That *"these desertions took place under marching orders"* was quite distressing; so was the direct connection between desertion and disaffection. "It is with regret," Ruggles reported, "that it has become my duty to state that there is a general and apparently well-founded conviction that a portion at least of the 4th Mississippi State Troops now in Confederate service have become so demoralized from various causes and influences that they are unreliable for service requiring prompt and energetic action." In an aside that was a harbinger of the morale problems ahead, he said, "To what extent this disaffection has gone is not yet clearly manifest."[35]

The demoralization of soldiers and civilians was to play a significant role in both the timing and the terms of Vicksburg's surrender. Grant would exploit such disaffection after the surrender of Vicksburg when he agreed to parole the Southern army rather than make them prisoners of war. He sent toward home thirty thousand demoralized ambassadors of disaffection.

Informants, Spies, and Slaves Aiding the Union Command

Grant's fourth offensive cemented his place in the annals of military history; his maneuvering demanded the nerves of a high-stakes gambler, the organization of a logistics magician, and the skill of a consummate strategist. Having failed either to bombard Vicksburg into submission or to overwhelm it from the northeast, and thwarted in efforts to find a secure water route around the city, Northern forces had to embark on a spectacular strategic ploy or abandon the campaign to open the Mississippi altogether. Grant left his base camps and swung his entire army around Vicksburg's western, southern, and eastern perimeters in a daring move that put the Northern army astride the city's overland supply link. His commanding position then forced Pemberton into a siege that would produce a climactic Northern victory. Grant took an army of fifty thousand soldiers on a forced march through more than fifty miles of unmapped Louisiana marshland and moved this huge force across the rain-swollen Mississippi to flank the Confederate army before Pemberton could react, at the same time keeping his own army supplied from their Union base camps. It was one of the stellar campaigns in all military history.[36]

How was Grant able to overcome obstacles similar to those that had befuddled George McClellan during the Peninsula Campaign? James McPherson explains, "Operating amid a hostile population, the Union army was at a distinct disadvantage in the matter of military intelligence." The network of Southern country roads had never been mapped, and "only local knowledge could guide troops along these roads, many of which ran through thick woods that could shield the movement from an enemy but where a wrong turn could get a division hopelessly lost." As it turned out, the necessary local knowledge was supplied; a continuous flow of essential military intelligence arrived from disaffected Southern citizens. One paid Southern informant made it possible for Colonel Benjamin Grierson to execute his famous cavalry raid, which helped conceal Grant's whereabouts during the most delicate phase of his flanking maneuver. Significant credit for the Grierson raid, which severed telegraph lines and cut road links north of Vicksburg, must go to the author of a "secret report" sold to Grierson by a Southerner in January 1863, apparently for fifty dollars. "This report," according to Carroll S. Root, "described routes by which a cavalry column might move through Mississippi, locations of well-stocked plantations, Confederate warehouses, the varying loyalties of the people in different sections of the State, the probable presence of guerillas, the geography of the country, and the distance between towns."[37]

Likewise, a Southern double agent's information provided advance warning to Grant of a surprise attack, permitting him to turn the tables on Pemberton and Johnston at the battles of Clinton and Champion's Hill. An officer in the 75th New York Infantry, William Root, in his diary for April 5, told of one such incident: "An 'Intelligent Contraband' [runaway slave] came into our lines, and reported that Captain Fuller . . . was coming down to attack us, so we were ordered up there to be ready." And when Captain Frank Crawford, a "commissary of subsistence," returned from a successful foraging expedition around Vicksburg with 136 cattle and 700 bushels of corn, he explained to his superior, Captain G. J. Taggart: "I was informed at various points on the river that the inhabitants had removed large quantities of their produce to a distance . . . into the country for the purpose of preventing the Union army from obtaining the same. This information was obtained from contrabands and is I believe reliable."[38]

Some of the information from contraband intelligence moved up the Union chain of command with impressive speed. On March 26, 1863, Colonel Charles Abbott dispatched to Grant's headquarters an urgent message along with seven blacks "who came over from Vicksburg last night. . . . The men are bright and intelligent, and can give a great deal of information in regard to the condition of affairs at Vicksburg. One of them has been in the artillery service since the war and can tell you the position and number of almost every gun from Vicksburg around to Warrenton." The group brought along copies of "yesterday's Vicksburg and Jackson papers." The men demanded compensation, but "they desire to go North." The next day Grant passed this information on to his superior, the Northern general in chief, Henry W. Halleck: "I get papers and deserters frequently from Vicksburg"; "I have just learned from a reliable source that most of the forces from Vicksburg are now up the Yazoo, leaving not 10,000 in the city today. . . . I have no doubt of the truth of the information because it is substantiated by Southern papers and by deserters."[39]

General G. W. Dodge, writing from Corinth, Mississippi, in May 1863, asked Grant's adjutant for advice on Secret Service funds for behind-the-lines intelligence: "There are citizens living in the South who give us the most valuable information that will not sign a voucher for fear of consequences in the future and I have to pay them considerable money." "It is important for me to keep these men about their homes, they work for money." For their part, the Confederates missed a golden opportunity to foil Grant's elaborate plan when a Union courier who had deserted from Sherman's army, as W. H. Tunnard told it, "gave the information that the enemy was not strong enough to assault our works, and that the movement was a mere feint to keep our forces occupied, and to prevent their reinforcing the army at Grand Gulf, where a formidable demonstration was being made by General Grant to land his troops." Unfortunately for the Confederate force, "the information was not credited at the time" and apparently never reached Pemberton's ears.[40]

With Confederate fortifications guarding the two principal river crossings south of Vicksburg, Grant devised a plan whereby Porter's gunboats would run past the Vicksburg river batteries to silence the artillery, but ten hours of heavy pounding failed to knock out a single Southern gun. If Grant were to land his army at an impassible point, his bridgehead could become a trap. His experience at Shiloh had shown him the dangers of being trapped with a rain-swollen river at one's rear, but just at this most critical juncture, information from a runaway slave showed him a way out. "A negro man came in who informed me," Grant recalled later, "that a good landing would be found at Bruinsburg . . . from which point there was a good road leading to Port Gibson some twelve miles in the interior. The information was found correct, and our landing was effected without opposition." With typical understatement Grant wrote, "The move to Bruinsburg undoubtedly took the enemy much by surprise." Grant could move with the assurance of a native defending his home soil because black and white Southerners shared their intimate knowledge of local terrain with him. Such information enabled him to adopt the kind of tactics employed so successfully by Lee and Jackson in the Virginia theater, dividing his forces to make long sweeping runs around the enemy. Grant seized on this advantage to gain an element of tactical surprise he never relinquished.[41]

Pemberton, Johnston, and Davis struggled to develop a strategy to turn back Grant's bold moves, but as in perhaps no other major campaign, the glaring absence of a Southern command system was to exert a profound influence on the outcome of battle. In late 1862 Davis had appointed Johnston supreme commander in the west, but he failed to make Johnston's authority over departmental commanders explicit, and Pemberton and Braxton Bragg were left unsure whether the primary command responsibility was held by Johnston or by the War Department in Richmond. Confused lines of authority and responsibility led in turn to indecision and vacillation, and Davis found himself having to act as arbiter across a distance of almost a thousand miles. Also, Pemberton was a foil in a bitter personal rivalry between Davis and Johnston, with Davis in favor of defending certain key positions at all costs, and Johnston for avoiding decisive conflicts in favor of piecemeal engagements. Pemberton saw eye to eye with Davis on the need to hold Vicksburg, even if a siege was the result.[42]

How much responsibility did Pemberton bear for the debacle at Vicksburg? One possible answer can be found by comparing his performance with Lee's reaction to Grant's maneuvers in the aftermath of Cold Harbor. Lee had been forced into defending an elongated perimeter, much as Pemberton had been by Sherman's presence north of Vicksburg. Lee waited patiently for Grant to reveal his plans; in the interim, Grant executed a brilliant strategic coup to lay siege to the Confederate capital. Grant's tactics at Richmond resembled his at Vicksburg, and Lee's reaction resembled Pemberton's. In both instances, Grant bought valuable time by diversionary raids; in both instances, he moved large armies across major rivers deep in the heart of Southern territory. Pemberton, under the circumstances, may well have done the best he could.

Private Osborn H. Oldroyd, of the 20th Ohio Infantry, in May 1863 captured the exuberant confidence now reverberating throughout the army of the North on its march toward Jackson: "The enemy are doing all they can to hinder us, but let Grant say *forward* and we obey." Such élan stood in stark contrast to the bitter cynicism that enveloped Southern troops under Pemberton's command. William Claiborne, the aide serving on the staff of Major General Carter Stevenson, saw clearly what would happen if Grant seized Jackson: "With the railroad in possession of the enemy and supplies cut off, the fate of Vicksburg, if not a matter of certainty, will scarcely be more than a question of time." "Dark clouds hover around us and I fear for Mississippi." "As for the imbecile at Jackson [Pemberton] who holds as it was the fate of Mississippi in his hands," Claiborne wrote in his diary, "a halter is almost too good for him."[43]

Many Southern units fought stalwartly during that critical fortnight, but many other regiments were reluctant to fight. During the pivotal engagement at Champion's Hill, many broke and ran, precipitating a rout sealing the fate of Vicksburg. A Southern double agent further compromised Southern chances at Champion's Hill by giving Grant advance warning about Pemberton's and Johnston's plans to isolate a Northern corps and join in piecemeal assaults against Grant's widely scattered forces. Back in January, Arkansas governor Harris Flanagin, begging Davis not to transfer newly conscripted Arkansas troops across the Mississippi, had warned, "There is already in the Army East of the Mississippi a very large proportion of the active Southern element, and those remaining on this side as a mass are less devoted to Southern rights in the first instance and less disposed as well as less capable of defending them in the second." "In the early stages of this war the fighting men were enlisted and went across the Mississippi; those remaining left are comparatively peace men." Flanagin acknowledged that Arkansas troops "now in service on the East side of the Mississippi, should this State be overrun, in a great number will desert in order to protect their property and families as far as they can."[44]

Surrender of a Demoralized Army

Having abandoned his heavy supply train to live off the land, Grant could move quickly to capture Jackson, sever the rail link between Jackson and Vicksburg, and block Pemberton's escape route back into Vicksburg. Marching the bulk of his force out of Vicksburg to try to cover as many bases as possible, Pemberton hoped to lure Grant into attacking on ground that Pemberton had chosen, but the plan ran afoul of Davis's frantic directive that Pemberton and Johnston unite to defeat Grant before he could reestablish communications with base camps north of the city. Davis pressed Johnston to strike as quickly as possible, a plan that appealed to Johnston's preference for fighting the enemy in detail rather than in a single decisive engagement. On May 13 Johnston notified Pemberton, "if practicable," to come up in the rear of Sherman's corps between the two Southern armies. "Time is all important." But Pemberton, complaining that Johnston "did not fully comprehend the position that Vicksburg will be left in," waited two days before committing himself to join with Johnston before attacking Sherman's isolated corps.[45]

A successful combined assault by Confederate forces against Sherman might well have forced Grant to pause, giving Southern forces time to bring in reinforcements. Indeed, so high were the risks Grant took that a major repulse might even have cost him his command of the Army of the Tennessee. But Pemberton committed two grave tactical errors, not only by temporizing for over a day, then summoning a council of war to poll his generals, but also by not abandoning his line of retreat back into Vicksburg. He set his army on a path headed south of Jackson instead of north, as Johnston had asked. Had everything else remained static, Pemberton's errors might not have been pivotal, but everything else did not remain static.

A Southern double agent made the difference. Johnston had trusted three couriers to reach Pemberton with his request for a coordinated attack, but one, a Southerner from Memphis, was loyal to the Union. To provide a convincing cover story, the commander of the Northern forces occupying Memphis had contrived a great show of expelling the man for his Southern sympathies; the tactic took in the Southern command completely, and the courier had worked his way into a position of trust in the Confederate army. He took a copy of Johnston's original order and Pemberton's reply and set forth, presumably to Johnston's headquarters. Instead, as an aide-de-camp to Grant recounted later, "The national spy . . . brought it direct to McPherson, and McPherson forwarded both dispatch and messenger to Grant." Grant directed Sherman to strike at Johnston's forces, and Johnston retreated north out of Jackson, whereupon Grant moved swiftly westward toward Vicksburg, encountering Pemberton's forces at Champion's Hill. There, several regiments of raw Georgia recruits, caught in the open by veteran volunteers, broke and ran, followed by other conscripts who saw them turn and run, and soon General Stevenson sent word he could hold no longer.[46]

At Big Black Bridge, Southern fortifications had been erected to foil a cavalry raid not an infantry assault, and the battle was even more disastrous than the engagement at Champion's Hill. Pemberton's dispirited troops fell back into Vicksburg. A Northern soldier who participated in the assault, Robert G. Shrcey, wrote in a letter of May 18 (later found in his clothing after he was killed) to his brother that some Confederate prisoners had told him "that they were deceived and the southern Confederacy would soon be played out." A civilian resident of Vicksburg, Dana Miller, was shocked at what she witnessed that day: "I shall never forget the woeful sight of a beaten, demoralized army that came rushing back—humanity in the last throes of endurance. Wan, hollow-eyed, ragged, footsore, bloody, the men limped along unarmed, but followed by siege guns, ambulances, gun carriages, and wagons in aimless confusion."[47]

Vicksburg's defeat came with awful suddenness and lingered for what seemed an eternity, a forty-seven-day siege after a disorderly retreat. After two attempts to take the city failed, Grant settled down to the task of wearing out the defense, shelling the city incessantly. Eventually, in July, once it grew clear that Johnston could not force Grant to lift the siege, Pemberton surrendered his thirty thousand soldiers. In trying to explain to Johnston his decision to disobey a direct order to remove the army from Vicksburg, Pemberton offered perhaps the best explanation why he had accepted so long a siege. After a council of war to consider Johnston's order to withdraw, Pemberton and his general staff had concluded unanimously, "It was impossible to withdraw the army from this position with such morale and material as to be of further service to the Confederacy."

The demise of slavery was at the core of this eroding process of defeat and disillusionment. Slaveholders were engaged in protecting their own interests; numbers of slaves had run to Northern camps, and the proximity of Northern detachments had undermined any remaining slave discipline. A Wisconsin artilleryman, Jenkin Lloyd Jones, engaged in reconnaissance patrols along the Coldwater River north of Vicksburg, had encountered numerous groups of slaves in April of that year: "An occasional darkey to be seen with mule and plow in the fields, but in most cases the darkey had 'hung up the hoe.'" Alfred Quine, overseer at Benjamin Wailes's Fonsylvania plantation, wrote in his plantation journal:

> May 9, 1863—Grate confusion. . . . Holiday in the evening no Yankees come yet.

> May 11, 1863—So much confusion today cant tell what was dun. Some little plowing and hoeing of corn.

> May 12, 1863—Confusion and excitement today. Some little plowing and hoeing of corn today.

> May 22, 1863—So much confusion today not mutch work dun

> May 25, 1863—All hands went to work and worked up to 12 O'Clock and the Yankees came and set the negroes all free and the work all stopped

> May 26, 1863—Negroes all free No work dun

> June 1, 1863—Negroes all riding about and doing nothing

> June 4, 1863—Some of the negroes went to working out corn on their own

> June 5, 1863—Negroes all forlican [frolicking]

> June 5, 1863—Holiday all the time now with the negroes.[48]

From his older brother Joseph, who remained with Johnston throughout the Vicksburg siege, Jefferson Davis received a series of graphic letters revealing the decomposition of Southern society and culture. Writing on June 17, Joseph criticized both Pemberton and Johnston for their inability to inspire confidence among the soldiers. "Our army will therefore moan under the feeling being whipped, under this impression I wish to move what I can to some place east of Pearl River. . . . The negroes that are here are listless and seem unwilling to do anything." On June 21 Joseph wrote, "Affairs here are depressing—the greatly superior force of the enemy, and no certainty of reinforcements, has produced a feeling of alarm, and flight is on the countenance of most that you meet; and the prospect of the country east is but little better." Nor was the mood good among the common soldiers. James Shelton, serving with Johnston's force near Yazoo City, wrote to his wife Emily, describing the area as "a rich landed country and I suppose rich people live in it." "There is one thing I am sure of they are a very selfish people they think all soldiers ought to support themselves and the Confederacy support its own armies and not bother them or anything they have." "Fight its own battles and let they stay at home and make all they can by speculation or any other way they choose and I dont think they are very conscious of how they do it."[49]

The state of discipline among the troops outside Vicksburg may well offer the key to the paradox of the Vicksburg siege: Johnston's conspicuous failure to make any attempt to rescue Pemberton. Morale had held up inside Vicksburg primarily because of hopes that Johnston would create an exit. Johnston never did launch an attack, despite Davis's frantic attempts to reinforce him for that very purpose. The acerbic relationship between Johnston and his commander in chief was a factor, but perhaps most telling was the unexplained absence without leave of thousands of Southern troops. Davis had scoured the Confederacy for troops to send to Johnston to lift the siege, but desertions on the way left these regiments significantly weaker on their arrival in Mississippi than they had been on their departure. Neither Davis nor Johnston seemed aware of this, hence the disparity between Davis's reckoning of the numbers dispatched to Johnston and Johnston's count of those on hand and ready for duty.

Davis engaged in a testy correspondence on the matter with Johnston throughout these trying weeks. One week after Pemberton retreated into the city, Davis told Johnston, "The disparity of numbers renders prolonged defense dangerous. I hope you will soon be able to break the investment. Make a junction and throw in munitions." Three days later, Johnston sent a fierce response: "We cannot break the investment without an army. . . . When all the reinforcements arrive shall have but 23,000. Tell me if additional troops can be furnished." Davis spotted a glaring inconsistency in Johnston's reckoning; "The reinforcements sent you exceed by, say 7,000, the estimate of your dispatch. . . . We have witheld nothing which it was practicable to give. We cannot hope for numerical equality and time will probably increase the disparity." Johnston insisted, "Pemberton can be saved only by beating Grant. Unless you can promise more troops, we must try with that number. The odds against us are very great. Can you not add 7,000?" Davis shot back a heated reply: "The Secretary of War reports the reinforcements ordered to you as greater than the number you request. . . . He states your whole force to be 34,000, exclusive of militia." Johnston, apparently stunned by Davis's thinly veiled accusation that he was undercounting his troops in order to avoid attack, ordered a new tally, but the recount showed an effective force of 25,000, not the 34,000 Davis claimed. When Davis disputed the new report, Johnston replied: "The Secretary of War is greatly mistaken in his numbers. The total of the above is 24,100."[50]

Nothing but massive numbers of desertions would seem to explain the disparity in these figures. Edwin Hedge Fay, who had served in a Louisiana infantry regiment sent from the Army of Tennessee to reinforce Johnston, said his regiment had encountered a company that "had run away and come down here and were going across the river to Louisiana. All had deserted but 4 men I believe. Capt. [William] Harrison was endeavoring to get Gen'l Johnston's consent but if not said he was going anyhow. They have effectually played out I think." And from the 4th Mississippi Cavalry, more than two hundred men—including two officers and eighteen noncommissioned officers—learning that they were bound for duty with Johnston, deserted in one June week.[51]

Grant knew that hunger alone might compel surrender. "Deserters come out daily. All report rations short." Pemberton had reduced the rations to prolong the time his army could wait for a relieving force, but reports of civilian hoarding promoted more grumbling within the ranks. General Kirby Smith urged Pemberton to undertake an accounting of "the quantity of provisions in the hands of dealers and if necessary provisions [should be] searched out and held subject to governmental control." "The impression is that a considerable quantity of flour etc. held by speculators may be hid away, thus lost to the cause unless such steps be taken." Supplies of potable water were also scarce, and the captain of a ranger company urged Pemberton to seize control of all private cisterns and wells, but Pemberton demurred, on the advice of a staff officer that "should orders be issued in accordance with the writer's request—no citizen would have sufficient water for his family." "The troops in the trenches are drinking water from the river, which has always been considered excellent water."[52]

Arson, too, demonstrated the alienation between Vicksburg's yeoman defenders and its affluent residents. Emma Balfour recorded one such fire in her diary for June 2: "It is the third fire that has taken place in that neighborhood and is doubtless the work of an incendiary." The Louisiana soldier W. H. Tunnard echoed her suspicions. "Last night a large fire occurred in the city, the result of incendiarism, destroying several buildings." Of the same event, Private Hugh Moss wrote that the fire had destroyed "flour, sugar and other articles that the poor soldiers ought to have had."[53]

A steady flow of desertions proceeded toward the Northern lines. One Union private, Isaac Jackson, wrote "that Deserters from there daily say they will have to give it up." During a truce called to allow Northern soldiers to bury their dead, Jackson noticed that large numbers of Southern soldiers, seeing an opportunity, deserted. "The rebels came out of their forts and had a talk with our boys. A great many never went back. They say they will have to give up." "Not a circumstance transpired within our lines," he said, "that the enemy did not know and they were informed of the true condition of affairs, knowing full well and confidently expecting, that the gaunt skeleton of famine, then seizing the besieged forces, would ultimately prove the conqueror."

Confederates discovered that their incomplete fortifications would not allow an exchange of fire with Northerners shielded by well-constructed entrenchments. The surgeon Dr. James Dill Allison described the situation as "desperate." "No place of safety," he wrote; "if you stand still there is danger from the pieces of shell that fill the air, if you move the danger becomes greater. . . . The air is filled with missiles of destruction." A combination of factors had undermined morale inside the garrison: exposure to sudden death, hunger, a lack of confidence in Pemberton, and corrosive disaffection among backcountry conscripts. "Provisions scarce and men put on ¼ rations from the first day arrived," William Claiborne recorded in his diary. "Now they dont even get that much. . . . Many of the troops—especially the Georgians—much demoralized by repeated defeats and the fact that no confidence exists in the ability of the Cmdg. Genl. of this Dept. Lt. General Pemberton."

A Missouri volunteer said of the fighting spirit of one ravenously hungry Mississippi conscript: "The location of his patriotism could not be mistaken and there were some others like him."[54]

Pemberton finally surrendered the Vicksburg garrison on July 4, 1863. Only dire circumstances could have compelled him to yield so great a victory on the national birthday. Pemberton gained from Grant the surprising agreement that the Army of Mississippi be allowed to march out of the city, on their parole of honor not to fight again until each man was properly exchanged. There had been many acts of heroism and patriotism on both sides. Claiborne's diary recorded the death of a first cousin, Captain Ferdinand Claiborne, from a Northern mortar shell. Shortly after his cousin's funeral, Claiborne reflected that "a nobler, kinder, truer heart never ceased to beat—a braver spirit never winged its flight from Earth. But he fell as he wished to fall—at the point of duty, with his face to the foe, on his native soil, and in defense of a cause he dearly loved."[55]

Such a poignant evocation of the spirit of duty formed an eloquent counterpoint to an anonymous note thrust beneath General Pemberton's door on July 1, three days after Captain Claiborne's death, a note that was evidently a crucial factor in Pemberton's decision to surrender. Signed "Many Soldiers," the letter congratulated Pemberton for his generalship and then got down to hard cases. "We are actually on suffrance, and the consequence is, as far as I can hear, there is complaint and general dissatisfaction throughout our lines." "Men dont want to starve and dont intend to, but call upon you for justice, if the commissary department can give it; if it can't, you must adopt some means to relieve us soon. . . . If you can't feed us," said the anonymous writers, "you had better surrender us, horrible as the idea is, than suffer this noble army to disgrace themselves by desertion. I tell you plainly, men are not going to lie here and perish, if they do love their country dearly. Self-preservation is the first law of nature, and hunger will compel a man to do almost anything." The letter closed with a blunt warning. "The army is now ripe for mutiny, unless it can be fed. . . . see if I have not stated the stubborn facts, which had better be heeded before we are disgraced." Pemberton did take heed of the letter and, two days later, wrote the following note to his divisional commanders:

Unless the siege of Vicksburg is raised or supplies are thrown in, it will be necessary very shortly to evacuate the place. I see no prospect of the former, and there are very great, if not insuperable, obstacles in the way of the latter. You are, therefore, requested to inform me with as little delay as possible, as to the condition of your troops, and their ability to make the marches and undergo the fatigues necessary to accomplish a successful evacuation.[56]

The general staff concluded that surrender was their only viable option. Major General John S. Bowen inspected his men and reported, "I am satisfied they cannot give battle and march over 10 or 12 miles in the same day." If Johnston could not lift the siege, "I see no alternative," Bowen said, "but to endeavor to rescue the command by making terms with the enemy." Major General Martin L. Smith offered the bluntest assessment: "A secret evacuation I consider almost impossible, on account of the temper of many in my command. . . . I would really expect the enemy to become aware of the movement before my command had cleared the right of our line." Smith's men would continue to resist a direct assault on their fortifications, but demoralization had sapped their fighting spirit. "I do not think they would do as well out of them and in the field."[57]

Grant and Pemberton's initial face-to-face meeting to discuss surrender was testy, but subordinates worked out terms that would spare the Southern army the losses of a frontal assault and a Northern army prison camp. Grant agreed to parole the army rather than ship them to such camps, violating General Halleck's direct orders. One of those involved in the discussions, Assistant Secretary of War Charles Dana, wrote of Grant's decision for parole not imprisonment, "In its favor was urged that it [i.e., having to imprison so many Confederate soldiers] would at once demoralize Grant's whole army for offensive operations, while to guard and transport so many prisoners would require a great portion of [our army's] strength." Grant was gambling that Confederate demoralization would render moot Halleck's fears about a speedy return of the Army of Mississippi to active service.[58]

A report to the Confederate ordnance department by Eugene Hill, an ordnance messenger trapped in Vicksburg, denied that hunger had played a role in the defeat: "There were 90,000 lbs of Bacon and Pork when the surrender took place. Officers and men of General Shoup's Brigade threw away their arms." The chief ordnance officer, Josiah Gorgas, pointed out to Secretary of War Seddon: "I think it worthwhile to call attention to the inexplicable abandonment of surplus arms and ordnance stores. These should have at all events been destroyed, before the surrender." On entering Vicksburg Grant found "considerable ammunition and about four days' rations of flour and bacon and 250 pounds of sugar. The small arms are of good quality and over 50,000 in number." The abandonment of so many rifles points to a hasty surrender.

After Vicksburg's surrender on July 4, and the victory at Gettysburg on July 3, Grant proposed a line of policy to his congressional patron, Illinois representative Elisha Washburne. Many Northerners were now speculating about the terms Confederates might seek in return for a negotiated peace, and Washburne was concerned that the South might demand Union renunciation of emancipation. "The people of the North need not quarrel over the institution of slavery," Grant wrote. "What Vice President Stephens acknowledges the cornerstone of the Confederacy is already knocked out. Slavery is dead and cannot be resurrected. It would take a standing army to maintain slavery in the South if we were to make peace today, guaranteeing to the South all their former constitutional privileges."[59]

Grant, keenly aware more than a year before that Southern society was decomposing, had written to his sister Mary in August 1862, "The war is evidently growing oppressive to the Southern people. Their *institutions* are beginning to have ideas of their own and everytime an expedition goes out, more or less of them follow in the wake of the army."[60] The peculiar institution of slavery was at the core of the demise of the Confederacy, and both the prolonged fighting and the dying of the Cause also caused the death of the institution of slavery. Neither Cause nor slavery could be resurrected.

Chapter Nine   **"A War Fought by the Weak"**

Desertions, Brigandage,
Counterinsurgency, Anarchy, and
the Rise of an Antiwar Movement

T he dispersal throughout the South of the defeated Vicksburg garrison of thirty thousand men contributed to the unraveling of frayed morale and the spread of anarchy on the home front. Four days after the fall of Vicksburg, a doubtful General Halleck wrote to Grant, "I fear that your paroling the prisoners at Vicksburg . . . may be construed as an absolute release and that the men will be immediately placed in the ranks of the enemy. Such has been the case elsewhere." Grant assured him that would not happen: "General Pemberton's acceptance of the terms proposed to him bind the Confederate Government not to accept the services of any man who formed part of the garrison on the morning of the 4th instant until properly exchanged. The object of the parole is to make each individual feel the same obligation."[1] Grant had required each man the Yankees had captured at Vicksburg and Port Hudson to affix his signature to an individual parole. If obeyed, it would withdraw them, at least temporarily, from further service to the Confederate cause.

"Thus Melted Away the Gallant Army of Vicksburg"

On July 8 Private Hugh Moss of the Vicksburg force wrote in his diary, "We have received our paroles, and crowds of men are crossing the river to try to get home. Several of our company have attempted similar expeditions but only two have succeeded." "Great discontent exists among the troops," he wrote the next day, "fearing they may have to go to parole camps." Union officers sought to implement Grant's strategy of dispersion by encouraging the spread of unrest among the paroled troops. "The Confederates crossed the river in numbers," Private W. H. Tunnard wrote in his diary entry for July 7, "being permitted to do so by the federal officers, who well knew that it was a most effectual method of demoralizing and destroying the efficiency of the army." The Southern general staff did what it could to stem the massive desertions, but one of Pemberton's brigade commanders, Brigadier General F. A. Shoup, reported failure. "Numbers of the men of my brigade have crossed the river for their homes, and their officers represent that it will prove utterly impossible to prevent the remainder from leaving in like manner as soon as we get beyond federal lines." "This conduct on the part of the men results from no disaffection to our service, but from a determination not to go into a 'parole camp' and a belief they can now be absent from their commands without injury to the service." Shoup closed his July 10 letter with the discouraged disclaimer, "all has been done to counteract the latter that was possible." Pemberton found himself in the awkward position of appealing to his opponent for assistance in retaining control over his troops: "Many of my men have been crossing the river this afternoon and are still crossing notwithstanding all that has been said on the subject, and again [I] request that this be stopped, if possible."[2]

The Confederate soldiers were leaving in grief and bitterness. Officially, the Union allowed a march out of Vicksburg on July 11, but Grant permitted Pemberton to leave with his men the night before, and some paroled prisoners were already leaving. "Tears rose to my eyes and my very heart swelled with emotion," wrote Moss in his diary, "being a prisoner did not in the least affect me, but the loss of the place which was such a great downfall to the Confederacy and what some of the citizens would have to endure caused me much pain." William Claiborne noted in his journal the same day, "Well, a week of humiliation has past away and thank God we are to leave to-morrow. . . . It is deeply humiliating to see our beautiful and fallen little city—in possession of her foes—her streets trod by the footsteps of an enemy—her palatial residence occupied by officers and soldiers foreign to her soil and our slaves standing guard at the doors of their owners." On the march out of the citadel, Claiborne wrote sardonically, "Men marched much more rapidly than we generally expected proving conclusively that they would have been much better able to endure the fatigue necessary 'to accomplish a successful evacuation' than most of the generals supposed." After this stinging reference to Pemberton's final council of war, which had endorsed his decision to surrender, Claiborne added a more direct indictment: "I am confident the movement could have been successfully accomplished and look upon the surrender of Vicksburg at the time at which it was surrendered as the most disgraceful occurrance of the war."[3]

Once outside Vicksburg, all discipline among the veterans seemed to dissolve. "General Pemberton desires that the army be kept together and maintain its organization," Claiborne wrote, "in order that men may be supplied with rations on the march," but despite promises of a furlough once they reached their rendezvous with General Johnston, the general in command "has no influence whatever with the men—two thirds of them have never *seen* him—and they are leaving the column singly and in squads of from two to fifty as fast as they reach the points on the road nearest their homes." Three days after the army exited Vicksburg, "a third of the army (including officers) had already gone and hundreds leave daily." By July 21 Pemberton recognized the reality and granted a general furlough of thirty days. "A general scattering of the men over different States" promptly began. Private Tunnard wrote mournfully on July 21: "Thus melted away the gallant army of Vicksburg, and the Confederacy lost the services of some of her bravest, most heroic and truest defenders." Many "exhibited a disposition to interpret" the meaning of their paroles "in its literal and closest signification." "Gen. Grant could not have employed a more effective method of disbanding and disorganizing an army than the course he pursued. It was as effective as if a scourge had swept them from his [Johnston's] path."[4]

General Richard Taylor, who had sought valiantly to create a diversion on the Louisiana side in hopes that Pemberton could break out of Vicksburg, was compelled to fall back when desertion reduced his own ranks. A Texas private wrote home on July 21, when word reached his force about the simultaneous loss of Vicksburg and Port Hudson, "We will nearly all of us go home, if we have to fight our way through." "I do not know anything about where we will go or when we will make the next stand," James Skelton wrote his wife Emily the same day. "It looks like this is the Darkest hour we have ever had and a great many of the soldiers are entirely out of heart and I believe would be willing to give it up and many of the officers are in the same situation." On the victorious Yankee front, Grant sent Sherman in pursuit of Johnston and reported to Halleck on July 18 that the relieving "force is now in full retreat east. Sherman says that most of his [Johnston's] army must perish from the heat, lack of water and general discouragement. The army paroled here have to a great extent deserted, and are scattered over the country in every direction." In response to Halleck's request for clarification, Grant replied that he had authorized the Confederate provost marshal to furlough "all paroled prisoners who have returned to our lines when it is their desire to receive furloughs."[5]

Three weeks after Vicksburg's fall, Grant's letter to Halleck was triumphant about the success of his strategy:

> Johnston's army was much demoralized and deserted by hundreds. I do not believe that he can get back to Mobile or Chattanooga with an effective force of 15,000 men. The army paroled here was virtually discharged from service. At last account, Pemberton had but 4,000 left with him and they were no doubt men whose homes were in the States east of here and are only waiting to get near them to desert too. . . . The country is full of paroled prisoners, swearing they will not take up arms again if they are exchanged. Thousands have crossed the Mississippi and gone west.[6]

Grant waited for his efforts to bear further fruit, the decay of Southern civilian morale in the wake of the influx of thousands of demoralized parolees.

Amnesty and Pardon for Returning Deserters

In February 1863 Jefferson Davis, recognizing the flagging sense of Confederate purpose, had issued a proclamation designating Friday, March 27, 1863, as a "day of national fasting, humiliation and prayer." After the fall of Vicksburg, on July 15, Davis called for yet another day of "fasting, humiliation and prayer." "It is meet that when trials and reversals befall us we should seek to take home to our hearts and consciences the lessons they teach, and profit by the stern self-examination for which they prepare us." The Confederate president hoped to contain parolee defeatism and provide a new infusion of men and a renewal of spirit. He picked up the option provided by the amended conscription bill and extended conscription from an upper age limit of thirty-five years to forty-five: "In my judgment the necessities of the public defense require that every man capable of bearing arms . . . should now be called out to do his duty in the defense of his country, and in driving back the invaders now within limits of the Confederacy." He threatened resisters with the "pain of being held and punished as deserters in the event of their failure to obey this call," but at the beginning of August he extended an olive branch with a second presidential proclamation offering amnesty and pardon to all deserters who reported back to the army within twenty days. If they "should promptly repair to the post of duty, should stand by their comrades now in front of the foe," victory would come; they would "so strengthen the armies of the Confederacy as to insure success." Otherwise, the Confederacy would be "in imminent peril." "I repeat that the men who owe duty to their country, who have been called out and have not yet reported for duty, or who have absented themselves from their posts are sufficient in number to secure us victory in the struggle now impending."[7]

The prospect of losing the services of veterans involved in the Vicksburg campaign was intolerable. Thirty thousand men had been captured there and paroled; 16,000 more men had been seized at Port Hudson and 10,000 at Arkansas Post. These 56,000 were at least fully one-fifth of the men available for duty. If to these 56,000 parolees were added the more than 136,000 soldiers reported by the Confederate War Department as absent without leave during the summer of 1863, it becomes clearer why Davis's August proclamation was both stern and conciliatory. The effective date of the pardon, August 21, coincided precisely with the date Pemberton had set for reassembling the parolees, a conjunction that could hardly have been accidental.

So devastating was the potential impact of losing the combat veterans of Vicksburg, Port Hudson, and Arkansas Post that the Davis government, six weeks after these defeats, sought to force the Vicksburg parolees back into service in open violation of Grant's stipulation, and their agreement, that forbade them to bear arms against the North until properly exchanged through the prisoner of war cartel. With the South in no position to complete so large an exchange within the terms of the cartel—that is, without an equivalent number of Northern parolees to exchange for their own—the Confederate War Department simply chose to ignore the cartel and on August 19 ordered their parolees to report back for duty "as far as practicable into their former regiments and battalions."

Dispensing with the protocol that commissioners from North and South agree in advance on each exchange and issue a joint announcement of the prisoner exchanges, Richmond now published a unilateral declaration. It read in part, "The Following officers and men captured at Vicksburg on July 4, 1863, and subsequently paroled have been duly exchanged and are hereby so declared." The unilateral action precipitated a bitter dispute between North and South, and on September 19 Halleck sent Grant a stinging letter of denial: "No such exchange has been made. The act of Commissioner Ould [the Confederate representative to the cartel] is entirely exposé and in violation of the cartel. Our commissioner has protested against this act of bad faith and deception on the part of the rebel authorities." Whereupon the North suspended all further prisoner exchanges until the Confederacy could present acceptable explanations for its action. After a heated round of charges and countercharges, it became clear by mid-October that the North would thereafter refuse to enter into any new exchanges of groups of parolees or prisoners; thus, in practice, soldiers captured by either side would be compelled to spend the balance of the war in prisoner-of-war camps.[8]

Confederate General Carter Stevenson anticipated much difficulty in getting his soldiers to comply with the special order of August 19 directing parolees to report for duty. "The men are under the impression," he told Pemberton, "that they cannot be held to serve under their parole and are encouraged in it by many people in the country, some I am told are prominent men." Soldiers in the 30th Alabama Infantry who received such notifications were confused, and many did not report back as ordered. S. J. Nelly, the commander of Company I, 30th Alabama, admitted to his wife on September 28 that many of the men in his outfit were resisting the order. "I look for all the boys. I hope they will come soon, as they will otherwise be counted and treated as deserters." One month later, Nelly placed an advertisement in the local paper, the *Democratic Watchtower*, announcing, "By order of Colonel Shelly I have returned to Talladega for the purpose of forwarding absent members of the Regiment (in squads of five or more as they report) to parole camps at Demopolis." Jefferson Davis's brother Joseph wrote to him from his new refuge near Lauderdale Springs, Mississippi: "The return of the paroled prisoners of V. B. [Vicksburg] come in very slowly, and fears are entertained that a large part will not voluntarily return." Robert Alexander Smith, a private serving with a cavalry detachment near Gadsden, Alabama, told his wife Eliza, "We kept guard all night, watching for deserters from the Army if any, we did not take up any."[9]

Lawlessness of Bands of Deserters and Resisters

With the return home of Vicksburg veterans came a rapid descent into social anarchy led by roving bands of deserters and resisters. John W. C. Watson, a civilian near Meridian, Mississippi, complained bitterly in a letter to General Samuel Cooper on August 5 about an "alarmingly great" increase in lawless deserters and stragglers. Alabama governor John Shorter wrote to Davis that same week: "Already are many of our counties filled with deserters and a restless, dissatisfied population, which the dissatisfied spirit of the Army at Vicksburg is calculated to increase." In a letter to the commander of the Department of the Gulf, General Dabney Maury, Shorter appealed for aid, apologizing for sending a lengthy recital, "but the evil is great and threatening and is portentous of mischief to our cause." General Kirby Smith, who had assumed command of the Trans-Mississippi Department in February, acknowledged that "the disaffection existing and growing in the parishes of Jackson and Winn, Louisiana [is] caused in the main by deserters and stragglers from our army."[10]

According to General Pillow, then head of the Conscript Bureau, in northern Georgia alone between 25,000 and 30,000 men had evaded the draft by the end of July 1863. A parallel report on northern Alabama estimated the strength of that region's resistance movement as of July 25 at between 8,000 and 10,000. In Louisiana, Governor Henry Allen expressed deep concern that the country south of Alexandria was "full of deserters and runaway conscripts." He cited one report that said, "They number 8,000—a terrible state of affairs."[11]

Davis's appeal for "stern self examination" in his July proclamation did not inspire the loyalty and high moral purpose he had in mind. The week after Vicksburg, responding to Kirby Smith's call for a "self-sustaining" Trans-Mississippi Department, Davis expressed considerable concern about the determination of prominent citizens to achieve a western destiny apart from the rest of the Confederacy: "You now have not merely a military but also a political problem involved in your command. I have been warned against a feeling which is said to exist in favor of a separate organization on the part of the States west of the Mississippi." A Texas civilian had estimated that a group of more than two thousand armed deserters had fortified an island in the Red River country near the Louisiana-Texas border as a base for raiding neighboring farms and plantations, and Kirby Smith had reported that large areas of Texas were in virtually open revolt. Brigadier General Henry E. McCulloch, commander of the Bonham district of northern Texas, announced in September that "deserters and conscripts . . . have gone into the brush in large numbers." He investigated and concluded that "these men live off the property and produce of the people near their camps and are a terror in the country about them and in many instances our best friends are in danger from them." Kirby Smith embarked on an inspection trip of his own in early October in the Bonham area, and informed Lieutenant General T. H. Holmes, commander of forces in Arkansas, that disaffection in northern Texas had expanded "beyond my expectations. Some 2500 to 2800 deserters with arms have collected in that country." Kirby Smith directed Brigadier General Smith P. Bankhead to bring up his division "to prevent their organization being perfected," and issued orders for a comprehensive plan to cope with insurgents: "Affairs have now reached such a crisis in some parts of your district the question now is whether they or we shall control. The deserters must be won back, the disaffected disposed of, the stern hand employed." "The deserters must be arrested and brought back to their commands or exterminated," he wrote to McCulloch. "Disaffection and disloyalty, too, must be silenced. Any enemies in our midst who by their acts or public expressions clearly evince disloyalty must be disposed of. Arrest and send them beyond the Rio Grande. The higher their position and influence the more prompt should be your action."[12]

McCulloch had planned to move against local deserters, but only when ready: "If we begin before we are sufficiently prepared and make a failure in the first move, it will embolden them, and give them additional strength." As a first step, he dispatched a threatening letter to Henry Boren, the leader of a large band of resisters: "In addition to the offense committed in leaving the army, you are now banded together in defiance of the laws of our country, creating fear among the civil and quiet citizens of the country, causing some of them to leave their homes and families exposed to pillage and outrage." He offered Boren a chance to surrender or face attack by regular army troops. This combination of bluster and conciliation won a measure of peace for the Bonham area, but at a heavy price for the national war effort, for McCulloch had had to promise that Boren and his men would not be compelled to serve at any distance from their homes. When his superiors questioned his decision to negotiate, McCulloch pointed out in his defense that fighting might have produced "a domestic war, which though small in proportion, would have been so magnified by our enemies as to have invited and caused an invasion of our State from Fort Smith." Six hundred and fifty deserters accepted his offer of pardon in exchange for signing up again. Yet, in going beyond the terms of Davis's proclamation of amnesty and pardon, McCulloch had conceded to disaffection.[13]

In North Carolina counties bordering on eastern Tennessee, morale was at such low ebb in September 1863 that the head of conscription for that state,

Lieutenant Colonel George W. Lay, dispatched a graphic report to his superiors in Richmond. It concluded that desertion, draft resistance, and anarchy had reached the point where "there is danger of marked political division and something like civil war if the military evils reported be not at once met with strong military repression." John Campbell, the assistant secretary of war, in an endorsement appended to Lay's report, warned that "the condition of things in the mountain districts of North Carolina, South Carolina, Georgia and Alabama menaces the existence of the Confederacy as fatally as either of the armies of the United States." In South Carolina, C. D. Melton told Colonel John S. Preston in late August that deserters and draft resisters had transformed the mountainous border between North and South Carolina into a secure haven. "The evil has gone on increasing, until there can be found few families which have not a husband, son, a brother or a kinsman, a deserter in the mountains." "The tone of the people is lost; it is no longer a reproach to be known as a deserter; all are ready to encourage and aid the efforts of those who are avoiding duty, and to refuse information and thwart and even resist those who seek to make arrests." Anarchy threatened lives and property: "Lawlessness pervades the country; the lives and property of the well-affected are endangered . . . ; the necessities of mutual protection has thrown them into bands; resistance to arrest is organized; they know their leaders and have their signals of danger and distress." Preston forwarded this report on to his superior, Secretary of War Seddon, who in turn forwarded it to Lee. Preston added a note, "I fear it is as truthful as it is graphic," and even more disquieting, "In other States, the condition is worse, if possible." If the Conscript Bureau was to provide badly needed manpower to the Southern army, it needed help. Seddon concurred. "The matter appears to me grave enough for the active interference of higher authority," he wrote. "Some decisive measures are essential to arrest this fearful evil."[14]

General Lee agreed that counterinsurgency seemed called for but was pessimistic about remedying the "evil." "I do not know that anything more can be done at present," he told Davis on August 17. He referred to his warnings after desertions spoiled his own plans at Antietam, and continued: "Now, the number of desertions from this Army is so great, and still continues to such an extent, that unless some cessation of them is caused, I fear success in the field will be endangered." Many soldiers were, in deliberately dissembling ways, "choosing to place" on the president's July 1863 proclamation of amnesty and pardon "a wrong interpretation," and employing it as a pretext for absenting themselves from their commands. "In one corps, the desertions of North Carolinians, and to some extent of Virginians, has grown to a very serious matter." Lee came to the painful conclusion that Confederate survival rested on a vigorous pursuit of deserters, and the ultimate punishment. "I now respectfully submit to your Excellency," Lee told Davis, "that all has been done which forebearance and mercy calls for, and that nothing will remedy this great evil which so much endangers our cause excepting the rigid enforcement of the death penalty in future cases of desertion."[15]

Fighting "Our Aged Fathers, Mothers and Poor Widows": Counterinsurgency on the Home Front

The longer the Army of Tennessee remained in camp, first at Tullahoma and then near Chattanooga, the more prevalent desertion and unauthorized leavetaking by the soldiers became. A recent study of wartime desertion among North Carolina troops has found that soldiers, particularly poorer soldiers, were likely to take leaves after about two years of field service. Faced with a wave of desertion, Bragg had done what was necessary, initiate a rigorous campaign to compel deserters to return to the ranks. When Johnston visited his camp in February 1863 he reported back to Davis, "The brigades engaged at Murfreesboro are now stronger than they were on the morning of the battle. Mainly by the return of absentees brought back by the General's vigorous system." At the head of his "vigorous system" Bragg had put General Pillow, who had been banished homeward to command the Volunteer and Conscript Bureau.

As head of the Conscript Bureau in the Army of Tennessee, Pillow had struggled as best he could against the resolute resistance to conscription, but almost as quickly as he caught resisters and forced them back into military service, many deserted again, taking their weapons with them and urging others to do likewise. When he ordered cavalry detachments to storm mountain hideouts in northern Alabama, the pursued fought back: "They have killed a number of my cavalry, and in several instances have driven small bodies of cavalry . . . from the mountains." Pillow requested a full regiment of veteran cavalry to even the odds.

When several citizens of Tennessee who were swept up in Pillow's dragnet sought relief via writs of habeas corpus, Pillow took matters into his own hands. In March 1863 he issued a general order—but on a matter the provisional Congress had itself debated and resolved in a contrary manner. "Officers of the Bureau will cause all Justices of the Peace—constables, deputy sheriffs and deputy clerks within the conscript ages to be enrolled and sent to the army," Pillow decreed. He promised that conscript officers under his command in Mississippi, Alabama, Tennessee, and Georgia could "remain on duty at their residences unless or until the exigencies of the Service shall make it necessary to order them into the field." Determined that "something ought to be done to punish these domestic traitors," and finding that the civil courts "have no *present vitality* and the danger of these judgments is so remote as to inspire no respect, much less fear," Pillow directed Conscript Bureau officers to try all disputed cases in military instead of civil courts. He ordered a detachment to proceed to one of the hotbeds of disaffection in Winston County, Alabama, "for the purpose of thoroughly conscripting this county" and rounding men up. "Please have the officers instructed to examine for and bring in *all public arms,* no matter where found or into whose hands they may have fallen."[16]

Word of Pillow's campaign against constitutional government speedily reached Richmond, and the War Department ordered him to bring his unauthorized operations to an immediate halt. "Cut up by the root all power to enforce the Conscript Law through the agency of this Bureau," Pillow responded, asking "to be relieved from further labor in this Bureau." Still, his results were impressive; although he brought few conscripts into the Army of Tennessee, Bragg would credit his bureau with a 25 percent increase in the army's strength. During its two-month active period, Pillow's Volunteer and Conscript Bureau had added ten thousand men to Bragg's force, raising its effective strength, by April 1, 1863, to a few more than fifty thousand. After the War Department shut down Pillow's bureau, "within ten days after his bureau ceased to function," the effective strength of the Army of Tennessee fell by five thousand men.

Confederate leaders had resolved certain staffing problems on the front lines by reassigning ineffective officers to duties on the home front. While understandable, this policy had the unfortunate result that officers who lacked the training or skills to command troops in combat frequently found themselves in charge of even more difficult strategic tasks at home. Alabama's Governor Shorter received complaints from Alabama soldiers outraged by oafishly mismanaged counterinsurgency raids on the home front. On July 20, 1863, soldiers of the 54th Alabama Infantry dispatched a scathing letter to the governor from the front, where they were fighting "the vandal foe," complaining sharply about the treatment meted out to their families by Confederate cavalry detachments out chasing deserters and resisters: "They are arresting our aged fathers, mothers and poor widows and dragging them to prison on pretense they are not loyal." The soldiers' litany went on: "More Soldiers families are insulted, their stock killed their homes plundered their little farms which have been cultivated by the weak hands of mothers and helpless children are laid waste." "Is the above treatment what 'State Authorities' intend to deal out to those not able to protect themselves?" After another group of Alabama soldiers who had learned of similar abuses threatened to take matters into their own hands, their commander, Brigadier General H. D. Clayton, urged Shorter to take prompt remedial action. "If it is not done at once," he warned, "it is feared [such abuses] will have a damaging effect upon the army."[17]

Governor Shorter, discovering direct evidence of linkages between Vicksburg parolees and bands of deserters and resisters, on September 3 asked General Maury to assign a battalion to the heavily infested southeastern corner of his state. The governor sent along copies of complaints by "leading citizens of Henry County, in This State, in reference to the existence and continued boldness of deserters and Tories in that County, and Dale and also adjoining Counties in Florida." Vicksburg veterans were using their paroles as a pretext for claims of exemption from any further service; in addition, they were joining groups hiding out in the swamps and bayous. Shorter felt compelled to confess, "I am powerless to execute the laws of the State, if resisted."[18]

The governor of Arkansas, Harris Flanagin, had pleaded with Davis in June 1863 not to commit the folly of attempting to transfer conscripts across the Mississippi; Arkansans would serve faithfully, he advised, "only when they know their homes are defended. If they believe their homes and families are within the enemy's lines, their commands, like many of those from Missouri, Kentucky, and West Tennessee, will melt into thin air." By September, Major General J. M. Schofield, commander of Northern forces in Arkansas, warned that "the rebel army west of the Mississippi is rapidly breaking up into small bands for guerrilla operations in the vicinity of their homes." He reported, in a letter to General Halleck, "The habit of waging guerrilla warfare, which amounts to a passion with the western people, will, I apprehend, give us more serious trouble than the organized rebel armies have done." The com-

mander of the conscript department for Arkansas, B. F. Danley, was petition-
ing Governor Flanagin for a cavalry regiment: "There are a great many deserters and refractory conscripts in the country who are running at large, and
will continue to do so until an armed force can be procured to arrest them." "I
am powerless," Danley ended his letter of September 30 to Flanagin, "to do
anything in the premises." Such expressions of impotence in the face of anarchy confirmed the judgment of an *Arkansas True Democrat* editorial: "Civil
Law, if not dead, is very sound asleep."[19]

Guerrilla warfare, though a possible source of social anarchy, was a necessary tactic in certain circumstances. After Vicksburg, Northern officers serving on the Mississippi's eastern shore had encountered much hit-and-run
guerrilla warfare. "It is reported that [General James] Chalmers is coming
South toward Brandon with his cavalry," Sherman had warned Grant in August 1862, "burning cotton and gathering conscripts and negroes as he goes
along." Six weeks later, Grant was warning Sherman in turn, "The rebels have
at present a small force on Silver Creek collecting cattle and negroes and burning cotton." Sherman dispatched a cavalry expedition to hunt down the guerrillas, informing Grant, "We know of some parties of rebels engaged in forcing
conscripts and punishing negroes, burning cotton, etc." In Arkansas, General
Thomas Hindman, also in the summer of 1862, authorized formation of partisan units to attack river shipping "day and night . . . using the greatest vigor
in their movements."[20]

The military resort to guerrilla raids provoked ruthless Yankee troop retal-
iation. A Southern civilian near Huntsville, Alabama, related how the Union
commander, Brigadier General Ormsby M. Mitchel, two months before
Vicksburg, incensed at "cutting of telegraph lines, the tearing up of tracks,
firing into trains," and the killing of several soldiers on routine patrol near
Paint Rock, condoned retaliation by the slain soldiers' comrades, who burned
Paint Rock to the ground. Sherman himself, after partisans near Randolph,
Tennessee, had fired on the steamer *Eugene,* ordered a regiment to Randolph
for the express purpose of destroying the town, "leaving *one* house to mark the
place." Two days later, Sherman wrote, "The regiment has returned and Randolph is gone. . . . The town was of no importance but the example should be
followed upon all similar occurrences."[21]

Guerrilla warfare therefore added to the lawlessness on the home front in
occupied areas, both from troop retaliation and from social anarchy. "The
people in the interior," Sherman observed, "are getting pretty tired of the

guerrillas and partisan rangers who are not particular about horses and provisions but help themselves liberally from friend and foe." In July 1863 General Stephen A. Hurlbut, commander of the 16th Army Corps, explained to Grant that "the people are more afraid of the guerrillas than of our troops, and therefore the people refuse to report them." By September Hurlbut had authorized formation of civilian home guard troops in occupied areas along the Mississippi and Tennessee Rivers, "to put down and suppress all robbery, violence and irregular warfare."[22]

Dreading the Soldiers "as Much as the Coming of the Yankees"

There was a growing aversion, as 1863 progressed, among Confederate soldiers and civilians alike to what had become an irregular war of indefinite duration, an aversion strikingly similar to currents of resistance that sapped the energies of the Continental Army during the American Revolution. John Shy estimates that during the revolution, a fifth of the American population were "actively treasonous." "The years 1776–1782," he writes, "might indeed be recounted as horror stories of terrorism, rapacity, mendacity and cowardice, not to blame our ancestors for these things, but to remind us what a war fought by the weak must be like."[23]

In the tier of southside Virginia counties bordering on northwestern North Carolina, one resident, J. E. James, charged that "deserters almost invariably have their guns and accoutrements with them and when halted and asked for their furloughs or their authority to be absent from their commands they just pat their guns defiantly and say, 'This is my furlough.'" Brigands retaliated against persons thought to be informers and even against any with the temerity to criticize desertion: "The next thing his house is burned, he waylaid and murdered or beaten nearly to death." Even loyalists were "afraid to do anything, and then are so cowed and dispirited that they do not think it worthwhile to make any attempt in these matters." Such brigandage proved increasingly difficult to distinguish from official impressment. Richard J. Archer, a planter in Claiborne County, Mississippi, wrote to Governor Pettus, three weeks before Vicksburg, that his county was "a prey to thieves and robbers as infamous as the 'cowboys' and 'skinners' of the Revolutionary War. Armed organizations of men . . . are engaged in seizing on our stock of mule, horses, etc. and running them out of reach of the owners." Within days after stealing most of Archer's stock, the outlaws carted their booty to a neighboring town and proposed to hold an auction. Archer claimed that the outlaws were focusing on slaveholders, seizing "our mules, horses, and oxen." "Our plantations, and our fences are thrown down and stock led into the fields to destroy corn, potatoes, etc., on which we hoped to subsist."[24]

Nor was depredation confined to deserters and outlaws. Regular soldiers had engaged in the practice since early 1863. A Mississippi slaveholder, Hugh Torrance, had written as early as February 1863 that he and his neighbors "always dreaded the falling back of our army as much as the coming of the Yankees." The commander near Houston noted in March that "numerous complaints are received daily . . . of depredations and outrages having been committed by stragglers. . . . Pillaging is at all times and under all circumstances disgraceful to the soldier but when practiced upon our own citizens whom the Army is duty bound to protect, it becomes a crime of such gross character as to merit the severest punishment, even should it reach the ultimate penalty of the law." An Alabama planter, Edward Batley, wrote to his senator, Clement Clay, about the troops serving near his home. "The whole neighborhood was entirely laid waste in the course of a few days." He had gone to see the commanding general personally to tell him that his men were behaving "in every respect, as though they were in enemy's country." They had seized "all my beef cattle and *every one* of my hogs, not only without my consent, but even without my knowledge, leaving me utterly destitute of meat for my family." A brigade camped in May near the Batesville, Arkansas, plantation of A. J. Gaines, as Gaines lamented to Governor Flanagin, "commenced killing my hogs [and] burning the fences from around my orchard." The soldiers had even seized the carriage Gaines had left behind in case his family needed a quick escape from the Yankees. Henrietta Butler, a Louisiana slave, remembered later, "I knows the day dem Sojers come in, takin' all de meat out of de smoke house, got all de chickens an' turkeys." Her mistress had "raised hell with the Boss an' tol' him to run dem sons of bitches away. He didn' say anything to dem sojers 'cause he was too scared." Katie Rowe, a slave in Oklahoma, had similar memories: "Long about de middle of de War, after Old Master was killed, de soldiers began coming 'round de place and camping. Dey was Southern soldiers and dey say dey have to take de mules and de corn to git along." Suiting their actions to their words, the soldiers "jest go in de barns and cribs and take whatever dey want."[25]

When James Acklen, a planter, dashed from Nashville to West Feliciana

Parish, Louisiana, in an effort to save his beloved Angola plantation, he discovered that he could do little and wrote home despairingly, "I am in constant dread of its being burned. My mules and horses all taken and stolen by the Confederates and my neighbors." L. W. Hopkins, a South Carolina planter, wrote in an October letter, "I have suffered all kinds of deprivations and been subjected to all kinds of lies and slanders that malice could invent. . . . I have been informed by gentlemen of respectability that the poorer classes in Mississippi . . . are engaged in robbing and stealing everything that comes their way, and that people of property suffer more from these wretches than from the Yankees." Kirby Smith was so exasperated that he ordered a subordinate to "have *any and all* men who may be caught in the commission of such outrages shot down then and there." "This wholesale and indiscriminate system of plunder and depredations," he wrote to Brigadier General P. C. Herbert in October, "is becoming such a general practice that instant and decisive measures must be taken to check it."[26]

Since the Confederate War Department had seen fit to favor Lee's Army of Northern Virginia over the western forces in its allocation of supplies, between January and August 1863 General Bragg, in his slow retreat back toward his base at Chattanooga, found himself increasingly dependent on local commissaries in eastern Tennessee. But the summer had produced a hard drought after the lingering effects of the 1862 subsistence crisis, and the winter wheat crop harvested in the spring turned out to be the only normal crop to be grown in the highlands until 1864. Highland families, fearing depleted stores of food for their own needs, declined to comply with military requisitions, and a series of incidents between soldiers and civilians was the result. Hunger drove some of General Polk's men to "destroying the orchard and digging up the potatoes" of a civilian who lived near a cavalry encampment; soldiers in D. H. Hill's corps committed "daily and nightly depredations . . . upon the fields and gardens of civilians . . . some of whom are aged and helpless widows." Yeomen struck back, and Bragg's commissaries informed their field commander, in one instance, that "the bushwackers in the mountains are killing the cattle . . . set aside for the army to eat." Commissary officers urged Bragg to "send a good cavalry force . . . , otherwise the cattle or a large portion of them may be lost." But such retaliatory tactics simply damaged morale among yeomen soldiers, who could readily imagine their dependents being forced to yield up their own scanty provisions.

Growing Despair in the Army and on the Home Front

Marauding soldiers may well have felt justified in their lawless behavior by the behavior of the Richmond government toward them, that is, by the late payment of their already meager wages and the imposition of a hated new tax on farm production. An army that consistently failed to pay even meager wages to its soldiers could hardly expect hungry troops to abstain from taking what they could not afford to buy. A common soldier serving in Arkansas summed up such resentment with crude eloquence: "The Government feeds us Texains on Poor Beef, but there is too darn many hogs here for that, these Arkansas Hoosiers ask us for 25 to 30 cents a pound for there pork, but the boys generally gets a little *cheaper than that.* I reckon you understand how they get it."

The Confederate government itself blurred the distinction between lawful impressment of civilian resources and unlawful pillaging when, rather than accept the sacrifice of putting its fiscal house in order, it opted for a cynical policy of deliberate underbidding as a means of rationalizing forcible impressment of goods. Typical of this strategy were the August 1863 orders of the chief commissary, John T. Strong, to "make purchases of all cattle possible at 15 cents a pound, the price fixed by the Commanding General." Strong knew that farmers would be reluctant to part with their goods for a price far below market value, and indeed seemed to count on such resistance as an excuse for forcible seizure: "In the event you cannot purchase at that price, you will make impressments by virtue of authority contained in General Orders #30 A & I G [Adjutant and Inspector General], Richmond. . . . You will offer no more than 15 cents for cattle you propose to impress."[27] The Confederate government had resolved its short-term fiscal dilemma at the expense of radicalizing its soldiers and yeomen, simultaneously alienating more-affluent farmers and planters as well. Lemuel P. Conner, who faced hard times himself, wrote to his wife Fanny, "*Our plantations must not furnish the Government any more corn.*" Private Edwin Hedge Fay urged his wife Sarah in July 1863 to charge for their crops whatever prices prevailed in their neighborhood. He sought to resolve the shortages at home caused by his own pitiful salary as a private by directing his wife to "speculate, lawfully, honestly."[28]

During the winter of 1863, a veteran sent a lengthy anonymous letter to Secretary of War James Seddon, with this stark closing line: "from a soldier who has felt the affect of powder and lead twice." The unnamed soldier claimed that certain neighbors "[had] a lot of wheat on hand and they will not sell it at all they are holding it for a higher price." He posed a plaintive query: "How is a soldier to support his family when we have such men left at home we cant do it the way everything has got we cant cloath ourselves and family let along getting bread and meat." Word of speculation by exempts had spread quickly in the camps, along with reports of home-front destitution. "I hear a great deal of talk in the army about such men being left at home and the poor having to fight for them." The letter touched the core of class consciousness with these words: "Iff such men are not put into the armey and this extortion stopped it will be the cause of the armeys being weakened because what man is at home that would stay in the army and no that hiss family was sufring at home." The anonymous writer ended with an angry warning: "I hope for the sake of our country and the poor you will look into this and have these men put into the armey. . . . We dont want men at home to steal for it cant be cault anything else."29

The mood within the army and on the home front would grow uglier and uglier as the year 1863 lengthened. T. B. Banes, a young soldier, wrote his parents in August, "It is truly hard for the soldier to content himself in the field . . . when he sees his government give the speculator the advantage of him and his family speculation will cause desertion and desertion will be our ruin." The Alabama soldiers of the 54th, complaining passionately to the governor in late July, lamented the suffering of their families, "those helpless ones left to the mercy of the Rich Iron-Hearted speculator." An Arkansas judge, John Brown, wrote in his diary, "Most of those who were so willing to shed the last drop of blood in the contest for a separate Government, are entirely unwilling to shed the first." Davis understood the dangers posed by such claims and wrote, in a letter to W. Harmon, the president of the Confederate Society of Enterprise in Mississippi: "The passion for speculation has become a gigantic evil. It seems to have taken possession of the whole country, and has seduced citizens of all classes from a determined prosecution of the war to a sordid effort to amass money." "It destroys enthusiasm and weakens public confidence. It injures the efficiency of every measure that demands the cooperation of the people in repelling the public enemy" and "threatens to bring down every calamity which can befall freemen struggling for independence."30

Nor were yeomen and nonslaveholders the only ones dispirited by economic concerns. William Minor, who managed several large sugar plantations in southern Louisiana under Northern occupation, wrote in his diary, at the end of September, a sober prediction that the war would impoverish even the affluent: "If the war continues twelve months longer, all negro men of any value will be taken, the women and children will be left for their masters to maintain, which they cannot do. The owners of the soil will make nothing, the lands will be taken for taxes, and bot in by Northern men, and the original owners will be beggars." From this scenario, Minor drew a painful lesson: "This is the result of Secession and Abolitionism—Was There ever such a folly since the world began?" An end of slavery would mean loss of the property of the planter class. The Arkansas slave Katie Rowe told of the harangue unleashed by her former owner: "You niggers been seing de 'Federate soldiers coming by here looking purty raggedly and hurt and wore out . . . but dat no sign dey licked!" He would "free" his slaves with his shotgun before the Yankees got there. "Dem Yankees ain't gwine to git dis fur, but iffen dey do you all ain't gwine get free by 'em, 'cause I gwine line you on de bank of Bois d'Arc Creek and free you wid my shotgun!" "Anybody miss jest one lick wid de hoe, or one step in de line, or one clap of dat bell or one toot of de horn, and he gwine be free and talking to de debil long befo' he ever see a pair of blue britches."[31]

In September, General Kirby Smith dispatched a representative to visit his president to communicate the "emminently critical" state of affairs in the trans-Mississippi west. "The despondency of our people, their listlessness, their deafness to the calls of both civil and military authorities, the desertions from our ranks checked by neither rigor or clemency, all indicate despair and abandonment." "Unless a great change takes place, unless succor comes to us from abroad, or unless the Providence of God is strikingly exhibited in our favor, this Department will soon have but a nominal existence." Kirby Smith despaired that "without men, without arms, with a people so demoralized by speculation that submission is preferred to resistance, the immense efforts being made by the enemy must be crowned with success."[32]

A Houston lawyer, William Pitt Ballinger, had reported ten days after Vicksburg that the defeats "will lead I fear to the overrunning of Mississippi, Alabama, Tennessee, Arkansas, Louisiana and Texas, to the practical destruction of slavery in time." "The war has no prospect but of long continuance and our thorough exhaustion." When Ballinger learned of Lee's withdrawal from Pennsylvania, he paused for a considered assessment of the prospects of the Southern revolution: "They have immense reserves still; we have scarcely any. Our country will be overrun and property destroyed, the 'peculiar institution' will go almost absolutely by the board." He recognized that a war for independence would not be decided simply on the basis of relative resources. Will could make all the difference. "If there is the spirit of endurance in the people, we can be free and independent but will that endurance be displayed. There has always been the rub for me." Ballinger concluded, "I have never felt that the evils were such as affected the feelings of the *masses of the people without property* to the extent which will sustain the extremities of suffering and resistance." He was not sanguine: "I not only distrust its being done, but I fear a reaction against the leaders of the Revolution and the Slaveholders." To this pessimistic reassessment he added a poignant coda: "This is neither a high nor a hopeful view to take. I am aware of it and devoutly hope the crisis may never be reached and that we are of nobler and sterner stuff."[33]

Rebellion, Treason, and Atrocities

General James Chalmers wrote from his headquarters at Tupelo, Mississippi, in late July 1863, "I regret to say that I am informed that there is some disaffection among the people in the northern parts of the State and that a few persons are openly advocating a policy of reconstruction." "Is it advisable," he queried General Johnston, commander of the western theater, "to attempt to suppress such expressions of sentiment; and if so what course shall I pursue towards persons guilty of using them?" Johnston directed Chalmers to "arrest all those who openly advocate the policy of reconstruction." Ten days later, General Daniel Ruggles, writing to Johnston from Columbus, Mississippi, about "the political status of the people in this district," moved quickly to the point. "The spirit of volunteering," he said, "has ceased to exist and although there are numbers of men apparently within conscription limits, few go forward to swell the ranks of our armies, there being no sentiment sufficiently potent to impel them to enter the service." "This want of patriotic fervor," Ruggles believed, could be traced to "that class possessed of small estates." "They assume that if the more wealthy portion of our population, slaveholders especially, will not enter the ranks of the army to defend their rights of property, it is not incumbent upon them who have no such large interest at stake." Substitution providing exemption from the draft gave "greater plausibility" to this line of argument. "Unless something is done and that right speedily to arrest this growing spirit of discontent, we shall cease to have that cordial support of the citizens who constitute a majority of our fighting forces."[34]

The commander of the occupation force at Memphis, General Hurlbut, had informed Lincoln on August 11, 1863, that "the rank and file of the Southern Army have begun to awaken to the knowledge that they are not fighting their own battle, but the battle of the officers, the politicians, and the plantation class." As evidence, Hurlbut pointed to arrests in Georgia, Alabama, and Mississippi of soldiers and citizens "on suspicion of membership in secret Union societies." Furthermore, he said, "heavy bodies of deserters, with their arms, hold the mountains of northern Alabama and defy conscription." "Thus treason to their treasonable government is being inaugurated and the justice of Heaven presses to the lips of the struggling Confederacy the poisoned chalice of their own brewing."[35]

Since the beginning of the war, the mountain areas of several Southern states had been home to pockets of anti-Confederate resistance. In January 1863 Georgia governor Joseph Brown had issued a proclamation on resisters in the mountains of northern Georgia, charging that they had "associated themselves together with arms in their hands and are now in open rebellion against the authority of the State and the Confederate States, robbing loyal citizens of their property and threatening to burn their dwellings and do other acts of violence." The governor warned citizens "to cease to harbor deserters or encourage desertion or to commit further acts of disloyalty or hostility to the State or the Confederate States." "The law against treason will be strictly enforced against all who subject themselves to its penalties." North Carolina's Governor Zebulon E. Vance issued a similar proclamation on January 26, admitting in it that "a large number of soldiers from our armies are absent from their colors without proper leave in this hour of greatest need."[36]

But the use of force, including executions, by Confederate military leaders led to shameful atrocities at the hands of local forces. In *To Die Game*, William McKee Evans recounts one such atrocity. Members of a home guard of the local squirearchy of Robeson County, North Carolina, seeking revenge for several raids by hungry young draft evaders hiding in the swamp, cornered several members of the Lumbee Indian tribe and executed two, one a man at least twenty years beyond the reach of universal conscription.[37]

Another atrocity occurred in January 1863 in North Carolina, in an Appalachian hill community along the Tennessee border called Laurel Creek

Valley. Clan members who were subject to the draft had fled into the back-country. With men absent from home and the failure of the growing seasons of 1862, privation had come to a valley precariously balanced on the edge of subsistence even in the best of times. One mountain resident urged the editor of the *Raleigh Daily Progress* to summon "Jeff Davis and his Destructives" to end the misery in the mountains by calling up "a *few,* just a few of their exempted pets . . . to knock the women and children of the mountains in the head to put them out of their misery." The commander of the Department of East Tennessee, General Sam Jones, had tried to ease the suffering by getting a brief suspension of the "execution of the conscript law in East Tennessee," writing to Davis in October 1862, "There are, as you know, comparatively few slaves in east Tennessee. Agricultural and mechanical labor is performed chiefly by whites." That same month a similar plea came for relief for northern Georgia. Davis rejected both pleas on the grounds that "to exempt the unwilling would be to offer a premium for disaffection." His refusal set the stage for disaster.[38]

Resisters and deserters raided the Madison County seat and seized salt, food, clothing, and money badly needed by their impoverished families. When affluent residents of the town urged a counterraid, officers of the 64th North Carolina Infantry, who were kin to the victims of the raid, responded, and in late January Colonel Lawrence Allen led a detachment into Laurel Creek Valley. Several skirmishes ensued, with casualties on both sides. Some "relatives of the suspects were whipped and tortured and hanged until almost dead and then let down for more questioning" to force them to disclose the whereabouts of the raiders. One unit captured fifteen men, a motley group of males from thirteen to sixty years old, and along the road back toward departmental headquarters at Knoxville, Lieutenant Colonel James Keith ordered all fifteen executed without benefit of a trial. The soldiers divided the prisoners into small groups and proceeded to kill them as they begged for their lives. Thirteen-year-old David Skelton cried out, it was reported, "You have killed my father and brother. You have shot my father in the face: do not shoot me in the face." The detachment marched back to its duty post in eastern Tennessee, leaving fifteen dead prisoners buried in "a shallow mass grave."[39]

Less than three weeks after the Laurel Creek Valley affair, a similar atrocity occurred at Yadkinville, North Carolina, in a clash between a militia unit and a band of deserters and resisters. The officer in charge, Lieutenant Colonel

W. A. Joyce, and his fourteen-man patrol had encountered on February 16 about twenty armed resisters barricaded in a schoolhouse. Two of the resisters and "two of the best citizens of this county," members of the patrol, were killed. Four resisters surrendered. Soldiers at the front, hearing of the evasion of the draft in Yadkin County, deserted, procured arms and ammunition, and allied themselves with the resisters in open defiance of the law. A Confederate informant, R. F. Armfield, reported to Governor Vance that these bands "even sent messages to the militia officers, threatening death to the most obnoxious of them and all who arrest them."[40] The conviction of the four Yadkinville resisters who had voluntarily surrendered was upheld on appeal to the North Carolina Supreme Court, by a vote of two to one.

Chief Justice R. M. Pearson, a states' rights advocate, protested in his strong minority opinion that the trial had been unlawful because the North Carolina legislature had refused to enact legislation that would make draft resistance a crime in that state; and that therefore the act for which the resisters had been tried did not violate North Carolina law. His controversial minority opinion was more widely disseminated than the majority ruling. When it reached North Carolina soldiers serving in Lee's army, camp gossip recast it into a majority ruling prohibiting prosecution of draft resisters on the sweeping ground that universal conscription was itself unlawful. Soldiers looking for an excuse to desert fled in droves, and General W. D. Pender warned Lee, "Our regiments will waste away more rapidly than they ever have in battle." Lee forwarded this warning on to Secretary of War Seddon, with this message: "General Pender states to me that the men go off with their arms in squads. They can thus band together in the State with other malcontents, and produce great trouble, defy the law, etc."[41]

In late July 1863 Dr. Urban Owen, a surgeon serving in the Army of Tennessee, recounted a heart-wrenching execution at Chattanooga. "I saw two young soldiers hung last Friday for desertion and bushwacking our army," he wrote. "They were both youthful," confessed the shocked surgeon, "but I suppose were dealt with according to their just deserts." "I know some of my old neighbor boys would go the same way if our soldiers ever got hold of them for several of them have deserted our army and joined the Yankees." In the memoirs of Sam Watkins, a Maury County slaveholder and a soldier in the Maury Grays 1st Tennessee Regiment, is the story of the execution of two convicted Yankee spies near the regimental camp. Watkins rushed to the scene, drawn by the prospect of watching two traitors meet their fate, but was stunned to see how young they were. "After a while I saw a guard approach, and saw two little boys in their midst, but did not see the Yankees that I had been looking for. The two little boys were rushed upon the platform. I saw that they were handcuffed. 'Are they Spies?' I was appalled; I was horrified; nay more, I was sick at heart." The executioners quickly placed ropes around their necks; one was fourteen years old, the other sixteen. "The youngest one began to beg and cry and plead most piteously," Watkins said. "It was horrid." The elder boy sought to stiffen the younger's resolve, "kicked him and told him to stand up and show the Rebels how a Union man could die for his country. Be a man!" The young men stood bravely to their deaths. After the provost marshal read the "charges and specifications," "the props were knocked out and the two boys were dangling in the air. I turned off sick at heart."[42]

The escalating use of force begat an increasingly desperate response, particularly among the deserters. One of the most poignant of such incidents was a March 1863 suicide attempt related by Dr. Owen: "Tobe Sledge deserted & saw men hunting him coming in both ends of a lane & no chance to run drew his knife and cut his own throat but failed to kill & is now lying at home and will probably get over it." The decision to execute repeat deserters, however, also brought the unintended consequence of stimulating the enlistment of disaffected yeomen in the Union army instead, particularly in occupied areas. Dr. Owen described one such case: "Old Dick Harris deserted & was caught, deserted again & went to the Yankees & deserted the Yankees & our cavalry caught him, he was court martialed & Sentenced to be Shot and is here now in the guard house chained fast and awaiting his *awful doom.*"[43]

So commonplace did such enlistment in the Union army become that General Buckner asked Secretary of War Seddon for instructions. Seddon replied that "the Government cannot hold any opinion in reference to citizens of Tennessee who enlist in the service of the United States or who give aid and comfort in their war upon Confederates but that they are guilty of Treason." Seddon referred to the case of "Old Dick Harris" in east Tennessee, the same man Dr. Owen described, who had from the beginning of the war "selected the party of the United States as his own—He protested against being enrolled as a conscript and announced his determination to resist conscription—He was sentenced to death for leaving Tennessee and joining the Federal Army." Seddon advised Buckner, "It is not, however, desirable to prosecute many of these cases."[44]

Accusations of unequal treatment mounted amid talk of "military despotism." Private Edwin Hedge Fay reacted bitterly to news that the former captain of his company had taken advantage of his "Twenty Nigger" exemption to bring his sick spouse to Hot Springs, Arkansas, for medical treatment. "He can stay with his wife but if you are sick," Fay lamented to his wife Sarah, "I could not come to you. Our Confederate laws do not operate equally upon all men. Some favored few can occupy places of ease and emolument while others must bear all the suffering. If it is right I cant see it." After five months of further absence from home, Fay said of a newly tightened furlough policy, "I shall come home, leave or license when I have a mind to. I have submitted to military despotism almost as long as I intend to." "I will not support a govt. when my rights depend on the caprice of first this Gen'l then that. My family are nearer and dearer to me than any Confederacy could be. . . . My first allegiance is to my family, a second to the Country if it does not trample on my rights." By late September 1863, the accumulated frustrations of life in the Army of Tennessee led this embittered veteran to conclude, "There is no such thing as patriotism where the rights of the private soldier are trampled on every hour. No it is brute force and fear of public opinion that now holds together the armies of the Confed. States."[45]

A persistent regionalism and contempt for the yeoman majority continued to beset the Confederate cause throughout the war. From his encampment near Spring Hill, Tennessee, Private Fay wrote his wife that "the standard for virtue is not very high though a mountainous country is historical for easy virtue, a 'mountain girl' being synonymous with one of bad character." In the light of the high value set on female virtue in antebellum Southern society, his comments speak eloquently. Even the official correspondence of the Southern army reeked of such contempt. Captain V. Sheliha, chief of staff of the Department of Western Virginia and Eastern Tennessee, welcomed his new commander, General Buckner, with a letter about the recent arrest of three prominent mountain Unionists and advising Buckner to expel them: "The Tories of East Tennessee have strong prejudices, by no judgment but their own, they are hardheaded, implacable & obstinate. To undertake to convince them of the justice of our cause would be a hopeless task." "Civilization has brought many of its vices, but few of its virtues to these people, they are gross Sensualists rendered our enemy on account of being deprived of some of the less comforts of life which they enjoy." And Captain W. W. Blackford, trying to explain to his Virginia-born wife the difficulty of fighting a war in such an environment, noted that "the social conditions of the country in which we are camped are very strange. There are no gentlemen nor gentlemen's houses; the people live in cabins with little cultivated patches of ground around them. As to patriotism, there is none." "In East Tennessee, the people are about equally divided and there rages a real civil war, which causes much misery."[46]

Certainly, disaffection with the Confederate cause was rampant in the region. A study of the largest antiwar group, the Order of the Heroes of America, has noted that the secret order was apparently formed in 1861 in the Randolph-Davidson-Forsyth-Guilford area of Piedmont North Carolina's "Quaker belt" by a group of antisecessionists who modeled it after the rituals and structures of Freemasonry. William T. Auman and David D. Scarboro write that the order "was made up of the most militant Unionists of North Carolina, for whom loyalty to the national government was an expression of antipathy to the political and social elite who ruled the State and the Confederacy." The Heroes of America is said to have functioned through a series of loosely organized Unionist networks throughout the backcountry regions not only of North Carolina but also of east Tennessee and southwest Virginia. Dr. Lewis Johnson, a founder of the Heroes of America, had enlisted in the Confederate army in July 1862 not only to avoid the stigma of draft resistance but also to spread the doctrines of his secret group inside Lee's army. He was captured by the Yankees and returned home to North Carolina, where he organized the Grand Council of the Heroes of America at Raleigh.[47]

Private E. D. Meroney, a Confederate prisoner of war who escaped from a Northern prison about a month before Missionary Ridge to make his way back home to the northern Alabama county of Blount, "got an intimation while in prison," so the provost marshal general of the Army of Tennessee reported, "that there was a secret society organized between the Northern and the Southern armies, the object of which is to deplete our ranks by desertion." Northern Alabama, he said, was completely "disloyal and full of deserters." With his curiosity piqued and his patriotism aroused, Meroney had joined the society: "They swear not to give any aid or comfort to a Confederate soldier, nor give any enrolling officer or any one engaged in the Conscript Bureau, any satisfaction or aid, or comfort, nor to write any of the secrets or signs of the society upon paper, earth or earthenware." The resemblance between this so-called Peace Society and the Order of the Heroes of America was not accidental. Meroney discovered, so he reported, that "the enemy have a secret line of spies from Tennessee to Tallapoosa County, Alabama." Perhaps most disturbing of all was his testimony about Peace Society infiltration of the Conscript Bureau itself, with some society members said to be getting legal discharges with the collusion of disaffected Confederate officers.

When an attempted mutiny occurred at Pollard, Alabama, evidence about the causes went directly to Secretary of War Seddon, who ordered further investigation and added his hope that "the disaffection will not only not spread, but be entirely suppressed." The officer in charge of the investigation, Major General Maury, writing on January 11, 1864, after the defeat at Missionary Ridge, wasted little time in correcting Richmond's wishful thinking:

> The fact is established that an organized opposition to the war exists in our midst; that a secret organization has been formed in the army, and with many members in the country, seeking peace on any terms. . . . It is now developed that they have many of them bound themselves to each other by solemn oaths never to fight against the enemy; to desert the service of the Confederacy; to encourage and protect deserters, and to do all other things in their power to end the war and break down the Government and the "so-called Confederacy."

Many civilians were also said to be members of the organization. "The origins of the association is attributed to the enemy and is said to have first entered our army at Cumberland Gap," but "it is improbable that the organization can do us any more harm . . . than the other manifestations of cowardice and unpatriotic opposition to the war with which from the outset we have had to contend." But Maury also turned up testimony "that the Battle at Missionary Ridge was lost and the surrender of Vicksburg was occasioned by the order." The circumstances of the decisive engagements at both Cumberland Gap and Missionary Ridge do seem suspicious (see chap. 10), and any active subversion by the Order of the Heroes of America in Lee's Army of Northern Virginia and in the backcountry areas of the Mississippi Valley that fed men to Lee's army would extend the scope of antiwar sentiment from a local phenomenon to an east-to-west movement.[48]

The antiwar movement within the Confederacy was rooted in social unrest. Yeomen cared little about the survival of the institution of slavery, and although they wanted to preserve the existing racial order, this concern reached its limits when the questions of family welfare intruded. Thus, Confederate policies that threatened to undermine the yeomen's family economy incited passionate resistance, and only at their peril could Confederate officials ignore warnings that increased centralization of national authority and control, in the form of expanded conscription and the hated 10 percent tax-in-kind, was forcing highland families to a level of intolerable deprivation. The conviction that the draft was fundamentally inequitable made submitting to conscription and tax-in-kind seem equivalent to bending the knee to political slavery.

In one of its rare displays of unanimity, the Army of Tennessee's general staff, in late July 1863, dispatched a letter from the camp at Chattanooga to the Confederate War Department about the relationship between the perceived inequalities of conscription and the morale and performance of the men under their command. Signing this letter were Bragg's corps commanders, his division commanders, his brigadiers, and even several of his regimental commanders. Their missive pleaded for speedy action to reinforce the army lest "our cause be lost." They were "thoroughly satisfied that there is enough able-bodied young men out of the service" to bring victory. "The whole system of exemption is based upon a false assumption." Not only had the system of categorical exemptions sparked a proliferation of persons in exempted occupations, but substitution burdened army rolls with men either unfit for duty or else waiting "to desert at the first favorable moment." The remedy seemed clear, a truly egalitarian draft to enable the Confederacy to "drive back the invader" rather than "allowing ourselves to be beaten in detail and our soil to be everywhere overrun." Calling on the "timid and effeminate young men" of high social position who had evaded military service to stand shoulder-to-shoulder with the yeomanry seemed the only answer. Bragg and his officers acknowledged the burdens of fighting for occupied Southern turf: "The occupation of our soil weakens us in men as well as in the means to feed and clothe our troops." "Early and vigorous measures to recruit our wasted ranks may save us further loss of men and resources, and possibly the existence of the Southern Confederacy itself."[49]

There would be no "early and vigorous measures," no egalitarian draft in 1863. Fundamental revision of conscription policy proved too controversial, and it came too late to save the Confederate Cause.

Chapter Ten   "Every Man Says That Every
Other Man Ought to Fight"
Election Losses and the Debacle
at Missionary Ridge

T he timing of the 1863 by-elections in the Confederacy could not
have been worse as far as the Davis administration was concerned,
in view of the impact on popular morale of the recent military disasters. Voters had gone to the polls from July through October to vote
for congressional, state, and local officials. When the votes were
counted, many of the president's closest friends and firmest supporters had
gone down in defeat, particularly in backcountry districts, where voters responded to the inequities of conscription. Many of the men Davis had most
relied on for congressional leadership were ousted. Their defeats dramatized
the influence of antiwar organizations, such as the Peace Society and the Order of the Heroes of America; the organized peace movement was at work on
the home front as well as in the Southern army.

In early August, Reuben Davis, a pro–Jefferson Davis congressman from
Mississippi, took time from his own election struggle against the antiadminis-
tration electoral tide to write his president a long and astute analysis of the
connections between demoralization and the abuses of conscription:

> This war is a peculiar one and does depend for success, very much upon its
> being conducted in such a manner as to control the prejudices and approval of
> the people. We are seeking to establish a Government, and not to defend one.
> In a revolution (and this war is in the nature of a revolution) every man puts his
> neck in the halter, and subjects his property to confiscation, therefore every
> man who is able to bear arms should be required to do so, if the pressure
> becomes so great as to require it; this is the opinion of the great body of the
> people. They naturally ask the question why a certain section of the people

should be required to do all the fighting and endure all the hardships of the camps; and finally conclude it is better to resume their former allegiance than to fight for others.

Reuben Davis pointed out that a secret opposition was seeking to persuade the yeomanry that "it is a war for the defense of the institution of slavery, an institution in which they have no personal interest, and which they cannot be made to believe benefits them politically or socially." He saw only one answer to such class-based rhetoric: "Now to satisfy them upon this subject, you must have no substitutes, no exempts." Anticipating the president's response, he continued, "I know that private interest and to some extent public interest demands that there be substitutes and exempts. But when the indulgence of these considerations is endangering the success of the revolution itself, they must yield on the ground that it [is] better that a few interests should perish than the *Cause* should fail utterly." He asserted, "Every man says that every other man ought to fight in this war, and if all will go, he will go—The Conscript and the Militia says they ought not to be forced to fight, whilst others as able as themselves and more wealthy remain at home, and when they are forced into camp with this feelings, they go to desert and not to fight." Notwithstanding all of the above, Reuben Davis remained optimistic. "I still believe the convocation of Congress and the repeal of these laws would have a salutary effect and perhaps save us from subjugation."[1]

But by the time the president managed to call a special session of the Confederate Congress for the express purpose of amending the unpopular conscription laws, it was already too late to save the military position in the Mississippi Valley. Vicksburg would exact one final penalty, for it was Vicksburg parolees who would take the leading role in the flight from combat at Missionary Ridge on that fateful day in November 1863 when the Confederacy lost its last combat army of the western theater.

Within a week after predicting a political reaction against the Confederate leadership, William Pitt Ballinger witnessed a stunning upset during the election for Congress from his own Galveston district. The cause, he believed, was the incumbent's vote "in favor of the exemption of the owners of 20 slaves. A furor was kindled against him on the matter." "The soldiers and poorer people were carried almost to a man for the upset victor." The unsuccessful campaign waged by Arkansas representative Charles Royston also indicates how much support for the overseer exemptions was a liability for candidates running in districts with heavy yeoman populations. Royston, the only defeated member of the Arkansas congressional delegation, had been accused of supporting the exemption as a means of removing his own son from the Southern army. Charles Royston Jr., a six-foot, three-inch strapping young man, had received an overseer exemption but was widely reported to have spent most of his time not in overseeing but in "riding the fastest horses over the country, attending *stag* dances with his associates." Royston defended his son's exemption as "completely legal and justified," but he lost his electoral race decisively.[2]

But it was in Alabama that anti-Davis forces won their most sweeping victories. Senator Clement Clay had stood for reelection that summer, and with the death of the state's other senator, William Lowndes Yancey, the Alabama legislature was to choose two replacements. With the terms of all their representatives expiring in the regular process, Alabama voters now had an opportunity to replace their entire congressional delegation, House and Senate. One of Davis's strongest supporters in that delegation, Jabez L. M. Curry, was defeated in his congressional race, and several other Davis supporters lost. Even Governor John Shorter went down to defeat, by almost a 4-to-1 margin; his reputation as an earnest supporter of the war effort had apparently produced that negative landslide. Even more stunning was the dramatic reversal in the state legislature. Anti-Davis forces there were able to remove Clay and to elect Robert Jemison, an early opponent of secession, as Yancey's successor. This sweep testified to the power of the Peace Society in Alabama: the antiwar movement had succeeded in replacing one of the Confederacy's founding fathers with an antisecessionist and in displacing one of Jefferson Davis's closest friends.

So dramatic and unexpected were the electoral results in Alabama that the commandant of conscription wrote an extensive report about the intervention of the Peace Society. Major W. T. Walthal suggested, in an August 6 letter to Lieutenant Colonel G. W. Lay that "the result of the recent elections in this State has developed a degree of disaffection (to use the mildest possible term) which may lead to serious mischief." Elections in his section of the state (Talladega) "have been generally carried by an opposition known as the 'Peace Party.'" He found a similar pattern elsewhere in the state.

These results are mainly attributable . . . to a secret sworn organization known to exist and believed to have for its objects the encouragement of desertion, the protection of deserters from arrest, resistance to conscription, and perhaps other designs of a still more dangerous character. . . . But it is a significant fact that hostility to the conscription law has been one of the main elements of the opposition. It is perhaps still more significant that the rank and file of the paroled prisoners of the Vicksburg army, according to my information, contributed largely by their votes to the result of the election.

Walthal attested to alliances between Vicksburg veterans and deserter groups. "Strength was added also to the opposition by the host of deserters who swarm throughout the country, and who no doubt came forth from their lurking places on the day of the election wherever the polls were not guarded by military force." He observed, in addition, "The disposition is widely prevalent among the population at home to afford shelter and protection to these deserters, and insidious efforts are making to induce the paroled men generally to refuse to return into service."[3]

In Mississippi, two Davis supporters fell victim to voter backlash. Much as in Alabama, opponents organized to control the state legislature, hoping to deny reelection to Senator James Phelan, a strong advocate of the Davis administration. James Alcorn helped orchestrate the campaign that replaced Phelan with J. W. C. Watson, a former Whig known for his coolness toward secession. Alcorn himself was elected to the state legislature despite refusing to take any active part in his campaign. In the race for governor, the incumbent John Pettus was retiring, leaving the field open, and three veteran politicians campaigned to replace him. One of the three was Reuben Davis, who finished third in a field of three. A local paper explained his defeat simply, "Too well known to be elected." Writing his autobiography later, Davis spoke in his own defense, criticizing the "personal and political enemies" who charged "that I had voted for what was called the 'Twenty Nigger Bill,' in spite of the well known fact that my opposition had been made conspicuous." Joseph Davis, the president's brother, correctly connected such defeats to anger at the exemption system, writing his brother during the Mississippi election campaign, "I hope when Congress meets the necessity will be so apparent that demagoging will wane and the safety of the country be considered. The conscription law should be repealed."[4]

Ebbing Confederate Morale and Bold Union Strategy

The original Republican rationale for denying the Confederacy the right to secede assumed that the secession movement did not represent the will of the nonslaveholding majority. The *London Times*'s war correspondent, William Russell, reflected this rationale in attributing Lincoln's determination to control eastern Tennessee to the Republican "theory of the divided South." In the light of the exploits of east Tennessee Unionist exiles like Andrew Johnson, William G. Brownlow, and Horace Maynard, Davis had to demonstrate that his popular majority did indeed provide a united support for the Confederate cause. The Northern invaders, for their part, saw themselves as deliverers of a long-oppressed people. Their sense of mission was expressed in an exchange of letters in October 1863 between Lincoln and several Unionists in newly liberated Knoxville who had written imploringly: "In the name of Christianity and humanity! in the name of God and liberty! . . . the loyal people of Tennessee appeal to you and implore you not to abandon them again to the merciless dominion of the rebels by a withdrawal of the U.S. forces from upper East Tennessee." Lincoln had responded quickly, and with unaccustomed emotion, "You do not estimate the holding of East Tennessee more highly than I do." In a conversation between Charles Dana, his assistant secretary of war, and Andrew Johnson, the war governor of occupied middle and western Tennessee, it was hoped that liberation of Tennessee Unionists might prompt yeomen in the mountains of western North Carolina "to free themselves from the Confederate Government." "In this respect, the occupation of East Tennessee is of the highest importance," Johnson said. "This is the center of the whole mountain region with its population of a million and a half natural haters of slavery and of the rebellion."[5]

None of the covey of Northern generals who had earlier been assigned this task had been able to mount a successful invasion. When General Buell captured Nashville without a fight in February 1862, he tarried so long before moving to reinforce Grant that the Union army came close to annihilation during the first day at Shiloh. Later, Buell moved toward Chattanooga so ponderously that Braxton Bragg swung his army completely around him and invaded Kentucky; Buell's pursuit of Bragg's columns resulted in the stalemate at Perryville. After Lincoln replaced Buell with General William Rosecrans, Rosecrans also found multiple excuses for delaying a move toward Chattanooga; only by ordering him forward was Lincoln able to force an offensive that led to the bloody battle of Stones River on December 31, 1862. Lincoln had hoped that a forward movement in middle Tennessee would compel Davis to redirect some of the troops massing to relieve the beleaguered garrison at Vicksburg, but Rosecrans resisted fighting two decisive campaigns simultaneously, the strategy that Lincoln intended to exploit the North's superiority in manpower and resources. Coordination between General Ambrose Burnside's Army of the Ohio and Rosecrans's move toward Chattanooga finally achieved Lincoln's long-held goal, the two-pronged invasion aimed at the northern and southern gates of eastern Tennessee. Burnside's move and Confederate bungling produced two stunning Union successes: the seizure of Knoxville on September 3, and the capture of Cumberland Gap on September 9, 1863.

Thanks to the many Southern mountain Unionists serving among his troops, Burnside could move with ease through the labyrinth of mountain passes from Kentucky to Tennessee and emerge near Knoxville at Big Stone Gap more quickly and in greater strength than the Confederate commander, General Buckner, had any reason to expect. Buckner withdrew; he lacked the troops he needed, and he had to respond to Bragg's orders to join the main Confederate force near Chattanooga. The move reflected the South's stark inferiority in numbers, an inferiority related, in turn, to the epidemic of desertion and resistance throughout eastern Tennessee. In Knoxville on September 3, as Colonel Gilbert Kniffen recalled, "The East Tennessee troops, separated for many months from their families, were greeted with expressions of the tenderest affection by the people all along the line of march." Union flags suddenly appeared. "A feast awaited the troops at every village. Women stood by the roadside with buckets of water, fruit and cakes, which they gave freely, refusing all offers to pay." "Men who for months had been hidden in caves in the hills and in mountain fastnesses came in and were overjoyed at their deliverance." Knoxville's residents, slave as well as free, wrote George Phillips in a September 12 letter, were "running wild through the streets and shouting for joy insomuch that even our brave General Burnside gave vent to his feelings in a profuse shedding of tears." At Cumberland Gap, the Confederate commander General John Frazer had "boasted that he could hold it for at least a month," but he failed to take account of the overt and covert assistance offered by local citizens to the Northern invaders. Frazer surrendered on September 9 without a fight. Davis called it "a shameful abandonment of duty." The strategic balance of the entire east Tennessee campaign was altered thereby.[6]

One of the Confederate prisoners of war at Fort Warren in Boston Harbor said that nocturnal reconnaissance by a party of forty Northern soldiers had frightened the demoralized two hundred members of the 62nd North Carolina Infantry into abandoning their picket line at Cumberland Gap, most leaving their muskets behind. The next day, these same soldiers refused to stand to their posts. "I do not hesitate to say that their disorderly conduct and obvious want of confidence in themselves destroyed all hope of getting effective service out of them," reported Lieutenant Thomas O'Connor, a Confederate artillery commander. "Anarchy and confusion was supreme throughout that portion of the line. Desertions from the regiment were a daily occurrence and its *morale* very bad." Earlier, part of a detail from the 62nd North Carolina had absented themselves without leave "and the balance of them almost mutinous." An attempt to persuade them to do their duty evoked "much other abusive language toward both the officers and Government of the Confederate States."

Seeking to salvage his own reputation, Frazer condemned the quality of his troops. The colonel of the 62nd North Carolina, he said, had gone home and was "an open advocate of reunion in his county." Affairs in the 64th North Carolina were little better; after the atrocity at Laurel Creek Valley (see chap. 9), "the Colonel and Lt. Colonel had left in disgrace for dishonorable conduct." In the 54th Georgia, Frazer's "best" regiment, "the men did ride their colonel on a rail, which he never resented, but on promise to them of better behavior was allowed to resume his command." Frazer concluded that "the character, confidence and condition of the troops hastily collected to defend the gap were such as to justify no hope of a successful defense against an equal number of the enemy, much less the overwhelming force as threatened the position front and rear." He insisted that the arrival of Union reinforcements had persuaded him that "it would be a mad or wicked attempt to defend the post, or to attempt a partial fight with a view to escape. I might have some reputation for desperate courage," he said, "but so selfish a consideration at so great a sacrifice of life forbade me to entertain so rash a design and to prefer a Northern prison to the self-reproaches of a wounded conscience." Still, Frazer could not explain away the fact that word had come before the surrender that reinforcements were on the way; he had been expected not to give up "without a stubborn resistance."[7]

After the Confederate loss of Knoxville and Cumberland Gap, two principal engagements were fought that fall of 1863: at Chickamauga on September 19 and 20, and at Missionary Ridge on November 24 and 25. In between was Chattanooga. Astride the great bend in the Tennessee River and in the shadow of Missionary Ridge, the city of Chattanooga lay at the center of a mining, manufacturing, and transportation complex the Confederacy could ill afford to lose. Jefferson Davis had implored his feuding commanders Bragg and Buckner to acknowledge "how necessary" was "a success against the enemy in that quarter," "how disastrous it would be to lose possession of that mountainous region which covers the entrance into Georgia and Alabama and constitutes our best base for the recovery of Middle Tennessee." On the Union side, on September 21 Abraham Lincoln had urged the Union commander near Chattanooga, General Halleck, to keep "all Tennessee clear from the enemy" and break "one of his most important railroad lines." The Confederacy, Lincoln knew, would put up a desperate struggle. If the North could retain firm control of the mountain passes, "The rebellion can only eke out a short and feeble resistance, as an animal sometimes may with a thorn in his vitals."[8]

At Chickamauga, Confederates gained what should have been a decisive victory after Davis undertook the daring maneuver of detaching Longstreet's corps from the Army of Northern Virginia and dispatching it to reinforce Bragg. But Bragg's forces, unable to cope with the combined Northern troops, failed to follow up aggressively, although Bragg did manage to impose a siege that came within an ace of forcing a withdrawal in disarray from Chattanooga. Lincoln then did what his Southern counterpart could not: he replaced a failing commander with his most successful field general, Ulysses S. Grant for Rosecrans. Within a week Grant had lifted the Chattanooga siege, and within a month he had maneuvered into position for a decisive engagement. It was a dramatic volte-face that would erase any question about the genius of Grant's generalship. He would rescue a besieged Northern garrison and inflict a decisive defeat on the besieging force.

Davis ordered twenty regiments of Vicksburg parolees up to Chattanooga from bases in Alabama and Mississippi, but—much as at Cumberland Gap—an outnumbered, demoralized, and poorly led Southern army could not summon the esprit de corps to take maximum advantage of a superior defensive position. The dimensions of the evil of desertion had become starkly apparent in Bragg's and Buckner's strength reports filed in the weeks before Rosecrans's offensive in late June. Buckner reported as "absent without leave" 9,000 members of the 28,000-man contingent in upper east Tennessee; Bragg recorded the unauthorized "absence" of 24,000 soldiers from his 83,000-man contingent. These 33,000 absentees together accounted for fully 30 percent of

the nominal strength of the defensive force. And yet, both in absolute numbers of absentees and in their percentage of the total force, the Union army
rivaled the Army of Tennessee: the Army of the Cumberland listed 36,000
men out of its nominal strength of 133,000 as absent without leave, an absentee rate of 27 percent. The rough approximation between desertion rates for
Confederate and Union forces has led students of the Civil War to conclude
that class-conscious desertion in Confederate forces was not decisive in their
defeat. They have assumed that desertion rates computed for the entire war
explain much of the importance of absenteeism in particular campaigns. Yet
there were distinctive patterns of desertion between North and South, especially for the east Tennessee campaign. There, between June and November
1863, the absentee rate for the Union army of Tennessee doubled, then fell
precipitously, while that of its opponent remained stable throughout the
campaign and rose afterward, suggesting that Southern desertion may have
been more decisive at Missionary Ridge than the heavy disproportion in
manpower between the South and the North, to which most scholars attribute the rout.[9]

Scholars have also tended to underrate the political significance of the pattern of Southern desertions. Lincoln's Emancipation Proclamation had
changed the meaning of desertion. To Davis the proclamation was "the most
execrable measure ever recorded in the history of guilty man," encouraging
the slaves "to a general assassination of their masters," as he said in his June 12,
1863, message to the Confederate Congress. "Lincoln's proclamation is worth
three hundred thousand soldiers to our Government at least," Henry F.
Stone, the son of a slaveholding Kentuckian, serving in the Army of Tennessee, wrote to his father the following month. "It shows exactly what the
war was brought about for and the intentions of its damnable authors." Although Davis had moved boldly and decisively as the commander in chief,
disaffection had repeatedly undermined Confederate military efforts. In his
decision to send troops to Bragg via Atlanta not Knoxville, Davis was considering the risk of partisan violence of mountain Unionists. As he put it in a message to Lee on September 16, a week after the loss of Cumberland Gap, "The
disaffected population in East Tennessee and North Carolina will materially
aid the enemy and embarrass our future operations." Davis and Lee had jug-
gled the regiments slated for the trip to east Tennessee in an effort to prevent
desertions like those that had frustrated the attempt to reinforce Vicksburg
earlier. Lee decided to leave several regiments in Charleston rather than trans-

port them through the mountains of northern Georgia; Longstreet, he told Davis, "does not want to take them into Georgia, for fear of desertion."[10]

All the same, trouble erupted along Longstreet's route from Richmond to Atlanta. Private Turner Vaughn, serving in the 4th Alabama Infantry, wrote in his diary for September 12, "When we reached Raleigh a number of our boys went uptown with the intention of destroying the *Standard* Office. Colonel Scruggs, being informed of it by Governor Vance who came down to the cars in his buggy, took the remainder of the regiment to arrest the offenders." These soldiers had chosen their target deliberately, since Confederate officials viewed the *Standard* as the leading voice of North Carolina antiwar sentiment; North Carolina was the headquarters of the Order of the Heroes of America. Governor Vance had implored Davis to prevent such acts of violence: "For God's sake save us from this state of things. If you wish to save North Carolina to the Confederacy, be quick," and he tried to interpose himself between the enraged troops and the newspaper office but could do nothing; the Alabama brigade "even threatened my life if I interfered with them." He stood by while another mob, this time of anti-Confederate activists, destroyed a second paper, the *State Journal,* as if to even the scale after the destruction of the *Standard.* Vance hoped the incidents would let Davis "see what a mine I have been standing on and what a delicate and embarrassing situation mine is." He was outraged over the role Confederate officers had played in destroying the press and offices. Some junior officers had participated, and a Confederate general who knew about the threat had done nothing: "The distance is quite short to either anarchy or despotism when armed soldiers led by their officers, can with impunity outrage the laws of a State. A few more such exhibitions will bring the North Carolina troops home to their own State and her institutions."[11]

The two-day battle at Chickamauga produced thirty-four thousand casualties and ended in an indecisive Confederate victory for Longstreet's Army of Northern Virginia veterans. Men from the Army of Tennessee fought with reckless courage, inflicting defeat on an army of superior resources and manpower. Yet, in perhaps no other battle did absenteeism prove to be so costly. A more decisive victory at Chickamauga would undoubtedly have prolonged the war and given the Confederacy the one thing it needed most: time.

In the end, the circumstances surrounding the climactic battle at Missionary Ridge told a tale of demoralization. There the South faced an enormous Northern force commanded by Grant, Sherman, George Thomas, and Philip

Sheridan. Lincoln, reorganizing the entire Northern command structure in the Mississippi Valley, had dispatched three full corps to rescue the garrisons at Chattanooga and at Knoxville. Bragg had occupied his time after Chickamauga preparing elaborate accusations of misconduct against his senior generals. Once the Confederate general staff learned of his preoccupation with assigning blame, an undetermined number of generals met on October 4 to draft a petition to Davis calling for Bragg's removal from command of the Army of Tennessee. But other matters were competing for Davis's attention. Desertion again threatened. On October 5 Lee queried Davis about an apparent discrepancy between the number of men Bragg was listing as reporting for duty and the number supposedly available to him. Could Bragg's army have been weaker after the arrival of Longstreet's corps than before? The ever vigilant Davis had already asked Bragg for clarification in a telegram of September 30: "Am surprised at the statement of infantry force. Hope there is an error in the cipher." "There was probably no mistake in the cipher," Bragg admitted. "Heavy losses resulting from a desperate and prolonged fight and heavy straggling from the reinforcements have depleted us." Much as at Vicksburg, the attempt to reinforce a Southern army had run afoul of a disinclination to serve at the front.[12]

The service record of a private conscripted into the Army of Tennessee helps to explain why Davis's effort to reinforce Bragg achieved so little. Amos Ginn, who lived with his nonslaveholding family in the swamp country near Beaufort City, South Carolina, testified a decade later, in 1875, that "my father and all his children were against the war and we boys did not want to fight against the Union." He had found himself in the army after "three Confederate soldiers in uniforms and with guns came to my father's house and took me and my brother off." Apparently, Ginn spent most of his time in service looking for ways to escape, but "I did not desert because I did not want to bring trouble upon myself and my people at home." He searched for another method of escaping service and found it when he allowed himself to be captured. He told his captors: "I was glad I was in good hands and never had wanted to fight against them."[13]

Almost as soon as Rosecrans's army drew near Chattanooga, a steady stream of deserters appeared, and shortly after the city was seized, the provost marshal reported an increase in desertion, "2500 since leaving Tullahoma, mainly men of Kentucky and East Tennessee." Rosecrans told Stanton on September 11 that "the number of deserters from the rebel army is great" and sought Stanton's permission to enlist such men in the Northern army. Stanton approved his request. The information some of the deserters brought along was encouraging. Dana described one such incident to Stanton: "A sergeant of Fifth (rebel) Kentucky Regiment, who deserted to us this morning, says it was understood in the rebel camps . . . that the firing beyond Missionary Ridge on the 6th [October] was occasioned by the refusal of a brigade of Georgia militia, 5,000 strong, to cross the State line." The deserter, Sergeant G. H. Baughn, who had led his picket patrol into a Union camp, informed his liberators in an October 8 statement of "a great deal of dissatisfaction" "particularly among the Tennessee, Kentucky, North Carolina and Virginia troops," who were "ready to desert whenever an opportunity presents itself." "The Kentucky troops," he said, "are willing to play quits upon any terms. The soldiers are down on the rich men." Referring to the "Twenty Nigger Law," Baughn said, "The property qualification does not please the men. The troops are arriving at the conclusion that this is a war for the rich men of the South, and they are determined to get out of it." Soldiers like Ginn and Baughn were an obvious threat to Confederate efforts. In the race between North and South to see which side could get the most reinforcements to the front the fastest, the steady hemorrhaging from the Southern army was tipping the strategic balance.[14]

The Davis administration, noting the swelling number of evaders, had earlier called on the only man who seemed able to cope with desertion and resistance: General Gideon Pillow. But Secretary of War Seddon informed General Johnston in August that many civilians compared Pillow's bureau "to the press gang, sweeping through the country with little deference either to law or to the regulations designed to temper its unavoidable rigor." Although such tactics might work in the short run, if persisted in "for any length of time," Seddon warned, they "will probably cause in the end a degree of dissatisfaction and positive opposition that may reverse the public feeling of the country and operate most disastrously to the Confederacy and the cause." The tenure of Pillow's renewed authority should be a response only to "the exigency of the present time," Seddon told Johnston, to be regarded "as temporary and not to be permanently continued." Pillow did indeed labor to staunch the flow of deserters, but at the root of the problem was the Southern peace movement. "If these deserters are arrested again and sent to the Army of Tennessee," Pillow told Ewell, "as many of them have been a second, third and even fourth time, they will not stay." The only feasible solution seemed to be to transfer disaffected soldiers from the Army of Tennessee to the Army of Northern Virginia, separating the "deserters and tory conscripts" from their bases in highland communities. Pillow understood that "they cannot be kept in the army so near their homes." Writing to Seddon on October 5, Pillow reported that he had found no alternative but to send captured Army of Tennessee deserters to Lee's army, "the best that can be done under the circumstances." "The Army of Tennessee is at present so convenient to the homes of these men, that it is impossible to keep them in the army . . . *General Bragg is satisfied that these men will not stay in his army and there are so many of them that shooting them seems out of the question*" (emphasis mine).[15]

Davis struggled for some formula that might restore fighting spirit to Bragg's demoralized army. He lectured Bragg about his past failings, charging in a message of October 3, "The opposition to you both in the army and out of it has been a public calamity in so far as it impairs your capacity for usefulness," and dispatched a special emissary to Bragg's headquarters, South Carolina senator James Chesnut. For weeks, Davis had pondered the wisdom of a personal visit to the strife-torn Army of Tennessee. Chesnut quickly recognized that only Davis's personal intervention could save the day: "Your presence in the Army is urgently demanded. Come if possible." Davis reached Missionary Ridge in five days. His inspection tour of several front-line positions failed to receive the heartiest of welcomes, particularly at a brigade post along the picket line at Lookout Mountain, where "only one regiment cheered him." John Bratton wrote to his wife Bettie, "It seemed to me a cold reception." From a common solider, Sam Watkins, came a somewhat pithier version of the same incident. Recalling the "privations and hardships . . . we went through at Missionary Ridge," he wrote, and then "in the very acme of our privation and hunger, when the army was most dissatisfied and unhappy, we were ordered into line of battle to be reviewed by Honorable Jefferson Davis." Hunger had given a sharp edge to the discontent among common soldiers, for while the siege had imposed crippling food shortages on the Northern army, deployment dictated by the siege had also brought discomfort to the besieging Army of Tennessee; in addition, hungry soldiers had been forced to share "some of our rations with starving women and children in the mountains." Nor did it help matters that many soldiers suspected Confederate commissaries of shameless profiteering. Davis apparently failed to hear what his soldiers shouted. "When he passed by us," Watkins wrote, "with his great retinue of staff officers and play-outs at full gallop, cheers greeted them, with the words, 'Send us something to eat, Massa Jeff. Give us something to eat, Massa Jeff. I'm hungry! I'm hungry!'" Major General Lafayette McLaws wrote to his wife that Davis "has been here for some time, endeavoring to settle the difficulties among the Generals," but "to tell you the truth, I do not like him, although he is about the best man we have." "His manners are cold and repelling; I hope he may be able to settle the difficulties, so as to make the army homogeneous but I doubt it very much."[16]

Bold Maneuvers and Mistakes

Lincoln acted boldly, in sharp contrast to Davis's temporizing over Bragg, in ordering the creation of a unified western theater command that would link the armies of the Tennessee, the Ohio, and the Cumberland under Grant. Grant replaced Rosecrans with George Thomas, and in response to Grant's request that he hold on at Chattanooga until reinforcements arrived, Thomas said, "We will hold the town until we starve." Grant broadened his charge to encompass expelling the Army of Tennessee from the Mississippi Valley, and although suffering from the sort of painfully disabling injury that had led Lee to decline command at Chattanooga, he hastened from Louisville as fast as his condition and transportation would allow, "carried over places where it was not safe to ride on horseback." Within a week of his arrival he opened the Tennessee River, now a reliable supply line into Chattanooga. Five thousand Northern volunteers floated down the Tennessee from Chattanooga to seize Brown's Ferry, and Bragg's tenuous hold on the Union supply line was broken. Davis now ordered a bold maneuver of his own, a thrust at Knoxville to force Lincoln to detach troops from Chattanooga; if Lincoln took that bait it might bring on an engagement Bragg's outnumbered army could win. It was one of the Confederate president's most controversial command decisions, a gamble Grant would later ridicule in these words: "Mr. Davis had an exalted opinion of his own military genius."[17] The Knoxville expedition accomplished little. The decisive breakthrough at Missionary Ridge occurred instead.

Thousands of Vicksburg parolees had been made available for fighting. Comparing the Army of Tennessee's strength report for October 31 with the official list of units captured by the Union army at Vicksburg shows that more than twenty regiments not listed on the October organizational chart were there by November 20. If Davis could replace Longstreet's twelve-thousand-man corps with some twenty regiments of Vicksburg veterans, the attempt to regain ground previously lost at Knoxville and Cumberland Gap seemed perfectly reasonable, since a push toward Knoxville would almost certainly force Lincoln to detach at least one corps from Chattanooga. With Vicksburg veterans available to replace troops at Missionary Ridge, a Northern countering move probably would indeed have postponed Grant's offensive and worked to the advantage of the Confederacy. The gamble failed, but it came much closer than is generally acknowledged. It failed for the same reasons the east Tennessee campaign had also gone against the Confederacy: poor leadership and popular disaffection.

A Union network of well-paid Southern informants was also important. Brigadier General W. P. Sanders was authorized "to employ as many citizen scouts" as he needed. "You will lose no time," said General Burnside, "in procuring thorough information and are not limited as to expense." Through informants, Burnside learned about Longstreet's location in time to beat a hasty retreat toward Knoxville; but the guide Longstreet had retained to lead his men to cut off Burnside's route apparently connived with the enemy, and "when daylight came," reported a rueful Longstreet, "it was discovered that the guide had failed to put the troops upon the right road and that the enemy had during the night abandoned part of his wagon train and made a hurried retreat." Longstreet had to chase his prey into the fortifications at Knoxville rather than engage him in the open field, and he became bogged down in a siege he could not win. Possibly most damaging to the Southern cause was Longstreet's absence from the decisive engagement at Missionary Ridge, and most humiliating of all was his withdrawal in late December, in the face of a relieving force sent by Grant from Chattanooga. Disloyal local informants spelled the difference: at Knoxville, Cumberland Gap, and Lenoir's Station, Southern forces had been outmaneuvered as they lost their home advantage in the mountains of east Tennessee. An embittered Longstreet escaped in the spring of 1864 and returned to his friendlier Virginia homeland.[18]

During the lead-up to the climactic day at Missionary Ridge in late November, the problem of desertion showed no signs of abating. Private John Cotton tried to dispute his wife's reports about the numbers of Alabama deserters found near their home: "I cont think there is much deserting agoing on now I think most that is deserting from here is tennesseeans some of our regiment gos home but they dont stay long before they come back." Captain Samuel C. Kelly admitted, "Four men from Co. H deserted night before last, and went to the Yankees, and yesterday the Yankees on picket told us about it, and that they understood we were short on rations." General Carl Schurz, who served in one of the two Union corps transferred from the Army of the Potomac to Chattanooga, observed "great numbers" of Confederate deserters, "mostly from Alabama regiments which were camped opposite to us. . . . They would during the night crawl over a big tree which had fallen across the creek and surrender to our pickets, . . . so many of them that I sometimes, when I arose in the morning, found the space between my hq. tents filled with a dense crowd." True to his Republican ideology, Schurz emphasized the backcountry origins of the hungry deserters, but he focused on the class-based rebellion against the Confederacy: "There was a 'winged word' among the poor people of the South, which strikingly portrayed their situation, as they conceived it to be, in a single sentence: 'It is the rich man's war and the poor man's fight.'" The frequency of desertion communicated a clear message to the North of a rapid erosion of the Southern will to fight. Major James Connolly wrote his wife, "A picket from one of the outposts . . . came in with a rebel deserter who had just come through our lines; the General ordered him taken to the Provost Marshall and nothing further was thought of it, all despatched in a business-like way; it occurs so frequently that our soldiers think nothing of it." On the other hand, he said, "I couldn't help thinking, as I looked at him, 'Your're a cowardly rascal.'" "I like to see them desert; I wish they would *all* desert and go to their homes, but at that moment I respected his misguided comrades who remained at their posts more than I did him." Connolly saw the surrender terms Grant had imposed at Vicksburg as limiting the manpower of the Confederate forces: "I find a general disposition among the paroled prisoners, in which they are sustained by public sentiment, not to report until exchanged, and am convinced they can only be brought in by compulsory means."[19]

Lincoln's decision to send fifty thousand fresh troops to Chattanooga had forced the Confederacy to rush the reluctant veterans of Vicksburg back into service. Urged by Davis to take this step as early as August 23, General Carter Stevenson, a division commander under Pemberton at Vicksburg who had been captured, paroled, and later exchanged, wrote in September in General Order #33: "It now rests with them—soldiers of Georgia, of Alabama and of Tennessee—to show whether they will respond promptly to the summons to duty and once more rally to the support of our cause, or be forced into the ranks that they should glory in filling." Writing from his new Mississippi headquarters, General William Hardee tried to explain the difficulties to his superiors in Richmond in a message of October 12: "I have used every effort to reassemble the command, but so far with but discouraging results." Word of the arrival of Vicksburg veterans at Chattanooga spread so rapidly that in less than two weeks Grant had learned about it via Hooker from four Southern deserters from the Army of Tennessee: "The Tennessee brigade has been relieved on the top of Lookout Mountain by Stevenson's Division, made up principally of paroled prisoners from Vicksburg. The reason assigned for this change is that the rebel authorities were afraid to intrust the defense of Lookout Mountain to Tennessee regiments, owing to the defection known to exist among them."[20]

Bragg's extensive reorganization of his command in the presence of the enemy, in addition to satisfying a desire to separate his foe, might also have been part of a deliberate strategy to break up disloyal combinations among regiments from anti-Confederate backcountry areas. Thus Bragg disbanded Hilliard's Legion, an organization of men from the Alabama backcountry known for their reluctance to join the Confederate army. Little more than a week before Missionary Ridge, Bragg dispatched a long letter to his commander in chief, seeking to reveal as gently as he could the extent of absenteeism. He used the imminent expiration of enlistment of three-year volunteers to suggest to Davis that amendment of the draft act might help counter complaints about class discrimination: "I should propose to put the services of every man in the Confederacy at the disposal of the Government, and leave it to the Government to decide when, where and how it might employ them for the greatest public good." Enacting a truly equalitarian draft "would no doubt allay nearly all opposition on the part of the present soldiers, and induce them to submit cheerfully and contentedly to what they know to be a necessity and from which there is no escape." He referred to thousands of "officers and men remaining absent from their commands." "Our present effective force in the field will not exceed 40% of the aggregate strength on the muster rolls—This is frightful but it is too true."[21]

"A Defeat So Disgraceful": Rout at Missionary Ridge

A war correspondent for the *Richmond Dispatch*, writing under the pen name Sallust, filed on December 4, 1863, a battle report laden with incredulity at the behavior of troops defending a position even Northern officers thought invulnerable. Confederate soldiers at Missionary Ridge had thrown down their weapons, then turned and fled to the rear, many without ever firing a shot. Sallust wrote scathingly: "The Confederates have sustained today the most ignominious defeat of the whole war—a defeat for which there is but little excuse or palliation. For the first time during our struggle for national independence, our defeat is chargable to the troops themselves, and not to the blunders or incompetency of their leaders." "The ground was more in our favor than it was at Fredericksburg," he charged, "[a]nd yet we gained the battle at Fredericksburg and lost that of Missionary Ridge."

Why, indeed, did the Army of Tennessee, baptized and lauded for its service in the fires of Shiloh, Perryville, Stones River, and Chickamauga, fail to hold on to a ridge line five hundred feet above the Northern army? The difficulty of storming fortified high ground had in large measure explained the failure of the Northern assault at Fredericksburg, and that of Pickett's charge up Cemetery Ridge at Gettysburg. According to conventional military wisdom, an uphill charge against fortified high ground, such as the North would need to make at Missionary Ridge, was suicidal. Why then the Southern defeat?

Grant had about a 3-to-1 advantage in manpower, and at least as great an edge in artillery. The South held a seemingly critical advantage, the height of Missionary Ridge and the steepness of its slopes, but in the end these would work to its disadvantage. Only with difficulty could cannon on top of a natural crest fire effectively onto a plain below, and since the steepness of the ridge hampered use of the crest by troops, General Bragg may well have concluded that he had to position his troops across the plain to slow the pace of a Northern advance and thus provide and maintain an effective field for artillery fire. His deployment of Confederate soldiers in multiple lines remains an immensely controversial aspect of the east Tennessee campaign. Heavy absenteeism had sharply reduced the depth he could bring to bear along his extended lines. When Grant tried to account for the Union victory at Missionary Ridge, "won against great odds, considering the advantage the enemy had of position," he said it "was accomplished more easily than was expected by reason of Bragg's making several grave mistakes," among them the Knoxville expedition and the plan of deployment—a "grave" error—"placing so much of a force on the plain in front of his impregnable position."[22] In retrospect, the Confederate decision to place Vicksburg parolees and Tennessee yeomen on the plain in front of Missionary Ridge probably deserves right of place as the gravest of Bragg's many blunders.

In the valley below, more than a hundred thousand Northern soldiers from the Army of the Tennessee, the Army of the Cumberland, and the Army of the Potomac had maneuvered into position. As Private Ralph Neal described the frightening view from the crest of Missionary Ridge, "It was indeed a great spectacle for our little band to see—perhaps in modern times an entire army had not witnessed such a scene." A lunar eclipse two nights before the battle had imparted a sense of "impending disaster." Yet Private Neal asked, "Why should it presage defeat for us? Why not the Yankees?" The same question occurred to the Northern army camped in the valley below, Major Connolly wrote to his wife. An eclipse "was considered a bad omen among the ancients, on the eve of battle; we concluded that it was ominous of defeat, but not for us; we concluded that it meant Bragg because he was perched on the mountain top, nearest the moon."[23]

Much more critical than omens was the corrosive pessimism in the Southern army and the defeatism of the Vicksburg parolees. The Vicksburg parolees had behaved so badly in transit to Chattanooga that the president of the Mobile and Ohio Railroad complained to Johnston that soldiers riding the freight cars had conspired with brigands in return for an opportunity to escape. They simply tore "our cars to pieces so that thieves can jump on our cars and throw off freight to an extent that is perfectly ruinous." Defeatism and poor leadership were a lethal combination. An officer new to the situation, Captain W. W. Blackford, was stunned to discover, he wrote his wife at the end of October, that most of the army believed fervently that "whatever should be done will be left undone and whatever should not be done Bragg will do."[24]

In an attempt to raise sagging morale, Bragg undertook a typically clumsy gesture. If there was any subject about which Vicksburg parolees were uniformly anxious, it had to be the prospect of their treatment by Grant's army in the event of capture; taken literally, their paroles appeared to put their lives at risk if they were caught fighting before a proper exchange had occurred. Bragg took the unusual step of issuing a general order in mid-November about the consequences of a breakdown in the prisoner-of-war cartel, apparently assuming it would reignite fires of patriotic fervor. "If taken prisoner," he wrote to Longstreet, "those who survive their cruel treatment will be forced to languish in Northern dungeons until the close of the war." "If their liberty and their lives must be lost, the alternative of *Honorable Death* on the field of battle, nobly fighting for the cause of freedom, will be accepted by brave and patriotic Southern soldiers." One need only imagine the response to this announcement when it was read aloud at morning assembly to already disheartened Vicksburg parolees.[25]

Rather than exchange fire with the onrushing Northern soldiers, most of Bragg's men at the base of Missionary Ridge simply declined to give battle; some surrendered, others dove for cover, and still others raced up the ridge. Instead of the heavy hand-to-hand combat they had expected, the North's attackers found themselves exposed to firing from higher up the ridge and, in direct violation of orders, bolted up the ridge side by side with Confederates fleeing for the rear, conquering the second line of defense—more rifle pits about halfway up the ridge. Major Connolly described the stampede: "Over these we go, some of the rebels lying down to be run over, others scrambling up the hill which is become too steep for horses." Emboldened Northern soldiers pressed forward then paused, much as at Gettysburg, where Pickett's men stopped beneath the crest of Cemetery Ridge to gather themselves before a final push. "If we can gain that Ridge," Connolly wrote, "if we can scale those breastworks, the rebel army is routed, everything is lost for them, but if we cannot scale the works few of us will get down this mountain side and back to the shelter of the woods." The exhausted band of Union soldiers moved on to poke their battle flags above the crest, expecting a furious Confederate counterattack; but none came, and they clambered over the Southern fortifications, planted their flags, and awaited reinforcements. Shortly after, they seized Bragg's artillery position and turned the unmanned cannons against the rest of the Southern force below. The entire position at the top of Missionary Ridge disintegrated, and a general rout ensued.[26]

Why did the Army of Tennessee put up such feeble resistance after the initial breakthrough on the plain below? John Keegan argues, in *The Face of Battle*, that soldiers tend to behave in concert with their peers, usually a squad-sized aggregate of about six persons. The key factors in determining most soldiers' reactions to battle, he writes, are their "will to combat" and "group solidarity and individual leadership." For once, Bragg was blameless; he attempted to rally his troops for a counterattack, mounted his horse, seized a Confederate battle flag, and rode toward the Northern breakthrough to encourage his soldiers to stand. Private Neal described the scene: "We came to a field, and just across the field was General Bragg, sitting on his horse with a large flag, appealing to his men to stand." But for alienated yeomen soldiers, a cry of "Death before Dishonor" would hold less meaning than self-preservation. Then, too, the prolonged period of anti-Bragg propaganda within the Army of Tennessee virtually guaranteed that common soldiers would fail to coalesce around their commander. As Private Sam Watkins put it, "I felt sorry for General Bragg. The army was routed, and Bragg looked so scared. Poor fellow, he looked so hacked and whipped and mortified and chagrined at defeat, and all along the line, when Bragg would pass, the soldiers would raise the yell, 'Here is Your Mule,' 'Bully for Bragg, he's h——l on retreat.'" Thus did the Confederacy pay a heavy price for Davis's earlier refusal to relieve Bragg. Watkins described the scene as soldiers ran away: "Some were mad, others cowed, and many were laughing. Some were cursing Bragg, some the Yankees. It was the first defeat our army had ever suffered, but the prevailing sentiment was anathemas and denunciations hurled against Jeff Davis for ordering Longstreet's corps to Knoxville, and sending off Generals Wheeler's and Forrest's cavalry, while every private soldier in the whole army knew that the enemy was concentrating at Chattanooga."[27]

Throughout subsequent campaigns in Georgia, and even during the suicidal assault at Nashville, this proud Army of Tennessee fought with courageous distinction. The answer to why it showed such irresolution under fire during this, its most significant engagement, lies in the behavior of Confederate soldiers posted at the base of Missionary Ridge, according to most accounts the decisive killing zone. The headlong flight up the ridge provided cover for the pursuing Yankees and compelled Confederate units on the crest to fire high to avoid striking their own men. On November 30 Bragg described what had occurred: "A panic which I had never before witnessed seemed to have seized upon officers and men, and each seemed to be struggling for his personal safety, regardless of his duty or character." "The position was one which ought to have been held by a line of skirmishers against any assaulting column. . . . [The Yankees] who reached the ridge did so in a condition of exhaustion from the great physical exertion in climbing, which rendered them powerless, and the slightest effort would have destroyed them."[28]

Even Northern observers thought the assault up Missionary Ridge so difficult that its success must be a miracle. The omnipresent Charles Dana, who served as Lincoln's eyes and ears at the front and who stood with Grant and Thomas, watched the charge in stunned amazement, especially in view of orders that had looked only toward seizure of the first line of rifle pits. An awestruck Dana described the scene: "The storming of the ridge by our troops was one of the greatest miracles in military history. No man who climbs the ascent by any of the roads that wind along its front can believe that eighteen thousand men were moved in tolerably good order up its broken and crumbling face unless it was his fortune to witness the deed." "It seemed . . . a visible interposition of God. Neither Grant nor Thomas intended it." Sheridan, whose division led the charge up the ridge, told Dana: "When I saw the men were going up, I had no idea of stopping them; the rebel pits had been taken and nobody had been hurt and after they had started I commanded them to go right on."[29] In the light of their performance at Chickamauga, soldiers of the North had strong incentives to demonstrate courage under fire, which perhaps helps explain their refusal to accept Grant's order to remain at the base.

Fewer than three hundred Confederate soldiers lost their lives on all sectors of the Missionary Ridge battlefield. Only the lack of esprit de corps among soldiers manning the first line of rifle pits can explain the Southern failure to fight to repel the Northern charge. Reports from various Confederate commanders make it clear that the decisive breakthrough occurred along the segment of the line occupied by a division under command of General Patton Anderson. Anderson's official report is missing not only from the *Official Records* and the National Archives but also from his collected papers, yet Anderson did prepare such a report, referring back to it in 1865 when he criticized Bragg's multiple-line deployment, which he blamed for the debacle. In consequence of this deployment, he said, "The troops made no fight at all, but broke and ran as soon as the enemy's overwhelming columns advanced." Anderson's papers contain other information in reports submitted to him by his subordinates, one of whom, General A. W. Reynolds, praised his men for resisting fiercely but admitted that troops in the rifle pits "broke and fled in the utmost disorder," a "disgraceful and inexplicable panic." Colonel M. T. Tucker, too, found fault with Bragg's orders, and Brigadier General A. M. Manigault complained that many regiments on the plain did not know how strenuously Bragg wished them to resist before retiring up the ridge.[30]

Grant reacted quickly to news of his surprisingly easy triumph. Unlike Bragg after Chickamauga, he immediately recognized the opportunity to do to the Army of Tennessee what had already been done to Pemberton's Army of Mississippi—destroy it as a fighting force. An energetic pursuit by General Sheridan produced a large haul of prisoners and supplies. But Patrick Cleburne's skillful and gallant rearguard action for the Confederate forces surprised Sheridan's troops and inflicted heavy casualties, saving the Army of Tennessee from complete annihilation—it survived to fight another day—but the debacle in November 1863 at Missionary Ridge marked the low point in an otherwise glorious record.[31]

A British visitor who toured the battlefield, John Kennaway, highlighted the obvious explanation for the defeat at Missionary Ridge—"the unpopularity of Bragg and his inability to inspire his troops with confidence"—but he added a hitherto ignored but crucial factor: "the presence in the Confederate ranks of a large body of paroled prisoners, who had been re-drafted into the service much against their will, while there was some hitch about their exchanges." These reluctant parolees "proved themselves not to be relied upon in the hour of danger," Kennaway wrote. "From their desperate attempt to protect their own lives sprang the flight that led to a Result so unexpected, a Defeat so disgraceful." A number of soldiers captured at Missionary Ridge acknowledged that they were paroled prisoners from Vicksburg. These reports were reinforced by a report from the Union general Thomas. The Army of the Cumberland's sweep up the ridge netted more than two thousand Confederate prisoners, and when they were processed the next day, the identification of the regiments in which they served yielded the startling information, dutifully reported by Thomas in a telegram to Halleck on November 25, that "among the prisoners are many who were paroled at Vicksburg." Thomas inquired, "What shall I do with them?"[32]

Patton Anderson confessed the embarrassment of the panic at Missionary Ridge but denied that the cause was a loss of fighting spirit. Writing on December 18 to his wife, Henrietta Adair Anderson, who had sought to console him, he said, "I am not quite as despondent as you suppose. True, I was mortified at the conduct of some of our troops but have not lost confidence in their courage and patriotism." He referred to the broader "general crisis" of wartime society and pointed squarely at the role of disaffection. "If the people at *home,* men, women and children and servants, will only set their faces against deserters, absentees, skulkers, etc., not permitting them to eat, sleep or *speak* with them, our army may be made strong enough to cope with that of the enemy." "I can tell the people at home, they had better not require *too much* of the few who are in the army and who have up to this time borne the brunt of the war."[33]

Ella Lonn, commenting on a Missionary Ridge postmortem by Georgia senator Benjamin Hill, wrote that "Senator Hill's bitter claim that the Battle of

Missionary Ridge was lost because of absenteeism was doubtless not over-stated and was not an isolated instance." In fact, "the presence or absence of a hundred thousand men from duty was a factor of stupendous importance. It should be recalled that practically each man carried off his arms, equip-ment, and if mounted, his horse, with frequently additional ammunition bor-rowed from his comrades—all subtracted from the resources of the State."[34] Throughout the east Tennessee campaign, subversion by the Southern anti-war movement had reinforced the epidemic of desertion and outbursts of opposition to conscription. Disaffected yeomen soldiers had resisted re-assignment into the combat zone, and many had already deserted to enlist in the army of the North. So, too, many Southern civilians had offered aid and encouragement, even active collaboration, to the Yankee invaders. It seems reasonable to conclude that demoralization among Confederate soldiers and disaffection of yeomen civilians spelled the significant difference between vic-tory and defeat for the South in the long and closely contested campaign for eastern Tennessee, as in the war itself.

Epilogue   **Slavery and the Death of the Southern Revolution**

I n the aftermath of Missionary Ridge, a flood tide of war weariness overwhelmed Confederate resolve. The undertow sapped the will to independence among hardcore Confederate loyalists much as the disaffection among angry yeomen had earlier swamped the east Tennessee campaign. The administration of the Confederate States of America slowly and painfully concluded that it could tap the reserves of manpower needed to stall the Yankees only by purging class discrimination from its draft and tax policies. Although traditionally slavery had served as a means of removing class issues from Southern politics—with all free white men regarded as equals—slavery was now seen as reinforcing class division among whites and hence as alienating the Confederate regime from its bedrock of support. Conflicting class interests had stirred a divisive debate about the character of the Southern way of life. The accretion of alienation paralleled the series of military defeats that would lead to the Confederate surrender at Appomattox on April 9, 1865.

Try as it might, the Richmond regime could not decouple the struggle to retain nonslaveholders' allegiance from the struggle to sustain slavery. The Confederate army, the Richmond administration, and the Confederate Congress each in turn strove futilely to reconcile the competing interests of planters, yeomanry, and slaves. Ultimately, this debate would lead to the unwelcome conclusion that sustaining slavery was incompatible with winning national independence for the seceding South. But such a revolutionary discovery required a leap of perspective and policy so enormous that it could only be considered in extended congressional deliberation. The necessary legislation for the South itself to emancipate its slaves came too late: only weeks remained for the Confederacy. The new nation had foundered on the central contradiction of the generations-old way of life of the South, between slavery as the ally of the economy of the South and slavery as the enemy of its political democracy.

With Chattanooga won, the way was now open for a Yankee invasion of the Lower South. General Lee confessed, "I have considered with some anxiety the condition of affairs in Georgia and Tennessee. . . . There appears to me to be grounds to apprehend that the enemy may penetrate Georgia and get possession of our depots of provisions and important manufacturories." He warned President Davis that, "Upon the defense of the country now threatened by General Grant depends the safety of the points now held by us on the Atlantic." Davis moved quickly to accept General Bragg's resignation from command of the Army of Tennessee, sparing both men the agony of a forced removal. Davis preferred not to give the command to his old nemesis Johnston, but Hardee had forced his hand by declining the conversion of a temporary command into a permanent appointment, and in December Davis proffered to Johnston the independent field command he knew Johnston had coveted. He advised him that he would watch his performance closely. His top priority was to be "reoccupying the country upon the supplies of which the proper subsistence of our armies materially depends." Johnston's assignment resembled George Washington's in the aftermath of the defeat at Germantown, which drove the Continental Army into winter quarters at Valley Forge. Much as Washington sought to improve the conditions of his dispirited soldiers, so Johnston sought to resupply and reinvigorate the ragged and hungry veterans of the east Tennessee campaign while struggling to lure deserters and stragglers back into the fold. Private Sam Watkins described the result as "a revolution, sure enough."[1]

The 36,000 troops listed at Dalton, Georgia, where Confederate forces regrouped after Missionary Ridge, barely outnumbered the 34,000 men that were carried on the muster rolls as absent without leave, and nothing could obscure the urgent need for reinforcements. Johnston asked Davis to permit the substitution of slaves "for all soldiers on detached or daily duty. . . . This would give us 10,000 or 12,000 men, and the other armies of the Confederacy might be strengthened in the same proportion." It would give the slave "a portion of the pay" and also punish "the master for not returning him if he deserts." "My experience in Mississippi," Johnston said, "was that impressed negroes run away whenever it is possible, and are frequently encouraged by their masters to do so, and I never knew one to be returned by his master." Johnston, taking no chances, dispatched his message simultaneously to Davis and to Senator Louis Wigfall of Texas, one of Davis's bitterest enemies in the Confederate Congress.[2]

Of revolutionary import for the institution of slavery was "A Memorial from the Army of Tennessee" produced by the general staff on December 29, 1863, a month after the debacle at Missionary Ridge. The staff took the extremely unusual step of sending its proposal directly to the Confederate Congress, bypassing both the normal channels between army officers and elected officials and also the back channel to Davis that Johnston was accustomed to use. The memorial began with the plea, "In the existing state of affairs, it is hoped your honorable bodies [the Senate and House] will pardon the variance from custom of addressing you directly from the army." The officers wasted few words in calling on the emergency session of the Confederate Congress, convened on December 7, to draw on the only two untapped sources of manpower left to the South—exempted white men and slaves—and to enact a truly egalitarian *levée en masse,* placing "in service immediately . . . all other white males between eighteen and fifty years of age to perform military duty." They demanded that the new conscription act prohibit substitution and "exemption, except for the necessary civil and military officers and employments of the Confederate States and the Several States." Congress should also "place in the service as cooks, labourers, teamsters and hospitals, with the army and elsewhere, able-bodied negroes and mulattoes, bound or free." There was no reference to blacks as soldiers. The word *slavery* did not even appear. With most of the Army of Tennessee general staff signing the memorial, the Congress could hardly afford to ignore its demands.[3]

The memorial from the Army of Tennessee was closely followed by another event, one of surpassing importance in the history of the Confederacy: the presentation to the general staff of a draft proposal for emancipation from a battlefront hero. The proposal came from the only member of the Army of Tennessee's general staff to emerge from the debacle of Missionary Ridge with an enhanced reputation, Major General Patrick Ronayne Cleburne, whose command had staged a brilliant rearguard maneuver at Ringgold Gap that halted Northern troops' pursuit of the fleeing Confederate forces, probably saving Bragg's army from total annihilation.

Cleburne's proposal of January 2, 1864, to the general staff dealt explicitly with disaffection among white yeomen and with the need to enlist slaves in the service of the South. The preamble to the draft memorial, sent to the "Commanding General, the Corps, Division, Brigade, and Regimental Commanders of the Army of Tennessee," pointed to the "fatal apathy" into which hopelessness about prospects for victory had drawn the army encamped at

Dalton. This apathy sprang, in turn, from "three great causes": first, a wide disparity in manpower between the competing armies; second, an insufficient number of white men in the South to fill the demand for soldiers; and third, and most important, the belief that "slavery, from being one of our chief sources of strength at the commencement of the war, has now become, in a military point of view, one of our chief sources of weakness." Slavery had become an asset "of great and increasing worth to the enemy . . . for information." "As between the loss of independence and the loss of slavery, we assume that every patriot will freely give up the latter—give up the negro slave rather than be a slave himself." Cleburne argued that ending slaveholders' property rights in slaves would eliminate "the fear that sealed the masters' lips and the avarice that has, in so many cases, tempted him practically to desert us." Cleburne insisted that emancipation could "remove forever all selfish taint from our cause and place independence above every question of property."[4]

A foreign-born émigré from Ireland like Cleburne might seem, at first, the unlikely author of so revolutionary a break with the canons of Southern society. But Cleburne's role may have been similar to that of the Prussian-born drillmaster Baron von Steuben during the American Revolution. Von Steuben had helped to create an esprit de corps among the Continental troops at Valley Forge, using European close-order drill to enable Washington's undisciplined troops to stand their ground against the best troops of the British. But Davis, unlike Washington, rejected the bold strategy proposed to him. Not until November 1864, after the fall of Atlanta, would he embrace the concept of emancipation he spurned in January.

Patrick Cleburne had left Ireland in 1849, but not to flee the potato famine that was causing such suffering among his countrymen. He was apparently not a member of any group fighting for Ireland's freedom, but Ireland had no doubt enhanced his sympathies toward the poor and the downtrodden, though he himself was of the minor gentry and his father a member of England's Royal College of Surgeons. Cleburne fled from Ireland after the disgrace of failing his medical entrance examinations, joined the British army at eighteen, then left the army to join his family in emigrating to America after British tax policy threatened the small family estate. "The elements of decay and destruction" in Ireland, he told his grandmother later, "seemed to me to be so deeply seated in the heart of the body social or politic that to stay would only be to witness a lingering dissolution." In his new home in Helena, Arkansas, he experienced a sense of rebirth as "a free man, knowing no superior, acknowledging no aristocracy except that of intellect or moral worth." He became a moderately successful lawyer but refused to purchase slaves. When his brother Robert, who lived in Cincinnati, asked why he had nonetheless cast his lot with the South, he answered, "I am with the South in life or in death, in victory or defeat. I never owned a Negro and care nothing for them, but these people have been my friends and have stood up to [for] me on all occasions."[5]

A furious debate over Cleburne's memorial ensued, first within the Army of Tennessee's general staff and then throughout much of the Confederate elite. General Johnston declined to send the proposal on to Richmond because "it was more political than military in tenor." To Major General James Patton Anderson it was a "monstrous proposition." Major General W. H. T. Walker found it so obnoxious that he sent a copy directly to Davis, thwarting Johnston's attempt to bottle it up. Davis, recognizing immediately the mortal threat it represented, imposed a ban on public dissemination. "Deeming it to be injurious to the public service that such a subject should be mooted, or even known to be entertained by persons possessed of the confidence and respect of the people," Davis wrote to Walker, "I have concluded that the best policy under the circumstances will be to avoid all publicity. . . . If it be kept out of the public journals its ill effects will be much lessened." Johnston informed his general staff of Davis's order; there was to be no further discussion of emancipation by the Confederacy. Cleburne, too, ceased all public discussion of the matter.[6]

Davis apparently quashed Cleburne's memorial in part because it appeared during congressional deliberations over his own carefully crafted plan for tight control over the Southern economy. The effect of its suppression cannot be assessed. Whether either plan, Cleburne's for emancipation of the slaves or Davis's, might have saved the Confederacy at such a late date can only be speculated on. But although Davis would wait another year before considering jettisoning slavery to save an independent Confederate nation, he did take steps now to reduce the inequities of the conscription process.

When the Confederate Congress convened in emergency session on December 7, 1863, the fourth session of the First Congress, it received a lengthy message from President Davis drawing on the annual report of the secretary of war, in which Seddon had written, "It may be safely assumed that one-third of our Army on an average are absent from their posts, and may with due efforts, be returned." "Due efforts" alone would be unavailing; a more systematic change in conscription was required, especially the repeal of "the provision allowing substitutes and the exemption law," since substitution had "produced among the less fortunate and poorer classes repining and discontent," and exemptions had "caused some dissatisfaction among those whose services are exacted in the field." More effective use should be made of slave labor, Seddon had recommended, so that every possible white soldier could be closer to combat. "Compulsion in some form will be necessary" because slave labor "could not be obtained by voluntary engagements of service or hire from their owners."[7]

Davis's preamble put the matter succinctly. "Whatever obstinacy may be displayed by the enemy in his desperate sacrifices of money, life, and liberty in the hope of enslaving us, the experience of mankind has too conclusively shown the superior endurance of those who fight for home, liberty, and independence to permit any doubt of the result." A Confederate will to fight for "home, liberty, and independence" could overcome Yankee resources. But important to a sustaining will was an increase in "effective force," and in a remarkable passage Davis acknowledged the connection between "effective force" and a challenge to the primacy of slaveholder property rights. He called for "restoring to the Army all who are improperly absent, putting an end to substitution, modifying the exemption law, reducing details, and placing in the ranks such of the able-bodied men now employed as wagoners, nurses, cooks and other employees as are doing service for which the negro may be found competent." For the first time, the Confederate president made common cause with yeomen angry that the draft system sheltered many of the young men of the affluent class from dangerous service in combat. And to suggest that slaves might be "competent" to perform in essential service jobs, thereby reinforcing men at the front, was to endorse Seddon's argument that slaveholders be compelled to provide slaves for military labor. Davis acknowledged the frequent desertions from the Confederate army and the legitimacy of the "dissatisfaction . . . excited among those who have been unable or unwilling to avail themselves of the opportunity thus afforded" to slaveholders by the substitution system "for avoiding the military service of their country." Not that Congress had intended class discrimination—no, "the object of your legislation has not been to confer privileges on classes"—still, Congress must heed the consequences of privileges and alter the draft laws to compel all able-bodied men to enlist.[8]

Davis's proposal stopped short of both the general staff memorial from the

Army of Tennessee and Cleburne's memorial on the political question of how far the national government ought to continue to sustain slaveholders' property rights. Cleburne would have eliminated rights to slave property altogether, while the Army of Tennessee had finessed the issue of slavery by taking no notice of it. Davis did not now challenge slavery as an institution, but he would require slaveholders to provide slave labor for public needs. All three proposals shared an avid desire to remove from the planter-dominated Confederate Congress the authority to grant categorical exemptions based on class privilege. In response, the lame-duck Congress enacted a dismal round of legislation that suggested that slaveholders regarded surrender of the power to protect their interests as too desperate a remedy to embrace. As long as it seemed that piecemeal reform might support the army long enough to gain military victory, the slaveholding elite would withhold legislative sanction from Davis's proposed core reforms of the draft system. While they did repeal substitution and expanded the War Department's discretionary power to impress slaves, they refused to abolish exemptions of overseers for plantations with twenty or more slaves and instead gave the Davis administration the power to further suspend habeas corpus as a means of countering dissident resistance to service. In a hot debate in the Confederate Congress on whether to make the repeal of substitution retroactive, Senator Edward Sparrow of Louisiana admitted, "Our affairs [have] reached the point when we should show the soldiers in the field that there [are] no favorite classes." Senator Wigfall urged, "Let us close the mouths of the demagogues. Let no man say this is a poor men's fight and a rich men's war."[9]

On February 17, 1864, the day of adjournment, the Congress passed two laws, "An Act to Increase the Efficiency of the Army by the Employment of Free Negroes and Slaves into Certain Capacities," virtually a draft of free blacks, and "An Act to Organize Forces to Serve during the War," which extended universal conscription to all white males from seventeen to fifty years old and required them to remain "in the military service of the Confederate States for the war." No more twelve-month or three-year stints. South Carolina representative William Miles, backing repeal of categorical exemptions, proposed to give the power of detailing to the War Department, since "Congress could not make an exemption law. . . . Local influence and pressure would be too potent." But Waller Staples of Virginia expressed the sentiments of the majority in disputing Miles's contention. "The whole subject of conscription and exemption belongs to Congress and to Congress alone," Staples argued. "It is a legislative power, a legislative discretion and a legislative obligation." The Congress kept the categorical exemptions and revised the number of slaves a planter needed to qualify for overseer exemption down from twenty to fifteen, although the fifteen had to be field hands, and thus slaveholders generally had to have about thirty slaves in total in order to gain overseer exemption.[10]

The exemption was now effectively more discriminatory than ever in favor of the affluent, and a major defeat for President Davis. The chief clerk of the War Department, John B. Jones, had confided to his diary at the end of November 1863 that the rich must join the poor in fighting or the cause could be lost. "The want of men is our greatest want, and I think it is probable Congress will repeal the Substitute Law, and perhaps the Exemption Act. Something must be done to put more men in the ranks, or all will be lost. The rich men have contrived to get out, or to keep out, and there are not poor men enough to win our independence. All, with very few exceptions . . . must fight for freedom, else we may not win it." In early January, Jones wrote of the congressional vote to make repeal of substitution retroactive, "The army is delighted with the measure. The petition from so many generals in the field intimidated Congress, and it was believed that the Western army would have melted away in thirty days, if no response had been accorded to its demands by the government."[11]

The president's request of February 3 for power to suspend the writ of habeas corpus reflected his conviction that it would take extraordinary authority for martial law to counter the antiwar movement. In noting the "discontent, disaffection, and disloyalty manifested among those who, through the sacrifices of others, have enjoyed quiet and safety at home," Davis spoke of "secret leagues and associations," with many prominent persons advocating "peace on terms of submission and the abolition of slavery."[12] By choosing to ignore the full draft reforms Davis had proposed, with concessions sufficient to meet the growing unrest within Confederate territory, Congress may well have forced him to resort to denial of traditional due process.

The Confederate Congress had gambled that Lincoln would not raise the ante in the war enough to overwhelm the South's augmented military force. But when the spring 1864 campaigning season opened in May, the Confederacy discovered, to its dismay, that in the five-month interval after the east Tennessee campaign, the Northern war machine had been revamped and an intensive and coordinated offensive was now underway. Lincoln, knowing he could not wait for the Confederacy to collapse of its own weakness, had vigorously reorganized the Northern war effort, appointing Grant as general in chief. For the first time the North had a unified command.

Much of the impetus for this impressive burst of organizational motivation in the North had come from the increasingly powerful activities of the Northern peace movement. The broad compass of draft riots during the spring and summer of 1863, in New York City and elsewhere, demonstrated the breadth and depth of discontent. The July 13–17 draft riots in midtown Manhattan in New York were, Eric Foner has said, "the largest civil insurrection in American history other than the South's rebellion." Huge pillaging crowds, primarily poor and Irish, had stampeded in the streets, enraged by the draft, by the continued increase in prices, and by the fear that freed slaves would compete for their jobs. With draft substitution costing three hundred dollars, families making five hundred dollars a year or less had no chance to escape military service. During the riots in New York more than a hundred people were lynched, and many atrocities were committed against blacks; thousands were injured. Federal troops were summoned from Gettysburg to restore order. The unrest transformed the 1864 presidential election into a referendum on Lincoln's conduct of the war.[13] Had Lincoln failed to follow up aggressively on the North's smashing victory in eastern Tennessee, war weariness might even have forced him from office and ceded independence to the Confederacy precisely as British war weariness during the Revolution had led to American independence. But he did not fail.

Necessity compelled the North to exert maximum pressure on the already hard-pressed Confederacy. In early May 1864 Sherman launched a coordinated offensive from his bases near Chattanooga, his task to smash the southeastern supply complex on which Lee's army depended. Lee had to give priority to defense of the capital at Richmond, and the South's only hope for averting a major defeat was to stall Sherman's march. Johnston planned to withdraw in order to draw Sherman farther and farther from his supply base and perhaps lure him into a tactical error. But in early July, Davis replaced Johnston with the impulsive John Bell Hood, who did what Davis wanted: he took the offensive. Too late to save Atlanta, Davis discovered the wisdom of Johnston's strategic plan. In the wake of the fall of Atlanta, Lincoln's reelection was now assured; it sealed the fate of the Confederacy. A saddened and chastened Southern president delivered a rambling oration to a large meeting in Macon, Georgia, on September 29, 1864. "Our cause is not lost," he said, but he made a startling admission: "It is not proper for me to speak of the number of men in the field. But, this I will say, two-thirds of our men are absent—some sick, some wounded, but most of them are absent without leave."[14] The time had come, Davis decided, to move toward emancipation.

In the two months between the fall of Atlanta in September 1864 and Davis's message to the second session of the Second Confederate Congress in November, a spate of emancipation proposals had appeared from politicians, newspaper editors, and private citizens. Davis's message of November 7 proposed a "radical modification in the theory of the law" of slavery. He asked his Congress, in effect, to recognize that slaves were persons, not only property. If the South wanted to elicit their enthusiastic cooperation as laborers working for the Cause, then it must consider "engaging to liberate the negro on his discharge after service faithfully rendered."[15]

By Davis's scheme, therefore, slaves had to earn their freedom by saving their masters from national defeat; those who did not serve would remain slaves. But the Confederate president had waited far too long for this partial, if revolutionary, step. Cleburne had warned him on January 2, 1864, "There is danger that this concession to common sense may come too late," and Cleburne was right.[16] The intense congressional debate that followed lasted from November until mid-March 1865, much too late for emancipation to be of any practical assistance to the South, since the North had not meanwhile granted the customary winter respite from battle. Appomattox was to come in April.

The debate was impassioned, its participants aware that the ideology that had supported their slave society was at stake. Major General Howell Cobb, for example, maintained to Secretary of War Seddon that "the proposition to make soldiers of our slaves is the most pernicious idea that has been suggested since the war began. . . . You cannot make soldiers of slaves, nor slaves of soldiers. The moment you resort to negro solders, your white soldiers will be lost to you." "The day you make soldiers of them is the beginning of the end of the revolution. If slaves will make good soldiers our whole theory of slavery is wrong."[17] Only by giving his countrymen time to recover from the blow of the proposal to use slaves as soldiers might Davis have retained the allegiance of hard-core loyalists like Cobb. Similarly, the delay in offering an emancipation proposal robbed it of its effect on the disaffected and disloyal. Acting in January 1864 might have reconciled some of the wavering yeomanry, but waiting until the aftermath of Atlanta's fall made such a gesture seem a futile last gasp, a gesture unlikely to induce the disaffected to resume active allegiance to the cause.

Eventually, despite the tenor of the debate, Sherman's northward thrust compelled a reluctant Confederate Congress to grant Davis the authority he requested—but not until March 1865 and only after an endorsement by Lee himself. Of Lee's two letters on the matter, only one was made public at the time, that of February 18, in which he replied to Representative Ethelbert Barksdale of Mississippi on his opinion on the issue of freeing and arming the slaves. "I think the measure not only expedient but necessary," Lee said without equivocation. More candid still was his earlier letter, drafted in mid-January and sent to a member of the Virginia General Assembly but not made public; in it he acknowledged that the North's action on emancipation had made any survival of slavery chancy at best. Lee had preferred that the South not the North take the initiative in freeing and arming the slaves to avoid "evil consequences." "If it end in subverting slavery," he said, "it will be accomplished by ourselves, and we can devise the means of alleviating the evil consequences to both races. I think therefore, we must decide whether slavery shall be extinguished by our enemies and the slaves used against us, or use them ourselves at the risk of the effects which may be produced upon our social institutions."[18]

But would slaves fight for the Confederacy on a promise of freedom after the war if they could fight for the North and gain freedom immediately on enlistment? And would rank-and-file hard-core Confederate loyalists in service in the spring of 1865 accept such a plan? The behavior of the first organized army unit of Confederate slaves—who turned themselves over to the Northern conquerors of Richmond—suggests that the answer to the first question was no: emancipation by the Confederacy would probably have failed to provide many loyal black soldiers for the Confederate cause. And the fact that Lee's army melted away after evacuating Richmond rather than fight to the bitter end suggests, in turn, that Confederate loyalists too were voting with their feet against an altered Southern way of life. With slaves struggling for freedom from planters' control over their persons and their labor whether on the plantation or on military duty, with planters struggling to retain control over their chattel property and real estate, and with white yeomen struggling to defend themselves from subjugation to what they saw as political slavery, the wartime South could no longer command the minimal consent required for social order. Anarchy and retaliation follow such circumstances, for governments in deep trouble tend to rely on escalating levels of coercion as a substitute for consent denied by the governed.

The isolation in which the Davis regime concluded its reign is exemplified by an impassioned plea sent to Pendleton Murrah, the governor of Texas, by a loyal Confederate. "In God's name," he wrote, "let us not forget the cause of this war (the assertion of state sovereignty) and loose in the struggle through military dictatorship the principle of State Right." Once the Davis government alienated itself from its most loyal base among slaveholders, it could no longer maintain the struggle for independence. Therein lay the central paradox of the Confederate experience. Slaveholders attempted to employ the egalitarian ideology of the American Revolution to justify the Southern quest for national independence, but this ideology was diametrically opposed to the nonegalitarian social structure of the antebellum and wartime South. Only by winning independence quickly, politically or on the battlefield, could the South have avoided fundamental confrontation with that immanent contradiction. The interests of the slaveholding minority were in direct opposition to the interests of the slaves and to the interests of the majority of free citizens of the South, the white nonslaveholding yeomanry. Once the struggle became a prolonged war of attrition, the Confederacy could not fend off a sustained and massive invasion while simultaneously coping with a slave freedom struggle on the one hand and a yeoman revolt on the other—in effect conducting a three-front war. These contradictions resolved themselves, in the end, in the only way possible: by destroying slavery and, at the same time, by thwarting the slaveholders' quest for national independence. The vice president of the Confederacy, Alexander Stephens, abandoned the Confederate capital at Richmond rather than participate in desecration of the sacred altars of states' rights. And a prominent Florida loyalist, David L. Yulee, in October 1864 criticized proposals for arming slaves in these words, "Whenever the Confederate Government treats slaves in the states otherwise than *as property,* a social revolution is begun in the South, the end of which may not be foreseen."[19]

These reflections on the causes and consequences of wartime class conflict suggest the need to revise once again the inscription on the tombstone of the Confederacy. Rather than reading "Confederate States of America, 1861–1865, Died of State Rights," or "Died of a Theory," or "Died of Democracy," or "Died of an Imbalance in Resources," a proper epitaph to the failed struggle for Southern independence should read instead:

Confederate States of America

1861–1865

Died of Class Conflict

Notes

ABBREVIATIONS AND SHORT TITLES

AAAG	Acting Assistant Adjutant General
AAG	Assistant Adjutant General
AG	Adjutant General
AHR	*American Historical Review*
AlaDAH	Alabama Department of Archives and History, Montgomery
AlaHQ	*Alabama Historical Quarterly*
AoT	Army of Tennessee
AotT	Army of the Tennessee
Collected Works	*The Collected Works of Abraham Lincoln,* ed. Roy P. Basler
Compilation of the Presidents	*A Compilation of the Messages and Papers of the Presidents,* ed. James D. Richardson, 20 vols. (New York: Bureau of National Literature, 1897)
CSA	Confederate States of America
CWH	*Civil War History*
DMEL	Department of Mississippi and Eastern Louisiana
DotT	Department of the Tennessee
DUL	Duke University Library
DWT	District of West Tennessee
ETHSP	*East Tennessee Historical Society Publications*
ISH	Index of Slave Holding
JAH	*Journal of American History*
JDPP-RUL	Jefferson Davis Papers Project, Rice University Library, Houston, Texas
Jefferson Davis	*Jefferson Davis, Constitutionalist: His Letters, Papers, and Speeches,* comp. and ed. Dunbar Rowland, 10 vols. (Jackson: Mississippi Department of Archives and History, 1923–32)
JNH	*Journal of Negro History*

JSH	*Journal of Southern History*
LC	Library of Congress
LLMVC	Louisiana and Lower Mississippi Valley Collection, LSU Libraries
LR	Letters Received
LS	Letters Sent
LSUL	Louisiana State University Libraries
MDAH	Mississippi Department of Archives and History, Jackson
Messages and Papers	*The Messages and Papers of Jefferson Davis and the Confederacy, Including Diplomatic Correspondence, 1861–1865,* ed. James D. Richardson, 2 vols. (New York: R. R. Bowker, 1905)
MVHR	*Mississippi Valley Historical Review*
NA	National Archives
NA-CSA	War Department Collection of Confederate Records, Record Group 109, National Archives
NA-USA	Records of the United States Army Continental Commands, 1821–1920, Record Group 393, National Archives
NCHR	*North Carolina Historical Review*
OA	Official Archives
OR	U.S. Department of War, *The War of the Rebellion: A Compilation of the Official Records of the Union and Confederate Armies,* 128 vols. (Washington, D.C.: GPO, 1880–1901)
RG	Record Group
SHC	Southern Historical Collection, University of North Carolina, Chapel Hill
SHQ	*Southwestern Historical Quarterly*
SHSP	Southern Historical Society Papers
TexSLA	Texas State Library and Archives
THQ	*Tennessee Historical Quarterly*
TMD	Trans-Mississippi Department
TSLA	Tennessee State Library and Archives
TUL	Tulane University Library
UTexL	University of Texas Library
VCB	Volunteer and Conscript Bureau

Introduction

1. Robert Penn Warren, *The Legacy of the Civil War: Meditations on the Centennial* (New York: Random House, 1961), 3–4.

2. A full description of this mathematical model was originally in an appendix that has unfortunately been lost.—ED.

3. Charles H. Wesley, *The Collapse of the Confederacy* (Washington, D.C.: Associated Publishers, 1937), vii–x; Jaime Vicens Vives, "The Decline of Spain in the Seventeenth Century," in *The Economic Decline of Empires,* ed. Carlo Cippolla (London: Methuen, 1970), 120–22. For an introduction to the literature on the collapse of the Spanish empire, see Earl J. Hamilton, "The Decline of Spain," *Economic History Review,* 1st ser., 8 (1938); J. H. Elliott, *The Revolt of the Catalans: A Study in the Decline of Spain, 1598–1640* (Cambridge: Cambridge University Press, 1963); R. Trevor Davies, *Spain in Decline, 1621–1700* (London: Macmillan, 1957).

4. Josef V. Polisensky, *The Thirty Years War,* trans. Robert Evans (Berkeley: University of California Press, 1971), 5. See also Christopher Hill, introduction to Trevor Aston's *Crisis in Europe, 1560–1660* (New York: Basic Books, 1965), 1–4; Geoffrey Symcox, *War, Diplomacy and Imperialism, 1618–1763* (New York: Harper Torchbooks, 1973); Theodore K. Rabb, *The Thirty Years' War,* 2nd ed. (Lexington, Mass.: Heath, 1972).

5. Wesley, *The Collapse of the Confederacy,* vii–x.

6. Bell Irvin Wiley, *Plain People of the Confederacy* (Baton Rouge: Louisiana State University Press, 1949), 70–104; Wiley, *Southern Negroes, 1861–1865* (New Haven: Yale University Press, 1938); W. E. B. Du Bois, *Black Reconstruction in America* (New York: Harcourt, Brace, 1935), 17–127.

7. Albert B. Moore, *Conscription and Conflict in the Confederacy* (New York: Macmillan, 1924), 361.

8. Joshua Burns Moore, 22 February, 30 April 1862, Diary, AlaDAH.

CHAPTER 1. A "Most Un-Civil War"

1. Edmund Ruffin, 12 April 1861, in *The Diary of Edmund Ruffin,* ed. William K. Scarborough, 3 vols. (Baton Rouge: Louisiana State University Press, 1972, 1977), 2:588.

2. *The Diary of Miss Emma Holmes, 1861–1866,* ed. John F. Marszalek (Baton Rouge: Louisiana State University Press, 1979), 26.

3. Lincoln, Proclamation to Governors, 15 April 1861, in *The Collected Works of Abraham Lincoln,* ed. Roy P. Basler, 9 vols. (New Brunswick, N.J.: Rutgers University Press, 1953), 4:331–32; George Ticknor, *Life, Letters and Journals* (London, 1876), 2:433–34.

4. Lincoln, speech at Chicago, 10 July 1858, *Collected Works,* 2:498; Lincoln-Douglas debate, Charleston, IL, 18 September 1858, in Paul M. Angle, ed., *The Complete Lincoln-Douglas Debate of 1858* (Chicago: University of Chicago Press, 1991), 258. On the political realignment of the 1850s and the rise of the Republican Party, see William E. Gienapp, *The Origins of the Republican Party, 1852–1856* (New York: Oxford University Press, 1987).

5. Lincoln, "A 'House Divided' speech at Springfield, IL," 16 June 1858, *Collected*

Works, 2:461–62; "Last Speech of the Campaign at Springfield, IL," 30 October 1858, ibid., 3:334.

6. Lincoln to Nathan Sargent, 23 June 1859, *Collected Works,* 3:387–88; Lincoln, Speech at Columbus, Ohio, 16 September 1859, ibid., 3:356–57.

7. Lincoln, "Seventh and Last Debate with Stephen A. Douglas at Alton, Illinois," 15 October 1858, *Collected Works,* 3:312.

8. Rhett, quoted in *Charleston Mercury,* 7 July 1859.

9. Stephen B. Oates, *To Purge This Land with Blood: A Biography of John Brown,* 2nd ed. (Amherst: University of Massachusetts Press, 1984), 307–61.

10. Ruffin quoted in Avery Craven, *Edmund Ruffin, Southerner: A Study in Secession* (Baton Rouge: Louisiana State University Press, 1932), 171.

11. Oates, *John Brown,* 351; Randal W. McGavock, 18 October 1858, 19 November, 2 December 1859. [Perhaps from McGavock's *Pen and Sword.* —Ed.]

12. For the Dred Scott decision, see Don E. Fehrenbacher, *The Dred Scott Case: Its Significance in American Law* (New York: Oxford University Press, 1978). Jefferson Davis, campaign speech at Portland, Maine, 11 September 1858, in *The Papers of Jefferson Davis,* ed. Lynda L. Crist (Baton Rouge: Louisiana State University Press, 1989), 6:214–25.

13. B. F. Perry quoted in William W. Davis, *The Civil War and Reconstruction in Florida* (Gainesville: University of Florida Press, 1964), 37.

14. For Breckinridge's background and political perspective, see William C. Davis, *Breckinridge: Statesman, Soldier, Symbol* (Baton Rouge: Louisiana State University Press, 1974).

15. Edmund Ruffin, 15 November 1860, *Diary,* 1:495.

16. Letter from "Ladies of Broward's Neck," *Fernandina East Floridian,* 5 December 1860.

17. James Phelan letter, and "A Voice from a Montgomery Lady," *Montgomery Daily Mail,* 9 November 1860.

18. For L. Virginia French's petition, 13 January 1861, see *AlaHQ* (1941): 65–67; Augusta J. Evans to J. L. M. Curry, 20 December 1862, J. L. M. Curry Papers, LC.

19. On the Montgomery convention, see Emory M. Thomas, *The Confederate Nation, 1861–1865* (New York: Harper & Row, 1979), 37–60.

20. Edwin De Leon, "The Position and Duties of 'Young Americans'" (Charleston, 1845); Merle E. Curti, "Young America," *AHR* 32 (1926): 34; Benedict Anderson, *Imagined Communities: Reflections on the Origin and Spread of Nationalism,* rev. ed. (London: Verso, 1991); Hugh Seton-Watson, *Nations and States: An Enquiry into the Origins of Nations and the Politics of Nationalism* (Boulder: Westview Press, 1977), 5.

21. Wesley, *The Collapse of the Confederacy,* vii–x.

22. Jefferson Davis, in *Jefferson Davis, Constitutionalist: His Letters, Papers, and Speeches,* comp. and ed. Dunbar Rowland, 10 vols. (Jackson: Mississippi Department of Archives and History, 1923–32), 5:48.

23. Reuben Davis to Jefferson Davis, JDPP-RUL.

24. Allan Pinkerton, *The Spy of the Rebellion, Being a True History of the Spy System of the United States Army* (New York: G. W. Carleton, 1885), 180, 187.

CHAPTER 2. "Playing Thunder"

1. For general background, see Avery O. Craven, *The Growth of Southern Nationalism, 1848–1861* (Baton Rouge: Louisiana State University Press, 1953), 312–401; Charles S. Sydnor, *The Development of Southern Sectionalism, 1819–1848* (Baton Rouge: Louisiana State University Press, 1948). A useful guide to the older literature on the secession movement is C. E. Cauthen and Lewis P. Jones, "The Coming of the Civil War," in *Writing Southern History: Essays in Historiography in Honor of Fletcher M. Greene,* ed. Arthur S. Link and Rembert W. Patrick (Baton Rouge: Louisiana State University Press, 1956), 224–48. Also useful for traditional interpretations is Thomas J. Pressly, *Americans Interpret Their Civil War* (Princeton: Princeton University Press, 1954). For more recent interpretive trends, see Eric Foner, "The Causes of the American Civil War: Recent Interpretations and New Directions," *CWH* 20 (1974): 197–214. For R. S. Finley, see Ollinger Crenshaw, "The Psychological Background of the Election of 1860 in the South," *NCHR* 19 (1942): 265.

2. See Wesley Norton, "The Methodist Episcopal Church and the Civil Disturbances in North Texas, 1859–1860," *SHQ* 68 (1964–65): 333. For Dr. Hampton, see Frederick D. Williams, ed., "The Civil War Recollections of Cornelia Hampton," *Michigan History* 40 (1956): 170–72; Samuel Andrew Agnew, 24, 25 December 1860, Agnew Diary, SHC.

3. Stephens to J. Henry Smith, 10 July 1860, in Ulrich B. Phillips, *The Correspondence of Robert Toombs, Alexander H. Stephens, and Howell Cobb* (1913; rpt. New York: Da Capo Press, 1970), 487, 501. For background on secession, see Phillips, *The Course of the South to Secession: An Interpretation,* ed. E. Merton Coulter (1939; rpt. New York: Hill and Wang, 1964), 128–49. Like Phillips, most Civil War scholars cite heightened Southern anxiety over the slavery issue as the foremost stimulus for the Fire Eaters' efforts to create a Southern nation. William Barney attempted to demonstrate the effects of adverse economic trends on the growth of Southern nationalism during the 1850s. Barney, *The Road to Secession: A New Perspective on the Old South* (New York: Praeger, 1972), and *The Secessionist Impulse: Alabama and Mississippi in 1860* (Princeton: Princeton University Press, 1974). His thesis is challenged by William J. Cooper Jr., "The Cotton Crisis in the Antebellum South: Another Look," *Agricultural History* 49 (1975): 381–91, and also by Gavin Wright, *The Political Economy of the Cotton South: Households, Markets and Wealth in the Nineteenth Century* (New York: W. W. Norton, 1978), 128–57. For a revisionist synthesis of the national political crisis of the 1850s, see Michael F. Holt, *The Political Crisis of the 1850s* (New York: John Wiley, 1978), 219–59, which locates the causes of the Civil War more in the collapse of interparty competition than in Southern anxiety over slavery.

4. Nathaniel Macon, "The Destruction of the Union Is Emancipation: Letters to Chas. O'Connor," *Campbell's Pamphlets, Pamphlet #4,* ed. John Campbell (Philadelphia: John Campbell, 1862), 20–24.

5. Lillian A. Pereyra, *James Lusk Alcorn: Persistent Whig* (Baton Rouge: Louisiana State University Press, 1966), 38–42. According to Nathaniel W. Stephenson, this counterrevolution left enduring scars: Yancey "passed rapidly into futile and bitter an-

tagonism to Davis," and Rhett became "the great unavailed genius of the opposition." Stephenson, *The Day of the Confederacy: A Chronicle of the Embattled South* (New Haven: Yale University Press, 1902), 24–27.

6. The impact of the Haitian revolution on Southern racial consciousness is explored in Phillips, *The Course of the South to Secession,* 100–27; George Fredrickson, *The Black Image in the White Mind: The Debate on Afro-American Character and Destiny, 1817–1914* (New York: Harper & Row, 1971), 8–9, 52–54. Jefferson Davis, 10 January 1861, *Jefferson Davis,* 5:30. See also Phyllis Moore Sanders, "Jefferson Davis, Reactionary Rebel, 1808 to 1861," Ph.D. diss., UCLA, 1976. In this important psychobiography, Sanders argues that Davis's first experience with the concept of murder came about because of the slave revolt and subsequent massacre at Fort Mims, Alabama, during the War of 1812. For Davis's own memories of the Fort Mims incident, see Jefferson Davis, "Autobiography," in *The Papers of Jefferson Davis,* ed. Haskell M. Moore Jr. and James T. McIntosh (Baton Rouge: Louisiana State University Press, 1971), 1:lxix.

7. Ulrich B. Phillips, "Racial Problems, Adjustments and Disturbances," in *The Slave Economy of the Old South,* ed. Eugene Genovese (Baton Rouge: Louisiana State University Press, 1968), 60–61; Genovese, *Roll, Jordan, Roll: The World the Slaves Made* (New York: Pantheon, 1974), 596; Clement Eaton, "Mob Violence in the Old South," *MVHR* 29 (1942–43): 366–69. For a seminal study of Afro-American slave revolts, see Herbert Aptheker, *American Negro Slave Revolts* (New York: International Publishers, 1935), 18–52; see also Genovese, *From Rebellion to Revolution: Afro-American Slave Revolts in the Making of the Modern World* (Baton Rouge: Louisiana State University Press, 1979). For Stephens after Montgomery, see Benjamin Quarles, *The Negro in the Civil War* (1953; rpt. New York: Da Capo Press, 1988), 42–43.

8. Pinkerton, *The Spy of the Rebellion,* 187; narratives of Mary Woolridge and Dora Franks in George Rawick, ed., *The American Slave: A Composite Autobiography,* 22 vols. (Westport, Conn.: Greenwood, 1972), 16:107, 7:52.

9. Franks in Rawick, *The American Slave,* 7:52. For recollections of former slaves, see B. A. Botkin, ed., *Lay My Burden Down: A Folk History of Slavery* (1945; rpt. Chicago: University of Chicago Press, 1958), 16, 17. In *Roll, Jordan, Roll,* 272–79, Genovese focuses special attention on the millennialist character of slave religion. For a careful study of Afro-American religious life during the antebellum period, see Albert Raboteau, *Slave Religion: The "Invisible Institution" in the Antebellum South* (New York: Oxford University Press, 1978), 212–321; also Lawrence Levine, *Black Culture and Black Consciousness: Afro-American Folk Thought from Slavery to Freedom* (New York: Oxford University Press, 1977), 136–38.

10. Alexander Pugh, 24 February 1861, Alexander Franklin Pugh Papers, LLMVC, LSUL. For slave testimony, see Lemuel Conner to Brother, 11 March 1861, Lemuel P. Conner and Family Papers, LLMVC. Conner sent his brother, who lived in Texas, a copy of the transcript of secret testimony given to the Natchez Vigilance Committee by condemned plotters so that it could serve as a confidential record of the committee's proceedings. Connors probably transcribed what he heard as faithfully as he could.

11. Howard Hines to Governor John Pettus, 14 May 1861, OA, MDAH.

12. Daniel R. Hundley, 18 May to 30 May 1861, Hundley Diary, AlaDAH. See also Daniel R. Hundley, *Social Relations in Our Southern States* (New York: Henry B. Price, 1860).

13. Nancy Williard <or Willard> to Micajah Wilkerson, 26 May 1861, Wilkerson Papers, LSUL. For the Monroe County incident, see Harvey Wish, "Slave Disloyalty under the Confederacy," *JNH* 23 (1938): 443. For evidence of other revolt plots, see Coulter, *The Confederate States of America, 1861–1865* (Baton Rouge: Louisiana State University Press, 1950), 255; and Aptheker, *American Negro Slave Revolts*, 359–67.

14. On slaves from middle Tennessee, see Joseph Farley in *The Unwritten History of Slavery: Autobiographical Accounts of Negro Ex-Slaves*, comp. and ed. Ophelia Egypt, J. Masuaka, and Charles S. Johnson (Fisk University, and Washington, D.C.: Associated Publishers, 1945), 121–25.

15. For Iberville Parish jury decree, see Charles P. Roland, *Louisiana Sugar Plantations during the American Civil War* (Leiden: E. J. Brill, 1957), 32–33, 34.

16. Fifth Legislature of the State of Louisiana, 5 March 1861, *Acts of the State of Louisiana;* called session of the Mississippi Legislature, July 1861, 1 August 1861, *Mississippi Laws;* 1st called session of the Alabama Legislature, 30 January and 8 February 1861, *Acts of the General Assembly of the State of Alabama;* special session no. 4 of Arkansas Legislature, 1861, *Acts of Arkansas, 1861,* Sec. 1E; 9th Legislature of the State of Texas, 1862, *General and Special Laws of the State of Texas.* See also, on state legislatures' supervision of slaves and free blacks, Wiley, *Southern Negroes, 33;* Bernard Nelson, "Legislative Control of the Southern Free Negro, 1861–1865," *Catholic Historical Review* 32 (1946): 28. The best overall study of the wartime treatment of free blacks is Ira Berlin, *Slaves without Masters: The Free Negro in the Antebellum South* (New York: Pantheon, 1974), 369–80.

17. J. B. Mannary to Pettus, 18 May 1861, OA, MDAH. On Arkansas slaveholders, see Pinkerton, *Spy of the Revolution,* 187.

18. Felts to William Woodruff, 24 May 1861, in Ted Worley, ed., "At Home in Confederate Arkansas: Letters to and from Pulaski Countians, 1861–1865," *Pulaski County Historical Society Bulletin* 2 (1955): 8; Pugh, 7 May 1861. For a parallel experience from the Upper South, see George Washington Smith, 25 May and 15 June 1861, George Washington Smith Papers, Special Collections Department, University of Kentucky Library, Lexington. Alexander Pugh, Pugh Papers, LLMVC. For Wailes and the Natchez home guard, see Elizabeth M. Fox to Mrs. Thomas Affleck, 7 May 1861, Affleck Papers, LSUL; see also Charles S. Syndor, *A Gentleman of the Old Natchez Region: Benjamin L. C. Wailes* (Durham: Duke University Press, 1938), 35–36; John K. Bettersworth, *Confederate Mississippi: The People and the Policies of a Cotton State in Wartime* (Baton Rouge: Louisiana State University Press, 1943), 18; Felts to Woodruff, 28 July 1861, "At Home in Confederate Arkansas," 9–10.

19. Kate Stone, 19 June 1861, in *Brokenburn: The Journal of Kate Stone, 1861–1868,* ed. John C. Anderson (Baton Rouge: Louisiana State University Press, 1955), 28; Pugh Papers, LLMVC.

20. J. D. L. Davenport to Pettus, 14 May 1861, OA, MDAH; Daniel Pratt to Governor A. B. Moore, 10 July 1861, OA, AlaDAH. For state control over raising troops

and seized weapons, see Frank Vandiver, *Rebel Brass: The Confederate Command System* (Baton Rouge: Louisiana State University Press, 1956), 5–7; Coulter, *Confederate States of America*, 199–200.

21. For anonymous letter of 30 May 1861, see Aptheker, *American Negro Slave Revolts*, 362. Felts to William Woodruff, 29 May 1861, "At Home in Confederate Arkansas"; C. J. Mitchell to Jefferson Davis, 27 April 1861, JDPP-RUL.

22. The statistics used to produce the map [This map was not found with the rest of the manuscript.—ED.] are derived from the 1860 U.S. Census; the data were produced by the Confederate Food Self-Sufficiency Project [which was described in the lost Appendix A—ED.]. This project sought to determine whether the antebellum South had a "dual economy." Dividing the counties in the Mississippi Valley into categories defined by the percentile contribution of slaves to the population of each county revealed geographically bound patterns of land use and economic activity that demonstrate the existence of a "dual economy," by which I mean an economic system characterized by sharp distinctions in degrees of participation in the export-oriented commercial economy. The table below reports the most significant of the descriptive statistics derived from this analysis.

The strength of the relationship between Cotton Production and Perslave demonstrates that counties without a significant proportion of slaves probably did not produce sufficient cotton to participate in the antebellum South's commercial economy, a useful method of determining whether a "dual economy" existed in the antebellum South.

Descriptive statistics for percentage slaves

Level (%)	Total slaves	Total white pop.	White males 15–40	Cotton prod.
<10	50,359	879,952	182,009	84,529
>10–<25	140,867	744,209	149,752	276,589
>25–<50	573,622	1,000,594	215,879	1,070,013
>50–<75	739,023	466,469	103,103	1,786,580
>75	263,265	63,698	15,460	884,472
TOTAL	1,767,136	3,154,912	666,203	4,102,183

Note: Bivariate correlations are for 349 counties. Percentage of slaves and cotton production: .70/.001/for 344 counties.

The pioneering work on Southern economic dualism is Morton Rothstein, "The Antebellum South as a Dual Economy: A Tentative Hypothesis," *Agricultural History* 41 (1967): 373–82. For more-recent discussions, see Wright, *Political Economy of the Cotton South*, 10–42; Armstead L. Robinson, "Beyond the Realm of Social Consciousness: New Meanings of Reconstruction for American History," *JAH* 68 (1981): 276–97.

23. D. D. Ranch to Pettus, 30 April 1861; B. G. Terry to Pettus, 30 April 1861; Citizens of Panola County to Pettus, Petition, 29 April 1861, OA, MDAH. For similar

correspondence, see D. C. Knight to Governor Isham G. Harris, 5 June 1861, OA, TSLA. John M. Crockett to Governor Edward Clark, 5 May 1861, OA, TexSLA. The 8.5-to-1 ratio was computed as follows: total slave population in counties with +50 percent slaves equals 1,002,288; total of white males 15–40 in same counties equals 118,473.

24. Cornelia McDonald, *A Diary with Reminiscences of the War and Refugee Life in the Shenandoah Valley, 1860–1865* (Nashville: Cullon and Ghertner, 1935), 21; Kate Stone, 1 March 1862, *Brokenburn*, 95; Robert A. Moore, *A Life for the Confederacy, as Recorded in the Pocket Diaries of Pvt. Robert A. Moore*, ed. James W. Silver (Jackson, Tenn.: McCowat-Mercer Press, 1959), 43, 61.

25. Magnolia Plantation Journal, 4 March 1862, SHC. Lee to Indian Commissioner Dale, 15 March 1862, in Annie Heloise Abel, *The American Indian as Slaveholder and Secessionist: An Omitted Chapter in the Diplomatic History of the Southern Confederacy* (Cleveland: Arthur H. Clarke, 1915), 78; Joshua Burns Moore, 19 April 1862, Diary, AlaDAH.

26. Plaquemines Parish *Weekly Rice Planter,* 22 March 1862, Manuscript Department, TUL; John D. Winters, *The Civil War in Louisiana* (Baton Rouge: Louisiana State University Press, 1963), 74.

27. The absence of reliable statistics on Confederate enlistments has long frustrated efforts to analyze patterns of service in the Southern army. In an effort to measure planter participation in the army, Wiley used a Confederate army register that listed approximately 9,000 Southern soldiers by their prewar occupations. Wiley reported that eleven soldiers listed their occupation as "planter," approximately 1/10 of 1 percent of the soldiers on the register. The 1860 U.S. Census estimated that plantation families accounted for 3 percent of all free families in the South. Wiley, *The Life of Johnny Reb: The Common Soldier of the Confederacy* (Indianapolis: Bobbs-Merrill, 1943), 413n. [Appendix A contained formulas used to compute the variable Index of Slave Holding, ISH—Ed.].

Descriptive statistics for index of slave holding

Level (%)	Total slaves	Total white pop.	White males 15–40	Cotton prod.
<10	23,015	581,009	113,989	76,606
>10–<30	314,649	1,289,950	269,895	613,353
>30–<50	548,412	827,657	181,645	1,015,034
>50–<66	427,098	291,693	63,783	953,238
>66	452,903	148,658	34,753	1,443,834
TOTAL	1,766,077	3,138,967	664,065	4,102,065

Note: The variables perslave and ISH are very highly intercorrelated. Their bivariate correlation for 349 counties is .95/.001/343.

28. H. A. McPhail to Clark, 21 April 1861; R. D. Meanelly to Clark, 25 April 1861, OA, TexSLA.

29. R. B. Hubbard to Clark, 13 May 1861; Walker to Governor Clark, 16 April 1861, OA, TexSLA; Clark to Walker, 20 May 1861, in *OR*, series I, 3:550.

30. Thomas O. Moore to Jefferson Davis, 9 May 1861, JDPP-RUL; Andrew Moore to Clement C. Clay, 18 June 1861, Clay Family Papers, DUL. For Andrew Moore's official correspondence with the War Department, see A. Moore to Walker, 4 March 1861, and Walker to Moore, 4 July 1861, *OR*, IV, 1:121 and 420. Andrew Moore to General Albert Sidney Johnston, 23 September 1861, and Moore to General Braxton Bragg, 8 November 1861, OA, AlaDAH. See 2nd called and regular session 1861, Alabama Legislature, *Acts of the General Assembly of the State of Alabama*, 86–87; regular session 1861, Texas Legislature, *General and Special Laws of the State of Texas*, 11–27; 1861 session, *The Mississippi Legislature, 1861–1862*, 193; 1st session 1861, Tennessee General Assembly, *Public Acts of the State of Tennessee;* 1861 session, Louisiana Legislature, *Acts of the State of Louisiana.* Lincoln had similar problems with governors who put their local interests ahead of those of the national government in allocating manpower and matériel. For a careful examination of this problem, see William Best Hesseltine, *Lincoln and the War Governors* (New York: Alfred A. Knopf, 1948).

31. M. E. Weaver to Omer Weaver, 9 June 1861, "At Home in Confederate Arkansas." See also Michael B. Dougan, *Confederate Arkansas: The People and Policies of a Frontier State in Wartime* (University: University of Alabama Press, 1976), 68–70. McCullough to Walker, 20 May 1861; Rector to Walker, 11 June 1861; and Walker to Rector, 22 June 1861, *OR*, I, 3:579–80, 590–91, 597.

32. Walker to Davis, 24 July 1861, *OR*, IV, 1:497. Grady McWhinney and Perry D. Jamieson's argument, in their *Attack and Die: Civil War Military Tactics and Southern Heritage* (University: University of Alabama Press, 1982), 3–24, that Confederate strategic blunders were a consequence of the South's Celtic heritage remains controversial. Frank Lawrence Owsley, *State Rights in the Confederacy* (1925; Gloucester, Mass.: Peter Smith, 1961), 272.

33. Davis to General Joseph Johnston, 13 July 1861, *OR*, I, 2:976. See Wiley, *Life of Johnny Reb*, 288.

34. Clement Eaton, *A History of the Southern Confederacy* (New York: Macmillan, 1954), 87; B. Franklin Cooling, *Symbol, Sword, and Shield: Defending Washington during the Civil War* (Hamden, Conn.: Archon Books, 1975), 60. See also Coulter, *Confederate States of America*, 199–200.

35. Benjamin to Bragg, 4 November 1861, *OR*, I, 5:829–33, 886, 896; Miscellaneous Manuscripts, University of Rochester Library, Rochester, N.Y. For similar confrontations in other states, see General Benjamin McCulloch to Rector, 25 September 1861, Manuscript Department, University of Arkansas Library, Fayetteville; Pettus to Walker, and Harris to Walker, 28 May 1861, *OR*, IV, 1:484, 358–59.

36. For the Southern home front, see Mary Spencer Ringold, *The Role of the State Legislature in the Confederacy* (Athens: University of Georgia Press, 1966), 23; James L. Roark, *Masters without Slaves: Southern Planters in the Civil War and Reconstruction* (New York: Norton, 1977), 14.

CHAPTER 3. "A People's Contest"?

1. Jefferson Davis, "Inaugural Address 18 February 1861," *Messages and Papers,* 1:35; see also Davis, "Address to Second (Called) Session of the Provisional Confederate Congress 29 April 1861," ibid., 1:77. Abraham Lincoln, "Inaugural Address 4 March 1861," *Compilation of the Presidents,* 7:3206–7. See also James M. McPherson, *Ordeal by Fire: The Civil War and Reconstruction* (New York: Knopf, 1981), 149–59; and William C. Wright, *The Secession Movement in the Middle Atlantic States* (Rutherford, N.J.: Fairleigh Dickinson University Press, 1973), 21–97. Lincoln to O. H. Browning, 22 September 1861, *Collected Works,* 4:532.

2. Abraham Lincoln, "Special Message 4 July 1861," *Compilation of the Presidents,* 7:3231.

3. For July 21, 1861, see Carl Sandburg, *The War Years,* vol. 3 of *Abraham Lincoln,* Sangamon Ed. (New York: Charles Scribner's Sons, 1959), 300–309. For a persuasive presentation of the view that much of Lincoln's wartime policy toward the South was shaped by his determination to control the later peace, see William Best Hesseltine, *Lincoln's Plan of Reconstruction* (1960; rpt. Chicago: Quadrangle Books, 1967), 11–72; Herman Belz, *Reconstructing the Union: Theory and Policy during the Civil War* (Ithaca: Cornell University Press, 1969), 1–40.

4. Lincoln, "Memorandum of Military Policy Suggested By the Bull Run Defeat 23 and 27 July 1861," *Collected Works,* 4:457–58. See also Sandburg, *The War Years.* For evidence of Lincoln's awareness of and participation in the arming of western Virginia unionists, see *Collected Works,* 4:443, 464, 481, 491, 511. Unionist activity in eastern Tennessee is discussed in Secretary of War Simon Cameron to General in Chief Winfield Scott, 27 June 1861, *OR,* III, 1:299–300.

5. Lincoln, "Special Message 4 July 1861," *Compilation of the Presidents,* 7:3230.

6. Ruffin, 3 December 1859, *Diary,* 1:373.

7. Davis, "Speech 16 February 1861," *Jefferson Davis,* 5:48.

8. William Lowndes Yancey, 12 October 1860, in Fredrickson, *The Black Image,* 61. Davis had expressed a similar position during a speech at Aberdeen, Miss., in 1851; see *Jefferson Davis,* 2:74.

9. Davis, "Speech 20 July 1861," *Messages and Papers,* 1:120, 124.

10. V. O. Key Jr., *Southern Politics in State and Nation* (New York: Vintage Books, 1949), 15–17, 551; Holt, *The Political Crisis of the 1850s,* 238–39. For a perceptive analysis of American Whiggery, see Daniel W. Howe, *The Political Culture of the American Whigs* (Chicago: University of Chicago Press, 1980). For a discussion of the difficulties experienced by Southern Know-Nothings, see J. Mills Thornton III, *Politics and Power in a Slave Society: Alabama, 1800–1860* (Baton Rouge: Louisiana State University Press, 1978), 348–65. Yeoman anxiety about "political slavery" is lucidly analyzed in ibid., xviii–xix.

11. George Fitzhugh produced the most extreme formulation of these trends in proslavery thought; see Eugene D. Genovese, "The Logical Outcome of the Slaveholders' Philosophy: An Exposition, Interpretation and Critique of the Social Thought of George Fitzhugh of Port Royal, Virginia," in *The World the Slaveholders*

Made: Two Essays in Interpretation (New York: Pantheon Books, 1969), 118–244. For Spratt, see Thomas, *The Confederate Nation,* 44.

12. For campaign circular, see Dougan, *Confederate Arkansas,* 44, 75. For Hudson, see Paul D. Escott, *After Secession: Jefferson Davis and the Failure of Confederate Nationalism* (Baton Rouge: Louisiana State University Press, 1978), 29.

13. John Berrien Lindsley, 20 April 1861, Lindsley Diary, TSLA. See Paul D. Escott, "An Irrepressible Conflict within the South? Class Influences on the Balloting for Secession," unpublished paper presented at OAH convention, 1979.

14. Editorial, *Morgantown Star,* 20 April 1861, reprinted in *The National Intelligencer,* 25 April 1861.

15. Lindsley, 8 June 1861, Lindsley Diary, TSLA.

16. J. Reuben Sheeler, "The Development of Unionism in East Tennessee, 1860–1866," *JNH* 29 (1944): 182. It is worth noting that in the late 1850s Brownlow, in the *Knoxville Whig,* assumed a militantly proslavery position, going so far as to warn that the South would defend its rights, with arms if necessary. For a discussion of the connections between the use of code terms like "military despotism" and "European monarchy" and the emergence of anti-secessionism in the Upper South, see Marc W. Kruman, "Dissent in the Confederacy: The North Carolina Experience," *CWH* 27 (1981): 293–313.

17. See Gordon B. McKinney, *Southern Mountain Republicans, 1865–1900: Politics and the Appalachian Community* (Chapel Hill: University of North Carolina Press, 1978), 12–29; Mary Campbell, *The Attitude of Tennesseans toward the Union, 1847–1861* (New York: Vantage Press, 1961); James Patton, *Unionism and Reconstruction in Tennessee* (Chapel Hill: University of North Carolina Press, 1934); James Fertig, *The Secession and Reconstruction of Tennessee* (Chicago: University of Chicago Press, 1898); Charles H. Ambler, *Sectionalism in Virginia from 1776 to 1861* (New York: Russell and Russell, 1964). The pioneering analysis of this "double revolution" appears in Michael P. Johnson, *Toward a Patriarchal Republic: The Secession of Georgia* (Baton Rouge: Louisiana State University Press, 1977), xx. See also two discussions of politics and society in nineteenth-century Georgia: Steven Hahn, *The Roots of Southern Populism: The Transformation of the Georgia Up Country, 1850–1890* (New York: Oxford University Press, 1983), 86–116; and Edward L. Ayers, *Vengeance and Justice: Crime and Punishment in the Nineteenth-Century American South* (New York: Oxford University Press, 1984), 141–45. See Carter G. Woodson, "Freedom and Slavery in Appalachian America," *JNH* 1 (1916): 132–50, for a provocative interpretation of the social origins of the tension over issues of economic and political equality that had existed from the colonial period onward between nonslaveholding highlanders and slaveholding lowlanders.

18. In his study of the social origins of political violence in eastern Tennessee, James B. Campbell concludes, "In many respects the war in east Tennessee assumed the character of a class struggle between the rural smallholders and the plantation owners of the towns." Campbell, "East Tennessee during Federal Occupation," *East Tennessee His-*

torical Society Publications 14 (1947): 65. This analysis confirms Sheeler's description of east Tennessee prosecessionists as wealthy urban slaveholders in a deadly struggle against the rural yeomanry who formed the backbone of mountain unionism. Sheeler, "Development of Unionism," 185. For an impressionistic account of these trends in western Virginia, see Pinkerton, *Spy of the Rebellion*, 206–10. A. I. Boreman to Governor Pierpont, 26 July 1861, OA, West Virginia Department of Archives and History.

19. See E. Merton Coulter, *The Civil War and Readjustment in Kentucky* (Chapel Hill: University of North Carolina Press, 1926), 18–56, 87–91, 147–49; A. C. Quisenberry, "Kentucky's Neutrality in 1861," *Kentucky State Historical Society Register* 15 (1917): 9–18.

20. Coulter, *Civil War and Readjustment in Kentucky*, 18–34; William H. Townsend, *Lincoln and the Bluegrass: Slavery and Civil War in Kentucky* (Lexington: University of Kentucky Press, 1955); William Earl Parrish, *Turbulent Partnership: Missouri and the Union, 1861–1865* (Columbia: University of Missouri Press, 1963), 1–14; Jay Monaghan, *Civil War of the Western Border: 1854–1865* (New York: Bonanza Books, 1955), 117–227; Hans C. Adamson, *Rebellion in Missouri, 1861: Nathaniel Lyon and His Army of the West* (Philadelphia: Chilton, 1961); McPherson, *Ordeal by Fire*, 153–59. On the Frémont proclamation of 30 August 1861, see *OR*, I, 3:466.

21. Morris Sheppard's narrative in Rawick, ed., *The American Slave*, 7:288–89. See also Coulter, *Confederate States of America*, 49–55. Annie Heloise Abel, "The Indians in the Civil War," *AHR* 15 (1909): 282–89; Abel, *The American Indian as Slaveholder and Secessionist: An Omitted Chapter in the Diplomatic History of the Southern Confederacy* (Cleveland: Arthur Clarke, 1915), 13–14, 22, 88–95, 108–17, 216; Edward E. Dale, "The Cherokees in the Confederacy," *JSH* 13 (1947): 162–66; and Abel, *The American Indian as Participant in the Civil War* (Cleveland: Arthur Clarke, 1919), 62–67. For more recent treatments, see Daniel F. Littlefield, *Africans and Seminoles: From Removal to Emancipation* (Westport, Conn.: Greenwood, 1977); Littlefield, *Africans and Creeks: From the Colonial Period to the Civil War* (Westport, Conn.: Greenwood, 1977); and R. Halliburton Jr., *Red over Black: Black Slavery among the Cherokee Indians* (Westport, Conn.: Greenwood, 1977).

22. For the situation in Maryland, see Barbara Jeanne Fields, *Slavery and Freedom on the Middle Ground: Maryland during the Nineteenth Century* (New Haven: Yale University Press, 1985); also Charles Wagandt, *The Mighty Revolution: Negro Emancipation in Maryland, 1862–1864* (Baltimore: Johns Hopkins University Press, 1964).

23. Thomas R. R. Cobb to wife, 24 July 1861, in Coulter, *Confederate States of America*, 345; Jones, 22 July 1861, in John B. Jones, *A Rebel War Clerk's Diary at the Confederate State Capital*, ed. Howard Swiggert, 2 vols. (New York: Old Hickory Bookshop, 1935), 1:66.

24. Robert M. T. Hunter to James W. Mason, 8 February 1862, L. Q. C. Lamar Papers, OA, MDAH.

25. On the Peace and Constitutional Society, see Georgia Lee Tatum, *Disloyalty in the Confederacy* (1934; rpt. New York: AMS Press, 1970), 24–25; Ted R. Worley, "Doc-

uments Relating to the Arkansas Peace Society of 1861," *Arkansas History Quarterly,* 17 (1958): 82–111; Dougan, *Confederate Arkansas,* 84. Beford County declaration: John Huddleston (et al.) to Davis, 12 July 1861, LR, NA-CSA.

26. E. Merton Coulter, *William G. Brownlow: Fighting Parson of the Southern Highlands* (Chapel Hill: University of North Carolina Press, 1937), 137–207; Eaton, *A History of the Southern Confederacy,* 41. For partisan warfare in eastern Tennessee, see *OR,* II, 1:823–66; Tatum, *Disloyalty in the Confederacy,* 143–50. For a summary of the military problems caused by disaffection in the backcountry, see Coulter, *Confederate States of America,* 84–99.

27. On the bridge burning, see Jones, 11 November 1861, *Rebel War Clerk's Diary,* 1:91–92.

28. Benjamin to Carroll, 10 December 1861, *OR,* II, 1:854; *OR,* I, 7:439–684.

29. See Thomas L. Connelly and Archer Jones, *The Politics of Command: Factions and Ideas in Confederate Strategy* (Baton Rouge: Louisiana State University Press, 1973), 93–95; Clement Eaton, *Jefferson Davis* (New York: Free Press, 1977), 187–95.

30. Lincoln, "First Annual Message 3 December 1861," *Compilation of the Presidents,* 7:3256.

31. See Carl Degler, *The Other South: Southern Dissenters in the Nineteenth Century* (New York: Harper & Row, 1974).

32. Editorial, *Richmond Examiner,* 19 July 1861.

33. See the interpretation of the Southern "aversion to slavery" in Kenneth Stampp, "The Southern Road to Appomattox," in *The Imperiled Union: Essays on the Background of the Civil War* (New York: Oxford University Press, 1980), 246–69.

34. Harry Smith, *Fifty Years of Slavery in the United States* (Grand Rapids: West Michigan Publishing Co., 1891), 116; Cecil George, "Narrative," in Louisiana WPA Narratives, Louisiana State Library, Baton Rouge. Walters's narrative in Rawick, ed., *The American Slave,* 7:312.

35. For Committee of Constables, see Dickerson to Pettus, 18 May 1861, OA, MDAH. Woodcock to Pettus, 5 May 1861, OA, MDAH. Harrison to Clark, 23 April 1861; and Meanelly to Clark, 25 April 1861, OA, TexSLA.

36. The Southern tradition of low taxation and laissez-faire in local expenditures combined to make the South the national leader in adult illiteracy. In 1850, for example, 20 percent of the Southern population described itself as illiterate; this compares with 3 percent in the middle states, and 0.42 percent in New England. Clement Eaton, *A History of the Old South* (New York: Macmillan, 1949), 416–21. See also Aptheker, *American Negro Slave Revolts,* 360. The best exposition of the worldview of the up-country yeomanry is found in Hahn, *Roots of Southern Populism,* 15–85. For a perceptive comparison of the varied influences that up-country and low-country milieus exerted on attitudes toward Southern nationalism, see Ayers, *Vengeance and Justice,* 73–150.

37. W. L. C. Musgrove to Governor Moore, 16 July 1861, OA, AlaDAH; P. C. Winn to Governor Shorter, 7 December 1862, ibid. See also Hugh Bailey, "Disaffection in Early Confederate Alabama," *JSH* 23 (1957): 522–28.

38. John Bell to Henry Bell, 11 April 1861, James Bell to Henry Bell, 21 April 1861, and Robert Bell to Henry Bell, 10 June 1861, in Bailey, "Disaffection in Early Confederate Alabama," 524–27; Irvin to Moore, ibid., 527–28. Apparently, Henry Bell gave these letters to his local postmaster, a man named Irvin, who in turn mailed them to Governor Moore along with the two affidavits.

39. Elissay Bell to Henry Bell, 21 April 1861, in Bailey, "Disaffection in Early Confederate Alabama," 525. See also James Oates, *The Ruling Race: A History of American Slaveholders* (New York: Knopf, 1982), 229–32, for his analysis of the effects of shifting patterns of upward mobility on the aspirations and the ideologies of younger Southern men "on the make." As Eric Foner's *Free Soil, Free Labor and Free Men: The Ideology of the Republican Party before the Civil War* (New York: Oxford University Press, 1970) makes clear, Northern men on the make saw the expansion of slavery into the territories as an unacceptable threat to their own main chance, in contrast to their Southern counterparts, who saw the expansion of slavery as necessary to their dream. The distinctive social bases of the free labor economy of the North and the slave labor economy of the South may well have led to these contradictory perspectives. Escott, *After Secession,* 19–32, identifies as a problem the wide compass of disaffection among the Lower South yeomanry, to which Johnson, *Toward a Patriarchal Republic,* Hahn, *The Roots of Southern Populism,* and Ayers, *Vengeance and Justice,* give more detailed attention.

40. For Jim Jeffcoat, see Tom Terrill and Jerrold Hirsch, eds., *Such as Us: Southern Voices of the Thirties* (1978; rpt. New York: W. W. Norton, 1979), 61.

CHAPTER 4. "This War Is Our War, the Cause Is Our Cause"

1. The pioneering analysis of the deleterious effects of states' rights ideology on the Confederacy is in Wesley, *The Collapse of the Confederacy,* esp. xi–xii. For an early elaboration of Wesley's thesis, see Owsley, *State Rights in the Confederacy;* for a more recent treatment, see George M. Fredrickson, "Blue over Gray: Sources of Success and Failure in the Civil War," in *A Nation Divided: Problems and Issues of the Civil War and Reconstruction,* ed. Fredrickson (Minneapolis: Burgess, 1975), 69.

2. Davis, "Proclamation of 17 April 1861," and "Message 29 April 1861," *Messages and Papers,* 1:60–62, 63–69, 81.

3. See David Potter's penetrating critique, "Jefferson Davis and the Political Factors in Confederate Defeat," in *Why the North Won the Civil War,* ed. David Herbert Donald (Baton Rouge: Louisiana State University Press, 1960), 91–112. In 1860 the legislatures of the seven Lower South states had widely divergent percentages of slaveholders among their membership: South Carolina (82%), Alabama (76%), Mississippi (73%), Georgia (72%), Louisiana (64%), Florida (55%), and Texas (54%). Ralph A. Wooster calculates these percentages in *The People in Power: Courthouse and Statehouse in the Lower South, 1850–1860* (Knoxville: University of Tennessee Press, 1969), 41. As soon as the Confederacy came into existence, however, slaveholders assumed even greater prominence.

The unicameral provisional Congress of February 1861–February 1862 was derived from the Constitutional Convention, whose delegates assumed constituent powers. Of its 105 members, 91 percent were slaveholders [SH] (95), 9 percent were not [NSH] (10); data on the remaining is unavailable [ND]. The division in the first full Congress, and the second, shows the following pattern:

First Confederate Congress (February 1862–February 1864)

	House	*Senate*	*Total*
SH	90 (92%)	28 (93%)	118 (92%)
NSH	8 (8%)	2 (7%)	10 (8%)
ND	11	0	11
TOTAL	98	30	128

Second Confederate Congress (February 1864–February 1865)

	House	*Senate*	*Total*
SH	83 (86%)	23 (96%)	106 (88%)
NSH	13 (14%)	1 (4%)	14 (12%)
ND	13	0	13
TOTAL	96	24	120

Source: Thomas B. Alexander and Richard E. Beringer, *The Anatomy of the Confederate Congress: A Study of the Influences of Member Characteristics on Legislative Voting Behavior, 1861–1865* (Nashville: Vanderbilt University Press, 1972), 354–89.

4. William M. Brooks to Davis, 13 May 1861, *OR*, IV, 1:318–19.

5. Harry St. John Dixon, 18 May 1863, Dixon Family Papers, SHC; Fay to Sarah Fay, 21 April 1862, in *"This Infernal War": The Confederate Letters of Sgt. Edwin H. Fay,* ed. Bell Irvin Wiley (Austin: University of Texas Press, 1958), 37–38.

6. Frank Richardson to Father, 4 September 1861, Richardson Family Papers, SHC; Oliver P. Temple, *East Tennessee and the Civil War* (Cincinnati: Robert Clarke Co., 1899), 76.

7. Theodore Mandeville to Family, 15 April and 31 August 1861, 17 March 1862, Mandeville Family Papers, LSUL.

8. Nathaniel Dawson to Elodie Todd Dawson, 10 May 1861, Dawson Family Papers, SHC; L. D. Poe to William M. Morris, 1 April 1862, William Morris Papers, SHC.

9. Frank Richardson to Mother, 14 December 1861, Richardson Family Papers, SHC; Maria Southgates Hawes, "Reminiscences," 11, SHC; for an analogous case, see

William Curtis's narrative in Rawick, ed., *The American Slave,* 7:51. Robert A. Moore, 18 October 1861, in *A Life for the Confederacy,* 63. For Robert M. Gill, see Wiley, *Life of Johnny Reb,* 337–38.

10. William Miller Owen, *In Camp and Battle with the Washington Artillery of New Orleans: A Narrative of Events during the late civil war from Bull Run to Appomattox and Spanish Fort* (Boston: Ticknor & Co., 1885), 7–8, 13, 21; James W. McHenry to Governor Harris, 4 August 1861, OA, TSLA; Alcorn to Amelia Alcorn, 6 June 1861, in Pereyra, *James Lusk Alcorn,* 46. On slaves hiring out for personal service, see also Frank Richardson to Mother, 23 September 1861, SHC; Dunbar Affleck to Parents, 6, 22, 29 April 1862, Affleck Family Papers, LSUL; and Wiley, *Life of Johnny Reb,* 103–4, 117, 327–28.

11. Gus Smith's and Perry McGee's narratives in Rawick, ed., *The American Slave,* 2:325, 231. McGee did receive eighteen dollars in change from the soldiers for his services.

12. Albert Taylor Bledsoe to John Sale, 17 June 1861, *OR,* IV, 1:380.

13. On War Department regulations, see R. H. Chilton to A. C. Myers, 15 June 1861, *OR,* IV, 1:379. See also Harry N. Scheiber, "The Pay of Confederate Troops and Problems of Demoralization: A Case of Administrative Failure," *CWH* 15 (1969): 226, 229–30; and Scheiber, "The Pay of Troops and Confederate Morale in the Trans-Mississippi West," *Arkansas Historical Quarterly* 18 (1959): 350–65.

14. Mollie Shoemaker to Governor John Pettus, [Fall 1861], OA, MDAH.

15. Davis, "Message 18 November 1861," *Messages and Papers,* 1:136–44; William Brooks to Jefferson Davis, 13 May 1861, *OR,* IV, 1:318–19.

16. Lincoln to Buell, 13 January 1862, *Collected Works,* 5:98.

17. Secretary of War Benjamin to Davis, 30 November 1861, *OR,* IV, 1:763–64. James M. Matthews, ed., *Statutes at Large of the Provisional Government of the Confederate States of America* (Richmond, Va., 1864), 223–24.

18. Bragg to Adjutant General Samuel Cooper, 20 December 1861, *OR,* I, 6:784–85. Marcus Cunliffe challenges John Hope Franklin's thesis about the uniqueness of the Southern militia tradition, in *Soldiers and Civilians: The Martial Spirit in America, 1775–1865* (Boston: Little, Brown, 1968). The role that militias played in nineteenth-century American military affairs is discussed in Allan R. Millett and Peter Maslowski, *For the Common Defense: A Military History of the United States of America* (New York: Free Press, 1984), 165–66; and in T. Harry Williams, *The History of American Wars from 1745 to 1918* (New York: Knopf, 1981), 136, 213, 219–20.

19. Bragg to Cooper, 20 December 1861, *OR,* I, 6:784–85.

20. Wilfred Buck Yearns, *The Confederate Congress* (Athens: University of Georgia Press, 1960), 63.

21. Johnston to Benjamin, 18 January 1862, *OR,* I, 5:1037; Lee to [Magrath, delegate to the South Carolina state convention], 24 December 1861, *OR* I, 6:350.

22. Benjamin to Johnston, 25 January 1862, *OR,* I, 5:1045–46.

23. Benjamin to Bragg, 5 January 1862, *OR,* I, 6:794–95.

24. Davis apparently expressed these reservations as early as April of 1861. See Yearns, *Confederate Congress,* 61–62. In the immediate postwar period, Davis's critics

blamed their former president for the eccentricities of the December reenlistment act. See Edward A. Pollard, *The Lost Cause: A New Southern History of the War of the Confederates* (New York: E. B. Treat & Co., 1866), 219–20. His other vetoes were May 17, May 21, and August 22. *Messages and Papers,* 1:59, 100, 101, 130. Eaton, *Jefferson Davis,* 216, points out that Davis vetoed thirty-nine bills in all and that only one of his vetoes was overridden.

CHAPTER 5. The Failure of Southern Voluntarism and the Collapse of the Upper South Frontier

1. Johnston to Benjamin, 25 December 1861, *OR,* I, 7:793–94. See also Thomas Lawrence Connelly, *Army of the Heartland: The Army of Tennessee, 1861–1862* (Baton Rouge: Louisiana State University Press, 1967), 3. Together with its companion study, *Autumn of Glory: The Army of Tennessee, 1862–1865* (1971), Connelly's two volumes have replaced Stanley Horn's *The Army of Tennessee,* 2nd ed. (Norman: University of Oklahoma Press, 1955), as the standard study of the Civil War along the Upper South frontier.

2. Pillow to Walker, 15 May 1861, *OR,* I, 52, pt. 2: 99–100; Special Orders #140, 26 May 1861, Provisional State Army of Tennessee, Gideon Pillow Papers, Generals' Papers, NA-CSA.

3. Kate Stone, 22 January 1862, *Brokenburn,* 83.

4. Daniel S. Donelson to General Sneed, 15 June 1861, Pillow Papers, RG #109, NA. Ulrich B. Phillips argues that antebellum slaveholders disliked sending slaves to construction camps because "their lack of sanitation, discipline, domesticity and stability were at the opposite poles from the plantation as places of slave residence." *American Negro Slavery* (Baton Rouge: Louisiana State University Press, 1916), 380. So numerous were the complaints about the treatment of fortifications workers that Secretary of War Benjamin asked Attorney General Thomas Bragg for an opinion on the government's liability for illness, injury, or deaths that occurred without fault or negligence on the part of the army. Bragg's opinion exempted slave property from the normal obligation to pay for consequential damage to private property, arguing that since "a slave is a rational being, his death, injury or loss may be caused by his own fault or misconduct, and in such cases, it seems to me that the government ought not to be responsible." See Bragg to Benjamin, 25 November 1861, in Rembert W. Patrick, ed., *The Opinions of the Confederate Attorneys General, 1861–1865* (Buffalo, N.Y.: Dennis, 1950), 51–53. On the increasingly querulous relationship between the governors and the slaveholders over the use of slaves as military laborers, see Harrison A. Trexler, "The Opposition of Planters to the Employment of Slaves as Laborers by the Confederacy," *MVHR* 27 (1940): 211–24.

5. John Houston Bills, 8 October 1861, Bills Family Papers, SHC; Francis Terry Leak Jr., 30 August and 21 September 1861, Leak Journals, SHC.

6. Leonidas Polk to Johnston, 28 November 1861, *OR,* I, 7:710–11. The problems that resulted from the paucity of competent engineers in the Confederate army are dis-

cussed in Colonel J. F. Gilmer's Chief of Engineer Bureau Report to Seddon, 26 December 1862, *OR*, IV, 2:259–62. The engineering mistakes at Forts Henry and Donelson are indicative of the relatively low level of incentive within the antebellum South for mechanical and industrial pursuits. For the role of slavery in limiting Southern entrepreneurship, see Eugene Genovese, *The Political Economy of Slavery* (New York: Vintage, 1965), 124–53, 180–239.

7. W. W. Mackall to Tilghman, 17 November 1861, *OR*, I, 4:560; Tilghman to Mackall, 29 November 1861, *OR*, I, 7:719. For community leaders, see S. D. Weakley and James Saunders to Benjamin, 22 November 1861, ibid., 692–93.

8. Montgomery Lynch to Polk, 1 December 1861, *OR*, I, 7:728–29. Johnston called on Governor Harris for help in procuring slaves for Forts Henry and Donelson and for Nashville. Johnston to Harris, 19 November 1861, *OR*, I, 4:864. See also Colonel William Preston Johnston, *The Life of General Albert Sidney Johnston, Embracing His Service in the Armies of the United States, the Republic of Texas, and the Confederate States* (New York: D. Appleton, 1878), 343, 410–22. Charles P. Roland, *Albert Sidney Johnston: Soldier of Three Republics* (Austin: University of Texas Press, 1964), offers a useful corrective to the tone of W. P. Johnston's apologia for his father's failures in Tennessee. Connelly attributes the incomplete state of the inland river defenses to the reluctance of slaveholders to donate slaves; see *Army of the Heartland*, 72–74. Mackall to Gilmer, 29 November 1861, *OR*, I, 7:724; Gilmer to Mackall, 7 December 1861, *OR*, I, 52, pt. 2: 233.

9. Harris to Johnston, 31 December 1861, *OR*, I, 7:811–12. The situation was actually much worse than Harris cared to admit; the engineer in charge of the project at Nashville reported that only seven of the three hundred laborers needed had been sent; see G. O. Watts to Hugh McKrew, 6 December 1861, ibid., 739. The figures on slave population are derived from the 1860 U.S. Census, part of the Confederate Self-Sufficiency Project [described in the lost Appendix A—Ed.].

Total slave population for the three states

Alabama	Mississippi	Tennessee	TOTAL
435,074	417,390	275,719	1,128,183

Total slave population in the vicinity of Nashville

County	Total slaves
Cheatham	1,882
Davidson (Nashville)	14,790
Dickson	2,201
Hickman	1,753
Humphreys	1,463

Total slave population for the three states (cont.)

County	Total slaves
Lawrence	1,160
Maury	14,654
Montgomery	9,554
Perry	548
Robertson	4,861
Rutherford	12,984
Sumner	7,700
Williamson	12,367
Wilson	7,964
TOTAL	97,565

10. Dixon to Gilmer, 21 November 1861, *OR,* I, 7:599; Gilmer to "The Citizens of Nashville," 11 December 1861, ibid., 757; and Gilmer to Harris, 11 December 1861, LS, Western Department, NA-CSA. On Johnston's order, see Mackall to Lindsay, 27 January 1862, ibid.

11. Gilmer to Mackall, 24 November 1861, LS, Western Department, NA-CSA; M. Jeff Thompson to Polk, 16 December 1861, *OR,* I, 8:715–16. Two studies by the economist George Tucker describe the folkways that designated certain tasks as "nigger work." See Tucker, *Progress of the United States in Population and Wealth in Fifty Years . . .* (Boston: Little and Brown, 1843), and *Political Economy for the People* (Philadelphia: C. Sherman and Sons, 1859). The Joseph Carson reminiscence (see below) helps explain the decision to ban all blacks from fortifications labor. He touches on an important feature of the culture of Southern honor: the potential for social schisms within the army if the customary distinction between the public (civic) and private (familial or personal) dimensions of honorable behavior was undermined by experiences in the camps. White men were expected to conform their behavior in public and private spheres of life to community standards, and participation in civic rituals went hand-in-hand with appropriately deferential behavior toward family and households. The ideology of popular democracy was grounded on a presumption of equality of status before the law underlying the civic obligations of white men, such as voting, taxation, and militia and patrol duty.

12. Hinson McVay to Mr. Weekly, 15 January 1861, Andrew Johnson Papers Project, University of Tennessee Library, Knoxville. On soldiers unwilling to work with Negroes, see John Q. Anderson, "Joseph Carson, Louisiana Confederate Soldier," *Louisiana History* 1 (1969): 48–49. The distinction Carson makes between "official drudgery" and personal service is consistent with antebellum standards. However, the attempt to apply these standards to life in army camps had the practical effect of providing a basis for social conflict. Body servants and military laborers were slaves, even if their functions differed. Allowing body servants to perform a "civic duty," to substi-

tute for their masters on construction details alongside yeomen soldiers, threatened the presumption of racial superiority and could lead to personal insult sufficient to prevent an offended white male from performing *his* civic duties. Once it became clear that yeomen would refuse to work with any blacks, the army had little choice but to make concessions. Bertram Wyatt-Brown, *Southern Honor: Ethics and Behavior in the Old South* (New York: Oxford University Press, 1982), 25–27, 59–61.

13. On Johnston's urging of civilians to provide arms, see Johnston to Benjamin, 8 and 22 January 1861, LS, Western Department, NA-CSA.

14. Stone, 30 June, 2 and 5 July 1861, *Brokenburn,* 33–37; Mary Wilkerson to Micajah Wilkerson, 1 August 1861, Micajah Wilkerson Papers, LLMVC. Even though this account refers to the victim as a white male, the letter does not explicitly identify Joe Day as white. Pugh, 26 August 1861, Pugh Family Papers, LSUL. For reports of arson scares in Mississippi and Kentucky, see D. C. Nichols to Governor Pettus, 28 October 1861, and Jackson Light to Pettus, 29 October 1861, OA, MDAH; also Aptheker, *American Negro Slave Revolts,* 365.

In Alabama three white men decided, during the summer of 1861, to try to nab a slave named Isham in the act of harboring runaway slaves. They disguised themselves by "blackening" their faces and "went near the negro house and made a noise there and struck on it with a stick." When Isham demanded that they identify themselves, one of the men yelled out, "A Partner!," whereupon Isham shot through the door, killing one. Isham (A Slave) vs. State, 38 Alabama 213, in Helen Catterall, comp. and ed., *Judicial Cases Concerning American Slavery and the Negro,* 5 vols. (Washington, D.C.: Carnegie Institution, 1926–37), 3:252.

15. For Higgins, see Felts to Woodruff, 25 July 1861, in Worley, ed., "At Home in Confederate Arkansas," 9–10. Edward Ayers makes a persuasive case that the customary antebellum practice was to accord "procedural fairness" to a slave, even one accused of capital crime; see Ayers, *Vengeance and Justice,* 131–36.

16. S. D. Weakley et al., to "Fellow Citizens of North Alabama and North Mississippi," 23 November 1861, *OR,* I, 7:694–95.

17. Blount to Benjamin, 19 January 1862, *OR,* I, 7:840; Clark to Benjamin, 16 November 1861, *OR,* I, 52, pt. 2: 209; Brown to Benjamin, 17 November 1861, ibid.; Carroll to A. S. Johnston, 5 December 1861, ibid., 228–29.

18. Lincoln to Buell, 31 December 1861; Lincoln to Buell and Halleck, 1 January 1862; and Lincoln to Buell, 4 and 6 January 1862, *Collected Works,* 5:84, 86–87, 90–92. Congressional Republicans grew sufficiently concerned about the prolonged stalemate after First Bull Run that they created a Joint Committee on the Conduct of the War; this committee began summoning witnesses, including McClellan, in January 1862. For a careful discussion of the origins and membership of this committee, and of the concern about its potential for mischief, see J. G. Randall, *Lincoln the President: From Springfield to Gettysburg* (New York: Dodd, Mead, 1945), 2:62–64; and Benjamin P. Thomas, *Abraham Lincoln* (New York: Alfred A. Knopf, 1952).

19. On 8 November 1861 the *San Jacinto,* a U.S. naval vessel on blockade duty, fired a shot across the bows of a British mail steamer, the *Trent,* while both were in in-

ternational waters in the Bahamas Channel. The captain of the *San Jacinto,* Charles
Wilkes, used force to remove two Confederate commissioners, James Mason and John
Slidell, and their secretaries from the decks of the *Trent* and transferred them to federal custody in Boston. The British government reacted sharply to the removal, from
a neutral vessel in international waters, of diplomats bound for London and Paris. Secretary William Seward managed to prevent a war. Norman B. Ferris, *The Trent Affair*
(Knoxville: University of Tennessee Press, 1977); Brian Jenkins, *Britain and the War
for the Union* (Montreal: McGill-Queens Press, 1974); Glyndon Van Deusen, *William
Seward* (New York: Oxford University Press, 1967).

Financial affairs reached a crisis in the North on 30 December 1861 when the U.S.
Treasury Department and the principal Northern banks suspended specie payment.
The uncertainty spawned by the Trent affair played a major role, but the burden of
expenditures to support the war meant that the treasury could not pay its bills in gold
and silver, as required by law, and the private banks could not cover their deposits.
See Bray Hammond, *Sovereignty and an Empty Purse: Banks and Politics in the Civil
War* (Princeton: Princeton University Press, 1970); Allan Nevins, *Ordeal of the Union,*
vol. 5: *The War for the Union: The Improvised War, 1861–1862* (New York: Scribner,
1947–71), 405. President's General War Order #1, 27 January 1862, *Collected Works,*
5:111–12.

20. Halleck to Lincoln, 6 January 1862, *OR,* I, 7:533; Ulysses S. Grant, *Personal
Memoirs of U. S. Grant,* ed. E. B. Long (1952; rpt. New York: Grosset & Dunlap,
1962), 146; Johnston to Pettus, 24 December 1861, and Johnston to Benjamin, 22 January 1862, *OR,* I, 7:788–89, 844–45.

21. See General Orders #1, 1 January 1862, and Special Orders, 15 December 1861
to 15 April 1862, NA-CSA.

22. Polk to Cooper, 27 December 1861, *OR,* I, 7:798; Johnston to Benjamin, 8 and
12 January 1862, ibid., 824–25, 827–28; Polk to Benjamin, 24 December 1861, 22 January 1862, ibid., 789–90, 846. Arkansas governor Hiram Rector made a similar request
to Benjamin for financial assistance to encourage reenlistment: Rector to Benjamin,
6 February 1862, *OR,* I, 8:748.

23. Tilghman to Williamson [Polk's AAAG], 2 January 1862, *OR,* I, 7:817–18.

24. For "suspicious persons," see Jones, 8 November 1861–20 February 1862,
Rebel War Clerk's Diary, 1:90–111. For spies in the Tennessee Valley, see Pinkerton,
Spy of the Rebellion, 194; see also Grant to General C. F. Smith, 1 September 1861, and
Grant to Colonel Johnson, 13 October 1861, LS, District of Southeastern Missouri,
Records of the Continental United States Army Commands, RG #393, NA.

25. Johnston to Benjamin, 8 January 1862, LS, Western Department, NA-CSA.
See also Johnson to Josiah Gorgas, 27 January 1862, *OR,* I, 7:849.

26. On the abandonment of Fort Donelson, see Connelly, *Army of the Heartland,*
113–25; Horn, *Army of Tennessee,* 85–98; Grant, *Personal Memoirs,* 150–61.

27. G. A. Henry to Brigadier General William Hardee, 21 January 1862, *OR,* I,
7:842–43; Lindsley, 16 and 17 February 1862, Lindsley Papers, TSLA.

28. Davis, "Message 25 February 1862," *Messages and Papers,* 1:189–91; Davis to

William Brooks, 13 March 1862, *Jefferson Davis*, 5:216–19. However justified Davis may have been in declining to hold Johnston personally responsible for the debacle along the Upper South frontier, he seems to have felt bound by personal honor to support friends so long as they remained loyal; conversely, he did not feel bound to extend support to persons he considered personally disloyal or unfriendly. Davis often retained loyal friends in official positions despite strong evidence of their incompetence, and exiled others he suspected of disloyalty or unfriendly behavior, even because of incidents many years old. See Eaton, *Jefferson Davis*, 270–76. For a generally sympathetic critique of Davis's strategy, see Grady McWhiney, "Jefferson Davis and the Art of War," *CWH* 21 (1975): 101–12.

29. Seddon to Davis, 3 January 1863, *OR*, IV, 2:281.

30. Fortinberry to Pettus, 1 December 1862, OA, MDAH. Normal mean rainfall for January and February in the eastern Mississippi Valley was 11 inches. During January and February 1862, this mean increased to 16 inches, 46 percent above normal. Mean rainfall for June, July, and August for the area east of Austin, Texas, was 12.26 inches. Only 4.47 inches fell during the same period in 1862, a reduction of 64 percent. These rainfall figures were supplied by a network of Smithsonian Institution volunteer weather observers using instruments on which they made daily recordings of rainfall and temperature. Center for Polar and Scientific Archives, RG #106, NA. Mean rainfall totals come from Charles A. Schott, "Tables and Results of Precipitation in Rain and Snow in the U.S. . . . ," *Smithsonian Contributions to Knowledge* 18 (1872): 44–45; 24 (1881): 10–11.

Reports of rainfall and melted snow (in inches) for January and February 1862

| Location | January 1862 | | | February 1862 | | |
	Mean	*Actual*	*% Change*	*Mean*	*Actual*	*% Change*
Clarksville, TN	3.94	5.13	+30%	4.29	8.23	+92%
Columbus, MI	5.61	8.01	+43%	6.20	8.88	+43%
Chilesburg, KY	4.33	9.25	+114%	4.22	7.00	+66%
Nicholasville, KY	5.74	7.98	+39%	4.42	6.41	+43%
Greensboro, AL	5.00	8.89	+78%	5.45	10.43	+91%

31. R. C. Parker to Governor Shorter, 25 February 1862, OA, AlaDAH; *Tuscaloosa Observer*, March 1862, OA, AlaDAH; Susannah Clay to Senator Clement Clay, 5 March 1862, C. C. Clay Papers, DUL Manuscript Department.

32. Jonathan F. Bailey to Governor Watson, 31 March 1862, OA, AlaDAH.

33. Edward H. Moren to Fannie Moren, 5 June 1862, Edward Moren Papers, AlaDAH; *Weekly Rice Planter*, 22 March 1862, TUL Manuscript Department.

34. Lawrence M. Jones to Governor Shorter, 17 March 1862, OA, AlaDAH.

35. *Selma Morning Register,* 31 May 1862, 27 September 1862, cited by H. E. Sterkx, *Partners in Rebellion: Alabama Women in the Civil War* (Rutherford, N.J.: Fairleigh Dickinson University Press, 1970), 145; S. K. Rayburn to Shorter, 10 July 1862, OA, AlaDAH.

36. Samuel Tate to Hon. A. M. Clayton, 1 May 1861, *OR,* IV, 1:276; G. W. Brame to Moore, 14 November 1861, OA, AlaDAH; *Memphis Daily Appeal,* 18 and 19 February 1862.

37. Brown's resolution to Congress, and Wigfall's response, SHSP 44 (1923): 147.

38. Rector to Pickens, 11 April 1862, University of Arkansas Library; Shorter to "Planters of Alabama," 16 March 1863, OA, AlaDAH. *Arkansas True Democrat,* 27 January and 24 April 1862, cited by Dougan, *Confederate Arkansas,* 87.

39. Francis Leak to John W. Clapp, 5 February 1862; Leak to Pettus, 5 May 1862, Leak Journals, SHC.

40. James Lusk Alcorn to Amelia Alcorn, 17 December 1861, 25 November 1862, 18 December 1862, cited by Pereyra, *Alcorn,* 56–57, 62–63.

41. Roark, *Masters without Slaves,* 38–41.

42. See [missing—ED.] Appendix A for 1862 weather statistics and crop forecasts. The evidence suggests that the following general estimates are appropriate calculations of the effects on various crops: winter wheat, −66 percent; cotton, −33 percent; corn, −20 percent.

43. William Brooks to Shorter, 29 March 1862, OA, AlaDAH; R. K. Rayburn to Shorter, 10 July 1862, OA, AlaDAH. The continuation of a three-year drought similarly damaged winter wheat in Texas. Magnolia Plantation Journal, 20 June 1862, SHC; Philip Henry Pitts, Plantation Book, 10 April, 12 June 1862, SHC; Coleman to Brother, 8 August 1862, Homer H. Coleman Letters, DUL. For epidemics, see Magnolia Plantation Journal, 29 May–31 July 1861, SHC; Leak, 13–18 March 1861, Leak Journals, SHC. Effingham Lawrence, owner of the Magnolia plantation, reported that losses of more than one-quarter of work stock were common; Leak reported similar trends.

44. John Houston Bills, Plantation Journal, 2 June–11 July 1862, SHC.

45. The formula used for the calculation is as follows:

$$C_{62} = (C_{60} \times A_R)(1{-}L_S)(1{-}D_C)$$

C_{62} = 1862 cotton yield; C_{60} = 1859 cotton yield from the 1860 census; A_R = acreage reduction, −10% for yeomen and +/−15% for slaveholders; L_S = 30% reduction in slave labor efficiency; and D_C = 33% loss of cotton due to weather.

If civilians had made no effort during the 1862 planting season to compensate for the loss of access to imported food stuffs and for the absence of men at the front, in non-cotton-producing areas food production would have met only 48 percent of pre-war needs. Such a steep drop would help explain the puzzle of Confederate desertion at Antietam in 1862, as soldiers in Lee's Army of Northern Virginia came close to poverty on the home front. Within the cotton-producing regions of the noncommercial backcountry, there could have been a food deficit of 35 percent, in the commercial low country a shortfall of approximately 40 percent. But even with the most optimistic set of assumptions about the success of converting Mississippi Valley agriculture to meet wartime subsistence needs, human food consumption would have been reduced to one-third below prewar norms. The noncommercial backcountry would still have encountered a severe subsistence crisis in 1862, although the commercial low country would have been able to survive in relative comfort.

If we recognize that each bale of cotton represented approximately fifty bushels of corn, and that fifty bushels of corn could have fed a woman and four children for a year while a man was fed in camp, then the political importance of the 1.5 million bales of cotton actually produced in 1862 becomes clearer, both in symbolic and in practical terms.

46. Andrew Patrick to wife, 26 October, 2 November 1862, cited in Wiley, *Life of Johnny Reb,* 376n.

47. Frank Ruffin to Northrop, 18 October 1862; Ruffin to Randolph, 8 November 1862; endorsement by Randolph, 12 November, and by Davis, 13 November 1862, Frank G. Ruffin Papers, Virginia Historical Society. F. J. Cummings to Northrop, 12 November 1862; Brent to Cummings, 1 December 1862; Walker to Cummings, 4 December 1862; Cummings to Northrop, 5 December 1862, Ruffin Papers.

48. Ruffin to Northrop, 3 November 1862, *OR,* IV, 2:158–60; endorsement by Northrop, 15 December 1862, on letter; Brent to Cummings, 4 December 1862, Ruffin Papers; Northrop to Seddon, 12 January 1863, *OR,* IV, 2:350–51; Edwin Fay to Sarah Fay, 9, 14, 18 December 1862, in Wiley, ed., *"This Infernal War,"* 182, 185, 189.

49. Thirty-third Mississippi Volunteers to Pettus, July 1862, OA, MDAH; Lucresy Simmons to Governor Shorter, 11 July 1862; and Nancy Brazwell to Shorter, 10 August 1862, OA, AlaDAH.

50. Thomas Moore to Davis, 11 November 1862, JDPP-RUL.

51. Richard Winter to Pettus, 6 June 1862, OA, MDAH.

CHAPTER 6. Invasion of the Heartland and the Failure to Achieve Universal Conscription

1. John B. Jones, 28 February 1862, *Rebel War Clerk's Diary,* 1:112. Bell Irvin Wiley argues persuasively that the first major break in Southern morale occurred as a result of the disastrous winter–spring campaigns of 1862; see Wiley, *The Road to Appomattox,* 120. Emory Thomas, on the other hand, emphasizes the disastrous summer of 1863; see Thomas, *Confederate Nation,* 247–51.

2. Davis, Second Inaugural Address, 22 February 1862, *Messages and Papers,* 1:183–88.

3. Edmondston, 20, 22, and 24 February 1862, in *"Journal of a Secesh Lady": The Diary of Catherine Devereux Edmondston, 1860–1866,* ed. Beth G. Crabtree and James W. Patton (Raleigh: North Carolina Division of Archives and History, Department of Cultural Resources, 1979), 124–25; see also 10–16 February, on pp. 114–19.

4. Edmund Ruffin, 27 February 1861, *Diary,* 1:557–58. For a comprehensive dis-

cussion of the Southern refugee experience, see Mary Elizabeth Massey, *Refugee Life in the Confederacy* (Baton Rouge: Louisiana State University Press, 1964).

5. Johnston to Harris, 19 November 1861, *OR*, I, 4:564. Mary Jones to Lt. Charles C. Jones, 21 February 1862, in Robert Manson Myers, ed., *The Children of Pride: A True Story of Georgia and the Civil War* (New Haven: Yale University Press, 1972), 852–53.

6. Samuel Agnew, 11 February 1862, Agnew Family Papers, SHC. Stanley F. Horn, "Nashville during the Civil War," *THQ* 4 (1945): 8–9.

7. Elizabeth Pendleton Hardin, *The Private War of Lizzie Hardin,* ed. E. Glenn Clift (Frankfort: Kentucky Historical Society, 1963), 33; Stanley F. Horn, comp. and ed., *Tennessee's War: 1861–1865, Described by Participants* (Nashville: Civil War Centennial Commission, 1965), 61–62; Lindsley, 17 February 1862, Lindsley Papers, TSLA.

8. Beatty, 13 February, 20 March 1862, in John Beatty, *Memoirs of a Volunteer, 1861–1863,* ed. Harvey S. Ford (New York: W. W. Norton, 1946), 83, 93–94. Mary A. Newcomb, *Four Years of Personal Reminiscences of the War* (Chicago: H. S. Mills Berry, 1893), 24.

9. Wiley, *Plain People of the Confederacy,* 75–76; Louis Hughes, *Thirty Years a Slave: From Bondage to Freedom* (Milwaukee: South Side Printing Co., 1897), 120–22. For analyses of antebellum master/slave relations, see Kenneth M. Stampp, *The Peculiar Institution: Slavery in the Antebellum South* (New York: Alfred A. Knopf, 1956), 141–91; John W. Blassingame, *The Slave Community: Plantation Life in the Antebellum South* (New York: Oxford University Press, 1979), 132–83; Genovese, *Roll, Jordan, Roll,* 3–7; Leslie H. Owens, *This Species of Property: Slave Life and Culture in the Old South* (New York: Oxford University Press, 1976). The background of wartime emancipation is ably recounted in John Hope Franklin, *The Emancipation Proclamation* (Garden City: Doubleday, 1965). For a challenging reinterpretation of Lincoln's position on the question of emancipation, see LaWanda Cox, *Lincoln and Black Freedom: A Study in Presidential Leadership* (Columbia: University of South Carolina Press, 1981). For a useful analysis of Union army interaction with Southern slaves, see Louis B. Gerteis, *From Contraband to Freedman: Federal Policy towards Southern Blacks, 1861–1865* (Westport, Conn.: Greenwood Press, 1973).

10. For a pioneering examination of the liberating effects of plantation abandonment, see Willie Lee Rose, *Rehearsal for Reconstruction: The Port Royal Experiment* (1964; rpt. New York: Vintage, 1967), 3–31.

11. John W. Clay to Clement Clay, 30 March 1862; see also Julia Bates to Virginia Clay, 31 March 1862, Clay Family Papers, DUL. Owsley describes the resentments spawned by plantation abandonment: "Rape, murder and other nameless violations always hovered as a dark specter in the minds of soldiers from the invaded districts." Yeomen felt the same emotions as did their wealthier mates; but while their wives and children had to remain and face the hazards of occupation, "the rich could move their women if they felt the need." Frank Lawrence Owsley, "Defeatism in the Confederacy," *NCHR* 3 (1926): 449.

12. John Park in the *Memphis Daily Appeal*, 28 December 1861. For the "Nashville Gods," see Alfred Leland Crabb, "The Twilight of the Nashville Gods," *THQ* 15 (1956): 291–305; and Connelly, *Army of the Heartland*, 137. In the rowing party were Mayor R. B. Cheatham, John M. Lea, John M. Bais, Russell Houston, and R. C. Foster.

13. Joshua Burns Moore, 17 and 22 February 1862, Moore Papers, AlaDAH.

14. Eliza McHatton-Ripley, in Ripley, *From Flag to Flag* (New York, 1889), 34–36.

15. Narratives of Simpson, Gray, and Childress in Rawick, ed., *The American Slave*, 11:312, 16:25, 16:9. The estimate of 250,000 transported slaves comes from Barry A. Crouch, "Hidden Sources of Black History: The Texas Freedmen's Bureau Records," *SHQ* 83 (1980): 211–26.

16. Joshua Burns Moore, 19 April 1862, Moore Papers, AlaDAH.

17. James Allen, 6 June 1862, James Allen Papers, MDAH. Joseph Davis to Jefferson Davis, 13 June 1862, JDPP-RUL. See also Janet Sharp Hermann, *The Pursuit of a Dream* (New York: Oxford University Press, 1981), 37–39.

18. Harrison N. Butler (aide-de-camp to Davis) to Pettus, 16 May 1862, and Moore to Davis, 6 June 1862, JDPP-RUL.

19. Buckner to Grant, and Grant to Buckner, 16 February 1862, in Grant, *Personal Memoirs*, 158–59. The brusque manner in which Grant disposed of the request for a traditional ceremony of capitulation offended Buckner. In 1854, shortly after an impoverished Grant had resigned from the army, Buckner had extended a personal loan so that Grant could pay his New York hotel bill and travel home by train. See McFeely, *Grant*, 56, 101–02.

20. Davis, "Message 25 February 1862," *Messages and Papers*, 1:189–92.

21. For the wish list, see Davis to Speaker of the House of Representatives, 4 March 1862, *Messages and Papers*, 1:194–95.

22. For War Department reports, see Cooper to Benjamin, 1 March 1862, and V. D. Groner to W. H. Richardson, 27 March 1862, *OR*, IV, 1:962–63, 1029.

23. Christopher Memminger, "Report 14 March 1862," in Raphael P. Thain, comp. and ed., *Reports of the Secretary of the Treasury of the Confederate States of America, 1861–1865* (Washington, D.C.: GPO, 1878), appendix 3, 59–66. In a comparison of Confederate and Union methods of financing the war, James McPherson observes, "Whereas the Confederacy raised 60 percent of its funds by printing paper money and less than 5 percent by taxes, Union war finances included 13 percent paper money and 21 percent taxes. While the Confederacy suffered an inflation rate exceeding 9000 percent, the cost of living rose about 80 percent in the North and fell gradually but steadily after the war was over." McPherson, *Ordeal By Fire*, 205. For the Montgomery convention vote, see Confederate States Constitution, Article 1, Sec. 8, Par. 5, and Article 1, Sec. 9, Par. 5, *Messages and Papers*, 1:42–43.

24. Memminger to Thomas S. Bocock, 14 March 1862, in Todd, *Confederate Finance*, 106. See also Eugene M. Lerner, "Money, Prices and Wages in the Confederacy, 1861–1865," in *The Economic Impact of the American Civil War*, ed. Ralph Andreano, 2nd ed. (Cambridge, Mass.: Schenkman, 1967), 35.

25. Using statistics derived from Appendix A [missing—ED.], I have estimated the effects in the Mississippi Valley of a 5 percent tax in kind on slaves and foodstuffs. If we assume a 20 percent level of noncompliance, the effective yields would be about 4 percent of 1861 grain yields and total slave population. The 1861 yields have been adjusted to reflect the effects of reduced wartime levels of available labor power. These yields are stated in bushels on constant unmilled corn, that is, by converting all foodstuffs into corn equivalents. Total 1861 production of unmilled corn then equals 174,863,557 bushels; at an effective tax rate of 4 percent, this yields approximately 7 million bushels, enough grain to provide prewar diets for approximately 140,000 yeomen families. Also, had the Confederacy delegated responsibility for collection and distribution of grain to county-level relief societies, it probably would not have been necessary to transport a drastically larger volume of supplies than was already being moved for military purposes. Assuming a 20 percent noncompliance, a 5 percent tax on slaves in the seceded states of the Mississippi Valley would have yielded 72,000 slaves. If these blacks were males of military age, this total tax would certainly have been adequate to perform the labor required for constructing defensive installations. The resource problem facing the Confederacy probably sprang less from its lack of capacity and more from the difficulty Southerners encountered in summoning the will to create a central government capable of enforcing the measures needed to win independence.

26. Luraghi, *Rise and Fall*, 121–23. Davis saw fiat financing as a positive development: "To the extent that Treasury notes may be issued the Government is enabled to borrow money without interest, and thus facilitate the conduct of the war." Davis, "Message 18 November 1861," *Messages and Papers*, 1:139.

27. Davis to Johnston, 26 March 1862, *OR*, I, 10, pt. 2: 365. See also Herman Hattaway and Archer Jones, *How the North Won: A Military History of the Civil War* (Urbana: University of Illinois Press, 1991), 152–58; Connelly, *Army of the Heartland*, 145–81.

28. Douglas Southall Freeman, *R. E. Lee: A Biography*, 4 vols. (New York: Charles Scribner's Sons, 1934–35), 2:8–16; Hattaway and Jones, *How the North Won*, 158–62.

29. On egalitarian nationalism, see Cyril B. Falls, *The Art of War from the Age of Napoleon to the Present Day* (New York: Oxford University Press, 1961); J. F. C. Fuller, *The Conduct of War, 1789–1861: A Study of the Impact of the French, Industrial and Russian Revolutions on War and Its Conduct* (New Brunswick: Rutgers University Press, 1961); Trevor N. Dupuy, *The Evolution of Weapons and Warfare* (Indianapolis: Bobbs-Merrill, 1980); William McNeill, *The Pursuit of Power: Technology, Armed Force, and Society from A.D. 1000* (Chicago: University of Chicago Press, 1982). Radical egalitarianism played a critical role in sustaining the élan and esprit de corps of the armies of Napoleonic France; see George Lefebvre, *Napoleon: From 18 Brumaire to Tilsit, 1799–1808*, trans. Henry F. Stockhold (New York: Columbia University Press, 1969), 214–23; and Lefebvre, *Napoleon: From Tilsit to Waterloo, 1807–1815*, trans. J. E. Anderson (New York: Columbia University Press, 1969). See also Leo Gershoy, *The French Revolution and Napoleon* (New York: F. S. Crofts,

1933); Louis R. Gottshalk, *The Era of the French Revolution, 1715–1815* (Boston: Houghton Mifflin, 1929).

30. Davis, "Message 28 March 1862," *Messages and Papers,* 1:205–6.

31. "Proceedings of the First Confederate Congress," SHSP 45 (1925): 26–35.

32. For the April 16 and 21 draft laws, see James M. Matthews, *Public Laws of the Confederate States of America . . . 1862* (Richmond: R. M. Smith, 1862), 29–32.

33. Shorter to Morgan, 14 February 1862, OA, AlaDAH; Thomas R. R. Cobb to wife, 24 April 1862, in Coulter, *Confederate States of America,* 39.

34. Albert B. Moore, *Conscription and a Conflict in the Confederacy* (New York: Macmillan, 1924), 27. Special Orders #51, 5 March 1862, War Department, *OR,* IV, 1:971. Lee assumed an active role in formulating the conscription system proposed by the Davis administration. He proposed conscription of all white men eighteen to forty-five; he wanted to end the reelection of officers and reorganization in the field by compelling conscripts to fill up existing regiments. Lee's proposals were sent to Congress, which drastically revised them. For an account of Lee's involvement, see Charles Marshall, *Aide-de-Camp of Lee: Being the Papers of Colonel Charles Marshall, Sometime Aide-de-Camp, Military Secretary, and Assistant Adjutant General to Robert E. Lee, 1862–1865* (Boston: Little Brown, 1927), 30–32. See also Louis H. Manarin, "Lee in Command: Strategical and Tactical Policies," Ph.D. diss. Duke University, 1964.

35. Wigfall, 29 March 1862, "Proceedings of the Confederate Congress," SHSP 45 (1925): 27.

36. William G. Webb to Governor Clark, 26 June 1861, OA, TexSLA.

37. *Acts of the State of Louisiana 1862,* 61–62. Governor Moore issued Order #191, which directed that one able-bodied white man per plantation be exempt from compulsory militia service. See Winter, *Civil War on Louisiana,* 72. R. H. Todd to Major General Lewis, 10 March 1862, *OR,* I, 6:850–51. Slaveholders in Mississippi pressed Governor Pettus to adopt a similar plantation exemption plan. See G. W. Humphreys, 6 May 1862, David Harrison, 5 May 1862, and Benjamin Bedford, 3 May 1862, to Pettus, OA, MDAH.

38. Kate Stone, 1 March 1862, *Brokenburn,* 95.

39. Bushrod Rust Johnson to Col. Thomas Jordan, 21 April 1862, *OR,* I, 10, pt. 2: 431.

40. William H. Mott to Lila Mott, 21 June 1862, in Charles R. Mott, ed., "War Journal of a Confederate Officer," *THQ* 5 (1946): 240–41.

41. William Creagh to wife, 13 May 1862, Creagh Family Papers, SHC.

42. On abuse of the draft law, see Seddon to Davis, 26 November 1863, *OR,* IV, 2:997. Confederate officials disagreed about the actual number of substitutes. In a July 1863 letter to Adjutant and Inspector General Samuel Cooper, Braxton Bragg and a group of officers from the Army of Tennessee estimated the total at 150,000. See Cooper's reply to Bragg et al., 6 August 1863, *OR,* IV, 2:695–96.

43. Matthews, *Public Laws, 1862,* 52; Eaton, *A History of the Southern Confederacy,* 91. For a thoughtful history of the Northern draft and popular resistance to it, see Grace Palladino, "The Poor Man's Fight: Draft Resistence and Labor Organization in Schuylkill County, Pennsylvania, 1860–1865," Ph.D. diss., University of Pittsburgh,

1983; Peter Levine, "Draft Evasion in the North during the Civil War," *JAH* 67 (1981): 816–34; Eugene Murdock, *One Million Men: The Civil War Draft in the North* (Madison: State Historical Society of Wisconsin, 1971).

44. *Vicksburg Whig* advertisement in A. C. Moore, *Conscription and Conflict,* 30n.

45. Edwin Hedge Fay to Sarah Shields Fay, 21 April, 20 May, 25 May, 15 June, 18 June 1862, in Wiley, ed., *"This Infernal War,"* 35, 36, 55, 58–59, 84–86, 90.

46. Figures for map 6.1. For ISH, Index of Slave Holding, see chap. 2, n. 27.

Per-family average wealth (PFAW)

Level ($)	White pop.	Slave pop.	White males 15–40	Cotton	Free families	ISH
<2,000	916,609	70,092	189,682	192,486	170,959	08%
2–4,000	902,659	212,631	184,170	350,108	164,304	20
4–10,000	946,489	670,364	204,154	1,360,232	172,846	39
10–20,000	279,009	466,080	62,513	1,114,949	51,923	57
>20,000	94,237	342,578	22,877	1,081,984	17,754	81
TOTALS	3,154,912	1,767,136	666,203	4,102,183	577,686	

Bivariate correlations for PFAW and other variables (351 cases):

	ISH	Perslave	Cotton	ICP	PFIMPAC
PFAW	.73	.69	.64	.90	.9*
	.0001	.0001	.0001	.0001	.000*
	341	342	342	342	342

Perslave = percentage of slaves; ICP = index of cotton production; PFIMPAC = per-family impact.

47. Joshua Burns Moore, 30 April 1862, Moore Papers, AlaDAH.

CHAPTER 7. In the Wake of Military Occupation

1. Cordelia Scales to Louly Itly, 4 August 1861, Lummkin Papers, LLMVC; Stone, *Brokenburn,* 105, 96, 120.

2. E. J. Launders to Johnston, and Johnston to Launders, 30 March 1862, Western Department, NA-CSA; Stone, *Brokenburn,* 120.

3. Davis to Joseph E. Davis, JDPP-RUL; L. G. Wollard, 22 March 1862, Wollard Diary, LLMVC.

4. W. H. Sholar to Rector, October 1861; Sholar to Rector, March 1862.

5. Governor Shorter to Randolph, 11 June 1862, *OR,* IV, 1:1149 (OA, AlaDAH). Kirby Smith to Davis, 8 April 1862, JDPP-RUL. Declaration of martial law in East Tennessee by Davis, 8 April 1862, *Messages and Papers,* 1:224–25. Wigfall, 27 February 1862, SHSP 44:65.

6. For criticism of suspension of habeas corpus, see, e.g., Phillips, *Correspondence of Toombs, Stephens, and Cobb,* 633, 637–38, 640, 643. Ruffin, *Diary,* 2:246. For congressional amendment of martial law, 19 April 1862, see Yearns, *Confederate Congress,* 150–51.

7. For Seward and Hammond, see *Congressional Globe,* 35th Congress, 1st sess., 4 March 1858, 68–71 (quotation on p. 70).

8. Mr. Alexander to Davis, JDPP-RUL.

9. Congressional debate of 1, 5, 15 March 1862, Henry, Miles, Foote, Curry, Pryor, SHSP 44:72, 99, 101–2, 163–65. See Frank Lawrence Owsley, *King Cotton Diplomacy: Foreign Relations of the Confederate States of America* (Chicago: University of Chicago Press, 1931); and Gustavus Henry, letter to wife, 17 December 1861, Henry Papers, SHC.

10. Ruffin, 28 April 1862, *Diary,* 2:289; E. E. Porter to General Beauregard, 6 June 1862, *OR,* I, 10, pt. 2: 591–92.

11. Stone, *Brokenburn,* 100–101.

12. Warren Cole to General Polk, 11 May 1862, *OR,* I, 10, pt. 2: 515–16.

13. John Houston Bills, Plantation Journal, 16 April 1862, 28 July 1862, 26 August 1862, Bills Family Papers, SHC.

14. Davis to Jefferson Davis, JDPP-RUL; Jefferson Davis to *Raymond Gazette,* 12 June 1862, *Jefferson Davis,* 5:274.

15. See Leon F. Litwak, *North of Slavery: The Negro in the Free States, 1790–1860* (Chicago: University of Chicago Press, 1961).

16. Lincoln to Seward, 28 June 1862, *Collected Works,* 5:292; governors' memorial to Lincoln, 5:294; Lincoln's response to memorial, 2 July 1862, 5:304.

17. George P. Sanger, ed., *Statutes at Large, Treaties, and Proclamations of the United States of America* (Boston: Little, Brown, 1865), 12:319, 354, 376–78, 589–92 (quotation on p. 591).

18. Lincoln, Appeal to Border State Representatives to Favor Compensated Emancipation, 12 July 1862, *Collected Works,* 5:318.

19. Lincoln, preliminary draft of Emancipation Proclamation, presented at cabinet meeting, 22 July 1862, *Collected Works,* 5:336–37. Objections of Blair and Seward in Francis B. Carpenter, *The Inner Life of Abraham Lincoln: Six Months at the White House* (Lincoln: University of Nebraska Press, 1995), 21–22.

20. Lincoln, "Order Making Henry W. Halleck General-in-Chief," 11 July 1862, *Collected Works,* 5:312–13; Halleck on fugitive slaves, General Order #3.

21. Booker T. Washington, *Up from Slavery* (New York: Penguin, 1986), 8; from Rawick, *The American Slave:* Mary Woolridge, 16:107; Talith Lewis, 9, pt. 4: 254.

22. Louisiana planter quoted in Charles P. Roland, *Louisiana Sugar Plantations during the Civil War* (Leiden: E. J. Brill, 1959), 11; Mary B. Eskeridge to Woodruff, 4 June 1861, *Pulaski County Historical Society Bulletin;* Lizzie Neblett to William H. Neblett, 5 August 1863, Neblett Papers, UTexL. *Montgomery (Alabama) Weekly Mail,* 15 March 1861, cited in James Benson Sellers, *Slavery in Alabama* (University: University of Alabama Press, 1950), 285–86.

23. Ida Henry, in *The American Slave,* 7:135. On slaves' hanging of overseer, see Coleman, *Slavery in Kentucky,* 267–68. For killing of Jim Rankin, see Charles Moses, in *The American Slave,* 7:115–16.

24. Pillow to Davis, 26 July 1862, Pillow Papers, NA-CSA; Mary Williard <or Willard> to Wilkerson, 15 May 1862, Wilkerson Papers, LSUL; Bowman Diary, 67–69, LSUL; James McCutcheon to Pettus, 21 February 1863, OA, MDAH.

25. Mrs. Bart Smith to Governor Shorter, 18 July 1862; Mrs. J. W. Lajlue to Shorter, 1 September 1862; and Addie Harris to Shorter, 16 October 1862, OA, AlaDAH.

26. Mrs. W. J. Whatley to husband, 23 November 1862, Whatley papers, UTexL; James F. Bailey to General Watson, 31 March 1862, OA, AlaDAH; Concerned Alabama Citizens to Shorter, 12 April 1862, OA, AlaDAH. Mrs. Boyce to W. W. Boyce, 12 April 1862, in Bell Irvin Wiley, *Confederate Women* (Westport, Conn.: Greenwood Press, 1975), 148.

27. Daniel Ruggles to Secretary of War, 3 October 1862, *OR,* I, 15:821.

28. Miles, Sexton, Chilton, Chambers, Foote, Herbert, 18–21 August 1862, SHSP 45:40, 176–82, 189–90, 199–211, 213.

29. For citations of Semmes, Moore, Randolph, and Sparrow, see next note.

30. Semmes, Sparrow, Phelan, Wigfall, Barnwell, Preston, Simms, 20, 29, 30 September 1862, SHSP 45:271–75, 46:3–7, 20–21, 64:182, 190; 47:7, 29; Moore to Davis, 6 June 1862, JDPP-RUL; Randolph to Davis, 12 August 1862, *OR,* IV, 2:42–49.

31. Semmes, SHSP, 18, 19, 10 September 1862, Journal of the Congress, II, 294–95; Yancey SHSP 64:182, 190.

32. Brown, SHSP 45:271–73; Phelan, SHSP 64:182, 190.

33. Wigfall, 20 September, 11 September 1862, SHSP, 45:190–95. For discussion of congressional debate, see also Franklin Barlow Sexton, 20, 22, 23 August; 10, 25 September; 5, 13 October 1862, in Mary S. Estill, ed., "Diary of a Confederate Congressman, 1862–63," *SHQ* 38 (1934–35): 276–77, 280–89. The first House vote was 54 to 29, although the vote on the concurring Senate bill was much closer, 47 to 34. SHSP 46:242–43, 251–52.

34. J. T. Terrell to parents, 16 November 1862, in Wiley, *Life of Johnny Reb,* 149.

35. Augusta Evans to Jabez L. M. Curry, 20 December 1862, J. L. M. Curry Papers, LC.

36. Phelan to Davis, 9 December 1862, *OR,* I, 17, pt. 2: 790.

37. Genovese, *Roll, Jordan, Roll,* 91–92.

CHAPTER 8. "The Carefully Fostered Hostility of Class against Class"

1. Henry C. Lay to Mrs. John Perkins, 23 February 1863, Lay Papers, SHC. The upas is a tree of the mulberry family with a poisonous juice, and figuratively the word means "a poisonous or harmful influence or institution" (*Webster's New International Dictionary,* 2nd ed.). The Russian poet Pushkin was censured for describing the tsar as a Russian upas.

2. For Lincoln quotation, see Admiral David D. Porter, "The Opening of the Lower Mississippi," *Battles and Leaders* (New York, 1887), 2:23–25.

3. Winters, *The Civil War in Louisiana,* 104–10.

4. Kate Stone, 5, 29, 30 June, and 24 July 1862, *Brokenburn,* 125–35; Farrar to Pettus, 17 July 1862, OA, MDAH.

5. *Vicksburg Whig,* 5 May 1862, quoted in Samuel Carter, *The Final Fortress: The Campaign for Vicksburg, 1862–1863* (New York: St. Martins, 1980), 36.

6. A. O. McCollom to "Dear Friends," 25 December 1862, cited by Dougan, *Confederate Arkansas,* 112; David Hubbard to Clement Clay, 28 January 1863, C. C. Clay Papers, DUL.

7. James Allen, 15 and 21 May, 6 June 1862, MDAH.

8. Roark, *Masters without Slaves,* 54, 80.

9. Alfred Quine, Fonsylvania Plantation Journal, 20 February–1 March 1863, MDAH.

10. *Clarksville Standard,* 23 January 1863, cited in Robert L. Kerby, *Kirby Smith's Confederacy: The Trans-Mississippi South, 1863–1865* (New York: Columbia University Press, 1972), 56.

11. James Garner to Pettus, 12 March 1863, OA, MDAH.

12. F. Dillard et al. to Pettus, 13 February 1863, OA, MDAH; *The Freeman's Champion* (Houston), 10 April 1865, cited by Wiley, *Southern Negroes,* 124; H. B. Lyons to Pettus, 24 April 1863, OA, MDAH.

13. Stafford to Quartermaster, 8 June 1863, OA, MDAH; Ewell to Buckner, 6 June 1863, OA, MDAH.

14. T. W. Ham to Pettus, 30 December 1862, OA, MDAH.

15. J. F. H. Claiborne to Major M. B. Clarke, 19, 31 August 1862, LR, DMEL, NA-CSA.

16. T. J. Hart to Clarke, 18 November 1862, LR, DMEL, NA-CSA; "A Soldier's Sister" to Governor Moore, 9 August 1862, Thomas O. Moore Papers, LSUL.

17. General Earl Van Dorn to Pemberton, 5 December 1862; James M. Porter to Colonel John Adams, 12 December 1862, LR, DMEL, NA-CSA. J. F. Llewellen to Turner, 4 December 1862; Bell to Llewellen, 3 January 1862, *OR,* I, 15:886, 925.

18. Webb to Major A. G. Dickerson, 4 January 1863, *OR,* I, 15:926–28. For Standing Order #35, District of Texas, New Mexico, and Arizona, 5 January 1863, see Bell to Llewellen, 28 November 1862, ibid., 931, 887. For further details on draft resistance among foreign-born Southerners, see Ella Lonn, *Foreigners in the Confederacy* (Chapel Hill: University of North Carolina Press, 1940), 431–37.

19. AAG Clarke to Pemberton, 18 November 1862, LR, DMEL, NA-CSA; Orders from Pemberton, J. C. Taylor, aide-de-camp to Brigadier General W. R. Beale, 11 December 1862, LR, DMEL, NA-CSA.

20. A. E. Reynolds to Davis, 20 January 1863, JDPP-RUL.

21. Alex Fitzpatrick to Davis, 19 November 1862, LR, War Department, NA-CSA.

22. Cyrus Boyd, 24 August 1862, in "Civil War Diary of Cyrus F. Boyd, Fifteenth Iowa Infantry, 1861–1863," ed. Mildred Throne (Iowa City: State Historical Society of

Iowa, 1953), 178. Lincoln, Annual Message, 1 December 1862, *Messages and Papers,* 6:140.

23. James K. Wells, 16 April 1863, "An Indiana Volunteer Advises His Neighbors," ed. Charles G. Talbert, *Indiana Magazine of History* 53 (1957): 178–79.

24. P. A. Willis to Samuel E. Carey, 3 February 1863, Harry W. Walter Letters, SHC; Dixon to Harry Dixon, 6 March 1863, Dixon Papers, SHC; Kate Stone, 22 March 1863, *Brokenburn,* 184; Grant to Halleck, 12, 19 April 1863, LS, AotT, NA-USA.

25. Stone, 25 April 1863, *Brokenburn,* 197, 199.

26. John Taylor to Pettus, 26 May 1863; A. S. Moyers to Pettus, 12 July 1863, OA, MDAH. *Shreveport Semi-Weekly News,* 25 August 1863, in Jefferson Davis Bragg, *Louisiana in the Confederacy* (Baton Rouge: Louisiana State University Press, 1941), 216–17.

27. Samuel Agnew, 13 October 1862; Stone, 30 August 1863, *Brokenburn,* 238. Charles Ramsdell, *Behind the Lines in the Southern Confederacy,* ed. Wendell H. Stephenson (Baton Rouge: Louisiana State University Press, 1944), 45.

28. Alcorn to Amelia Alcorn, 11 February 1863, in Pereyra, *James Lusk Alcorn,* 57; see also 64–65.

29. *Milledgeville Confederate Union,* 20 January 1863. Shorter to J. F. Dortch, 12 March 1863; and Shorter, "A Proclamation to the Planters of Alabama," 16 March 1863, OA, AlaDAH.

30. Pemberton to Seddon, 22 January, 8 April 1863, LS, DMEL, NA-CSA; Johnston to Davis, 9 January 1863, JDPP-RUL; Edward Tracy to Clay, 3 March 1863, C. C. Clay Papers, DUL.

31. *Arkansas True Democrat,* 21 January 1863, in Dougan, *Confederate Arkansas,* 99; *Milledgeville Confederate Union,* 29, 31, 24 March 1863; Stephen D. Lee to J. J. Reeve, 12 April 1863, *OR,* I, 24, pt. 2: 505–6.

32. Davis, "An Address to the Southern People," 10 April 1863, *Messages and Papers,* 1:331–35.

33. On Hindman, see Kerby, *Kirby Smith's Confederacy,* 35, 29. Kirby Smith to General Theophilus Holmes, 16 May 1863; and Kirby Smith to Taylor, 16 May 1863, LS, TMD, NA-CSA.

34. Wirt Adams to Pemberton, 6 April 1863; James Chalmers to Pemberton, 6 April 1863; Porter to Pemberton, 28 April 1863, LR, DMEL, NA-CSA. Thomas Conn Bryan, *Confederate Georgia* (Athens: University of Georgia Press, 1953), 144–46. J. F. White to AAG, Captain L. D. Sondridge, 18 April 1863; and L. Morris to Lieutenant Colonel Woodley, 5 February 1863, LR, DMEL, NA-CSA.

35. J. V. Harris to Captain Wade, 4 April 1863; Ruggles to Major Menninger, 5 April 1863.

36. Sir Edward Cressy and Robert Hammond Murray, *Decisive Battles of the World* (Harrisburg, Pa., 1943, 1955), 564.

37. McPherson, *Ordeal By Fire,* 187; S. Carroll Root, ed., "Experiences of a Fed . . . ," *Louisiana Historical Quarterly* 19 (1936).

38. William Root, 5 April 1863, in S. C. Root, ed., "Experiences of a Fed"; Frank Crawford to G. J. Taggart, 18 February 1863, LR, AotT, NA-USA.

39. See Grant to Halleck, 27 March 1863; and 4 April 1863, LS, DotT, NA-USA.

40. William H. Tunnard, *A Southern Record: The History of the Third Regiment Louisiana Infantry* (Baton Rouge, 1866; rpt. Dayton, Ohio: Press of Morningside Bookshop, 1988), 230.

41. Grant, *Personal Memoirs,* 251. See also Barton, *Autobiography of Dr. Thomas H. Barton* (Charleston: West Virginia Printing Co., 1890), 112; Charles A. Dana, *Recollections of the Civil War* (New York: D. Appleton, 1898), 43; Bruce Catton, *Grant Moves South* (Boston: Little, Brown, 1960), 424–45. Grant to Halleck, 3 May 1863, LS, DotT, NA-USA.

42. Pemberton to Davis, 1 May 1863, LS, DMEL, NA-CSA. For the rivalry, see Alfred P. Jones, "Gen. Joseph Eggleston Johnston: Storm Center of the Confederate Army," *MVHR* 14 (1927): 342–49. Pemberton to Davis, 1 May 1863, LS, DMEL, NA-CSA.

43. Oldroyd, 6 May 1863, *A Soldier's Story of the Siege of Vicksburg: The Diary of Osborn H. Oldroyd* (Springfield, Ill., 1885), 9; William Claiborne, 18 April, 1 May 1863, Claiborne Diary, SHC.

44. Flanagin to Davis, 5 January 1863, JDPP-RUL.

45. Pemberton to Johnston, 12 May 1863; Johnston to Pemberton, 13 May 1863; and Pemberton to Johnston, 15 May 1863, LS, DMEL, NA-CSA.

46. Adam Bodreau, *Military History of Ulysses S. Grant,* 3 vols. (New York, 1885) 1:252n. For Stevenson, see Pemberton to Cooper, 25 August 1862, *OR,* I, 24, pt. 1: 190.

47. Shrcey to brother, 18 May 1863; letter found on corpse and forwarded to Pemberton by Stevenson in letter of 23 May 1863, LR, DMEL, NA-CSA; Dana Miller, 17 May 1863, cited in Carter, *Final Fortress,* 206.

48. Jenkin Lloyd Jones, 7 April 1863, *An Artilleryman's Diary* (Madison: Wisconsin Historical Commission, 1914), 45; Quine, Fonsylvania Plantation Journal, 9, 11, 12, 25, 26 May; 1, 4, 5 June 1863, MDAH.

49. Joseph Davis to Jefferson Davis, 3, 17, 21 June 1863, JDPP-RUL; James Shelton to Emily Shelton, 6 June 1863, Shelton Papers, SHC.

50. Davis to Johnston, 24 May 1863; Johnston to Davis, 27 May; Davis to Johnston, 28 May; Johnston to Davis, 28 May; Davis to Johnston, 30 May; Johnston to Davis, 31 May; Johnston to Davis, 1 June 1863, *OR,* I, 24, pt. 1: 193, 194.

51. Fay to Sarah Fay, 13 June 1863, *"This Infernal War,"* 285; Headquarters, Jackson's Division, 11 June 1863, George Moarman Scrapbook, TUL.

52. Kirby Smith to Pemberton, LR, DMEL, NA-CSA.

53. Balfour, 2 June 1863, Emma Balfour Diary, MDAH; Tunnard, *A Southern Record,* 230.

54. James Dill Allison Diary, SHC; Claiborne Diary, SHC.

55. Claiborne Diary, SHC.

56. "Many Soldiers" to Pemberton, 28 June 1863, *OR* I, 24, pt. 3: 983; Pemberton to divisional commanders, 1 July 1863, ibid., pt. 2: 347.

57. Bowen to Pemberton, 2 July 1863, quoted in Pemberton, Report of Operations, 2 August 1863, *OR* I, 24, pt. 3: 282–83; Smith to Pemberton, 2 July 1863, ibid., 282.

58. Charles Dana to E. M. Stanton, 4 July 1863, *OR*, I, 24, pt. 1: 115.

59. Grant to Washburne, 20 August 1863, in *General Grant's Letters to a Friend,* ed. James Grant Wilson (New York: Crowell, 1897), 28.

60. Grant to Mary Grant, 19 August 1862, in *The Papers of Ulysses S. Grant,* ed. John Y. Simon et al. (Carbondale: Southern Illinois University Press, 1967–), 5:311.

CHAPTER 9. "A War Fought by the Weak"

1. Halleck to Grant, 8 July 1863, *OR,* I, 24, pt. 1: 62; Grant to Halleck, 8 July 1863, ibid., pt. 3: 489.

2. Hugh Moss, 8 and 9 July 1863, Moss Diary, 46; Tunnard, 7 July 1863, *A Southern Record,* 278; Shoup to Major John G. Devereux (Maj. Gen. Martin L. Smith's AAG), 10 July 1863, LR, DMEL, NA-CSA; Pemberton to McPherson, 8 July 1863, *OR,* I, 24, pt. 3: 488.

3. Moss, 11 July 1863, Moss Diary, 47; Claiborne, 11 July 1863, Claiborne Diary, SHC.

4. Claiborne, 18 July 1863, Claiborne Diary, SHC; Tunnard, 21 July 1863, *A Southern Record,* 280–81.

5. Texas private quoted from Kerby, *Kirby Smith's Confederacy,* 170; James Shelton to Emily Shelton, 21 July 1863, Shelton Letters, SHC. Grant to Halleck, 18 July 1863; Grant to Major General M. L. Smith (CSA), 24 July 1863, *OR,* I, 24, pt. 3: 550.

6. Grant to Halleck, 24 July 1863, LS, DotT, NA-USA.

7. Davis, proclamations of 27 February, 15 July, and 1 August 1863, *Messages and Papers,* 1:324–25, 326–27, 329–31. On men available for duty, see *OR,* IV, 2:615. The June 30, 1863, report showed 307,464 present and 135,998 AWOL.

8. Standing Order #197–A160, 19 August 1863, War Department, NA-CSA; *Richmond Enquirer,* 16 September 1863; Halleck to Grant, 19 September 1863, LR, DotT, NA-USA. For the tangled set of negotiations, see *OR,* II, 6:279–456.

9. Carter Stevenson to Pemberton, 22 August 1863, LR, DMEL, NA-CSA; S. J. Nelly to wife, 28 September 1863, in Nelly, "History of 30th Alabama . . . ," 146, 145; Davis to Jefferson Davis, 28 September 1863, JDPP-RUL; Smith to Eliza Smith, 30 August 1863, in William Robert Stevenson, "Robert Alexander Smith: A Southern Son," *AlaHQ* 20 (1958): 42.

10. Watson to Cooper, 5 August 1863, *OR,* I, 23, pt. 3: 1043–44. Shorter to Davis, 8 August 1863, JDPP-RUL; Shorter to Maury, 4 September 1863, OA, AlaDAH. For Kirby Smith on disaffection, see AAG-TMD to Lieutenant Colonel Ben, 4 September 1863, LS, TMD, NA-CSA.

11. On 25,000–30,000 draft evaders, see Pillow to General S. Cooper, 28 July 1863, *OR,* IV, 2:681. For parallel report, see Pillow to Colonel B. E. Ewell, 25 July 1863, ibid., 680–81. Allen quoted in Dougan, *Confederate Arkansas,* 91.

12. Kirby Smith to Davis, 16 June 1863, *OR,* I, 22, pt. 2: 872; McCulloch to Captain E. P. Turner, 18 September 1863, *OR,* I, 26, pt. 2: 236; Kirby Smith to T. H. Holmes, 2

October 1863, LS, TMD, NA-CSA; Kirby Smith to McCulloch, 2 October 1863, *OR*, I, 26, pt. 2: 285.

13. McCulloch to J. B. Magruder, 21 October 1863; McCulloch to Boren, 9 November 1863; and McCulloch to Magruder, 9 November 1863, *OR*, I, 26, pt. 2: 344–45, 352, 401.

14. George Lay to John Preston, 2 September 1863; C. D. Melton to Preston, 25 August 1863; and Preston to Seddon, and Seddon to Lee, 29 August 1863, *OR*, IV, 2:783–85, 769–70, 768–69.

15. Lee to Davis, 17 August 1863, *OR*, I, 29, pt. 2: 6.

16. General Order #12, Volunteer and Conscript Bureau, 16 March 1863, Orders, AoT, NA-CSA; Pillow to Major Falcone, 13 March 1863; Pillow to Woods, 17 March 1863; and Pillow to Falcone, 19 March 1863, Volunteer and Conscript Bureau, LS, AoT, NA-CSA.

17. Soldiers of the 54th Alabama to Shorter, 20 July 1863; Clayton to Shorter, 16 July 1863, OA, AlaDAH.

18. Shorter to Maury, 3 September 1863, OA, AlaDAH.

19. Governor Flanagin to Davis, 26 June 1863, JDPP-RUL; Schofield to Halleck, 18 September 1863, WA Collection, New-York Historical Society; B. F. Danley to Flanagin, 30 September 1863, OA, Arkansas History Commission and State Archives. *Arkansas True Democrat,* 29 April 1863, cited by Dougan, *Confederate Arkansas,* 102.

20. Sherman to Grant, 12 August 1862, LS, 15th AC, NA-USA; Grant to Sherman, 26 September 1862, LS, DotT, NA-USA; Sherman to "Commanding General, Co. Expedition," 27 September 1862, LS, 15th AC, NA-USA. General Order #17, 17 June 1862, *OR*, I, 13:835.

21. Sherman to Anthony, 24 September 1862, to Wolcott, 24 September 1862, and to John A. Rawlins (Grant's AG), 26 September 1862, DWT, 5th Division, NA-USA.

22. Sherman to Rawlins, 13 September 1863, ibid.; Hurlbut to Grant, 25 July 1863, 16th AC, NA-USA; Hurlbut to Steele, 26 September 1863, WA 16th AC.

23. Shy, *A People Numerous and Armed,* 14–15.

24. Richard J. Archer to Pettus, 17 June 1863, OA, MDAH.

25. Hugh Torrance to Mrs. T. M. Reid, February 16, 1863, George Davidson Papers, DUL; Batley to Clay, 23 January 1863, C. C. Clay Papers, DUL; General Order #6, Headquarters Eastern Sub. District of Texas, 2 March 1863, LR, TMD, NA-CSA; A. J. Gaines to Flanagin, 1 May 1863, OA, Arkansas History Commission and State Archives; Henrietta Butler, *Louisiana Narratives,* 1, Louisiana State Library; Katie Rowe, in *The American Slave,* 7:279.

26. James Acklen to Ada Acklen, 20 August 1863, Acklen Papers, TUL; L. W. Hopkins to James Gregorie, 11 October 1863, Gregorie and Elliot Papers, SHC; Kirby Smith to Herbert, 31 October 1863, LS, TMD, NA-CSA.

27. Tom D. Strong to Wallis, 13 August 1863, Wallis-Kalling Papers, TUL.

28. Conner to Fanny, 30 March 1863, Lemuel P. Conner Papers, LLMVC; Fay to Sarah Fay, 27 July 1863, in Fay, *"This Infernal War,"* 317.

29. Veteran to Seddon, February 1863, LR, War Department, NA-CSA.

30. T. B. Banes to parents, 8 August 1863, cited by Wiley, *Life of Johnny Reb*, 376; Soldiers of 54th Alabama to Shorter, 20 July 1863, OA, AlaDAH; Judge Brown diary, 31 July 1863, in Dougan, *Confederate Arkansas*, 111; Davis to W. Harmon, 17 September 1863, JDPP-RUL.

31. William Minor, 29 September 1863, Minor Papers, LLMVC; Katie Rowe, in *The American Slave*, 7:275–76.

32. Kirby Smith to Davis, 25 September 1863, LS, TMD, NA-CSA.

33. William Pitt Ballinger, 14 July, 29 July, 5 August 1863, William Pitt Ballinger Papers, UTexL.

34. Chalmers to Johnston, 29 July 1863, and Ruggles to Johnston, 10 August 1863, in J. S. McNiely, "War and Reconstruction in Mississippi, 1863–1890," *Publications of the Mississippi Historical Society*, Centenary ser., 2 (1918): 180–81.

35. Hurlbut to Lincoln, 11 August 1863, *OR*, I, 24, pt. 3: 588–89.

36. Governor Brown, 17 January 1863, *OR*, IV, 2:721–22; Governor Vance, 26 January 1863, *OR*, I, 18:860–61.

37. William McKee Evans, *To Die Game: The Story of the Lowry Band, Indian Guerillas of Reconstruction* (Baton Rouge: Louisiana State University Press, 1971), 3–18.

38. *Raleigh Daily Progress*, 31 March, 4 April, 29 September 1863; Sam Jones to Davis, 17 October 1862, *OR*, I, 16, pt. 2: 954–55. For northern Georgia, see Davis to General Benjamin Hill, 23 October 1862, *OR*, IV, 2:140.

39. For an account of the Laurel Creek Valley incident, see Phillip S. Paluden, *Victims: A True Story of the Civil War* (Knoxville: University of Tennessee Press, 1982), 84–98.

40. R. F. Armfield to Governor Vance, 19 February 1863, *OR*, I, 51, pt. 2: 709–10.

41. General Pender to Lee, forwarded by Lee to Seddon, 23 April 1863, *OR*, I, 25, pt. 2: 746–47.

42. Urban Owen to Laura Owen, in Enoch L. Mitchell, ed., "Letters of a Confederate Surgeon in the Army of Tennessee to His Wife," *THQ* 5 (1946): 50. Sam R. Watkins, *"Co. Aytch": Maury Grays, First Tennessee Regiment; or, a Side Show of the Big Show* (Jackson, Tenn.: McCowat-Mercer Press, 1952), 108.

43. Owen to Laura Owen, 17 March 1863, in Mitchell, "Letters," 147.

44. Buckner to Seddon, and Seddon to Buckner, 22 July 1863, War Department, NA-CSA.

45. Fay to Sarah Fay, 27 February, 27 July, 19 September 1863, in *"This Infernal War,"* 236, 305, 329.

46. Fay to Sarah Fay, 30 April 1863, in *"This Infernal War,"* 253; see Ann Firor Scott, *The Southern Lady: From Pedestal to Politics* (Chicago: University of Chicago Press, 1970); V. Shiliha to Buckner, 30 May 1863, LS, Department of Western Virginia and Eastern Tennessee, NA-CSA; W. W. Blackford to Susan Blackford, 29 October 1863, in Susan Leigh Blackford, ed., *Letters from Lee's Army; or, Memoirs of Life In and Out of the Army in Virginia . . .* (New York: Charles Scribner's Sons, 1947), 226.

47. William T. Auman and David D. Scarboro, "The Heroes of America in Civil War North Carolina," *NCHR* 58 (1987): 327–63; "Statement of Col. Jefferson Faulkner and Mr. A. R. Hill of Randolph County, Alabama in reference to a secret society," enclosure in H. W. Walter to General Bragg, 8 May 1864, *OR*, IV, 3:393, 396–98.

48. Dabney H. Maury to Seddon, 28 December 1863, Seddon to Maury, 9 January 1864, and Maury to Seddon, 11 January 1864, *OR*, I, 26, pt. 2: 548–52.

49. H. D. Clayton et al. to S. Cooper, 25 July 1863, *OR*, IV, 2: 670–71.

CHAPTER 10. "Every Man Says That Every Other Man Ought to Fight"

1. Reuben Davis to Jefferson Davis, 2 August 1863, JDPP-RUL.

2. Ballinger, 5 August 1863, William Pitt Ballinger Papers, UTexL. For Charles Royston, see Dougan, *Confederate Arkansas,* 122.

3. Walthal to Lay, 6 August 1863, *OR*, IV, 2:726–27.

4. Pereyra, *James Lusk Alcorn,* 65–67; Reuben Davis, *Recollections of Mississippi and Mississippians* (Hattiesburg: University and College Press of Mississippi, 1972), 434–35; Joseph Davis to Jefferson Davis, 24 August 1863, JDPP-RUL. See also Bettersworth, *Confederate Mississippi,* 52–53.

5. Jesse Burt, "East Tennessee, Lincoln and Sherman," pt. 1, *ETHSP* 34 (1962): 21; also, pt. 2, 35 (1963): 54–75; Alexander, "Strange Bedfellows: The Interlocking Careers of T. A. R. Nelson, Andrew Johnson, W. G. (Parson) Brownlow," *ETHSP* 24 (1952): 68–69. J. L. Williams et al. to Abraham Lincoln, 15 October 1863; and Lincoln to Williams et al., 17 October 1863, *OR*, 30, pt. 4: 401, 448–49; Dana to Stanton, 8 September 1863, *OR*, 30, pt. 1: 182–83.

6. For Kniffen, see Horn, *Tennessee's War,* 206–7; George Phillips to Hattie Carlin, 12 September 1863, Phillips Papers, Ohio Historical Society; Davis, 24 September 1863, *OR*, I, 30, pt. 2: 637.

7. "Report of Gen. John Frazer," 27 November 1863, *OR*, I, 30, pt. 2: 607–24, 635–59.

8. Davis to Colonel W. P. Johnston, ADC, 3 September 1863, JDPP-RUL; Lincoln to Halleck, 21 September 1863, *OR*, I, 30, pt. 1: 148.

9. On AWOL statistics, see *OR*, IV, 2:615; 23, pt. 1: 410–11.

10. Davis, "Message to Confederate Congress," 12 January 1863, in Richardson, *Messages and Papers,* 1:290; Henry F. Stone to Father, 13 February 1863, Stone Collection, Filson Club, Louisville, Ky.; Davis to Lee, 16 September 1863, *OR*, I, 29, pt. 2: 725–27; Lee to Davis, 9 September 1863, ibid., 706.

11. Vaughn, 12 September 1863, in "Diary of Turner Vaughn, Company 'C,' 4th Alabama Regiment . . . ," *AlaHQ* 18 (1956): 595. On antiwar activities, see Lieutenant Colonel George W. Lay to Colonel J. S. Preston, 2 September 1863, *OR*, IV, 2:738–85. Vance to Davis, 10, 11 September 1863, *OR*, I, 52, pt. 2: 763–65.

12. General Army of Tennessee to Davis, 4 October 1863, *OR*, I, 30, pt. 2: 65–66; Lee to Davis, 5 October 1863, ibid., 29, pt. 2: 771; Davis to Bragg, 30 September 1863, ibid., 52, pt. 2: 534; Bragg to Davis, 1 October 1863, ibid., 535.

13. "Testimony of Amos Ginn in the Case of Abner Ginn," Beaufort, S.C., 19 February 1875, Southern Claims Commission Case Files, General Accounting Office, 3rd Auditor, RG 217, NA.

14. Rosecrans to Stanton, and Stanton to Rosecrans, 11 September 1863, *OR*, I, 30, pt. 3: 529; Dana to Stanton, 14 September 1863, ibid., pt. 1: 186; Dana to Stanton, 8 October 1863, ibid., 211; Baughn's statement, ibid., 180.

15. Seddon to Johnston, 25 August 1863; Pillow to General Mackall, 14 July 1863; Pillow to Ewell, 28 July 1863; and Pillow to Seddon, 5 October 1863, *OR*, II, 2:748–49, 638, 680–81, 853–54.

16. Davis to Bragg, 3 October 1863, and Chesnut to Davis, 5 October 1863, *OR*, I, 52, pt. 2: 535, 538; John Bratton to Bettie Bratton, 23, 10 October 1863, Bratton Letters, SHC; Watkins, *"Co. Aytch,"* 121–22; Major General Lafayette McLaws to wife, 14 October 1863, McLaws Collection, SHC.

17. Grant, *Personal Memoirs,* 308–12, 312–21, 334, 344. See also Connelly, *Autumn of Glory,* 255–61.

18. Major General John Parks to Sanders, 9 November 1863, *OR*, I, 31, pt. 3: 106; Longstreet to Cooper, 1 January 1864, *OR*, I, 31, pt. 1: 457–58. See Organization of the Army of Tennessee, 31 October and 20 November 1863, *OR*, 31, pt. 3: 615–20, 656–66; Grant to Halleck, 24 October 1863.

19. John Cotton to Mariah Cotton, 12 November 1863, in Lucille Griffith, ed., *Yours till Death: Civil War Letters of John W. Cotton* (University: University of Alabama Press, 1951), 94; Samuel C. Kelly to wife, 11 November 1863, in Kelly, "A History of the 30th Alabama . . . ," *AlaHQ* 9 (1947): 178; Schurz, *The Reminiscences of Carl Schurz* (New York: Doubleday, 1917), 3:69–70; James Connolly to Mary Dunn Connolly, 19 November 1863, in Paul M. Angle, ed., *Three Years in the Army of the Cumberland: The Letters and Diary of Major James A. Connolly* (Bloomington: Indiana University Press, 1959), 141.

20. Davis to Bragg, and Bragg to Davis, *OR*, I, 52, pt. 2: 516–17; General Order #33, Stevenson's Division, 14 September 1863, ibid., 527; William Hardee to Cooper, 12 October 1863, ibid., 543–44. For the four deserters, see Hooker to Lieutenant Colonel Goddard, 17 November 1863, *OR*, I, 31, pt. 3: 174.

21. Special Order #25, Headquarters, Army of Tennessee, 12 November 1863, *OR*, I, 31, pt. 3: 685–86; Bragg to Davis, 16 November 1863, Davis Papers, DUL.

22. Grant, *Personal Memoirs,* 342–43.

23. For Ralph Neal, see Horn, *Tennessee's War,* 241–42; Connolly to Mary Dunn Connolly, 7 December 1863, *Three Years,* 152–53.

24. Milton Brown to General Joseph E. Johnston, 4 November 1863, OA, MDAH; Blackford to Susan Blackford, 29 October 1863, *Letters from Lee's Army,* 226.

25. General Order #208, Army of Tennessee, 16 November 1863, Orders, AoT, NA-CSA.

26. Connolly to Mary Dunn Connolly, 7 December 1863, *Three Years,* 157–58; see also Schurz, *Reminiscences,* 3:31–33.

27. For Neal, see Horn, *Tennessee's War,* 242; Keegan, *The Face of Battle,* 183; Watkins, *"Co. Aytch,"* 126–28.

28. Bragg to Cooper, 30 November 1863, *OR*, I, 31, pt. 2: 664–66.

29. Dana, *Recollections*, 150–51; Sheridan to Fullerton, 20 February 1864, *OR*, I, 31, pt. 2: 188–93.

30. Anderson, "Autobiography of Gen. Patton Anderson, CSA," SHSP 24 (1896): 69. The official report to which Anderson responded was accessioned at the University of Florida as part of Anderson's papers. However, Anderson's report is not now part of that collection, and the archivists admit their puzzlement at the mysterious disappearance. For congratulations by Reynolds to his men, see Reynolds to Major Wilson, 1863, Anderson Papers, University of Florida; also, Tucker to Wilson, 8 December 1863, and Manigault to Wilson, ibid.

31. For Cleburne's action, see Connelly, *Autumn of Glory*, 275–76; Howell Purdue and Elizabeth Purdue, *Pat Cleburne, Confederate General: A Definitive Biography* (Hillsboro, Tex.: Hill Jr. College Press, 1973), 237–66.

32. Kennaway, *On Sherman's Track*, 102–3; Thomas to Halleck, 25, 26 November 1863, *OR*, I, 31, pt. 2: 90–91.

33. Anderson to Henrietta Adair Anderson, 18 December 1863, in Margaret Anderson Uhlen, "Civil Wars Letters of Maj. Gen. Patton Anderson," *Florida Historical Quarterly* 56 (1977): 170.

34. Ella Lonn, *Desertion during the Civil War* (1928; rpt. Gloucester, Mass.: Peter Smith, 1966), 120.

Epilogue

1. Lee to Davis, 3 December 1863, *OR*, I, 29, pt. 2: 858–59; Davis to Johnston, 23 December 1863, *Jefferson Davis*, 6:136. Watkins, *"Co. Aytch,"* 131–32; see also Robert Middlekauff, *The Glorious Cause: The American Revolution, 1763–1789* (New York: Oxford University Press, 1982).

2. Johnston to Davis, January 2, 1864, *OR*, I, 32, pt. 2: 510–11; Johnston to Wigfall, January 4, 1864, Wigfall Papers, UTexL. There was a report that masters helped 1,200 slave laborers escape from Confederate service at Mobile in January 1864.

3. "Memorial from the Army of Tennessee," 29 December 1863, SHSP 50:140–42.

4. Cleburne's memorial, 2 January 1864, *OR*, I, 52, pt. 2: 586–92.

5. Purdue and Purdue, *Pat Cleburne*, 13–14, 74.

6. From *OR*, I, 52, pt. 2: Anderson to Polk, 14 January 1864, 598–99; Walker to Davis, 12 January 1864, 595; Davis to Walker, 13 January 1864, 596; Johnston to Hardee, et al., 31 January 1864, 608.

7. Seddon to Davis, 26 November 1863, *OR*, IV, 2:996–98.

8. Davis, "Message to 4th Session, 1st Confederate Congress," 7 December 1863, *Messages and Papers*, 1:348, 370, 377.

9. Edward Sparrow, 24 December 1863, and Louis Wigfall, 30 December 1863, SHSP 50:120, 155.

10. William Miles, 6 January 1864, and Waller Staples, 8 January 1864, SHSP

50:189–90, 204–5. For the two laws, see James M. Matthews, ed., *Public Laws, the Confederate States of America* (Richmond, 1864), 211–15, 235–36.

11. Jones, 29 November 1863, 2 January 1864, 29 November 1863, *Rebel War Clerk's Diary,* 2:108, 123.

12. Davis, "Message to the Confederate Senate and House," 3 February 1864, *Messages and Papers,* 1:395–400.

13. Eric Foner, *Reconstruction: America's Unfinished Revolution, 1863–1877* (New York: Harper & Row, 1988); also Robert F. Durden, *The Gray and the Black: The Confederate Debate on Emancipation* (Baton Rouge: Louisiana State University Press, 1972), 74–100. On the Northern peace movement, see Hattaway and Jones, *How the North Won,* 465–537.

14. Davis, "Speech in Macon, Georgia," 29 September 1864, *Jefferson Davis,* 6:341–44.

15. Davis, "Message to Confederate Senate and House," 7 November 1864, *Messages and Papers,* 1:493–94.

16. Cleburne to Johnston, 2 January 1864, *OR,* I, 52, pt. 2: 592; Cobb to Seddon, 8 January 1865, *OR,* IV, 3:1009–10.

17. See also SHSP 52. For Lee's two letters, to Barksdale, 18 February 1865, and to Andrew Hunter, 11 January 1865, see Durden, *The Gray and the Black,* 271–81 and 207–9.

18. Plummer to Pendleton Murrah, 25 May 1864, OA, TexSLA. See also Owsley, *State Rights,* 272–81; and Coulter, *Confederate States of America,* 374–404.

19. David L. Yulee to Davis, 24 October 1864, JDPP-RUL.

Index

Carter G. Woodson Institute Series